LOUIS SULLIVAN

THE POETRY OF ARCHITECTURE

By Robert Twombly

Frank Lloyd Wright: His Life and His Architecture

Louis Sullivan: His Life and Work

Louis Sullivan: The Public Papers (editor)

Power & Style: A Critique of Twentieth-Century Architecture in the United States

By Narciso G. Menocal

Architecture as Nature: The Transcendentalist Idea of Louis Sullivan

Keck and Keck, Architects

My Father Who Is on Earth: Including Comments, Responses, and Documents by Frank Lloyd Wright and John Lloyd Wright (editor)

The Tobacco Industry in Cuba and Florida: Its Golden Age in Lithography and Architecture

Wright Studies (editor)

LOUIS SULLIVAN

The Poetry of Architecture

ROBERT TWOMBLY

NARCISO G. MENOCAL

W. W. NORTON & COMPANY

NEW YORK   LONDON

Printed in Singapore by Tien Wah Printing
Design and typesetting by Katy Homans

Frontispiece: Louis H. Sullivan, circa 1900. Courtesy The Art Institute of Chicago

Library of Congress Cataloging-in-Publication Data

Twombly, Robert C.
Louis Sullivan : the poetry of architecture/ Robert Twombly and Narciso G. Menocal.
p. cm.
Includes bibliographical references and index.
ISBN 0-393-04823-3
1. Sullivan, Louis, 1856–1924–Catalogs. 2. Sullivan, Louis, 1856–1924–Philosophy.
I. Menocal, Narciso G. II. Title.
NA2707.S94 A4 2000
720'.92—dc21
00-020746

W. W. Norton & Company, Inc., 500 Fifth Avenue, New York, N.Y. 10110
www.wwnorton.com

W. W. Norton & Company, Ltd., 10 Coptic Street, London WC1A 1PU

1 2 3 4 5 6 7 8 9 0

Contents

LOUIS SULLIVAN

THE POETRY OF ARCHITECTURE

Introduction: On Dialogue

The origin of this book resides in a paper Robert Twombly read at the Sorbonne in February 1988. In "Tragic Facades: Five Dimensions of Louis Sullivan's Skyscrapers," Twombly argued that Sullivan's buildings were "multifunctional," outcomes and emblems of the architect's ongoing confrontation with a series of aesthetic, social, urban, metaphysical, and personal problems.

In light of the general understanding that Sullivan saw an aesthetic opportunity in skyscraper design, Twombly contended that the architect had developed not one but two—possibly even three—prototypes for the genre: one well know to historians based on a vertical aesthetic (which Sullivan called a "system of vertical construction"), a less familiar alternative based on a frame or skeletal aesthetic (which Twombly called a "system of skeletal construction"), and a short-lived intermediate approach linking the two. In addition, Sullivan had offered several compositional variations on each of these "types." Twombly then demonstrated that the tall building was also directed toward certain social, urban, and metaphysical issues weighing on Sullivan and that, as a result of his turning it into a vehicle for biting cultural criticism, it became a personal problem, since his critique prompted potential clients to withhold commissions, thus contributing to the poverty of his last years. Twombly further insisted that the ramifications of these five dimensions could be fully understood only by "reading" the buildings in close conjunction with Sullivan's literary work.

Twombly sent "Tragic Facades" to Narciso Menocal, who responded by focusing on one aspect in particular: the dichotomy—considered within the aesthetic dimension—between the expression of verticality and of the frame. Menocal maintained that only in the early 1890s was Sullivan fascinated by the question of height, for he soon came to realize that there was much more to the skyscraper, that there was "a very intimate rela-

tionship between form and structure—between the appearance of a body and the skeleton that supports it, to put it in [Leopold] Eidlitz's terms." It was the expression of the skeleton that became most important for Sullivan, Menocal wrote, especially "when one thinks of his perception of two important relationships, that of a building and the law of gravity, and the metaphysical [relationships] with geomorphism and anthropomorphism," not to mention "the dynamic possibilities that anthropomorphism opened."

Menocal pointed out that the Guaranty Building posed a problem because its 1894–95 design came after the development of the frame/skeletal model. "Why would Sullivan return to the first [vertical] style," he asked, "after he had been so close to defining the third style [Twombly's frame/skeletal] in the second [intermediate stage]?" The fact that the Guaranty was the only Sullivan building entirely clad in ornament "makes me consider," Menocal added by way of answering his own question, "that Sullivan may have been thinking in gynecomorphic terms as much as in anthropomorphic ones." Because we now know that Sullivan saw "the brown color of the Guaranty [as] definitely masculine," since he had characterized Henry Hobson Richardson's "masculine" Marshall Field Wholesale Store as "foursquare and brown," and that he also considered his own Bayard/Condict Building to be "maidenlike" because of its creamy hue, Menocal concluded that the Guaranty with its lush "feminine" ornament was the architect's attempt "at a new kind of synthesis," of the male and the female.

Thus, Menocal continued, by the late 1890s making a skyscraper lofty was a given for Sullivan, "but only if the design of the building demanded it." For he had come to see that "no two buildings should look the same, as no two specimens in nature are alike." Sullivan's last realized examples of the genre—the Bayard/Condict and Gage buildings and the Schlesinger & Mayer Store (all between 1897 and 1902)—prove the point by being "completely different from each other," Menocal wrote. "The question now was to express bones, sinew, and flesh, and to create with them a body that would be different from any other because it was the portrait of a unique personality. . . . Sullivan would never again turn his back to the truth of nature." He had entered, in Menocal's words, "the organic phase" of his career.

Menocal ended his letter to Twombly by proposing an organization for "Tragic Facades" that would have subsumed the five dimensions in an iconographical framework. Twombly replied that he was "content with the five problem approach" as it stood, adding that if he followed Menocal's advice he would be required to do one of two things: restructure the essay "along the lines of [your] outline . . . , or incorporate selected suggestions. To do the latter would be to emasculate the totality of the argument as you cast it. To do the former would be to write a different essay." So Twombly proposed an alternative: that Menocal develop his outline into an essay and that the two be submitted "in tandem" for publication. "The result would be two rather different—if sympathetic—ways [to assess] the same material," Twombly wrote, "a sort of dialogue, the likes of which is not often enough seen in American scholarly journals." Menocal agreed to do just that.

Prior commitments forestalled immediate progress. Twombly returned to the United States in August 1988 after a year in The Netherlands eager to resume work on a biography of Henry Hobson Richardson and with the idea of writing about the remarkable social housing he had seen. Menocal was hard at work on a study of Frank Lloyd Wright. But unknown to each other at first, both accepted invitations to speak at the "Louis Sullivan & the Architecture of Democracy" symposium at Grinnell College, one result of which was to encourage them to reconsider their publishing plans.

The Grinnell symposium proved to be of considerable importance. Speakers and the resident faculty and staff came together in what can only be described as an atmosphere of perfect collegiality; the intellectual atmosphere at Grinnell was anything but competitive or selfish. Issues were discussed and research shared without pretension or the goal of demonstrating "star" quality. Formal presentations and informal exchanges on the theme of Sullivan's "democratic" architecture disposed Menocal and Twombly to broaden their scope, to compose longer, more comprehensive texts on the meaning of Sullivan's entire oeuvre, to elaborate on the themes—the impulses—that drove him on, each author by his own lights, to be sure. Even though both had written on Sullivan, each sensed that he, and they, had not gotten from him all there was to get, that upon further reflection things remained to be said. So what began as a conversation about a single building type evolved after Grinnell into a discussion about Louis Sullivan himself.

Their plans accelerated when Menocal moved to Twombly's New York area as the 1989–1990 Senior Fellow at the Temple Hoyne Buell Center for the Study of American Architecture, Columbia University. Good talk often happens in the halls of academe, but it also occurs in the living room and over dinner, walking the streets, at exhibitions, and in bookshops. Some of Menocal and Twombly's best conversations took place at Twombly's house in West Nyack, New York; at Menocal's apartment in Butler Hall, Columbia University; at the Turning Point restaurant in Piermont, New York (where the final form of this book was worked out); and most of all at the Abbey Pub, an Upper West Side watering hole at Broadway and 105th Street where Menocal joined Twombly once a week for drinks and discussion about the progress of each other's work. While the dialogue was mostly about Twombly's "Richardson" and Menocal's "Wright," it was at the Abbey that the authors refined the idea for this book, and it was there that Menocal proposed gathering together for the first time all existing Sullivan drawings, some three dozen of which had never been published; nor had they ever been integrated in chronological order, thereby eliminating artificial classifications imposed by virtue of storage in disparate institutions. This new integration also contributes to the holistic sense of Sullivan that Menocal and Twombly tried to incorporate in their essays.

The dialogue between Twombly and Menocal, represented by their essays in this book, demonstrates that on several issues they reached different conclusions, which, however, are more complementary than oppositional. The reader will find two concerted efforts to pull from Sullivan's design and literary work the irreducible fundaments of his being, but the differing results reflect the authors' independence of each other's vantage points. In conventional academic terminology the one is known as a social historian of architecture, the other as an art historian of architecture, but in fact neither label accurately applies. Real difference lies in conceptualization, not in categories. Twombly interprets Sullivan's work as a call for cultural reform based on a revival of democratic instincts; Menocal sees it as an expression of an idealistic manner of thinking touching on the metaphysical. Sullivan's linking of style with iconography, in Menocal's view, aimed at creating an aesthetic response in the viewer that would urge him or her to become one with a transcendent nature; in Twombly's view, that linkage attempted to instill in the viewer the idea that human creativity knew no social boundaries. If Twombly stresses the social and political content in Sullivan's work and Menocal the aesthetic and intellectual, they agree that his fundamental objective was to revivify American democracy.

While Sullivan is the subject of this book, it is also, like any other book, about the intellectual development of its authors. Twombly delivered his first *conscious* sally at a comprehensive thematic interpretation of Sullivan in November 1989 at a Buell Center "luncheon seminar," the semester theme being the extent to which an architect's writings enhance understanding of his buildings and aesthetic ideals. In "Louis Sullivan and the Poetry of Cultural Reform," Twombly argued that

in a very real sense Sullivan's drawn and written work could not be distinguished, that sense being their objective: the resurrection of democratic life in America. This presentation turned out to be the fifth and last in an unplanned series of lecture—occasioned by speaking invitations following the 1986 appearance of *Louis Sullivan: His Life and Work*—in which Twombly, without realizing it, had been trying to determine the *raison d'être* of Sullivan's life as the architect himself understood it, a determination Twombly came to feel he had not satisfactorily made in that biography. Those five lectures became the basis for Twombly's text in this book.

In retrospect it appears that the first *unconscious* thrust in that direction had been "Tragic Facades," the Sorbonne lecture written in the Paris apartment of Twombly's wife, Professor Jeanne Chase of the Ecole des Hautes Etudes en Sciences Sociales, who commented on his interpretations, much to their improvement, in an ongoing intellectually fertile dialogue from which additional ideas sprang. Not only did she help hone his thinking while pointing out new directions it might take, but she also suggested emphases and connections he had missed, as she would do for "The Piazza in the Garden," written and read in Amsterdam; for "The Vision of His Life," delivered at Grinnell; and for "The Poetry of Cultural Reform." Without Jeanne Chase's considerable effort, taking valuable time away from her own work, "A Poet's Garden"—the culmination in this volume of the essays she strengthened— would be the lesser.

Menocal's development was roughly similar in that his perception of Sullivan broadened—as well as deepened—over the years. After publishing *Architecture as Nature: The Transcendentalist Idea of Louis Sullivan* in 1981, he devoted most of his attention to the study of Frank Lloyd Wright. But, like other historians, his interest was stimulated by new interpretations of mid-nineteenth-century French architecture offered by Neil Levine, David Van Zanten, Richard Chafee, Richard Etlin, Christopher Mead, Barry Bergdoll, and others, and of the formidable influence it had on U.S. architecture during Sullivan's formative years. This body of literature, along with Twombly's biography, kept Sullivan a secondary focus of Menocal's attention, as did the flurry of important new books on the architect himself: the collection edited by Wim de Wit as *Louis Sullivan: The Function of Ornament* (1986); Joseph Siry's *Carson Pirie Scott: Louis Sullivan and the Chicago Department Store* (1988); Larry Millett's *The Curve of the Arch: The Story of Louis Sullivan's Owatonna Bank* (1985), which serves as an excellent companion to Lauren S. Weingarden's *Louis H. Sullivan: The Banks* (1987); and two splendid volumes published by the Art Institute of Chicago: *Louis Sullivan in The Art Institute of Chicago: The Illustrated Catalogue of Collections* (1989), and *Louis H. Sullivan: A System of Architectural Ornament* (1990). In graduate courses at the University of Wisconsin–Madison, in symposia, and in a number of published essays, Menocal continued to explore Sullivan—all the while working on Wright—bringing his reading of the new literature into his discourse. His essay in this book, therefore, is a broadening as well as a refinement—and in the case of the banks, a correction—of his earlier interpretations of Sullivan's style and inconography.

That in this book the authors agree on the ultimate central meaning of their subject's work but often interpret it differently indicates not only divergent methods of scholarly operation but, most important, the fertility of Sullivan's mind. Unlike many present-day Americans, Sullivan lived ungrudgingly with his own contradictions and ambiguities, often not even aware of them. And indeed, it was in part because of them that he was able to construct a written and architectural body of work the authors believe must be understood as conceptually consistent. His buildings and his writings, they contend, however individually ambiguous or collectively self-contradictory they may appear, are, at bottom, a singular didactic process, consistent in its underlying tendency and purpose. And, needless to say, the authors hope their readers will construct yet another kind of

unity by organizing the literary and visual documents presented here into their own interpretive wholes, into their own understandings of the meaning of the work. Menocal and Twombly encourage their readers to open the same kinds of dialogue with the material in this book—that is, with Louis Sullivan himself—as they have had with him and with each other.

Louis Sullivan's drawings and the essays by Twombly and Menocal make up the bulk of this volume. But intrinsic to its integrity, and in some ways as important as anything else included herein, is the translation of Sullivan's "Etude sur l'inspiration," the only surviving copy of which is handwritten in French and dated 1893. This was a second and completely new version of his famous "Essay on Inspiration" of 1886: his first comprehensive statement of the centrality of nature to his philosophical and design work. The authors feel that the 1893 text merited translation and publication so that readers may trace changes in Sullivan's thinking and literary style during a seven-year period coinciding with the maturation of his creativity.

It will be noted that the structure of this book—Sullivan's "Etude," his drawings, their catalogue, textual illustrations, this introductory statement, and two quite different essays—does not adhere to conventional patterns of scholarly publication. The authors thank Jim Mairs at W. W. Norton & Company for his endorsement of idiosyncrasy, for welcoming something unusual, and for helping to stimulate the kind of collegiality that is not often enough present in academic life. For what began as a formal, professional relationship between two authors sharing similar scholarly interests ended up as a friendship based on respect for the personal and intellectual differences of the other. In more than the usual sense, then, *Louis Sullivan: The Poetry of Architecture* is the result of complete collaboration.

The authors also wish to thank Jim Mairs's many associates at Norton who contributed to the making of this book, especially Nancy Palmquist, whose stimulating inquiries, insightful suggestions, and impressive editorial skills are very much a part of these pages, and Ted Johnson for his impeccable copyediting.

The authors express their gratitude to the Graham Foundation for Advanced Studies in the Fine Arts for two generous grants that underwrote the cost of acquiring illustrations and to the Graduate School of the University of Wisconsin–Madison for a summer support grant for Narciso Menocal. They also take particular pleasure in thanking those who supplied photographs for the plates in this volume: at the Art Institute of Chicago, Mary Woolever; at the Avery Library, Columbia University, Janet Parks and Vicki Wiener; at the Bentley Historical Library, University of Michigan, Nancy Bartlett; at the University of Michigan Museum of Art, Terry Kerby; formerly at the Chicago Architectural Foundation, Carol J. Callahan; for the Richard Nickel Committee, Chicago, and from their own collections, Tim Samuelson and John Vinci; also from their own collections: Ruth Guyer and Wilbert and Marilyn Hasbrouck, Chicago; J. B. Muns and Jan Novie, Berkeley, California; Paul Sprague, emeritus, University of Wisconsin–Milwaukee; William and Karen Schuster, Cedar Rapids, Iowa; and Barbara Pine, New York City.

Finally, the authors thank those whose assistance advanced this project in other ways: Christine and Peter Livaudais, Reuil-Malmaison, France, for help in deciphering the text of "Etude sur l'inspiration"; Jeanne Chase, Paris and New York, for help with its translation; Robert M. Keuny, Kenosha, Wisconsin, for suggestions for locating drawings; and Alan K. Lathrop, Northwest Architectural Archives, St. Paul, Minnesota, and Lauren S. Weingarden, Florida State University, Tallahassee, for supplying illustrations for the texts. Menocal wishes to acknowledge the many stimulating comments of students in his Sullivan seminar and proseminar; Twombly is similarly grateful to those who contribute to "Organic Architecture: Richardson, Sullivan, Wright" at the City College of New York.

But most of all the authors thank their wives, Marta Menocal and Jeanne Chase, who with patience, humor, understanding, and insight helped bring this project to fruition.

ROBERT TWOMBLY & NARCISO MENOCAL
West Nyack, New York, and Madison, Wisconsin

A Poet's Garden:
Louis Sullivan's Vision for America

ROBERT TWOMBLY

Louis Sullivan was a visionary, given to utopian design, which he expressed in two ways. The one, his architecture, is much praised, but even when condemned, has had a profound impact, as strongly on his contemporaries as on subsequent generations. The other, his writing, is much condemned, but even when praised, has had a negligible impact, except on a handful of colleagues, and later on except for a single essay. By and large, architectural scholars have dismissed his writing—biographers and historians of ideas have been somewhat less remiss—claiming that since his thinking was unsystematic, his wording imprecise, his assertions contradictory, and, irony of ironies, his prose too poetic, they are without real value, perhaps impenetrable, and beside the point, especially because so much of what he wrote seems unrelated to design. Sullivan's pioneering buildings speak for themselves, it is said, so his writing—not the forte of many architects anyway—can safely be disregarded.

It is no doubt true that when directed toward nondesign matters most architects' ideas ought to be redeposited in "the dumpster behind the philosophy department," where they had been discarded, in the apt words of one observer.[1] But in Sullivan's case, scholarly dismissal leaves unconsidered the intimate connections between his writing—which was extensive (four books and some fifty essays and published lectures from 1885 to 1924)—and his designs. By ignoring those connections, and by refusing to accept him on his own terms and words, in his own time and place, scholars not only treat him ahistorically but also miss his fundamental meaning. Sullivan's buildings do, of course, speak for themselves, but in the light of his writing they resonate even more profoundly and imaginatively than is generally supposed.

A case in point is his skyscrapers, about which three interpretive errors have consistently been advanced: that Sullivan had but a single design objective in mind—an aesthetic one; that he realized it only one way—with his "system of vertical construction"; and that the explanation of that realization encapsulated in his phrase "form follows function" was in fact, as the critic/historian Sigfried Giedion and others have contended, a manifesto for a modernist future. But as the following pages will argue, Sullivan proposed *several* aesthetic solutions for a *contemporary* problem he believed to be, at bottom, not architectural but *social*, a conviction he stated unequivocally in his most famous publication, "The Tall Office Building Artistically Considered" (1896), the one essay scholars have never disregarded.

Apparently that essay has not been permitted to speak for itself, however, because its obvious social implications have usually been overlooked. But if we allow Sullivan's writings to say what they mean, not ignoring the nonarchitectural portions while keeping his buildings clearly in mind, we discover a kind of holistic edifice emerging from the totality of his oeuvre, which is to say that his mature life's work—from the writing desk as well as from the drafting table—was of a piece, was aimed at a single objective. That objective was the rebirth of democracy in the United States.

Based on an assessment of the world around him from the mid-1880s to the eve of World War I, Sullivan's architecture and writing addressed a variety of heavenly and mundane issues, but certainly the most pressing, decidedly the most important, was the declining quality of American life. In order to resuscitate flagging democratic principles, to save his nation from cultural death, he offered the healing power of architecture—as

Figure 1.
"Bits of Nature."
Photograph by
Louis H. Sullivan.
Forms and Fantasies, 1898.

imagery, as art, and in words. It is this vision of a reborn America that he wrote about and it is this for which he built. But in both cases, as a writer and a designer, he proceeded as a poet, for that is what he considered himself fundamentally to be. "Making a real building and making a real poem," he maintained, "are pretty much one and the same thing," since for him the poet had mastered the "power of seeing and doing."[2] If, like designing a building, writing a poem was also a way of "doing," and conversely making a building was also a way of "seeing," then it is reasonable to conclude that Sullivan saw no essential difference between the two, offering both his architecture and his writing as a single midwife for democracy's rebirth. Nor should *we* see a difference if we are to appreciate the richness of Sullivan's vision and understand how it impregnated his designs.

1. Sullivan's Vision

Louis Sullivan's vision for America is best approached by examining at the outset and in his own words what that vision was not. It was not that of a society, he wrote, in an unpublished manuscript of the early 1900s, in which the representative person was a "hermit," that is, someone who "can and does live within the retirement of his innate self, that, safe, within this sanctuary, he draws a veil impenetrable and inviolable." It was not a society in which people were without collective life and mutual connections. And, most especially, his vision for America was not one in which "torn and maimed men, women, and children, all the separated legs, and arms and heads, and the funerals, the weeping ones, the disconsolate, the crutches and the bandages, the surgeons, hospitals, coffins, paraphernalia and cemeteries must be brought to [the hermit], brought in thousands upon thousands, wailing, moaning, stiff and stark, ghastly and freshly ripped open, all brought in to the [hermit's] sanctuary, into the stillness, the quiet where the man is safe, inscrutable, —Alone with his secret soul, that he may see for sure that these human fragments, this human residue came from the grade crossings of his railroads; that he may know that he spells the word dividends with the identical letters that others use to spell the word murder. . . . [3]

"It is not customary to speak thus baldly," Sullivan continued, his anger accumulating as he contemplated what his vision for America was not: ". . . the word, murder, we dilute, in a sea of phrases, and evaporate in perfumed breezes of sentiment.

We attenuate it in speech, and make artistic distinctions, and we spin it into a delicate thread wherewith we weave a garment to hide its nakedness—and we paint it and powder it, and convert it and baptize it, and hide it in a religion, and have wise men to write beautiful books in which they spell it benevolence, political economy, and the laws of trade, and the survival of the fittest, and *laissez-faire*. And we infuse it [murder] into a body of laws—and we inject it into an army and a navy—and we erect it into a great system of business enterprise. And we have philosophers to sublimate it, and theologians to glorify it. And upon it we found a civilization, just as the man of the past founded civilizations upon it. But it is murder just the same, and the fear of life just the same, and the superstitious hatred of the neighbor just the same, and it is completely mutual, and completely universal, and individual just the same. In short it is you and I, and the secret thought we hold in common."

Sullivan wrote these lines between 1904 and 1908 in a manuscript called "Natural Thinking: A Study in Democracy" that was not published until thirty-seven years after his death and then under the title *Democracy, a Man-Search* (1961). They had been a difficult five years in which Sullivan received a paltry seven commissions leading to the realization of only two houses, a factory, and an out-of-the-way bank. This downturn in business had followed a brief upturn after the gloomy depression of the 1890s. Between 1897 and 1902 he had designed the Bayard/Condict Building in New York, and in Chicago, the Gage (or McCormick) Building facade and the Schlesinger & Mayer (now the Carson Pirie Scott) Store, his last major architectural works, as it turned out, although he hardly knew that at the time. But worse disasters struck soon enough, immediately after he finished "Natural Thinking": between November 1909 and January 1910 he would auction most of his household goods and his library, watch his wife leave him for another man, relinquish half his Ocean Springs, Mississippi, land to repay a loan, and then, in May 1910, lose to creditors his beloved winter residence there, "his paradise," he called it, his "other self"—this, perhaps, the worst blow of all. Even before he sank to this nadir in 1910, Sullivan had been on financial skids that he would escape only with death in 1924, leading some observers to maintain that personal misfortune accounts for the bitterness—the overt anger, in fact—of some of his late writing.[4]

Outspoken social criticism has frequently been discredited by attributing it to personality disorder or to "outsider" status, but it would be ill-advised to ascribe Sullivan's views to a resentment caused by material circumstance. For his unflinching assessment of what he saw around him was in fact the mirror image of a hopeful vision for his native land, an optimistic vision constructed during years of reflection before bad times arrived, but not fully articulated until they had. It could just as easily be said, if just as inaccurately, that his faith in the future was a reaction to his misfortune or, conversely, the outcome of his halcyon days. But none of this will do. His description of what was, like his insistence on what could be, was informed by contemplating the American character and reflecting on human nature, not by bemoaning his own situation, about which he usually remained rather dispassionate, in any event. But his vision for America's future was offered with all the passion he could muster, and it was this:

There was "a strange, far-off country," he continued in "Natural Thinking," "fair to look upon; well-watered, fertile, rich in every form of nature's bounty . . . on a scale simple, broad, impressive:— great plains, prairies, mountains, rivers and lakes— and a long, double-frontage on the seas. . . . Famine

is unknown. The broad-flowing land is crossed and re-crossed by railways, telegraph and telephone lines. . . . Nearly all the people read and write" the books, newspapers, and magazines that "are sown broadcast, like winged seeds upon the winds." The land is dotted with free public schools for children; and the seminaries, technical schools, and universities for young manhood and young womanhood are numerous. It is "a far-flung, sumptuous, inspiriting land . . . in its large serene isolation" that, if it will, "may be at peace . . . in tranquil strength."

"The activities of the people are varied and commensurate," he continued. Huge numbers are engaged in agriculture, business, and industry—"all on a basis of diversified immensity. The energy of the people is intense, quick-witted, practical and material." They call their government democratic: of, by, and for the people. "There are no acknowledged social castes; speech is asserted to be free; and religious tolerance is universal." Those to whom political power is delegated are "elected by a universal male suffrage. . . . A single language is used throughout . . . the noble land. Local divergences . . . are so slight as to be quite negligible. Never was a great multitude placed in so free, so expansive, so adequate, so bountiful, gracious and simple a setting. Never, to receive and nurture a vast people, were Nature's preparations so benign, so inclusive, so unspeakably gracious. . . . This land is known to you, no doubt, under its politico-geographical name: The United States of America."

This was Louis Sullivan's vision: that "a land so noble, a people so situate, so completely equipped with all the instrumentalities of advanced civilization, would surely bring forth out of themselves, life-results of simple, noble, strong and fruitful harmony."

But, sadly, they had not. The vision was in fact a mirage, a dream, an illusion. When Sullivan looked through the glass darkly at the people of this "strange, far-off country," he saw the opposite of his utopia. He saw, in his words, "decadent faces" with a look of "absence" in eyes "devoid of radiance," and with "complexions sodden." There was a "false note" to what they said, in speech that was either flat and dull or forced and artificial. There was something furtive and hidden, yet at the same time open and attractive, about them because they were leading double lives: one "as a concession to appearances," the other in search "of a something else." And that "something else" was in fact a two-sided search: for a sense of the spiritual life, and for "a sensibility concerning the true meaning of Nature, and of man's place therein." Because they failed to find "a something else," they drank too much, ate too much, took too many drugs. They were overstimulated and nervous; they suffered from anxiety, and from "every variety of self-induced disease." They poisoned themselves with adulterated foods, and as for mental food, they had created "not one" single philosophy or economic theory that met with general acceptance. They had failed to create out of their own lives "a valid statement of Democracy," allowing themselves instead to be infected with the "virus of feudal culture" wherein "right" was defined by "might" and only a few had power. The result, he concluded, was that the "key-note of the active aggressive American life is commercialism. And this means . . . the law of dog eat dog."

If the reality of American life was such that Sullivan's vision was not yet a dream but remained a nightmare, he nevertheless believed that the situation could change, that what he called the American "dance of death" could be turned into a festival of joy. "There is a fundamental urge in man which causes in him a deep desire to give his whole life-energy to the service of his fellow men.

. . . In other words, man's heart has always been right. All his confusion has been wrought by his vanity and absurdity of intellect. The splendid urge of his imagination and his will has been misconstrued by him, and it is his own intellect that has prepared the pitfalls into which he has sunk, even as he believed himself on the scent of something socially real. It is not that Feudalism represents what is bad in man's heart—for there is nothing bad there. . . . [I]t is merely because [men] do not clearly understand the essential and concrete nature of their relationship to their fellows, to the earth, and to the spirit of integrity" that they remain feudal.

"It will be seen therefore," he continued, "that what we are here choosing to call Democracy or The New Way, is but the ancient primordial urge within us of integrity or oneness. And it is this very urge of Nature . . . that is awakening within the heart of modern man the desire to seek a fundamental law of social integrity or oneness, wherein each man shall be truly a law unto himself. For that basic law shall imply the liberation of the free creative . . . spirit, . . . an organic law, . . . not for one man [monarchy] or a few men [feudalism], but for all men. This is the essential nature of Democracy. For Democracy and the oneness of all things are one." When that primordial urge bursts through—and Sullivan believed in 1908 that its time was near—"the American people will change, and rise at once, regenerate! to be the greatest, noblest people the earth has [ever] known." That was Louis Sullivan's vision for his nation.

2. Feudalism

It must be assumed that Sullivan believed all this or he would not have devoted so much time to "Natural Thinking" or told Chicago art critic Harriet Monroe early in its drafting that he intended to change the title to "The People," "for whom it will have been written," he said, "that is to say *all the people*."[5] And it must be assumed as well that "democracy" meant something precious to him or else his writing would not have been saturated

with the word and his thinking permeated with the concept. Yet, Sullivan has all too often been dismissed as an elitist, a Spencerian, a Nietzschean, as if reading authors like these could miraculously transform him into an antidemocrat or, as some have alleged, into so strong an advocate of late-nineteenth-century rugged individualism that he saw himself the cultural superman. But personal arrogance, of which he had plenty, does not an elitist make, and if Sullivan seemed to his contemporaries an unapproachable loner, a perfectionist, a man of highly cultivated tastes and unusually refined sensibilities devoid of intimate human contact, it was not because he harbored a patronizing view of average working people. Anything but. Albeit abstractly (as we shall see), Sullivan loved humanity as much as he hated plutocracy, which was for him the principal source of what was wrong with his nation. The overthrow of plutocracy—of "feudalism" or "neofeudalism," he called it—was the primary objective of his mature building and writing.

Sullivan divided history into two epochs: feudalism and democracy, with the birth of the United States as the great dividing point. His "feudalism" did not refer to what historians generally mean when they use the word: to those sets of social, economic, and political systems or arrangements characterizing the medieval period. Sullivan meant simply the absence of democracy or, more precisely, the accumulation, control, and manipulation of every kind of power by a privileged caste. Because of feudalism's rigid hierarchies, humanity was held in spiritual and intellectual bondage. It could not develop, make choices, create, educate itself; in short, could not realize its potential, collectively or individually. Economic serfdom mattered less to him than mental and spiritual serfdom. As serfs, people could never be real, whole, creative human beings.

But the American Revolution had changed all that. Humanity had begun the process of taking power into its own hands, abolishing aristocracies, elites, and privileged castes. For the first time in history a sizable number of people could choose their own life's work, be educated, develop self-defined potentials, and satisfy needs in self-determined ways. Becoming what the organism innately aspired to be also characterized the realm of nature, as Sullivan saw it, from which he concluded that democracy was the only "natural" form of social organization, and the United States, as established, the only nation in which life was "organic."

But then, at a moment he never precisely identified, but which seems to have been during his lifetime, the American democratic experiment went sour. The feudalism that should have been eradicated and seemingly was by the founding fathers resurfaced in the form of a monstrous accumulation of power—perhaps historically unprecedented in its dimensions—wielded by a new aristocracy with the complicity and complacency of the people. This aristocracy—the emerging industrially based entrepreneurial and financial elite—he occasionally labeled "the trusts" or "the barons" ("feudal" barons, he called them, not "robber" barons), but he never criticized capitalism *per se*, being a firm believer in private ownership and in laissez-faire. The aim of "Natural Thinking," however, and of much of his other writing, was to awaken the public, not by attacking the elite directly, but by urging readers to discover themselves, to understand that only in a democracy could they even imagine, let along fulfill, their human possibilities.

Sullivan's agenda was thus educational, implicitly but not overtly political, intellectually akin stylistically to that of his muckraking contemporaries, journalists Lincoln Steffens and Ida Tarbell, for example, who thought it sufficient to expose injustice, corruption, and exploitation without offering corrective remedies, leaving it to "the people" to do something someday. Sullivan's pedagogy was also unprogrammatic, aimed at arousing the public, which, learning the truth about itself and society, would act in its own best interest, would make democracy real. This was also the objective of his architecture.

3. The West: Locus of Democracy

Because of the continued existence of unspoiled nature and unsettled land, Sullivan was optimistic about his nation's democratic potential even though, in his opinion, it had once flowed but was now ebbing. It is not unlikely that he read or heard Frederick Jackson Turner deliver his extraordinarily persuasive and influential lecture "The Significance of the Frontier in American History" at the 1893 World's Columbian Exposition in Chicago, where Sullivan himself read a paper and for which he designed the building to house the transportation exhibit. But if he had, he would not have lamented with Turner the closing of the frontier, nor feared with him that as a result the great engine of democracy might be grinding to a halt. Perhaps there were no new geographical frontiers within national boundaries in 1893, or more particularly in 1901–2 when Sullivan published "Kindergarten Chats," on which the following paragraphs are based. But there certainly was open land, western land, even within cities like Chicago. If the East was hopelessly feudal, culturally tied too closely to Europe, to Sullivan's mind the West could still regain democracy, because it was not, and remained in part pristine. It was in the West, therefore, that Sullivan's vision might become his reality.

Born an Easterner, in Boston in 1856, Sullivan became a Westerner by choice, identifying with the region personally and intellectually. Arriving in Chicago as a teenager in 1873, he loved everything he saw, even grim reminders of the horrendous fire that two years before had destroyed the central city, recalling in his 1924 memoir that as he alighted from the train he shouted: "This is the Place for Me!"[6] An apocryphal tale perhaps, but it indicates his continuing belief in the city's promise half a century later. After a stint at the Ecole des Beaux-Arts in Paris and touring Italy in 1875, he returned directly to Chicago, never giving thought to remaining in his native East. Except for regular visits to his Mississippi winter retreat from 1890 to 1910, he spent the rest of his life in Chicago, where he died, at age sixty-seven.

His adopted West of the 1870s was in several important ways the architectural colony of an Eastern metropole. If aspiring architects were not trained by established professionals but instead joined the new trend toward academic studies, their only regional choice was the fledgling department of architecture at the University of Illinois (Champaign), opened in 1868. Otherwise they were obliged to attend the only other architectural program in America, at the Massachusetts Institute of Technology, then in Boston, or to travel across the Atlantic to England or Germany or to the Ecole des Beaux-Arts, upon which MIT's course of study was indirectly modeled. The profession's few major periodicals and the American Institute of Architects were Eastern-based, furthermore, and building styles Eastern-generated. When large structures were to be erected in Western cities, responsible parties more often than not looked outside the region for architects.

On the other hand, the West was arguably *tabula rasa*, a clean slate upon which to build, Chicago especially, because the 1871 fire had raged through 1,688 built-up acres, destroying 18,000 structures, leaving 100,000 people homeless. The original participants in what came to be called the Chicago School of architecture (meaning a dozen or so prominent firms specializing in commercial construction from roughly 1880 to World War I) were almost all Easterners who had flocked to the city like bees to pollen, some shortly before, but more immediately after, 1871: Dankmar Adler, Louis Sullivan, William Le Baron Jenney, Martin Roche, William Holabird, John Root, and Daniel Burnham were all recent arrivals. Adler wrote that he could literally measure his buildings "by the mile," so much work was there to do in the conflagration's aftermath.[7]

The fire created a sense of urgency: reconstruction had to be fast and without frills. Extraordinary demographic growth and a dangerously high water table had already generated an experimental spirit—prompting early innovations in foundation systems and lightweight wood construction, for example—that broadened after 1871 into an even greater receptivity to other new technologies, such as fire-resistant vaultings and iron and steel framing. Chicagoans took great pride in their speedy reemergence, like a "phoenix rising from the ashes," the boosters among them insisted; no other city, they boasted, had ever accomplished so much so quickly. If Eastern-born architects took charge of the rebuilding, Chicago soon took charge of them, in the process making them Westerners, often determinedly so.

By the 1880s a vigorous regional consciousness was emerging within the profession. In short order came *Inland Architect* magazine (Chicago), the Western Association of Architects (Chicago), architectural clubs and sketch clubs (in several cities), and finally *Western Architect* (Minneapolis). The University of Illinois professional training program began to flourish under the leadership of Professor Nathan C. Ricker, soon to be followed by another at Chicago's Armour Institute (today's Illinois Institute) of Technology. All this assumed that there was something different about the West, and if that difference was not so easily defined it was nevertheless characterized by separate and distinct organizations with separate and distinct publications calling for separate and distinct design work. It was in this climate that Louis Sullivan matured to articulate that regional difference, self-consciously Western, deliberately not Eastern. It is therefore important to think of the West as he did: as an idea as much as a place.

It is necessary to understand what "West" and "East" symbolized for him, because being "Western" informed his social thinking, his architectural work, and as a result his vision of democracy. By attempting to create an indigenous, nonhistorical, American style of design, Sullivan was also decolonizing the West, fighting an architectural war of independence, struggling to define the meaning of his nation. His battle was not over territory but about how to build the democratic utopia.

His clearest statement of the issue is in "Kinder-garten Chats" (1901–2), a fictional dialogue between an architectural master and his pupil, published in fifty-two installments of Cleveland's *Interstate Architect and Builder*. "Fortunately for us," the master intoned in an early Chat,[8] as he and his apprentice inspected a Chicago department store, buildings like this are "more rampant in the East than in the West." Designed in "the current jargon of architecture," that is, in a revived style, probably neoclassic, it showed "the incapacity of the insufficiently educated, the unleavened, the half-baked to express in simple well-chosen language the casual, current experiences of life." Though erected in Chicago, it was "not characteristic of the West" because it utterly lacked "western frankness, directness. . . . It is merely the weak-rooted cutting from the eastern hothouse." If the West was frank, direct, and honest, the East was glib, vague, and dishonest. If Westerners built to satisfy real needs, Easterners built to perpetuate tradition.

New York and Chicago epitomized East and West for Sullivan because they "stood in a certain polaric opposition in our civilization." Like other observers of the day, he understood New York (and much of the East) to be an extension of Europe, a purveyor of aristocratic and therefore antidemocratic values, a repository of feudalism, the locus of tired cultural ideas that, having once served well, were now degenerate. During a whirl-wind tour of Manhattan, Sullivan's literary master explained the inflated size and cost of a typical office building to his pupil as "*sui generis*, part of New York," which by definition was "Gomorrah" not Democracy, growling "the growl of the glutton hunt for the dollar." Highly ornate and fussy, this "tainted" building was "*profoundly anti-social*," a kind of "outlaw," "evidence of forces that are undermining American life," proof that "New York is the plague spot of American design."

Sullivan believed that architecture was "a social manifestation." "Behind the screen of each building is a man," its designer; collectively, buildings formed a larger screen called the city which was, he wrote, "the material reflection of the character of its inhabitants, who will it, who suffer it to be, whose thought it is. . . . [The city] is their image, their materialization." So what lay behind this screen called New York? Embarrassing social truths. "Where we should by seeming virtue of money-power be led to expect the best," Sullivan declared, "we find the worst; . . . where standards should be highest, we find them lowest; . . . where we should find the highest type of responsibility and honor, we find the grossest exhibition of irresponsibility and dishonor. . . ." If there was stewardship attached to wealth, it did not exist in the East, where Sullivan found only the complete absence of social conscience. In a word, the East was corrupt.

But what of Chicago, his symbol for the West? "We are here," the kindergarten master explained, "because I wish to show you extremes. . . ." Chicago was hardly perfect. Many of its buildings were sycophantic reiterations of ancient European styles, and many of its citizens were lustful money-grubbers. But "the case 'Chicago' is not the case 'New York,' " he assured his young charge, "and is not to be judged by it. . . . New York is old—its sins are fixed, the damage is done. Chicago is young, clumsy, foolish, its architectural sins are unstable, captious, fleeting; it can pull itself down and rebuild itself in a generation, if it will. . . . There can be no new New York, but there may be a new Chicago."

Why this faith in Chicago, in the promise of the American West? Because Chicago "at least has youth, and where youth is, there is always hope. . . . [A] tremendous understrength is here," Sullivan contended, recalling that the city had in fact "pull[ed] itself down and rebuil[t] itself in a generation" when it raised its grade up to ten feet in the 1850s and 1860s. That was its reality, and its hope was informed by three additional realities: the glorious, expansive lake; the endless, silent prairies; and the sky, that "big" Western sky, all of which formed, he said, "a trinity in one, dreaming." Here in the West, nature's trinity of life was still accessible—air, water, and earth—to which he might have added fire (the fourth element of creation), the

fire of 1871 that had given such impetus to Chicago's architectural progress. "Great minds may go to the great cities," he observed, but "all great thought, all great ideas, all great impulses are born in the open air, close to Nature." The promise of Chicago and the rest of the West was that its natural environment—the source and model of creativity—was still available, ready to be plumbed for its lessons.

Like other nineteenth-century romantics, Sullivan believed that cities were destructive but that nature was redemptive. He agreed with his contemporary Ebenezer Howard, who wrote in the introduction to *To-morrow: A Peaceful Path to Real Reform* (1898) that the "country is the source of all health, all wealth, all knowledge." And he also agreed when Howard wrote that the city, repository of art, culture, science, religion, and refined social relations, having removed itself from nature, *"must be remarried"* to it, so that "out of this joyous union will spring a new hope, a new life, and a new civilization."[9]

Appropriating Howard's famous term from *To-morrow*, which was published only three years before the "Kindergarten Chats" series, Sullivan dubbed Chicago "the Garden City." "Encircled and enfolded" by Lake Michigan, the prairies, and the sky, Chicago was also young, only seventy years old in 1901; it had once renewed itself, and it could do so again. Sullivan saw the West, in fact, as still in a state of nature, as an almost uncorrupted clean slate upon which to build a new architecture and, more important, a new society. The East was lost, its future nonexistent, having capitulated completely to Gomorrah, to the new feudal barons who represented themselves with European-derived architecture, some of it based on buildings of the original feudal era. But in the West the abundance of still untainted nature, of still virgin land, and of youthful open minds meant that feudalism was not so deeply rooted, could yet be rooted out. In the West alone resided the possibility of American utopia.

4. The Poet: Agent of Democracy

Nature was there, in the West, waiting for democracy. But how could democracy be instituted? How could the needs of the people and the power of nature be united to create the American utopia? Louis Sullivan's answer was through a process to which the poet had surest access. The poet would lead the way, not because he was a superior being, but because he was organically rooted in his culture, was of the people, and, moreover, was not simply a man of words but was, at the same time, a man of deeds.

Sullivan was a poet in the literal sense that he wrote a good deal of verse. "Natural Thinking" and "Kindergarten Chats" are liberally laced with it, and several of his essays are actually long prose poems in whole or in part–his 1886 "Inspiration," for example, as well as his 1893 revision, "Study on Inspiration" (published for the first time in this volume). But it is not in this literal sense that we should speak of Sullivan, for he considered poetry to be a much larger and more fundamental endeavor than composing rhyming lines. Like Frank Lloyd Wright, who once remarked that his buildings were his *real* children, Sullivan might have said that *his* buildings were really poems. For poetry is what he claimed to produce, in written and in architectural form, meaning that in his own mind his words and his designs had the same nonarchitectural–beyond architectural–objective.

"Poetry is not verse," Sullivan wrote, "although some verse may be poetic." Poetry "stands for the highest form of intellectual scope and activity." Poetry "means the most highly efficient form of mental eyesight. That is to say, it is that power of seeing and doing which reveals to Man's inner self the fulness and the subtle power of Life."[10]

The poet sees and does; the architectural poet conceives and builds. And he creates, which leads us to a consideration of Sullivan's epistemology. Knowledge and creativity originated solely in the poet's province, he contended, that is, in the "Imagination," which he defined as "a sympathy [toward all that is and was] that lives both in our senses and in our intellect." It is a "divine faculty which, in an illuminated instant [he called "Inspiration"], in that supreme moment," gives birth to ideas. "Second in this [epistemological] Trinity [after Imagination] comes *Thought*, the faculty that doubts and inquires" into what Imagination has yielded "and eventually arrives at a science of logical statement that shall shape and define the scheme and structure that is to underlie, penetrate and support the form of an art work." Third comes "Expression" that "clothe[s] the structure of art with a form of beauty; for she [Expression] is the perfection of the physical, she is the physical itself, and the uttermost attainment of emotionality. . . ."[11]

Art, then, is the Expression of Thought-refined Imagination. But from whence does Imagination come? From two well-springs: "The power of imagination and the science of expression become limitless," he wrote, "when we open our hearts to nature and to our people as the source of inspiration." If you would create an indigenous architecture for this nation, he told a group of young practitioners, "you must take the pains truly to understand your country, your people, your day, your generation, the time, the place in which you live; if you seek to understand, absorb, and sympathize with the life around you, you will be understood and sympathetically received in return." To create an indigenous architecture, he wrote elsewhere, "the American architect must himself become indigenous . . . in the sense that he must absorb into his heart and brain his own country and his own people." "Poetry is life," he wrote in "Kindergarten Chats," and "I have a dawning suspicion that making a real building . . . and making a real poem, are pretty much one and the same thing."[12]

But absorbing popular life and nature's principles into the heart and the brain was only the initial task of the poet/architect. At the present stage of democratic development, according to Sullivan, the public needed help, since "it can only partially and imperfectly state what it needs." Because the senses and intellect of the architect-as-poet had been sharpened by openness to nature and to life—because he had imagination and certain skills—he therefore had the duty to be the people's interpreter and spokesman. But in this role he must never lose touch with his source of inspiration: "No architectural style can become a finality," Sullivan warned, "that runs counter to popular feeling." The relationship, rather, must be reciprocal: "The desire at once to follow and to lead the public," he contended, "should be the attitude of our profession."[13]

Having followed the people, how should the poet lead? What should he teach? Many things, of course, but one thing Sullivan took pains to emphasize was that the complete and perfect work of art was a *"harmonious system of thinking and an equally harmonious method of expressing the thought"*[14]—a statement he considered important enough to italicize—which can be taken to mean that the thing created and the act of creating it are the same, that content and process are one. Writing a poem and the poem itself, designing a building and the building itself, are, all four, one thing.

Thus as lines of poetry can be read for their intellectual content, so too can the facades, the ornament, and the various "lines" of buildings. And as poems reveal to the perceptive reader something of the processes involved in their creation, so too do buildings. But if, as Sullivan insisted, content and process are one, process being revealed as creativity, then content is also about creativity. This is surely what he believed about his own work: that the viewer on the street could learn to "read" his buildings as essays on creativity, would be able to see on his facades (which we will call examples of content)—as well as in the various structural, aesthetic, and compositional relationships (examples of process) resulting in those facades—fulfillments of human possibilities, statements about the integration of imagination, thought, and expression that was the creative act.

But Sullivan was not so naive as to think that the languages of architecture and of print were interchangeable. He knew that some "readers" would be able to comprehend the one but not the other, or perhaps have trouble with both, which is why he offered his writing as a kind of exegesis on his architecture, not on architecture per se as building, but on the underlying principles that were its ultimate meaning, its essence, he would have said. If as an architect he was unable to indicate clearly enough on his facades that all democracy's citizens were potentially poets, he stated it as a writer. If he was unable to declare convincingly enough in brick or stone that the poet was but the servant of the people, took his strength from them, accomplished no more than what anyone else might accomplish, then he said all that in words. Because he must have sensed that his buildings—like any buildings—were for the layperson troublesome and difficult to decipher as symbol and representation, he devoted almost as much effort to writing as to design, each being poetry, and as such the same project.

5. The Garden: A Model for Democracy

Democracy might best be achieved in the West, according to Louis Sullivan, through the agency of the poet, but where were his guidelines? To what could the Western poet—the democratic architect—look to help him chart his course? In a heretofore neglected 1897 lecture only recently published,[15] Sullivan offered nature as the basis for a model, but not nature as he most often discussed it: as a set of processes akin to and illuminating human creativity; nor as it is usually associated with his work: as a source for his ornamentation; and not even in the fundaments that Narciso Menocal explains in this volume: as the foundation for a metaphysics underpinning his iconography and style. In this instance Sullivan spoke of nature as it entered into material relationship with humanity, drawing a parallel between the architect and the gardener.

Sullivan believed that nature was inherently individualistic: a pine was always a pine, a sparrow a sparrow, but no two specimens were ever alike, each evolving according to innate impulses and characteristics. Every thing in nature developed spontaneously from inchoate entities like seeds and embryos into mature forms conditioned only by function, environment, and its own idiosyncratic laws of being, and if left alone under congenial conditions it always fulfilled its potential. Of course, natural conditions were not always congenial. If the strong overwhelmed the weak or if the unforeseen overwhelmed both, that too was only natural. It was in this regard that Sullivan considered nature to be latently democratic: not because it was egalitarian or charitable but because it played no favorites.

As a skilled cultivator himself, he knew that nature was no bed of roses. In his own Ocean Springs, Mississippi, rose garden (fig. 1), "storms and frosts . . . and insect pests, blights, rust, drought and worm in the bud and worm at the root cause[d him], evermore, bitterness, anguish, disappointment [and] despair," while in untamed nature, angry seas, violent winds, predators, parasites, and the prospect of death sometimes made life as frightening as it could be serene. But if in the garden "disappointment [and] despair" were "ever followed by freshly budding hope," so also in the wild "storm clouds drift away . . . beneath the glory of the breaking day."[16] The difference was that nature could renew itself and its beneficence on its own, according to its own rhythms, but the garden could not because it depended on human intervention.

If left to its own devices, however, nature's way could mean survival of only the strongest or best-placed, as in society individualism could produce feudalism: the dominance of powerful elites. But for purposes of his model, Sullivan was not content to let nature take its course, proposing as an ameliorative the concept of the gardener, the interpreter of nature as the poet was of society, intervening to encourage natural potential as the poet encouraged it socially. "Eternal vigilance, patience, care are the price of a truly fine rose," he wrote from experience, and when he added that "few have seen a really fine rose, few know what are [its] possibilities," he was obliquely saying that the most perfect specimens did not exist in a state of nature but were nurtured by the "loving" gardener. To Sullivan, therefore, art and poetry (and gardening) could be superior to and improve upon nature, but only when they successfully transformed inchoate possibilities into more perfect realities.

And then, in what can be considered an extraordinary but for our purposes perfect juxta-position, Sullivan leaped directly from the horti-culturalist's realm into the architect's: "Should anything come fresher from the soil of a richly cultivated nature, should anything be more natural, more spontaneous, in its unfolding plan," he wrote, "should anything, can anything come straighter from the heart, the brain, of the artist than a truly fine building? . . . Surely the cultivation of a rose is not a more subtle one than . . . that of architecture," he continued in his 1897 lecture; "and may it not as truly be said that he who would cause a beautiful architecture to grow in the garden of this world, must [like the gardener have] a beautiful love of his art?"

The garden was a model for architecture but also for society. If cultivation unlocked nature's potential, it also stimulated human possibility, turning the former into art, the latter into democracy. And if the gardener knew how to wrench his plot from nature, the poet exemplified what could be extracted from feudalism. Under feudalism popular talents lay dormant, but in democracy they would spring to life. In nature, the seeds of democracy also awaited the nurturer's hand. For nature was only latently democratic while the garden was actually so, each individual specimen having achieved its fullest flowering.

It could surely be objected that Sullivan's garden analogy was inapt. The architect/poet, like the gardener, was self-selected, unilaterally dictating the best for his charges with a kind of benevolent despotism or, perhaps, with Louis Sullivan's own brand of elitism: that of the artist. Horticulture, after all, prunes out the weak and unaesthetic, eliminates the unwanted, makes ruthless decisions solely on the basis of individual taste and expertise. So, too, with architecture's own selecting and composing processes.

It is hardly surprising, however, that in an era elevating the entrepreneur's notion of "rugged individualism" and the Social Darwinist's corruption of "survival of the fittest" to the level of public policy, when "progressive" reformers often abstained from intimate contact with the great unwashed for whom they defined "best interest," that Sullivan absorbed at least some conventional sensibilities. But he would not have admitted it, would have shrunk from the suggestion of intellectual elitism with horror, in fact. For his intention was to oppose that very nexus of inegalitarian social relations—certainly its constraints on "equal opportunity" understood in the broadest possible existential sense—that may indeed have colored his thinking, albeit more in expression than in purpose.

For Sullivan believed the poet to be of and from the people, not above them. This means that although intervention—socially, which no Social Darwinist would have accepted, or horticulturally, which no Social Darwinist should have accepted—was required to improve the commonweal, it was not to be undertaken by those (conservatives or progressives) who "knew best," but in keeping,

rather, with the imperfectly articulated desires of the people, for whom the poet acted as nothing more than spokesman and exemplar. The purpose of pruning, therefore—to return to the realm of horticulture—was not to produce the ultimate rose but to create the ultimate garden. And the purpose of architectural poetry was not to create the ultimate edifice but to symbolize the ultimate in human possibility. Sullivan's roses and buildings were not ends, in the end, but means—symbols—of the individual components of the garden—the society—he envisioned.

The implication was that the model of the garden and the social role of the poet would one day no longer be necessary. For when democracy arrived, everyone would be a poet in society's garden, not a poet/architect, if that was not their bent, but a fully creative person. If locating democracy in the West was utopian, if offering the poet as its agent was idealistic, and if proposing the garden as its model was ethereal, it was perhaps because all three—location, agent, model—could exist only in an imaginary landscape, a fictive reality, where the not-yet could be the now.

But in fact Sullivan had already designed such a landscape, part of it at least, for the 1888–89 Pueblo Grand Opera House in Colorado. There, in a gardenlike setting in the West—made more gardenlike in its rendering—the poet proposed an architectural prototype for a democratic way of life.

6. The Piazza in the Garden

The most striking feature of the presentation drawings (fig. 2) for the Pueblo Opera House Block is that Sullivan provided a rural setting for an imposing edifice on Main Street in a city center. It is less the mountains in the background that attract attention than the greenery dominating the foreground, drawn in such a way as to obscure portions of the principal facade (as it encroaches upon the entry) as well as much of the neighboring city. Trees appear to be growing in the streets or, short of that, in vaguely delineated parkland, empty lots, perhaps even wilderness completely

surrounding the building. The angle of vision, furthermore, from slightly below, exaggerates the Western sky. The closest and most intimate companion of this temple of culture and commerce is nature, not the rest of Pueblo, for the Opera Block is made to stand apart from its urban milieu.

Key elements of the edifice as built reinforce the bucolic association, supporting Sullivan's contention that it was erected "in harmony with the climate."[17] Six-foot overhanging eaves act as sunscreens but also shelter the fourth-floor loggia, where strollers could be refreshed by mountain

Figure 2.
Pueblo (Colorado)
Grand Opera House
(1888–89).
Inland Architect and News
Record, 1893.

breezes. The view was even more spectacular from the observation deck atop the 131-foot tower and from behind it in the rooftop "summer garden," which was more fully fenestrated than any other part of the building. A shallow hipped roof—which Sullivan reserved mostly for locales with extreme temperature variation—provided dead air space for passive insulation. The building worked with nature as well as any other he ever designed.

Less than two years before receiving the Pueblo commission, Sullivan had written that good architecture was the "result of a prior and perfect understanding and assimilation of all the data," including, and this was his first consideration, "climate," which he said was "the arbiter of material things," and second, "locality, with all its accidental variations."[18] The Grand Opera House was, in fact, a consequence of its environment to a degree difficult to achieve in the East, where taller buildings would have blocked its views while putting it in shadow and where soot would have contaminated its cooling breezes. It opened to the outdoors as few urban structures could.

But it also addressed its social as well as its physical setting, attempting that "marriage" of city and country, of civilization and nature, for which Sullivan and Ebenezer Howard would later campaign. In the drawing, a formally dressed couple stroll in the shadow of trees—which partially hide other walkers across the street—toward the entrance of this sun-drenched symbol of culture and enterprise. Men and women in everyday attire approach and depart from its ground-floor shops. People of varying social conditions—with an assortment of purposes, in other words—cross paths congenially in its ambiance. But the most arresting figure is the cowboy, galloping across the foreground *away* from the Opera House, possibly escaping those civilizing influences which some pedestrians head toward but others seem not to notice. Is it too far-fetched to interpret all this as a mélange of attraction, indifference, and rejection—as the freedom to be one's self—all coexisting happily under the sunny sky of nature's benevolence? Is this not a depiction of an uncoerced marriage of individualism and the collectivity, a picture of Louis Sullivan's democracy itself?

The second striking thing about this drawing,

ness that sense of collective pride and interaction that Renaissance piazze implied for him, where they might also construct that union of individualism and agreed-upon values he understood to be democracy. This is what the images in the presentation drawing seem to suggest.

So it was not at all contradictory that in the drawing the new Opera House, symbol of an emerging civic sense, was positioned closest to, was virtually emerging from, nature, whereas the rest of Pueblo—off to a wrong start, in Sullivan's mind—was hardly visible. Because in a real way the Western city, literally and as the embodiment of civic spirit, was also just emerging, was hardly there, was not yet formed. Like the prototype Chicago mentioned earlier, it was still that *tabula rasa*, that state of nature, from which the garden city might grow.

Two years before he created this design, Sullivan had written that a building should reveal "a single, germinal impulse or idea" that "should permeate the mass and its every detail with the same spirit" so that "there shall effuse from the completed structure a single sentiment."[19] The sentiment here was certainly not to replicate Florence architecturally but to renew that essence of civic unity and possibility of individual choices that for Sullivan Florence represented.

It is the garden quality of the hoped-for city, however, that distinguished Sullivan from contemporaries like Charles Follen McKim, William Rutherford Mead, and Stanford White, whose firm also utilized Florentine forms and who were, in fact, primarily responsible for introducing them into the vocabulary of late-nineteenth-century American architecture, at the 1882–85 Villard Houses (fig. 3) in New York City, for example. Their stylistic counterpart to Sullivan's Florentine, in the East he so vehemently criticized, offers an opportunity to contrast the very different social purposes for which similar design mannerisms could be used.

In the architecturally disparate, indeed jungle-like, atmosphere of the American city, McKim, Mead & White was one of a number of prominent

and the realized building itself, is that while located in the Western garden, the Opera House Block refers directly to the Italian Renaissance. Its rusticated stone facade, its horizontal organization of masonry units and of floors diminishing in height and prominence toward the top, and its arches along the sidewalks suggest in particular the architecture of *quattrocento* Florence. In this light it is tempting to read the building as Sullivan's suggestion for Pueblo's future. Its rows of arched doors and windows recall arcades all over Italy whose functions include being quasi-public porches for collective activity, sheltering people from the elements, and defining civic spaces. If Sullivan saw his building as the model—as the first stage—of what might become a complete civic piazza, what better architectural memories to call up to get the project going than his own, assembled during a six-week visit to Florence—specifically to study the Renaissance—in 1875.

Sullivan thought of his design proposal in just this urbanistic way. Not only did it obscure the other civic structures—vaguely municipal or religious—in the drawing, but it also flew the American flag, surprisingly and rather too conspicuously for a nongovernment building. The flag served to designate the Americanness of the setting, whereas understating existing edifices suggested the possibility of a new civic center wherein the entire citizenry—not just a powerful new oligarchy—might experience through architectural orderli-

firms investigating ways to establish a visual order and clarity that would express the underlying social order. Henry Hobson Richardson, on the other hand, following the lead of his friend Frederick Law Olmsted, saw that ordering less in social than in spatial and functional terms: as distinctive commercial and residential zones linked by the railroad that Olmsted believed had come to define the modern American metropolis. Thus Richardson's interest in developing prototypes for the town house and business block, the suburban residence and library, and the commuter train station, each worked out in distant interpretations of northern Spanish/southern French Romanesque, styles offering that quality of burliness Richardson associated with industrializing America.[20] Richardson occasionally worked for aggressive new entrepreneurs like Marshall Field of Chicago and the Ames family of eastern Massachusetts, but the people with whom he preferred to associate, including many of his clients, represented an older, socially established, often Harvard-educated Yankee elite involved with regional commerce and manufacturing, philanthropy, public service, and the arts, men like John Hay, Henry Adams, Phillips Brooks, William James, and Robert Treat Paine.

Richardson's former employees Stanford White and Charles Follen McKim, collaborating with William Rutherford Mead, were more interested in legitimizing the social order. They attached themselves to a newer and more powerful but socially less secure oligarchy—that very class of New Yorkers (and others) Louis Sullivan condemned in "Kindergarten Chats"—composed of nationally oriented industrial and financial barons: railroad promoter Henry Villard, traction magnate William C. Whitney, Oliver Payne of Standard Oil, Jay Gould's broker Charles Osborn, members of J. P. Morgan's family, Cyrus McCormick, and the like. To order this elite's city, McKim, Mead & White looked to the Renaissance palazzo, a particularly appropriate choice under the circumstances.

The fifteenth-century "boom in the construc-

tion of family *palazzi*," historian Lauro Martines writes, was the result of "a growing concentration of wealth." Some one hundred new palaces plus expansions of many older villa were erected in Florence alone in the 1400s. This building and rebuilding "craze," he says, was "the very process of élite consciousness, . . . a growing resolution to remake or reshape the things around. . . . In effect, this was the quest for greater control over immediate environments." Princes, oligarchs, and other rich men "sought to affirm themselves by means of imposing *palazzi*, more organized and splendid facades," more elaborate interiors, decorations, and objects. The "passion" with which they "displayed their high status or proved their virtue," Martines continues, extended beyond the palazzo to other "architectural projects such as churches, chapels, . . . and new public buildings. . . . As the political and monied élite spread out and preempted more urban space, all others had to be content with less." Ultimately, "the rising awareness that élites could reapportion or remake the urban space if they so willed" led to an interest in ideal cities which were "politically a deeply conservative conception, a response to the rising demand, voiced by princes and urban élites, for grandeur and show, order and ample space, finesse and finished surfaces."[21]

And so too in late-nineteenth-century United States. The new industrial owning class, still first and second generation in the 1880s, had a nagging sense of social inferiority, wanted to make its cultural mark, wanted—as Jeanne Chase has observed—to distinguish itself from the rest of society, to express its impressive power, perhaps also to disguise from itself and from others the often grubby ways in which it had accumulated that power. "There is nothing about a château after the manner of Blois," Chase wrote, or a palazzo after the manner of Florence, she might have added, "to remind its occupant about the railroad on which that château is based."[22]

Sullivan looked to the Florentine piazza, as opposed to the palazzo, for entirely different reasons. Like McKim, Mead, and White, he hoped to bring visual coherence to the chaotic city, but unlike them he aimed to offer an example of collective civic endeavor to help unite the citizenry. Unfortunately, he confused architectural with social harmony by assuming the piazza to have been an expression of peaceful republicanism; nor did he seem to appreciate that oligarchy-sponsored architecture was by definition antidemocratic. And if he intended the tower on the Grand Opera House to symbolize civic virtue, to represent pride in place, he may not have realized that in medieval Italian cities towers were a consequence of interdynastic war. Like most architects, Sullivan was not a good historian.

Sullivan might have confused republicanism with democracy, but since it was a sense of *civilitas* that he wished to foster in Pueblo akin to what had been quite real in Florence, he consciously or unconsciously overlooked certain inconveniences. He may have interpreted the Florentine past with considerable imprecision, but he had absolutely no wish to use it to endorse or legitimize the prevailing social order. "Until the trusts and special privilege are overthrown," he wrote to Harriet Monroe in 1905, "democracy . . . will have but little show, and a democratic art least of all."[23] When McKim, Mead, and White revived the Florentine palazzo, they gave new merchant princes a more princely veneer, confirming their control over the social order. Sullivan used the piazza not to applaud entrepreneurial power but to instill a sense of civic pride in *all* the people. But to work, the piazza had to be in a garden.

Living close to nature, influenced at every moment by intimate contact with it, Westerners could learn by observation and osmosis that creativity, individuality, and the ability fully to develop human potential were nothing more than natural characteristics, natural rights presently denied them by the social order. Observation would also teach them that individual growth was in part conditioned by social interdependency. For just as flora and fauna provided each other with food and homes, just as Western pioneers had helped erect each others' houses and barns, so should society enable its members to build and grow. Sullivan's reading of the natural world may have been as romantic in this instance as his reading of the Renaissance was selective, but it was *his* reading, and it informed his contention that peacefully achieved social harmony was preferable to a social order maintained by might. As he wrote in a 1902 essay: "I am of those who believe that gentleness is a greater, surer power than force. . . ."[24]

It was too late for the East to learn these things. Divorced from nature, it used the architectural past, like McKim, Mead, and White, to valorize the few who controlled an unnatural neofeudalism. Sullivan drew on the Florentine past not to emulate its design forms but to resurrect what he understood to have been its civic sense, in order to adorn Pueblo, where the availability of still uncorrupted nature made it possible, he believed, to build democracy. So if he colonized the Renaissance he did so to decolonize the West, where, in garden cities, a new architecture, but above all a new way of life, might emerge. This is the fundamental meaning of the Pueblo Opera House.

7. The Tall Office Building Democratically Considered

Except for a building in Salt Lake City, designed and erected at roughly the same time, the Opera House in Colorado was farther west than anything else Louis Sullivan built, farther west than Chicago or St. Louis, where twenty-one of his twenty-four skyscrapers would have stood had all been realized. If in the Rocky Mountains he had found an accommodating locale for his vision of democracy, and if in the young city of Pueblo he had been given a garden site in which to plant its seed, Sullivan was not so fortunate with the settings of his high-rise buildings. But since his skyscrapers—his preferred architectural medium of expression during the 1890s—were erected in already built-up city centers, their distance from the garden mattered less to him than the didactic potential of their facades. Using them as blank tablets, he inscribed thereon two basic messages that stood for two social objectives. The first was to transform the skyscraper, which he regarded as the prototypical neofeudal manifestation, into an emblem of the democratic future, an emblem that, in conjunction with his writing, made his critique of plutocracy at the Pueblo Opera House even more pointed. The second objective was to suggest possibilities for a more diverse, amenable urbanism. Each message was closely associated with its own system of facade composition, and each in its way proclaimed democratic renewal.

Social Transformation

Sullivan did not consider the tall building in the abstract, nor solely—even primarily—as an architectural matter. To him it was fundamentally a social issue, the product of specific conditions he pinpointed exactly in time and place. "Architects of *this* land and generation are *now* [emphasis added] brought face to face with something new under the sun," he wrote in "The Tall Office Building Artistically Considered" in 1896, "namely that evolution and integration of social conditions . . . that results in the erection of tall buildings."[25]

"It is not my purpose to discuss the social conditions," he continued; "I accept them as the fact." But he did list some: the desire to transact business indoors in offices, the development of steel construction and the passenger elevator, increasing urban density, and escalating land rents. All this and more had produced the modern office building through the agency of three parties: the engineer and architect directed by the speculator. As the collaboration of a "modern feudal baron" with his two employees in their allied interests, the skyscraper took on its quintessential social meaning in service of entrepreneurial gain.

Sullivan's attitude toward the American businessman had gradually shifted from one of respect to one of contempt. In an 1885 speech analyzing the characteristics of national architecture, he had identified businessmen and financiers as his only fellow countrymen capable of taking risks in their chosen fields. Their "capacity to expand a single congenial idea . . . into subtle, manifold, and consistent ramifications is admirable," he had written, "and a shining example which we have often ignored." Their most singular characteristic was mental power, their ability to "develop elementary ideas organically" into complex material realizations.

Their implementation of ideas, however, that is, their business methods, was "usually so crude and harsh as to be revolting to a refined taste, and hence it is to be instinctively shunned." American entrepreneurs, he meant, cared not a whit about the damaging consequences of their own activities, like the impoverishment of working people, political corruption, or the ravishing of the landscape. Since it was not the mere possession of power that was so troublesome, Sullivan thought, but rather its abuse, he was optimistic: "Once subtilized, flushed with emotion, and guided by clear insight," he was sure, power would be "a worker of miracles." His hope in 1885 was twofold: that others, like artists, might emulate entrepreneurial use of power by "develop[ing] elementary ideas organically," and that the power itself might be redirected toward socially more beneficial ends.[26]

By the time he wrote his 1896 essay on tall buildings his attitude toward businessmen had changed dramatically, in striking contrast to the general public's changing perception of skyscrapers. For most observers, the tall building was no longer a novelty associated with national aspiration but a commonplace heralding national accomplishment. Dissenting strongly from this view, Sullivan condemned the skyscraper in 1896 as a hideous example of business malpractice, and therefore antisocial behavior; it was a flagrant abuse of power, the cruel egregious consequence of arrogance run amuck. The problem now confronting artists was not how to emulate or redirect entrepreneurial activity for the common good, as Sullivan had argued in 1885. It was now a question of complete social transformation, which he posed with some of his most compelling prose: "How shall we impart to this sterile pile, this crude, harsh, brutal agglomeration, this stark, staring exclamation of eternal strife," how shall we impart to this skyscraper "the graciousness of those higher forms of sensibility and culture that rest on the lower and fiercer passions? How shall we proclaim from the dizzy heights of this strange, weird, modern rooftop the peaceful evangel of sentiment, of beauty, the cult of a higher life?" How shall we transform this symbol of neofeudal power and greed into its opposite: a beacon of democratic renewal?

By discovering the true nature, or essence, of the skyscraper, was Sullivan's answer, and that discovery could be made by observing Nature—capital "N." Since the tall building had evolved naturally and organically from a specific set of social conditions, its transformation into a "peaceful evangel of sentiment" would also proceed in Nature's way as a logical outcome of its own evolution. "For it is my belief," he asserted, "that it is of the essence of every problem that it contains and suggests its own solution. This I believe to be natural law." The problem was that the entrepreneur had not allowed the skyscraper to realize its natural potential, making the task of the architect clear: just as the gardener intervenes in nature to help potential become reality, so the architect-as-poet (in this 1896 essay Sullivan called him an "artist") intervenes in society to help the skyscraper become its real self.

Nurturing potential required determining essence. Sullivan did not consider the tall building to be, in its fundaments, that pile of steel, glass, and masonry found on city streets; it was rather, "one of the most magnificent opportunities that the Lord of Nature . . . has ever offered to the proud spirit of man." Its essence could be determined only by "heed[ing] the imperative voice of emotion," and for this the poet was best equipped. On this spiritual plane, using his imagination—the source of knowledge and creativity, in Sullivan's view, we will recall—the poet discovered that the essence, "the chief characteristic of the tall office building," is that "it is lofty." This, Sullivan wrote, as lyrically as he ever wrote, "is the very open organ-tone in its appeal" and must therefore be "the dominant chord in [the poet's] expression of it. . . . It must be tall, every inch of it tall. The force and power of altitude must be in it, the glory and pride of exaltation must be in it. It must be every inch a proud and soaring thing, rising in sheer exultation . . . from bottom to top [as] a unit without a single dissenting line. . . ."

By declaring loftiness to be the essence of the tall building—as opposed to its commercial functions, its aesthetics, its municipal significance, or, most important, its assertion of entrepreneurial power—the poet unlocked its secrets. One of its secrets was that the skyscraper was not in truth a symbol "of most bald, most sinister, most forbidding conditions." In truth it was "the new, the unexpected, the eloquent peroration" of "the peaceful evangel of sentiment, of beauty, the cult of a higher life." By making the skyscraper be what it wanted to be, as architect Louis Kahn would have put it years later, the poet took it away from its owners, appropriated it on a spiritual plane, so to speak, and gave it to the people as their future.

The tall building had wanted to be lofty and the poet had made it so, realizing its potential, solving its problem, and as a result had revealed another secret: it was not its lofty *look* that made it a democratic building; it was the creative act of *achieving* that look. Since the poet was but the harbinger of democratic everyman, his act stood for everyman's potential creativity, exemplifying that "fundamental law of social integrity or oneness, wherein each man shall truly be a law unto himself," the law that guaranteed "the liberation of [man's] free creative . . . spirit," Sullivan wrote in "Natural Thinking," which was "the essential nature of Democracy."[27]

Loftiness therefore proclaimed that the poet had asserted creativity in everyman's stead, and Sullivan hoped that when people saw his lofty buildings standing before them on city streets they would understand that something had changed and that even more profound change was possible. For what had been an architectural lie shoring up personal self-aggrandizement was now an architectural truth prophesying collective salvation. The skyscraper had been liberated as the people ought to be. The poet had accomplished what the politician should.

Options

Sullivan's actual organization of the lofty facade, the aesthetic composition he made of it, is well known, partly because of his lucid description of it in 1896. It was based on his isolation and reduction of the building's primary functions to three, which he articulated separately and distinctly on each of his facades: a floor or two for circulation and commerce, a variable number of stories for clerical work, and an attic for mechanical systems, storage, and other service functions. At the same time, however, these three unities were subordinated to a governing "system of vertical construction," he called it, wherein fenestration and the horizontal elements framing it top and bottom—collectively the multistory window bays of clerical space—were recessed slightly behind their flanking columns, which were not subdivided horizontally in any way. This arrangement emphasized the facade's verticality, exaggerating its "syncopation," especially when seen from an acute angle down the street, the best position from which to view it in any case, given its height in relation to normal thoroughfare width. This "system" characterized almost half of the twenty-four high-rises he designed and five of the seven he saw to completion. Since most of what he actually built in this genre, as well as his best-known writing about it, had to do with expressing height, it has come to be understood that the "system of vertical construction" was all he cared about in this regard.

But there was for Sullivan another defining characteristic of the skyscraper. If the first was loftiness, the second was a tangible materiality: its steel frame. Many historians regard Chicago commercial architecture from the 1880s to World War I as the inauguration of a frame-determined design epoch, pointing to the work of William Le

Baron Jenney, Burnham & Root, and Holabird & Roche especially. Sullivan is usually omitted in this connection except for his 1898–1902 Schlesinger & Mayer Store and sometimes for his and Dankmar Adler's 1893 Chicago Stock Exchange. But in fact he devoted as much intellectual energy to letting the steel frame speak for itself as did any of his contemporaries, perhaps more consistently even, because there is an obvious determination to do so about all his proposals of this type, a haphazardly-arrived-at quality about many of theirs. This aspect of his work has been relatively unnoticed—and demonstrates the multiplicity of his aesthetic approaches to the skyscraper mentioned at the outset of this essay—but has important implications for democratizing the city.

Both height and steel stirred the imagination of Sullivan's generation, but they are obviously not synonymous. The steel frame is not inherently vertical, visually or structurally, because its horizontal and vertical members—its posts and beams, simply put—are mutually supporting and load-bearing. There is no implicit direction to it, a factor Sullivan apparently could not ignore, which is one reason why he distinguished between height aesthetics and frame aesthetics. Although he did not speak or write about the latter, over half his skyscraper designs addressed what we might call "form follows structure" in what we name here a "system of skeletal construction."

Sullivan's high-rises can be grouped according to these basic types of facade organization, with a small third cluster serving as a kind of bridge between them. The first has already been discussed as the vertical model. Varying in height from eight to sixteen stories, this group includes both single- and double-towered buildings, an I-shaped setback, freestanding, abutting, midblock, corner, and block-long structures. There are theaters, banquet halls, galleries, and observation decks requiring special facade treatment. Programs range from the standard mix of commercial and clerical facilities to light manufacturing, overnight accommodation, and private organizational activities. The buildings in this group (see figs. 4–12) are the 1890

Figure 4.
Wainwright Building,
St. Louis (1890).
Photograph by
Narciso Menocal.

Figure 5.
Schiller Building,
Chicago (1891).
Scribner's, 1894.

Figure 6.
Union Trust Building,
St. Louis (1892).
The Brickbuilder, 1894.

Figure 7.
Trust and Savings Build-
ing project, scheme 1,
St. Louis (c. 1892).
Western Architect, 1925.

Figure 8.
Trust and Savings Build-
ing project, scheme 2,
St. Louis (c. 1893).
Chicago Architectural
Photographing Company.

Figure 9.
Burnett House Hotel
project, Cincinnati
(c. 1894).
Art Institute of Chicago.

Figure 10. Guaranty
Building, Buffalo
(1894–95).
Chicago Architectural
Photographing Company.

Figure 11.
Bayard/Condict Building.
New York (1897–98).
Wurts Brothers.

Figure 12.
Gage Building, Chicago
(1898–99), on right.
Architectural Record, 1898.

Wainwright Building in St. Louis; the tower of the 1891 Schiller Building in Chicago; the 1892 Union Trust Building, St. Louis; also in St. Louis, two projects (c. 1892 and 1893) for the Trust and Savings Company (the name is conjectural); the 1894 Burnet House Hotel remodeling project in Cincinnati; the 1894–95 Guaranty Building, Buffalo; and somewhat tangentially but essentially in this manner, the 1897–98 Bayard/Condict Building in New York and the 1898–99 Gage Building facade in Chicago. These nine include his first and last realized skyscrapers and one for almost every year of the 1890s.[28]

Sullivan deployed the vertical model for all manner of situations and sites, suggesting that he found its form suitable for just about any skyscraper function and had no need to design in any other format. But this was not the case. The small cluster of "bridge" or transitional projects of 1891–92 exhibit vertical characteristics, to be sure.

At the 1891 Fraternity Temple (fig. 13) in Chicago, the four shortest and four medium-height towers are variations on the 1890 Wainwright Building. For the 1891 Mercantile Club (fig. 14) in St. Louis, Sullivan arranged the oriel window tiers near the corners to suggest a vertical motif. And at the 1892 Portland Building (fig. 15), also in St. Louis, the thin mullions running from bottom to top of the window banks have the same effect, as do the two-story openings above them.

But other portions of these three facades are not at all vertical. The surface of the tallest Fraternity Temple tower is flat and flush, wrapped tightly around its corners as if to diminish their upward thrust. Its taut skin reveals the location of the steel frame, making it impossible to employ the "false piers"[29]—that is, non-load-bearing mullions replicating and alternating with load-bearing columns—which served deliberately to override the construction system in order to emphasize verti-

cality on four of the first group's facades. At the Mercantile Club a similar flat treatment characterizes the expanse of facade between base and balcony, as well as at the corners, appearing at the Portland project in the center bay and on the two floors immediately above the base, not to mention on what can be seen of the side facade of the main tower. Those parts of the Portland's front facade mirroring the frame thoroughly surround, contain, penetrate, and therefore weaken the vertical elements, while on the rear setback, furthermore, the darkened sills and lintels seem almost to accentuate the horizontal.

This small group of skyscraper projects represents Sullivan's first sallies at making a literal correspondence between frame and facade, between structure and composition. It is noteworthy that two of them were proposed less than a year after he announced the Wainwright Building—his first exercise in architectural loftiness, on which he was still working, in fact, in 1891—and that by the 1892 Portland project he had designed only two other skyscrapers in the vertical manner (the Schiller and Union Trust buildings). Since only three of his first six high-rises expressed tallness, it seems reasonable to suppose that from the very outset of his skyscraper career, Sullivan never put all his design eggs in the one vertical basket, never saw the vertical *ipso facto* as the only way to design a tall building.

Another dozen or so skyscrapers designed between 1893 and 1904 reveal the frame clearly and directly and do not emphasize height, although as narrow shafts some are obviously tall. Whether narrow shaft or bulky block, however, Sullivan did not employ the "false pier" in a single instance, which is a clue to his intentions. As with the vertical model, Sullivan confronted a range of design situations involving differing lot sizes and locations, scales, and programs, for a department

store, office buildings, an apartment tower, and more. As a result this group contains several aesthetic strategies for clarifying the correspondence between the facade and its directionally neutral steel skeleton.

The 1893 Chicago Stock Exchange Building (fig. 16) is closest chronologically to the three transitional projects just discussed, and in it for the first time Sullivan made the steel frame manifest across an entire facade. The tendency of the oriel windows in combination with shadows and flanking columns is to suggest upward thrust, as do the thickened columns below. But that thrust is balanced by visually (not actually) linking the tops and bottoms of window frames on the oriels' three sides, by the attic colonnade, by the bold spandrels stretching across the facade, by the prominent second- and fourth-floor cornices, and by the deep, forward-tilting, entablature-like cornice at the roof. Yet this is not a horizontal building. It is both ver-

tical and horizontal at once; it is a balance between the two. Since the upper facade is internally consistent and not subdivided like those of the Portland, Mercantile, and Fraternity Temple projects, the Stock Exchange is Sullivan's first holistic articulation of the structural skeleton as such.

But it was by no means his clearest or purest statement. Two 1894 proposals for the Chemical National Bank in St. Louis perhaps were. The first scheme, for an eight-story building (fig. 17), features a highly ornate, dark-toned base separated from upper floors by a prominent cornice cutting across the columns (making it in this respect an early version of his Schlesinger & Mayer Store). The second scheme (fig. 18) raised the building by seven stories to fifteen, indicating that Sullivan did not consider skeletal expression suitable only for shorter structures (the Stock Exchange was twelve floors plus attic). But more important, in the taller version he eliminated the second-story cornice,

*Figure 19.
Unidentified office
building project,
St. Louis (c. 1897).*
Art Institute of Chicago.

*Figure 20.
Unidentified tall
building project, possibly
an apartment tower,
Chicago (c. 1900).*
Art Institute of Chicago.

further integrating base with superstructure by making them the same color. Except for what appear to be ornamental panels culminating in shallow, capital-like projections on the corners, this proposal is entirely unified from bottom to top ("without a single dissenting line," it might be noted). The upper floors of the eight-story project and the entire facade of the other do not so much balance verticals and horizontals—in the manner of the Stock Exchange—as dispense with them altogether.

Here we see crisp, smooth, skinlike wall planes —entirely unornamented except at base and attic— corresponding exactly to the frame's members and therefore neutral in direction. Unlike the vertical facade, the wall is stated flatly as a wall, not as

a gallery of columns, offering itself as a comparatively inconspicuous container for volume and space rather than an insistent proclamation of exterior mass. By rendering these Chemical proposals in pale monochromes against clear skies, furthermore, Sullivan may have been moving toward suggesting the weightlessness that would later be associated with glass curtain walls. His unrealized 1897 project for an unidentified St. Louis building (fig. 19) was almost identical to these 1894 Chemical schemes except for a heavy cornice at the level of third-floor windowsills and arched openings in the base, whereas in an unbuilt scheme c. 1900, possibly for a Chicago apartment house (fig. 20), tiers of oriels were worked into the basic skeletal format.

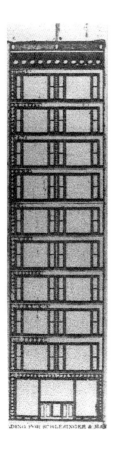

It would be ahistorical to label Sullivan a prophet of modernism on the basis of these designs, but it is nevertheless noteworthy that the ways in which they revealed the frame resembled the work of a later generation. The skinlike facade format might be familiar to modern eyes, but it was not Sullivan's final proposal for the high-rise facade, no doubt because finality was not his objective. If he had an objective with the skeletal model, it seems to have been finding viable options. An early scheme for a Wabash Avenue addition to Chicago's Schlesinger & Mayer Store in 1896 (fig. 21), for example, called attention to the horizontality of stacked floors as if ignoring both height and directional neutrality but without in any way compromising the clarity of the structural system. By contrast, a later version from 1898 (fig. 22) dramatized the neutral frame more than ever by deeply insetting the windows for a projecting, three-dimensional grid effect which, in addition,

closely resembled in miniature the shape of surrounding city blocks. To continue the urban reference, Sullivan turned the Madison and State Street corner with a vertically articulated arc, as if anchoring the store to what is in fact Chicago's most important commercial intersection, where, additionally, its quadrential street-numbering system originates.

As realized from another 1898 proposal (fig. 23), Schlesinger & Mayer became for modernist historians Sullivan's clearest, if not only, statement of form following structure. "In his typical buildings Sullivan picks out and emphasizes the vertical lines of force," Sigfried Giedion asserted in his monumental modernist apologia, *Space, Time and Architecture,* of 1941. "In the [Schlesinger & Mayer] store, however, it is the neutral and impartial equilibrium inherent in the skeletal construction which Sullivan chooses to project," directly influencing, he goes on to say, Walter Gropius's 1922

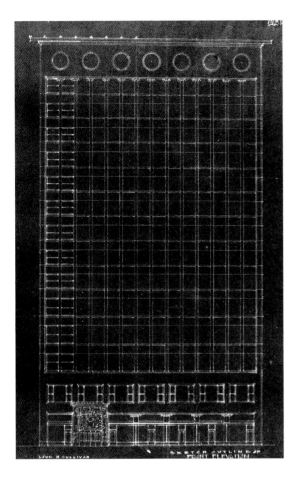

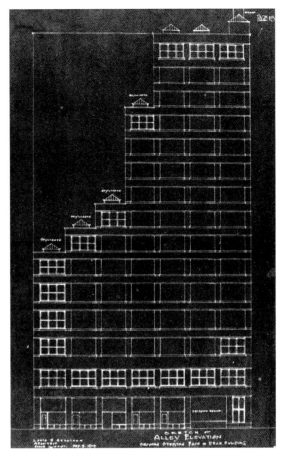

Figure 24.
*Project for a tall
building, Chicago (1904).
Front elevation.*
Northwest Architectural
Archives, University of
Minnesota Libraries, St. Paul.

Figure 25.
*Project for a tall
building, Chicago (1904).
Side elevation.*
Northwest Architectural
Archives, University of
Minnesota Libraries, St. Paul.

Chicago Tribune Building competition entry.[30] Unaware that because Sullivan had designed more often in the skeletal than in the lofty mode his vertical buildings were therefore not "typical," Giedion (who had not bothered to investigate the matter) nevertheless proclaimed it to be so.

This has confused historians more than it would have confused Sullivan, whose final proposal for a skeletal facade underscores the complexity of what Giedion found so simple. For a 1904 tall building project (fig. 24) in Chicago, Sullivan stated the principal, Michigan Avenue facade as a neutral skeleton possibly stressing the vertical; it is difficult to tell from the surviving blueprint. But the side alley elevation (fig. 25) has a decidedly horizontal layering. Here are two different possibilities given simultaneous treatment on different facades of the same building. Perhaps this repre-

sents a kind of concluding statement about Sullivan's consideration of the skyscraper: that there was no preferred treatment, no "true prototype," no "true normal type," despite what he wrote in his 1896 "Tall Office Building" essay. Altogether in addition to the strictly vertical, Sullivan had proposed the directionally neutral skinlike wall, horizontal layering, the directionally neutral projecting grid, the balancing of horizontals with verticals, and various combinations thereof, regardless of program or surroundings, sometimes on the same structure. What Sullivan was moving toward, and what his "system of skeletal construction" seemed to offer, was diversity, the possibility that each high-rise building could be unique, in anthropomorphic terms a unique individual.

If there was a tendency in Sullivan's work from the first skyscraper in 1890 to the last for which there is visual record in 1904, it was away from the vertical, not that he had ever concentrated exclusively upon it. Ironically enough, after insisting that skyscrapers should be lofty in 1896, Sullivan designed only two more buildings in that manner compared to eight of the skeletal type, six of the latter for Schlesinger & Mayer alone. (There are also three other proposals—making eleven in all after 1896—that cannot be discussed, since their drawings have been lost and there appears to be no written description of them.) And of those two vertical structures, the 1897–98 Bayard/Condict Building and the 1898–99 Gage Building facade differ from their genre predecessors. The columns are thinner and spaced farther apart in relation to facade width, and there are no "false piers." While opening larger voids for fenestration, the widening also placed somewhat greater emphasis on horizontal members, thereby subtly accentuating the structural grid. Bayard/Condict and the Gage remain determinedly vertical, to be sure, although architectural historian William Jordy felt that "in a way" the latter expressed "the gridded frame."[31]

Why Sullivan publicized only the vertical model remains a matter for conjecture. Perhaps he thought it distinguished him from his "Chicago School" colleagues, who by and large did not design in that manner. Perhaps he felt the concept of loftiness best captured that magical, romantic quality skyscrapers still conveyed, as depicted, for example, in Alfred Stieglitz's photographs of Daniel H. Burnham's Flatiron Building (1902) in New York City, dramatizing both its great height and its mystery. Perhaps working on the final stages of the Guaranty, his most insistently vertical edifice—and arguably his most aesthetically successful—while simultaneously writing "The Tall Office Building Artistically Considered" governed his public posture, even though, ironically, this would be his last "every inch of it tall" structure. Or perhaps there were more mundane factors at work: despite his reputation as the nation's most innovative high-rise designer, Sullivan had actually completed only four examples of the genre before 1896—the Wainwright, Schiller, Union Trust, and

Stock Exchange buildings—three stressing verticals, the other combining them with horizontals. (The rest of his projects remained on paper and were not widely known.) To have departed from this formula—in effect signaling a change in design direction—during a national depression when the recent termination of his partnership forced him to seek his own work for the first time in fifteen years might not have seemed to him the wisest business strategy.

Sullivan's reasons for not discussing skyscraper options may be unrecoverable, but he nonetheless appears to have felt that as an aesthetic, verticality had limited application. It could reveal the creative possibilities of the democratic citizen, to be sure, and probably to greater effect than something as pedestrian as steel frame members. But it did not seem to offer enough design variety, at least not in and of itself, running the risk of becoming an artistic straitjacket, which may have occurred to thoughtful readers of "The Tall Office Building." And that a city with only one kind of skyscraper might, like Corbusier's later proposals, end up dull and regimented, thereby inhibiting architecture's capacity to speak of democracy, may have dawned on Sullivan himself. Perhaps that was why he designed so often and in such different manners within the skeletal mode.

The Promise of the Setback

If we broaden our perspective at this point to consider Louis Sullivan's urban vision, we will better appreciate his painstaking exploration of the skeletal model. His 1891 essay "The High Building Question" in *The Graphic*, a popular Chicago pictorial magazine, opened by focusing on the skyscraper's usurpation of the city's light and air. At the heart of the matter was an unresolved conflict between "the public welfare" and the landowner's right to build "as he chooses." On the one hand, Sullivan did not want any "individual to trample on his neighbor," but on the other, he was disinclined to "suppress" those "brainy" businessmen who had made "our city . . . what it is . . . and guarantee its future."[32]

"The High Building Question" represents a halfway point between Sullivan's guarded respect for entrepreneurs in his 1885 "Characteristics and Tendencies of American Architecture" lecture and his not-so-guarded antipathy toward them in "The Tall Office Building" of 1896. From his position of "grudging respect"—shall we call it—of 1891, he proposed to regulate without suppressing, offering a three-part plan that would have restrained elite power, albeit minimally, in the name of public good.

When a skyscraper reached a specified height, he proposed, its owner would be allowed to build higher only on the equivalent of 50 percent of his lot. At twice the limit he could occupy only 25 percent, "and so on indefinitely, restricting the area as he progresses upward." But the problem with this, Sullivan noted, his sarcasm thinly veiled, was that "with his go-ahead proclivity, the average American citizen . . . would translate this to mean a thirty-story building on the street line with a great big hole behind." So we will have to teach our businessman "the manners he does not possess" and "gently inform him" of a second constraint: that the 50 percent limit applied to frontage as well as area. The building could be only half its lot width, in other words, at the first point of height limitation, a quarter as wide at the next, and so on upward. By this device, soon to be called the "setback" principle, we "will push him back unceremoniously from the street line to the middle of his ground," which will be acceptable, Sullivan was sure, if the businessman "can see a dollar in it."

Thus far his proposals left "the individual free to soar as high as it may please his lot, his purse, and his pride," Sullivan insisted, while ensuring "to the community the benefit of a . . . supply of light and air." But given a very large parcel of land, the owner's desire for profit might lead him nonetheless to erect a monstrously tall building. So there remained "the very practical question of the actual number of feet in these limits." Sullivan therefore added a third proviso: that skyscraper height at the first setback be no more than twice its street width—132 feet or about ten stories on a standard sixty-six-foot Chicago thoroughfare—

while at the corner of a wide and a narrow street its height at setback be equal to the combined width of the two, perhaps thirteen or fourteen floors. These proposals presupposed the principle of making private privilege (that is, building size) conditional on public right (unobstructed access to amenity). They were not terribly radical, but they challenged neofeudal power in the name of a civil urban democracy.

Sullivan had nothing to say about the intersection of two very broad avenues, or a building usurping more than a single corner, and one wonders what he would have done with something as capacious as the Champs-Elysées. It is ironic, furthermore, that when he published these ideas in December 1891, he had already designed the seventeen-story Schiller Building for a midblock site, as well as the 450-foot Fraternity Temple, neither of which could have been erected under his own guidelines. The Temple, with its deep lightwells, and the Schiller, with vertical and horizontal setbacks, did, however, permit generous amounts of light and air to reach tenants and pedestrians.

Sullivan was one of the first American architects actually to use setbacks and to offer them as a formal solution to an urban problem posed by tall buildings. Chicago legislated height restrictions from time to time around the turn of the century, but not Sullivan's; although ideas similar to his were included in New York City's 1916 zoning ordinance—the nation's first to require setbacks—it is doubtful that at that late date his twenty-five-year-old proposals were even remembered, let alone instrumental, in shaping it. Sullivan may not have influenced public policy, but the suspicion lingers that by advocating restrictions that would have prevented construction of his own designs, he sensed a fundamental contradiction about working in his preferred genre. And he may also have sensed that by suggesting even minimal restraints on business power he was causing himself trouble (see section 9).

Accompanying his 1891 essay was an intriguing sketch (fig. 26) showing a number of setback options.[33] All pulled back from the street and

Figure 26.
Imaginary streetscape
depicting setback options
for "The High Building
Question."
Graphic, 1891.

rose "from bottom to top [as] a unit without a single dissenting line" it could not be set back. Evidence that Sullivan thought this is that the most set-back portions of all his set-back edifices were in the skeletal mode: the main tower of Fraternity Temple, the side facade for the 1904 Michigan Avenue scheme, and the rear spines and blocks of the Schiller Building and the Portland project. (Not until 1923, the year before he died, when he praised Eliel Saarinen's second-place-winning entry in the 1922 Chicago Tribune Building competition, did he begin to understand that verticality and the setback could be reconciled, nor that the skeletal system could soar "without a single dissenting line," as he himself had demonstrated in one of the 1894 Chemical National Bank proposals.) So it appears that to Sullivan's mind the skeletal model offered more design variety than the vertical, or, to put it another way, that in design—not metaphysical—terms the vertical was but one aspect of the variety a city should represent, variety being *prima facie* a chief characteristic, in the form of individualisms, of democracy itself.

from adjacent neighbors, withdrawing in depth while retreating in width. But their many forms and styles suggested a multitude of possibilities for handling the problem of big, bulky structures, for what they all shared was the absence of verticality. By implication this means that if a building

8. *Democratic Architecture*

The prominent critic Montgomery Schuyler understood something of Louis Sullivan's objectives when he reviewed Adler & Sullivan's Chicago Auditorium Building (1886–90) in the 1895 *Architectural Record.* Commenting on its magnificent acoustics, universally good sight lines, its exquisite decorations, "its expanding arches above, and its expanding terraces below [fig. 27], extending and proclaiming a hospitality as nearly as may be equal and undistinguishing" for everyone, whether in the cheapest or most expensive seats, he concluded that the theater stood in marked contrast to "royal" or "imperial" opera houses as "a new kind of art, an art of democracy."[34]

The promise of the setback extended the democratic implications of the Auditorium Theater to the city at large. Not only did it enhance the public welfare directly, but as a skeletal form it also seemed to Sullivan a cornucopia of design options with which to create a democratic architecture. As a believer in the efficacy of laissez-faire capitalism, and amazed like many of his contemporaries by the stunning growth and power of American industry, he also believed, like many contemporaries, that the skyscraper had become capitalism's most compelling symbol and, in this commercial culture, the nation's representative edifice. Determining its proper aesthetic expression could serve as the basis for creating indigenous art forms—that still elusive "American style"—the absence of which weighed so heavily on members of his generation. In addition to everything else he demanded from it, therefore, Sullivan also saw the skyscraper as the means by which American art might be redeemed, made more American, made more democratic.

But as it turned out, Sullivan's career began its long, debilitating decline (see section 9) at just

Figure 27
*Auditorium Building,
Chicago (1886–90).
Theater.*
Architectural Record, 1892.

about the time he published "The Tall Office Building Artistically Considered" in 1896, and by the second half of the next decade he had no work more often than not. After 1900 he executed only one skyscraper commission, the 1902 extension to his own 1898 Schlesinger & Mayer Store, but if that had already been contractually arranged, the next extension was not. When Carson Pirie Scott & Company took over the business and decided to expand the building still farther south along State Street in 1905, it hired Daniel Burnham & Company, which copied Sullivan's earlier work almost to the letter.

Losing the commission must have been particularly hard on him, not the least of reasons being that he badly needed the fee. Then, too, he had produced at least thirteen designs for Schlesinger & Mayer since 1890 (only three of them during his partnership with Adler), making him something of

an in-house architect, so to be replaced by a firm that essentially did what he would have done must have seemed to him an insulting snub. But perhaps most important, losing the commission was also a galling reminder—not that he needed it—that he was no longer able to get any high-rise work at all, forcing him in his reduced circumstances to take small jobs he would never have previously taken in remote places he would not have previously visited. This proved to have rewarding as well as dire consequences: dire because once perceived to be "over the hill," consigned to the provinces, as it were, he could not reenter the lucrative urban market; rewarding because the little bit of work he was able to get broadened and deepened his concept of democracy.

Beginning in 1906 and continuing irregularly through 1922, Sullivan designed and saw to completion nine banks (one, the First National Bank in Manistique, Michigan, was a remodeling) in towns and small cities scattered across the Midwest from Ohio to Iowa. Although still praised today for their brilliance and beauty, their relatively small scale (the largest cost $125,000) made him little money. Nor did they generate work in other design genres. But his experience outside the metropolis spending time with representatives of every social stratum, participating in their daily lives while observing their communities at work, seems to have altered his thinking.

His ideas about democracy evolved in two basic ways from the 1890s to the 1910s, paralleling a shift in the contours of his practice. At first, as an increasingly prominent architect best known for high-rises, he set forth the poet's mission as reawakening the individual's awareness of his own creative possibilities in an undescribed but implicitly urban milieu. Later, as a decreasingly prominent designer of rural banks, he located democracy more explicitly in towns and small cities—in the Western garden—wherein creativity was associated with communal endeavor. Whereas at first he had stressed the individual's will to achieve, the poet being the agent to ignite that will, he later emphasized the democracy of the ensemble, the poet being the creative coordinator.

If in the 1890s, in other words, democracy meant total individualism—a kind of universal access to existential opportunity—realized through one's own self-discovery but left to develop independently of others', by the 1910s Sullivan's democracy meant the consonant collectivity in which individualism was enhanced by membership and contribution. In the 1890s, Sullivan had been content to inform individuals that they were capable of singing beautiful solos, but by 1910 he was thinking about their harmonious orchestration. "Individualism without collectivity means sure destruction," he wrote at the time he finished his first bank in 1908, "while collectivism without individualism is an abstraction."[35]

This evolution in Sullivan's thinking is reflected in his literary shift of attention away from professional matters and "foreground buildings"

toward the question of what architecture meant in a democracy. This could be interpreted as a sign of his downward-spiraling career, a kind of face-saving effort to change the subject, although it might as easily be argued that had he concentrated on the themes of "The High Building Question" and "The Tall Office Building Artistically Considered"–his only two essays for mass circulation magazines—he might have gotten additional skyscraper work by maintaining high visibility. Instead, he spent more than a year on the "Kindergarten Chats" essays for an obscure Ohio professional journal and four years laboring over his manuscript "Natural Thinking"–during the last two of those years designing and building his first bank–never to see it published. Thus he made his choice, out of conviction it seems, not to try to write his way back to celebrity. The more he worked in small Midwestern places, the more he concentrated on democracy, in his writing and in his designs.

The Banks

In order to understand what Louis Sullivan meant by democratic architecture, it is useful to examine his almost entirely neglected essay (published in a 1912 issue of *The Illuminating Engineer*) on his second bank, the 1909–11 Peoples Savings, in Cedar Rapids, Iowa. Explaining the exterior of the building (fig. 28), Sullivan (for the first and only time) employed language and relied upon concepts characteristic of early 1900s Progressive Era treatises on scientifically based governmental efficiency that many of his contemporaries believed would broaden democracy: by rationalizing the electoral process with the secret ballot and the direct election of United States senators, for example, or by replacing boss-chosen mayors with professionally trained city managers. In words that Wisconsin governor Robert M. La Follette might have used but that he himself had not when discussing skyscrapers in the 1890s, Sullivan noted that in his bank scheme nothing was without practical purpose, that there was no waste: the "simple lines and plain surfaces," he explained, achieved a

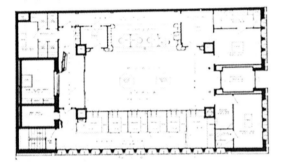

Figure 28.
*Peoples Savings Bank,
Cedar Rapids, Iowa
(1909–11).*
Illuminating Engineer, 1912.

Figure 29.
*Peoples Savings Bank,
Cedar Rapids, Iowa
(1909–11). Banking
room.*
Illuminating Engineer, 1912.

"quiet, dignified effect. . . . The exterior . . . is the logical outcome of the plan, the building being designed from within, outward, the prime governing consideration being utilitarian," so that the business of banking "should be, as nearly as possible, an automatically working machine."[36]

But "the high point of interest" for him, as it is for us at this point, "is the interior" (fig. 29), which he wrote, "may be called 'democratic' in plan." He meant, first of all, that the view upon entering was clear and unobstructed, everything important being in plain sight and every office easily accessible. The vault with its massive swung-open door (as it was usually photographed) was directly in line with the entry, a reassuring symbol of the availability of one's valuables and of the security of their storage place (echoed by the "strongbox" appearance of the cubelike brick container that was itself the building). Private offices for consultation or for the institution's executives were neither more luxurious than the public banking room or than waiting areas for men and women customers, nor were they made difficult to reach by

arduous detour, strategically placed barrier, or phalanxes of employees. Ornate metal wickets or simple handsome grilles made dealing with tellers an aesthetic adventure. In short, Sullivan aimed to promote a kind of dialogue between his banks and their patrons.

These features expressed for him "the modern 'human' element" because they promoted a "feeling of ease, confidence and friendship between officers, employees and customers." The general effect, he added, "is attractive and inviting, all repellent aspects of mystery, reserve, dullness and frigidity (so characteristic of the older banks) being carefully eliminated, and the social fact brought into prominence that banking is a function of society and not a secluded mystery apart from the people."

Just as the skyscraper was for Sullivan the result of "social conditions," so was banking and thus its building a "social fact." As with the skyscraper, this social fact was also deleterious—shall we call it feudal?—as presently constructed because of its inequitable power relationships. Had Sullivan not thought so, he would not have identified two sets of antagonists: officers *vs.* employees on the one hand, bank personnel *vs.* customers on the other. By replacing architectural symbols of power with an "attractive and inviting" "modern 'human' element," he aimed to instill "ease, confidence and friendship" among the three groups who heretofore had known only the opposite. Erecting a democratic bank meant for Sullivan building a democratic community.

By using words like "mystery," "secluded," "frigidity," and "reserve," Sullivan alluded to the superiority of the banker who, manipulating financial transactions "apart from the people," relied on esoteric expertise to prevent his business from being "a function of society," that is, an endeavor over which ordinary citizens might retain at least some sense of control. He alluded to the unfair advantage, the upper hand, to secrets, surprises, inside and hidden things known to the lender but not the borrower, enabling the one to dominate the other in economic and thus social relations. In this regard, Sullivan's thinking again reflected an aspect of Progressive Era *"mentalité,"* one that historian Richard Hofstadter was the first to examine. In their rebellion against formalism in social philosophy, an intellectual characteristic of the "genteel tradition" used by conservatives to stymie political reform, some Progressives gave a new meaning to the concept of "reality." "Reality [for them] was the inside story," Hofstadter wrote. "It was hidden, neglected, and off-stage. . . . It was rough and sordid: . . . the bribe, the rebate, the bought franchise, the sale of adulterated food. It was what one found in *The Jungle, The Octopus, Wealth Against Commonwealth,* or *The Shame of the Cities.*"[37]

Some Progressives believed, in other words, that what was seen, that which appeared to be, was more than likely a cover, a mask or disguise, for a "rough and sordid" reality beneath the surface of things. In this context, Sullivan's contention that the Peoples Savings Bank was "designed from within, outward," the exterior being "the logical outcome of the plan," takes on significance

beyond what was made of it above in relation to efficiency. Aside from defining architecture as the enclosed space and not as the enclosure, his statement means that the interior proclaims itself open to inspection on the exterior. Inside and outside become the same reality, meaning that the facade accomplishes iconographically what the plan does literally. With reality no longer "a secluded mystery apart from the people," as Sullivan had put it, it was cleansed of evil secrets and unfair advantages lurking in dark corners. Progressives hoped that by exposing those secrets and advantages they could rally the public around reform causes. Apparently aware of this political program, which was approaching its zenith when Sullivan was designing and building the Peoples Savings Bank, he tried to eliminate the hiddenness architecturally, so that reality, in this case the business of banking, was always in view, even from the outside, since to see the facade was to know the interior. Not only did Sullivan's design speak to Progressive Era interest in efficiency while being symbolically democratic, but his Peoples Savings Bank essay (unlike his writings on skyscrapers) also partook of that mode of thinking.

Because Sullivan knew that "most of the bank's clients are of the working class," he attempted by design to place them on a more equal footing in their business dealings. First, he made the public service space the aesthetic focus of the building (indeed, he made it the definition of the building, inside and out) through its superior scale and sumptuous embellishment. Second, he specified the finest materials for that and other rooms—marble, copper plate, quartered oaks, art glass—and insisted on "rich" decoration, abundant natural light, and the most up-to-date Prairie-style furnishings after the manner of Frank Lloyd Wright and his Midwestern contemporaries. Third, he paid tribute to working people with his choice of murals (fig. 30), themes of which were farm life and the relation of banking to labor and to local agriculture. "The entire scheme, therefore, is a complete inversion," Sullivan contended, "of the traditional notion of what a bank should be."

This was undoubtedly an exaggeration. Other institutions had majestic banking rooms, the finest furnishings, grand murals, and elaborate decorations. Architectural historian Wim de Wit has shown, furthermore, that in the early twentieth century, Midwestern bankers, trying to upgrade their image in the face of hostile farmer and labor movements, advocated the same "modern 'human' elements" Sullivan claimed as his own. In the towns and small cities where he built Peoples Savings and the rest of his banks, furthermore, it could easily be demonstrated that any number of community pressures and relationships were available—"progressive banking," in de Wit's phrase, being only one among them—to disguise or, in the best of circumstances, moderate (but without fundamentally weakening) the hold of the elite on the citizenry.[38]

Moderate, perhaps, but not abolish; in social relations, possibly, but not in economic. The problem was not the location of the bank but the structure of the industry. The issue was not handsome materials or "progressive" marketing strategies but the way society functioned. Sullivan's objective was to suggest by design and its imagery that the elite, nonetheless "feudal" for being small-town, was in no way intrinsically superior to the community at large. Sullivan knew he could not reform the way banks operated, but he hoped he could influence the way people thought.

He aimed with his bank interiors, therefore, to elevate the self-esteem of customers, of employees, of craftsmen who built them, and of other townsfolk whose only relation to them was visual. He was saying that in a democracy, important job titles, wealth, power, and social rank—privilege, in short—ought not to monopolize beauty or be thought to have the inside track to creative prowess. He was saying that the poet's province of emotional perception, imagination, refined thought, and eloquent expression was actually community property, part of everyone's birthright. The banks pointed toward democracy because Sullivan believed that in constructing, using, working in, and seeing them, the average person would be exalted, not

only by experiencing the best, or looking at it, but also by coming to understand that he could create the best himself. Through that kind of awareness, Sullivan believed, true democracy would be born again.

The Metaphor of the Brick

By focusing our attention now on the exterior of the banks, we can reconstruct Sullivan's thinking about the relation of individuals to community. The first thing to notice is that seven of the nine were built not in marble or granite, which was customary for banks, even small ones, but in a homey simple material in a new form he called "tapestry bricks." In "Artistic Brick," a little-known essay

Figure 30.
Peoples Savings Bank,
Cedar Rapids, Iowa
(1909–11). Banking room
mural over principal
entrance.
Banker's Magazine, 1912.

from 1910,[39] by which time he had designed two banking structures, Sullivan observed that new techniques of cutting and grinding hardened clay had produced a coarser texture that, after firing, "showed a veritable gamut of colors," a glorious range of tints and hues (fig. 31). The old, inexpensive, rough red paver had unexpectedly evolved into a beautiful object, making it economically feasible to abandon "shirtfront" construction wherein comparatively costly pressed brick was reserved for the principal facade with sides and rear left to cheaper dressing. It was now possible by treating all surfaces equally, Sullivan wrote, for the architect to "feel more sensible to the true nature of a building as an organism or whole: an individual or fully-expressed structure, rather than a mere slice showing one character for the front and another for the sides." The exterior could now become "the full expression of the plan," furthermore, "evidencing, instead of hiding, the working conditions of the building," thereby illustrating "nature's continuously operative law" by which everything seeks and finds "its form by virtue of its working plan, or purpose or utility."

Because of their infinite variations, it turned out, tapestry bricks could be laid in such a way as to form subtle patterns, tones, or textures depending upon the desired effect—to emphasize strength or density here, softness there, or the play of sun and shadow somewhere else—so that facades could now take on a more painterly or sculptural quality. Thus, in ensemble, tapestry bricks broadened the range of methods whereby interior requisites or even the social purposes of architecture might be represented on exteriors But the crucial point for Sullivan was this: the bricks "are at their best when laid up with a raked-out joint leaving the individual brick to play its part as a unity therein, and the mass free to express its color and texture in a broad way."

"So small a thing as a brick," therefore, contributed to the perfection of a building only by retaining its individuality. The whole would suffer were the uniqueness of the individual lost. Substitute the words "person" for "brick" and "society" for "mass" and we have Sullivan's democratic as well as his architectural vision: the ensemble— democracy—is composed of innumerable individualisms working together for the good of all but never losing their distinctive identities.

Sullivan himself hinted that his essay on bricks was actually about society. "It used to be said that it took two to make a building," he wrote: "the owner and the architect." But in fact, "it takes more than two": the owner and the architect, to be sure, but also "the intelligent brick manufacturer" and "the men working in their various ways and contributing technical support," referring most likely to masons, among other craftsmen. "Such is the development of modern society," he continued, "each [person] reacting upon each and all." By "modern society," Sullivan did not mean the new "feudalism" about which he had written so much, but referred, rather, to "what we are here [in "Natural Thinking," completed two years previously] choosing to call Democracy or The New Way." "Artistic Brick" was written shortly after Sullivan finished his first bank, the National Farmers' Bank in Owatonna, Minnesota (1906–8), and while he was constructing his second, the Peoples Savings Bank in Cedar Rapids (1909–11), a six-year period during which he executed only six small buildings, five of them in small cities or villages in the Midwest. It was during his experience of working in places such as these (which he had rarely done before) that bricks became his metaphor for individuals, putting up a bank his metaphor for building democracy.

Appropriately enough, all nine banks were sited with two or more facades exposed, enabling Sullivan to employ tapestry bricks (on the seven occasions he used them) to full advantage in order to express "the true nature of a building as a [whole] organism." But as exteriors they are more than examples of natural law, more, even, than illustrations of the social meaning of working with brick. As embodiments of democracy they put into practice in several ways what skyscraper facades could only anticipate. All the banks have strong civic—perhaps also civil—presence because they adjust themselves to, yet enter into friendly dialogue with, prevailing community norms. Far from rejecting what had already been locally

accomplished by blatantly heralding a new architectural order, they encouraged their communities to strengthen themselves by exploiting their own resources and remaining true to their own traditions.

On the matter of community norms, for example, each bank respects the scale and rhythm of its small-city streetscape (fig. 32); none ignores the cornice heights, widths, colors, shapes, or normal sidewalk features (size and location of openings, for instance) found among its neighbors. All provide walk-in customers with clear visual access, easy entry (there are no steps up to the "raised temple" of traditional banks), and legible signage, while their bases, set off near head height from superstructures by changes in color, string courses, sills, or other devices, offer pedestrians a comfortably human scale. Large windows in upper facades suggest airy, volumetric interiors suitable for congenial business transactions, eliminating the massive columns and pediments that often guarded more traditional repositories (see fig. 31). At Cedar Rapids and at the Peoples' Savings & Loan Association in Sidney, Ohio (1917), he placed

Figure 32.
Merchants National
Bank, Grinnell, Iowa
(1913–14).
Fourth Avenue setting.
Photograph by Robert
Twombly.

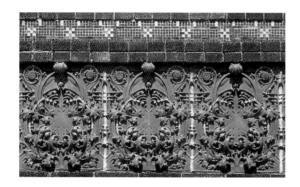

But in the very act of endorsing they also promised to strengthen the positive aspects of their social environments in ways the citizenry could readily comprehend. The banks, first of all, stand out from their milieus, but not in a monumental or majestic way, like more familiar expressions of finance in Greek-temple, Roman-domed, or Georgian-mansion style. They stand out, rather, as quietly powerful symbols of everyday life: for example, as "strongboxes" (fig. 35), called that because in a brilliant synthesis with the image of airy openness, they pledged themselves to be sentinels of working people's laboriously accumulated resources, and in that gesture underscored a second assurance, of the collective strength and security the town itself represented for its residents. As "jewel boxes" (fig. 36), so labeled because their sumptuous ornamentation immediately caught everyone's attention, they offered a higher standard for aesthetic aspiration than had previously been available, not only for cultivated individuals, but also for entire towns that, as collectivities, achieved elevated status precisely because Sullivan's banks were there. As emblems of civic pride—especially when sited as most are on the courthouse square, facing a park, or at a major intersection—they further dignified what were already considered to be important public places. Their ornamentation—sculpture, murals, art glass, terra-cotta, metal, and brickwork—were tributes to the community's artisanal skills, in some instances showcases for them (fig. 37), as one customer remarked about the recently restored Cedar Rapids bank: "I just love to come in here. I see something different every time. It's like a museum."[40]

At all times Sullivan's control over the lush, challenging decoration and the exquisitely executed detailing provided understated object lessons in art appreciation and in the importance of disciplined work. But even more important was his social lesson: that ordinary people, including those outside the metropolis, had the right to great art, not only to see it, but also in a sense to make it theirs. For if most city folk saw Sullivan's skyscraper facades at a distance or fleetingly en route to somewhere else,

streetlamps in the banks' vocabulary at curbside (see fig. 28); at Owatonna and at the Purdue State Bank in West Lafayette, Indiana (1914), he made grain and other local plant motifs the basis of his ornament (fig. 33); at the Farmers' & Merchants' Union Bank in Columbus, Wisconsin (1919), he slanted the window-framing side buttresses out into the sidewalk (fig. 34); at the H. C. Adams & Co. Land and Loan Offices in Algona, Iowa (1913–14), he flanked the entry with plant-filled urns; and he clad the Home Building Association in Newark, Ohio (1914–15), in greenish-gray terra-cotta to complement the greenish-gray limestone courthouse across the street. These were all simple, unprepossessing, but easily understood gestures linking edifice organically with community. In short, the banks were intended to fit gently into the established ambiance and traditions of their built surroundings.

small-town residents experienced and used his banks in much more intimate ways.

This was in part because their social relations made the meaning of a bank something different from that of an urban skyscraper. In Columbus, Wisconsin, Sidney, Ohio, and other places like them, the masons and carpenters who built the banks might well have been their customers. If not, they likely knew or were related to others who were, even including the banks' employees. Those employees and the directors, as well as the institutions themselves, were organic parts of their communities, not only because farmer and merchant dependence on credit made banks lifelines, but also because their financial prosperity (not to mention their architecture) stood in most everyone's mind for the success of their towns as collectivities. In addition to that, banks functioned as meeting places for farmers, shopkeepers, and many other members of the community, a social fact acknowledged by Sullivan (and his clients) with the nonbusiness spaces they provided, like the "farmers' exchange" at Owatonna and the men's and women's waiting rooms in several of the banks. So the edifice the townspeople used, helped construct, saw every day, and depended upon mightily was in substantial ways "theirs" as no skyscraper could ever be for urban dwellers. To Sullivan, therefore, and to the citizenry, in quite real ways, the bank represented community—the embodiment of dreams and of the recognizable labor of many individuals for the good of themselves and of the collectivity—working like a tapestry brick to make the ensemble better. Building the town bank was Sullivan's way of forging the democratic community.

Ornament

After 1910 that was just about all Louis Sullivan did: design small banks. Of his scant eleven executed commissions from then until his death fourteen years later, eight were banks. But it was not the kind of work he would have chosen for himself. Early in 1910, after finishing at Owatonna and while designing for Cedar Rapids, he wrote to a

Figure 35.
National Farmers' Bank,
Owatonna, Minnesota
(1906–8).
Courtesy Thomas A. Heinz.

Figure 36.
Merchants National
Bank, Grinnell, Iowa
(1913–14).
Northwest Architectural
Archives, University of
Minnesota Libraries, St. Paul.

Figure 37.
Home Building
Association, Newark,
Ohio (1914–15).
Photograph by Lauren
Weingarden.

friend that he did not want to take another bank commission, most likely hoping that larger jobs would again come his way. But they did not, and he later changed his mind, probably out of financial necessity at first, yet after a while developing a certain enthusiasm for the genre, it seems. In the end the legacy of his banks proved to be equal to that of his skyscrapers, perhaps not in the number of pages devoted to them in history books, but surely in their embodiment of his social thought.

Among their most visible features, certainly the most immediately obvious is their ornamentation. As early as 1902, some architecture observers deemed Sullivan the most accomplished American practitioner of "Art Nouveau," an inaccurate categorization that did justice neither to him nor to his European contemporaries, for there were considerable compositional, stylistic, and philosophical differences between his work and theirs. The comparison is apt only in the sense that both he and they regularly based their motifs on plant forms, he perhaps with greater verisimilitude. By 1910 or so, when Sullivan had little choice but to concentrate on bank design, he was criticized for clinging to a mode of decorative expression that was passing out of vogue, both among more progressive and more conservative architects. The Merchants National Bank (1913–14) in Grinnell, Iowa, the most elaborately decorated and best-known of all in this regard, has been ridiculed for being overdone, for having too much ornament for the size of its facade (see fig. 36). But if, as Sullivan believed, "the decorative ornamentation is the more intense" expression of the "emotional impulse" flowing through a building—more intense than even its "mass-composition"—then we had best pay attention to what that "*passé*," allegedly overdone ornament actually means.

In his 1892 essay "Ornament in Architecture," Sullivan declared it self-evident that a structure entirely without decoration could be noble and dignified by virtue of its mass and proportions alone, and that, given the contemporary proclivity to "vandalize" the past for usable motifs, it might be best if architects refrained completely from employing ornament for a few years in order to concentrate on producing buildings that were, in his now famous phrase, "well formed and comely in the nude." Ornament was "mentally a luxury, not a necessity," he observed, so why then, he asked, should we use it at all?[41]

Because "we have in us romanticism," he answered, "and feel a craving to express it. We feel intuitively that our strong, athletic and simple forms will carry with natural ease the raiment of which we dream, and that our buildings thus clad in a garment of poetic imagery . . . will appeal with redoubled power, like a sonorous melody overlaid with harmonious voices." In order to achieve this harmony, he went on, ornament should never seem to be "stuck on." "An organic system of ornamentation . . . should appear, when completed, as though by the outworkings of some beneficent agency it had come forth from the very substance of the [building's] material and was there by the same right that a flower appears amid the leaves of its parent plant. Here by this method . . . the spirit that animates the mass is free to flow into the ornament—they are no longer two things but one thing. . . . [T]he ornament should appear, not as something receiving the spirit of the structure," he advised, "but as a thing expressing that spirit by virtue of differentiated growth. . . . A decorated building, designed upon this principle, will require in its creator a high and sustained emotional tension," he continued, "an organic singleness of idea and purpose maintained to the last. . . . [T]he more intense heat in which it was conceived the more serene and noble will it forever remain as a document of man's eloquence."

So here is Sullivan emphasizing the intensity of creating ornament and of the ornament itself—process and content being one and the same—as well as underscoring its capacity to "redouble" the "power" of a building. It follows that the messages embedded in the massing and facades of Sullivan's structures were concentrated, distilled, and intensified in his ornament. Thus it becomes necessary here to demonstrate how his ornament, based on his understanding of natural law, encapsulated his vision for a democratic America.

Sullivan never detached human beings from the natural world. He did not believe that society had benefited itself by triumphing over nature. Quite the opposite: humanity civilized itself in direct proportion to the extent it absorbed natural principles, and in believing this Sullivan was an American romantic. It deeply disturbed him that modern man had lost touch with nature, hence with essential elements of himself. For it was nature, he knew, that in addition to providing clues about how creativity worked and how democracy was ordered also reminded human beings of their existentially tragic situation: that all lived to die. But it was also nature that exemplified humanity's great opportunity: the power to create in the face of death.

There was a cycle to all life that Sullivan said consisted of birth, growth, maturation, decay, and death. What distinguished humankind from other living things was its ability to comprehend this cycle and thus triumph over it, to live eternally in the sense that its creations could live forever, among other things instructing subsequent generations about the great secret of the universe, which was that death was not an obstacle to life but in fact urged it forward. For living was creating, making death in the cycle of life an essential part of re-creation, species re-creation, it could be said. Sullivan's vertical skyscrapers embodied this thinking.

By building on Narciso Menocal's analysis in *Architecture as Nature: The Transcendentalist Idea of Louis Sullivan* (1981),[42] which he develops further in section 5 of his essay in this volume, we can trace these ideas on the facade of the 1897–98 Bayard/Condit Building (see fig. 11) in New York. Bearing in mind Sullivan's insistence that ornament should "come forth from the very substance of the material" and not be "stuck on" the building, we allow our eyes to follow the projecting columns upward until they reach the attic, where their decorative fluting divides to form arches, returning by adjacent columns to the second-floor sill, which it crosses to its starting point, thus forming an unbroken circuit. At the spring points of the arch-

*Figure 38.
Bayard/Condit
Building, New York
(1897–98). Detail of attic
ornamentation.*
Photograph by Robert
Twombly.

es where the fluting divides, we see winged, vaguely angelic, apparently female figures with outstretched arms ever so slightly bent at the wrists, their presence confirming the inextricability of the human from nature's life cycle: the seeds in the ground at the sill are also human seeds; as their shoots turn into plants and our minds and bodies develop, the fluting rises to the curve of the arches; there, in maturity, everything flowers fully, the female figures bursting from the leafy efflorescence; but as their hands gently droop and the fluting begins its descent, the life force ebbs, returning to the sill—the earth—there to die where it is reborn.

Difficult to see from the sidewalk is vegetation reaching out as if to reclaim these female figures (fig. 38) at their feet, thighs, and portions of their wings, reminding us that in the end it is nature to which we return, that even here at the pinnacle of life's achievement, death beckons. The women's eyes seem purposefully ambiguous, either closed in death at the moment of their greatest glory or looking downward toward the source of their renewal. Either way, the message is regeneration: death cannot quench, only restore, the human spirit. Imagery such as this seems particularly appropriate for vertical facades—perhaps another reason Sullivan wrote about them so lyrically—but never appeared elsewhere with the intensity of Bayard/Condict.

This imagery was not suitable for low-rise banks, but by the time Sullivan was immersed in that genre, the message had changed—from an implicitly existential to an explicitly collective one—and it never appeared elsewhere as intensely as at the Merchants National Bank in Grinnell. Its ornamentation ought not to suggest to us, therefore, as it has to others, a lack of aesthetic restraint, a Sullivan out of control, but rather a Sullivan determined to make his point. Around the oculus (see fig. 36) over the entry, the decorative burst is meant to be eye-catching—is meant to make people stop, stare, and reflect—because it is meant to represent democracy unfolding. We might consider the interlocking network as an even more intense version of tapestry bricks in ensemble, that is, as the celebration of community wherein each interconnected geometry depends upon but bursts the bounds of the next, in proclamation of its freedom, of those many freedoms, whose other meaning is the final harmonious whole.

9. Sullivan's Reality

Louis Sullivan's skyscraper and bank designs were implicitly critical of an American order which he believed imprisoned human capacity, but if analyzed in light of his writing his critique becomes explicit. During the 1890s, unless one read "The High Building Question" or "The Tall Office Building Artistically Considered," his oppositional posture was difficult to discern, because it required deciphering skyscraper facades. But after the 1890s, when all the high-rise structures he ever built had been erected, writing became his principal means of social criticism, of proclaiming his vision of democracy. But it was not his only means, for beginning in 1906, even his much-diminished architectural output continued the themes of the previous decade. Like the skyscrapers, his banks presupposed that people were prevented by the social order from becoming full human beings, residence in small places notwithstanding. And like the skyscrapers, they alerted people to their own creative potential. But if anything, the banks were even more "subversive"— Sullivan would never have used the word—than his skyscrapers, because they said that democracy depended upon linking individualism to collective endeavor. This current of opposition and advocacy was central to his mature thinking, and the more it became known, the more it hurt him professionally.

A second characteristic of his intellectual position that did him no good was its abstract quality: his inability to put democratic principles into everyday practice, to apply them to known individuals as opposed to unknown groups, to live what he built and wrote. He could address the large, generalized requisites of a disembodied humanity but not the small, particularized needs of living human beings. Since it invaded his life to the point of saturation, intellectual abstraction coupled with personal detachment prevented him from forming individually close or collectively muscular relationships that might have sustained him after 1900 or so when his oppositional posture brought him into direct conflict with arbiters of the social nexus upon whom his livelihood depended. And in his vulnerable isolation, when arbiter withdrawal of patronage put him in dire financial straits, the rarefied nature of his life and thought also meant that he could not design livable, workable houses. Since potential clients knew this, he was infrequently asked, and since he himself also seemed to know it, he hardly bothered to pursue residential commissions even though middle- and upper-middle-class housing was a flourishing field that could have compensated him for the loss of commercial work. So his opposition to "neofeudalism" cost him dearly in two related ways: its critical *content* alienated the powerful, who cast him aside, and its abstract *quality* rendered him incapable of serving the middle class.

Therein lies the basis of his *material* problem, which worsened as the years passed. To put it bluntly, his outspoken criticism reduced him to poverty. His *intellectual* problem was that his vision of democracy was not based on close observation of life as lived. In point of fact, Sullivan seemed disinterested in the mundane needs of average people. He paid little attention—at least in his writing—to slum life, factory conditions, immigrant cultures, or family relationships at any class level, and when he touched on matters such as these, for instance in "Natural Thinking," he remained at a distance and said nothing specific. Just as in his autobiography he discussed himself always in the third person, the case study "Louis" observed as if under a microscope, so in his professional work he thought in terms of social categories.

This may explain why he excelled at bank and high-rise design where both interior accommodations and exterior imagery were intended for groups known to him as groups—office workers, borrower and lenders, "everyman," and "the public"—but why he failed at residential design, in which each client and every set of needs was unique. Nor was he able with houses to develop an iconography suitable for his democratic vision. That vision, it seems, did not allow for idiosyncrasy—all individuals being subsumed to the concept "people"—which is particularly ironic in that its richly creative everyman bore strong similarities to the richly creative Louis Sullivan himself, leading to the speculation, perhaps unfounded, that he would not have been happy in the utopia of his own making.

Houses

At the beginning of Sullivan's career, residential design took up much of his time. While working for, or in partnership with, Dankmar Adler from 1879 to 1895 he produced some sixty dwellings, a few of them multiple residences but most of them single-family. Like many young firms, Adler & Sullivan was at first obliged to take on more domes-

tic work than it would have preferred. But success changed its situation. Using as a litmus test the Auditorium Building of 1886–90—the point at which Adler & Sulllivan came to national attention and could be more selective about its commissions—this was the nature of its practice: through 1889, when work on the Auditorium was substantially completed, forty-two of its ninety-nine buildings (43 percent) were residential; from 1890 until the partnership dissolved in 1895, the figure fell dramatically to five of sixty-one commissions (8 percent). And from 1888 to 1893 Frank Lloyd Wright, who worked for Adler & Sullivan as chief draftsman beginning in 1890, was likely responsible for nine of the firm's twelve residences, two of which were multiple dwellings. The last private house from the partnership (which by Wright's time did them only as favors for friends and important commercial clients) was in 1891–92 (fig. 39) for Sullivan's mother, Andrienne.[43]

By and large these early Adler & Sullivan dwellings—all produced before Sullivan was thirty-

Figure 40.
Leon Mannheimer
House, Chicago (1884).
Photograph by
Robert Twombly.

Figure 41.
Louis H. Sullivan
Cottage, Ocean Springs,
Mississippi (1890).
Architectural Record, 1905.

five—were conventional inside and out. Relying on familiar architectural imagery with which their upper-middle-class clients felt comfortable, they spoke of the dignity and material well-being befitting their owners' accomplishments, standing, and ambitions (fig. 40). Never departing far from fashionable styles, these sturdy brick and stone buildings with prominent roofs and gables, occasional dormers, corner towers, and mansards, with elaborate capitals, spiky cornices, and tall, thin chimneys, were picturesquely predictable—even including Sullivan's ornament, which, early in his career, was mostly unremarkable—as predictable as his youthful assumptions about the lives of his clients, who, appropriately enough, superficially resembled each other: a high percentage were German-Jewish small manufacturers living on Chicago's South Side, members of the same one or two social clubs and of one of two temples. But since he was simply uninterested in the residential genre, it is not surprising that once the Auditorium was underway with Wright on board, he probably designed only three houses after 1887: in 1890 for his friend James Charnley in Ocean Springs, Mississippi, and for himself (fig. 41) next door to Charnley, and finally a year later for his mother in Chicago.

So it was eleven years—excluding these three quite personal undertakings, the least conventional of all his dwellings to 1891, by the way—before he accepted another residential commission: an 1898 vacation house for Albert W. Goodrich in Harbor Springs, Michigan. He took the job probably because he knew Goodrich and definitely because he needed work during a national depression—he landed the Schlesinger & Mayer Store and the Gage Building facade that year but had nothing else new in the office—a situation which only got worse, accounting for his accepting other domestic projects. Of the ten he designed from 1898 to 1911, one was a store with flats above, another an alteration of an existing structure, and a third a revision of a rejected first proposal. Of the last ten residential projects of his life, only seven would have been new private dwellings. But of the seven, only two were constructed.

The house in Harbor Springs was not, and for very good reason. It would have been a massive, monumental, classicizing edifice (fig. 42), much too formal for the Goodriches' relaxed manner of summer living and much too pretentious for the neighborhood. It was overly large and costly: nine bedrooms (including two each for servants and children and three for guests), a goodly amount of indeterminate wasted space, and a living room, master bedroom, gallery, and terraces of gigantic dimensions. Goodrich was a Chicago business-man, a close friend of the McCormicks, for whom at the moment Sullivan was designing the Michi-gan Avenue facade of the Gage Building. If Goodrich chose Sullivan after seeing the beautiful Gage drawings—and in all likelihood he did—he must have been disappointed when he inspected the residence plans. For along with everything else, the enormous, round, colonnaded dining room opening to the majestic entry sequence (exterior steps—porch—vestibule—interior stairs—grand hall) was far more suitable for a fashionable Michigan Avenue town house near the Gage Building than it was for a lakeside retreat two states away.

Goodrich got what he did not want, including the serious flaws Narciso Menocal discovered in the plan (fig. 43). The children's bath on the sec-ond floor was forty-five feet from their bedrooms and was to be shared with guests. Mrs. Goodrich Sr. had her own bathroom but no tub, and her bedroom had no closet. Although there were two servant and two guest rooms on the third floor, it was without bathing and toilet facilities: presum-ably, guests were expected to descend one flight and then compete with children, and servants to trudge three flights to the basement. The third-floor playroom would have faced north, its limited access to sun further diminished by a roofed, arcaded balcony, only five feet wide, surrounding its three exposed sides. The unroofed, sunny and warm, south-facing servants' terrace, by contrast, was seventeen feet by twenty-nine.[44]

Menocal's assessment of the Goodrich proposal was in fact rather forgiving in view of its addi-tional flaws: third-floor guests had no closets, an intimate rear terrace looked inside through win-dows but only at a stairwell from which one could not see out, and the hall was unnecessarily long and tortuous because it skirted a huge storeroom (of which there were two—right next to guests—despite ample storage in the basement). On the second floor, children could take unwanted

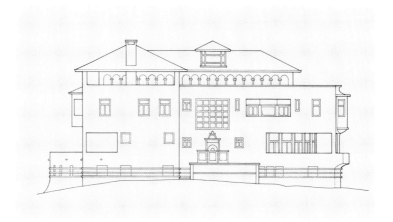

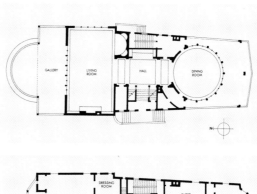

Figure 42.
A. W. Goodrich House project, Harbor Springs, Michigan (1898). Principal elevation.
Drawing by Hanque Macari after blueprint copy of original tracing in the State Historical Society of Wisconsin, Madison.

Figure 43.
A. W. Goodrich House project, Harbor Springs, Michigan (1898). First, second, and third floor plans (top to bottom).
Drawings by Hanque Macari after blueprint copies of original tracings in the State Historical Society of Wisconsin, Madison.

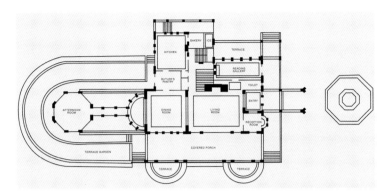

advantage of the master bath, which should not have opened on the hall, nor faced a banquette, the only purpose of which seemed to be to hide the servants' stairs. The second-floor guest room had but a single window, even though it was as large as or larger than the senior Mrs. Goodrich's room (three windows) and the children's rooms (four each, five counting another in the closet!). The kitchen was put in the basement—not unusual at the time but becoming more so in new designs, certainly those by Sullivan's Midwestern admirers—and the two small windows in the west living-room wall were too high up to look through. Menocal points out that this unlikely plan was adapted from an even more unlikely source: Henry Hobson Richardson's Billings Library (1882–86) in Burlington, Vermont. (The only two

dwellings Sullivan executed in the twentieth century were also derivative: his 1907 Henry Babson House in Riverside, Illinois, from Wright's 1899 Joseph Husser residence in Chicago, and his 1909 Harold and Josephine Crane Bradley House in Madison, Wisconsin, from Wright's 1901 "A Home in a Prairie Town" proposal for *The Ladies' Home Journal*.)

So it perhaps not surprising that when Sullivan took up his next house project after Goodrich he would again seek help: this time from McKim, Mead, and White's Isaac Bell residence (1881–82) in Newport, Rhode Island. The McCormick project (fig. 44) was also seriously flawed. Since there was no way to close off vestibule and entry, unexpected or unwanted callers could observe residents seated in the living room. Servants were required to traverse that large space, interrupting activity there, furthermore, whenever they answered the doorbell, because there was no alternative access route. Nor could they lay or clear the dining table without additional disruption, because Sullivan had provided no adequate means—pocket doors, screen, or curtains—for closing the fifteen-foot opening to the living room. The main stairs gave directly to that room, not to the adjacent hall where propriety would have it but could not, because it received the servants' stairs. And on the second floor, where this time all five bedrooms were given closet and bath, not to mention a fireplace, the octagonal hall had yet another fireplace, but no seating, no windows, and no provision for a skylight.

There is no reason to give further attention to the McCormick project or to list the practical problems with Sullivan's other houses. But it is useful in this consideration of social relations to examine his proposal for the Carl K. Bennett House (1911–12) in Owatonna, Minnesota, the same Carl K. Bennett that as vice-president of National Farmers' brought Sullivan his first bank commission in 1906. If in National Farmers'—considered by many to be his best bank—Sullivan had successfully built his version of democratic architecture, in Bennett's house he failed. The bank, after

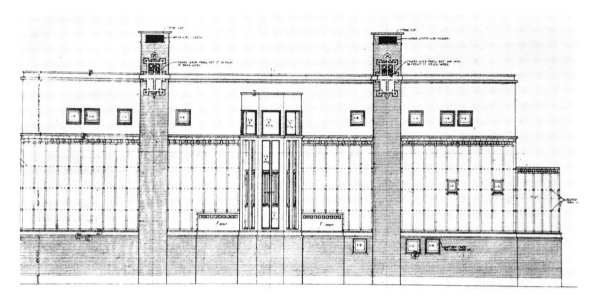

Figure 45.
Carl K. Bennett House
project, Owatonna,
Minnesota (1911–12).
Street (or north) eleva-
tion.
Northwest Architectural
Archives, University of
Minnesota Libraries, St. Paul.

all, served an anonymous group of customers, whereas in the house, people were all too real.

The Bennett project was impressive in several ways, perhaps too impressive. Its facade was symmetrical, tightly organized, and elegant (fig. 45), its main floor broad and sweeping, with long vistas through well-detailed Prairie-style rooms. Sited near the corner of a generous 135-by-444-foot lot (about an acre and one-third), its north or street elevation was virtually unglazed, appropriate for the climate and for privacy, Mrs. Bennett later recalled, while the south elevation looked over the garden with more than ample fenestration of continuous stained-glass window bands on all three floors. Like the Pueblo Grand Opera House, its facade was composed in a Renaissance manner but not entirely of Renaissance materials: a Roman brick base, a *piano nobile* of vertical redwood board-and-batten, and a stucco attic, all of which made it decidedly unusual. "I'm simply astonished at [this] Sullivan design," architectural historian James Marston Fitch wrote in 1973. "It certainly suggests a flare-up of creative energy . . . I'd never suspected."[45]

Flare-up or continuation, it was nevertheless grand inside, up-to-date, and handsomely appointed. The interior of the base contained entry, playroom, spacious servants' quarters with sitting

room, storage, workshop, and utilities, including an intercom, a gas-fired clothes dryer, and a central vacuum system (fig. 46). Within the *piano nobile* were living, dining, and music rooms and hall in a seventy-foot sequence, with kitchen and related services under a ten-foot ceiling. The uppermost floor had five bedrooms, two baths, dressing room, and balcony. All this was bisected by a minor north-south axis for stairwell, landings, balcony, and den. Had the Bennett House been built it would have been one of the most distinctive and luxurious in town.

And that would have been appropriate, because Carl K. Bennett was a distinctive man who loved luxury. As a member of one of the oldest and wealthiest local families, historian Larry Millett writes, he was something of a "patrician," "part of the monied class that dominated Owatonna's economic and cultural life," wealthier than his well-to-do father, who had been a founder of National Farmers' Bank in 1873. A product of private secondary schools and of Harvard College, Bennett "was a man who sought to live like a Renaissance prince in a world of Babbitts," Millet continues, and it was probably "because of his rather ostentatious life-style and cultural aspirations" that he seemed "not very well liked in Owatonna."[46] But he himself liked the design, at least

Figure 46.
Carl K. Bennett House
project, Owatonna,
Minnesota (1912).
Ground, main, and
upper floor plans
(top to bottom).
Northwest Architectural
Archives, University of
Minnesota Libraries, St. Paul.

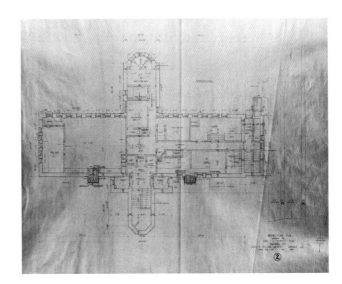

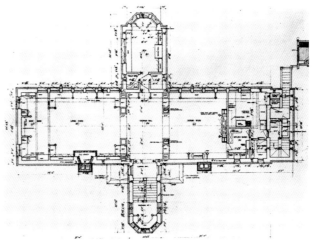

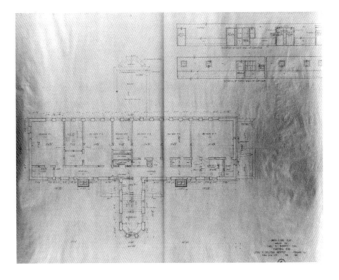

according to his widow's recollection in 1957: "We approved of everything [Sullivan] had planned, and suggested no changes. . . . It was a bitter disappointment that we were never able to build and occupy that house."[47]

Why it was never built remains something of a mystery. It was surely not because of ideological difference, for even if Sullivan thought of his client as a "modern feudal baron," he nonetheless happily gave him a "baronial" dwelling he (or his wife anyway) felt suitable for a "Renaissance prince" banker. Nor was it likely, as architect William Purcell suggested, that the house would have been too costly, calling "for an expenditure of nearly three times the maximum Bennett felt he could put in a home for himself."[48] What its price might have been in 1912 when the plan was completed is now unknown, but during World War I when he was still contemplating construction, Bennett received estimates of $20,000 in 1914 and $40,000 in 1918. Purcell and his partner George Elmslie, who had both worked for Sullivan, were hired by Bennett in 1914 to develop an alternative scheme, even though he had not yet rejected Sullivan's. So Purcell knew the client's financial situation, although on the face of it even the higher estimate seemed well within Bennett's capacity. Perhaps he was being tightfisted, holding fast to a fixed budget. Or perhaps other considerations prevented Bennett from going ahead.

What townspeople would have seen had the project been erected was something unrecognizable. From the street, it was a rigidly geometric, flat-roofed, boxlike structure of extremely formal demeanor with detailing that would have seemed peculiar. Raised high off the ground on its Roman brick base, its tall, vertically articulated *piano nobile* was capped with an elaborate, cornicelike string course broken by brick chimneys decorated near their tops with sawn wooden motifs. The front door was set at right angle to the facade plane out of sight behind a high, thick wall, while the only windows of note on this side were long, narrow slits on a landing in the projecting minor axis. The living, dining, and music rooms had no windows at all, making the street side exterior appear to be an impenetrable barrier between public and private realms. The corniced verticality of the *piano nobile* was in the tradition of a type of facade organization begun at Donato Bramante's Palazzo Caprini (the "House of Raphael," 1501–10) in Rome, Menocal has pointed out, adding that the Bennetts' stuccoed, minimally fenestrated "top story would not have looked at all like the bedroom floor of an American house."[49] Inside this attic, the rooms were strung in a line opening on a corridor along the street side, prompting one observer to call the arrangement "almost that of a club or a fraternity." Whatever the building might have seemed to Owatonnans, it would not have been a house, not an American house anyway, and surely not a house in their hometown. "Not only does it not resemble anything else [Sullivan] ever did," historian Fitch remarked, "it doesn't look like anything any of his contemporaries were doing . . . either."[50]

"Sullivan apparently did not have a feel for domestic design," a latter-day critic has written of this project. Others agree: one historian called it "formidable" and "uncompromising," another "extremely severe and monumental, with . . . [a] fortresslike appearance."[51] Words like these recall others, like "mystery," "secluded," "frigidity," and "reserve," words that Sullivan himself had used to describe traditional institutions in his essay on the Cedar Rapids bank published the very year of the Bennett design. And inevitably, the two Owatonna buildings, bank and house, would have been compared. Consider their facades: the one open and inviting while at the same time promising security for the community's assets, the other closed and uninviting, suggesting withdrawal from that community; the one ornamented with interpretations of local vegetation known to all, the other in the tradition of Bramante unknown to most; the one laden with recognizable banking imagery, the other virtually devoid of familiar domestic association. And, finally, if the one could be understood as a paean for democracy, the other might easily have been seen as a rich man's palazzo. Even

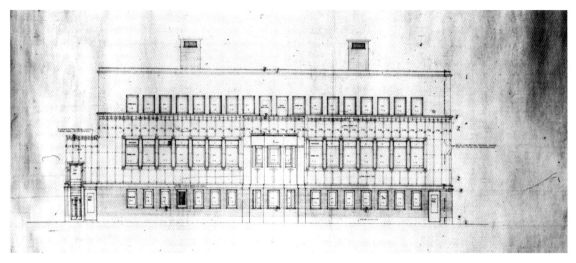

something as simple as the absence of windows, which in the abstract could be admired as an intelligent treatment of a north-facing facade subject to bitter Minnesota winters, might be seen in the particular by small-city neighbors as the antisocial gesture of an aloof aristocrat.

William Purcell sensed most of this when he wrote that the project seemed "wholly lacking in any feeling for the Bennetts as a living family, for their relations to the community or the relation of the building to its site in a farmer's village. It was much more in the nature of a Club House . . . on a city lot where one could look abroad on adjoining buildings. Mr. Sullivan simply had no concept whatever of American family life. The living room was the second floor cut off in both spirit and fact from the garden. The great windows [fig. 47] . . . seemed to interpose themselves like beautiful screens between the dwellers and the world."[52] These perceptive observations can be listed as follows: Sullivan had little understanding of how the Bennetts lived, their relationship with Owatonna, how the community might perceive the house, its social and physical environment, how it might take advantage of its land, and how American families functioned. Except for the last, these were project-defining specifics Sullivan could not grasp.

He could not understand in large part because of his own family history—*non*-family history would be closer to the mark—which left him ill equipped

to appreciate the emotional ties people have with one another and can have with their houses. As a boy he was raised primarily by his grandparents, roomed with their next-door neighbors for two years, and except for a few months on two occasions never lived with his mother and father after age eleven. And he was forever on the move: during the half-century from his sixteenth year until his death, he changed his address at least twenty-four times, from one hotel, rented room, club, or apartment to another (nine times from 1899 to 1909 alone), in addition shuttling back and forth at least once every winter from Chicago to Ocean Springs during the twenty years ending in 1910. He rented his brother's house for a while in the 1890s but knew that, like his spiritual and horticultural retreat in Mississippi, it could never be his permanent, primary home. Not since he was five had he resided full-time in a residence he could call his own, and not since grammar school had he lived in a family situation that the prevailing social mores could accept as "normal."

If Sullivan had a sense of "place" in life it was not before the hearth surrounded by loved ones but in this office surrounded by work. His inexperience with family and his nomadic existence could account for his skittishness about forming close personal connections. Or perhaps it was the other way around. Whatever the reason, his few long-term relationships were maintained at a safe, emotionally unengaged distance: with Dankmar Adler's family, for instance, which he enjoyed visiting but of which he could never be part; with artist and architect colleagues—usually younger than he—for whom he acted as mentor; with the married couple who for ten years shared his Chicago and Ocean Springs residences, probably as employees, but whose ultimate commitment was to each other; and even with his wife, Mary Azona Hattabaugh, who, barely half his age when he married in 1899 at forty-four, was in his mind a kind of cultural understudy. Otherwise, Sullivan had no close companions—he broke permanently with his brother, Albert, his only sibling, in 1896, and thus with his brother's children, his only other living relatives—preferring not to be intimate with anyone, it seems, at least anyone known to us, and as a result he had no knowledge about how to design for daily family life. To Louis Sullivan, the family and its residence were social and architectural mysteries.

Carl K. Bennett's rejection may therefore have been based on the perception that Sullivan's proposal would suit neither his family's manner of living nor his relations with the community in which he resided and from which he derived his income. In conception, the house was magnificent, but it would not have worked for the Bennetts in fact, as the disposition of the garden makes clear. William Purcell's observations indicate that outdoor activity was an important aspect of Bennett family life. But in Sullivan's plan the only routes to the garden from the main-floor living area were cumbersome ones: down stairs and out the front door along a walk next to the street and then around the house, or through the butler's pantry and kitchen to service stairs at their far side. Once outside, furthermore, family and guests would have been seen from the maid's ground-floor sitting room projecting well into the garden. There was no path to it, in other words, and no activity in it that would not have been subject to servant surveillance at every moment and public scrutiny at some moments. That, plus the remote elegance implied by the raised living and dining rooms "cut

off" from the view by stained-glass "screens," required a style of life too formal even for this "patrician" family, as Purcell suggested, an uncompromising formality proclaimed by the street facade. If Carl K. Bennett aspired to "live like a Renaissance prince," in Larry Millett's words, he was well served by Sullivan's palatial scheme. But Bennett undoubtedly knew that in his mundane "world of Babbitts," even an "ostentatious" patrician could overstep the permissible bounds of social pretentiousness, which would in the end be as detrimental to the business of banking with farmers as inadequate privacy and an overload of formality would be for life at home.

The Bennett and Goodrich projects shared several flaws. They were overly formal, solemn, and remarkably unworkable, inadequately addressing client desires. They were remote from physical milieu and insensitive to the social nexuses in which they were set. But perhaps their greatest failure was their sacrifice of practicality for elegance; their eye-catching forms seemed unrelated to function. Sullivan gave his clients beauty that neither facilitated daily activity nor accurately represented them to their communities. In his banks, gorgeousness contributed to practical and social success, but in his houses it became their substitute. Hence rejection in five of seven opportunities to build from 1898 to 1911, as well as on a sixth occasion when Sullivan was required to redesign the 1909 Harold and Josephine Crane Bradley House in Madison, Wisconsin, because his original proposal, the clients said, was too ostentatious "for the life of the average professor's family."[53] Unable to fathom household needs, Sullivan repeatedly offered inventories of luxurious elements that did not coalesce as working entities.

Nor did his dwellings carry the panoply of democratic imagery. Perhaps he believed that as private property intended exclusively for private use a house was not the place to address social issues, unlike privately owned banks or skyscrapers that were seen and used by sundry and all. If so, he was mistaken, because the appearance of a residence—which reveals a good deal about those inside as well as their attitude toward those out-side—is in truth public property, a kind of social signage offered to the world at large by owners who know it will be scrutinized and interpreted. It is more likely, however, that Sullivan simply did not recognize the family as an important social institution or as necessary in any way to the construction of democracy. His thinking on the subject, which, in its maturity, attempted to define the relationship between the individual and the community without compromising the integrity of either, nevertheless did precisely that. Because his thinking remained on the level of Olympian generality, it did not provide for certain kinds of particularity: not the particularity of a family or of its relation to society, not of the individual except as a unit working in and for and benefiting from the collectivity, and not particularity not as an absolutely unique personal characteristic. Just as he designed houses from abstract notions of program, aesthetics, and plan that found limited resonance in the real lives of actual clients, so in his vision for America democratic people were intellectually manageable only at a distance and in large numbers.

Although people always remained for him the great unknown, a remote abstraction, Sullivan's efforts on their behalf were nonetheless undertaken genuinely, seriously, and without compromise. By way of contrast, Frank Lloyd Wright liked to refer to "the masses" as "them asses," calling his 1949 book about Sullivan *Genius and the Mobocracy* a title its subject would most certainly have repudiated. Wright never wrote about people with anything resembling Sullivan's compassion, and his story suggests that while he was entirely capable of loving individuals and understanding their domestic needs—which no doubt contributed to his brilliance as an architect of private residences—it also suggests that his scorn for humanity in general knew few bounds. Sullivan, on the other hand, loved humanity but not individuals, which no doubt contributed to his inability to comprehend, let alone accommodate, their everyday desires. And he paid a price, because it was precisely that love—that remote, abstract, disembodied love of

humanity for which he could not design houses—that generated an opposition powerful enough to destroy his career. Had Sullivan not chosen to proclaim his vision of a democratic America by appropriating for this purpose the privately owned commercial buildings of "neofeudal" barons, and had he, like Wright, been able to please them as a residential architect, then he too, like Wright, might have been able to continue his work.

The Social Nexus

Sullivan's private war with the business class—with that "feudal" order he refused to call capitalist—was the underlying cause of his professional undoing, and his commitment to designing its architecture was the precipitating factor. That he was undone is painfully obvious. Associated in one way or another with Dankmar Adler from 1879 through 1895, he worked on at least 186 projects, almost eleven a year on average, a figure made artificially low by his not being a full partner with Adler until 1883 and by the national depression during the last two years of their association. During the halcyon days of the partnership from May 1883 to July 1895 Adler & Sullivan received some thirteen to fourteen commissions annually. From the beginning of his independent practice in 1895, on the other hand and in striking contrast, Sullivan was hired less than twice a year on average, only forty-six times, counting generously, during the twenty-nine years before he died in 1924. And of those forty-six jobs, two-thirds came in before 1909—when he turned fifty-three—after which he was hired less than once every twelve months during his last fifteen years, compared with more than once a month before 1893.

Many factors contributed to this dramatic reversal. There is his 1895 break with Dankmar Adler, who had landed and dealt with (and charmed) most of their clients, coupled with his own difficult, sometimes arrogant demeanor, which many found off-putting. There is the depression of the 1890s, which virtually halted construction (causing Adler briefly to leave architecture and thus the partnership). There is Sullivan's

bitter, very public attack on the professional establishment at the turn of the century, in particular
on the American Institute of Architects, whose
members, he said, were "unoriginal," producing
"nothing but imitations," and whose president, the
prominent Bostonian Robert S. Peabody, was
nothing less than a "plain public nuisance" for having given a "stupid paltry statement" as his 1900
convention address.[54] There is his inability (and
his disinclination) to master residential design
during the post-depression years when unprecedented suburban expansion enabled his Midwestern "disciples" like Wright—often called "Louis
Sullivan's followers" because they had either
worked for or been influenced by him—to take as
many commissions as they could handle.

There is, in addition, his disinterest in the public relations aspect of the architectural business,
his refusal to design in any style other than his
own, his alleged lack of experience with technical
matters (because Adler had handled most of this,
Sullivan was thought to be uninformed), his reputation as a remote aesthete, and the falling from
favor of his kind of ornament as the more geometrical Prairie style and the more astringent neoclassical became popular. There is, finally, his
drinking and gossip about his sexual preferences.
Each of these factors surely played its part, and
only a few in combination would have been
enough to undo anyone. But they mask the real
reason. Sullivan's professional undoing was the
outcome of his relationship with the business community, the consequence of his decision to concentrate on commercial architecture.

In 1908, about the time he completed "Natural
Thinking," Sullivan was hired to design what
proved to be his last skyscrapers. Newspaper
accounts described two schemes for completely
reconfiguring the Chicago Auditorium Building,
that vast hotel, theater, and office complex he and
Adler had realized from 1886 to 1890.[55] This monumental edifice not only was one of Sullivan's
finest, but also more than any other had established his national reputation. He had a particular
affection for it, for its tower, where since 1890 he

had had his office, its theater, one of his most stunning decorative achievements, and its oak-paneled
café, one of Chicago's (and Sullivan's) favorite
drinking establishments (fig. 48, and see fig. 27).
But his 1908 proposals would have altered the existing building beyond recognition, and in doing so,
we can only assume, wreaked considerable psychic
havoc with Sullivan himself. Had he not been so
financially strapped on the eve of selling his winter residence, his professional library, and most of
his household goods, he might never have taken
the job.

The less radical of the two schemes called for
a $500,000 transformation that would have added
four stories to the existing ten and completely
obliterated the original concept by converting
everything to offices. The $3 million alternative
would have turned the entire edifice into a luxury
hotel with a mammoth palm court, an interior car-
riageway, and a huge rotunda lavishly appointed
with statuary and fountains. Had the seventeen-
story tower been enlarged to twenty-two, it would

not only have eliminated the theater but also deprived Sullivan of his own office. Fortunately, although not for his depleted pocketbook, the project died and the building remained as it is today, more or less intact.

Those 1908 proposals live, however, as a cogent symbol of Sullivan's relationship to his employers. Not having control over the ultimate disposition of one's work is a frustration all architects face, but it becomes particularly acute when an architect considers his buildings to be something more than the mere satisfaction of everyday needs, to be, in fact, the embodiments of his profoundest beliefs. So it must have been tremendously painful for Sullivan to have been obliged not only to observe the planned destruction of his great Auditorium, but actually to design that destruction himself. Nothing else could have underscored his powerlessness with greater clarity. Nothing else could have demonstrated so vividly that in social terms Louis Sullivan was someone else's servant, someone else's "feudal" serf.

At best, his clients wanted handsome income-generating facilities. But Sullivan addressed his buildings to fundamental social and cultural issues. His high-rise and banking designs were, in his mind, object lessons constituting a kind of cultural map pointing the way out of feudal remains, out of a society in which a few held power, toward a society in which people acted collectively in their own self-interest, knowing they could because his buildings told them so. But it goes without saying that no entrepreneurial client would willingly donate a budget or a facade to any architect's personal agenda, no matter what it was, especially not an agenda as implicitly subversive as Sullivan's. As long as Adler was around to convince clients that good art was good business—which he was able to do as a much-respected professional known for his practicality—his partner could stay on course, from the safety of his remote corner office investing his designs with oppositional social content. But after Adler departed, leaving his former partner without a buffer, Sullivan was forced to deal directly—and by all indications uneasily—with the entrepreneur-

ial elite, who, scrutinizing his work more closely than ever, quickly abandoned him.

And from their point of view, with good reason, for almost immediately upon the end of the partnership, Sullivan burst out of his ideological closet. His indictment of entrepreneurs in "The Tall Office Building Artistically Considered" of 1896 was not consigned to some obscure architecture journal but boldly broadcast in *Lippincott's,* one of the nation's most influential journals of opinion. And his public attack on the AIA called into question the motives and intelligence of prominent individuals who were good friends, fellow club members, and business associates of his own potential clients, among them former clients from the now defunct partnership. Starting in 1896 and increasingly as time passed, Sullivan was considered a troublemaker. Commissioning him to design a commercial building, particularly a prominent one, was, from the point of view of the business elite, akin to hiring a Haymarket anarchist to guard the munitions dump.

The history of Sullivan's high-rise hirings confirms the elite's suspicions. During the six years prior to 1896, Sullivan designed at least fourteen skyscrapers for at least twelve different clients. But during the thirteen years from 1896 to his final projects in 1908, or to put it even more dramatically, during the twenty-eight years ending with his last commission of any kind in 1923, Sullivan found only six tall-building clients, three of whom decided not to proceed. Of the three that did, just one—Schlesinger & Mayer—returned from Adler's day. Stanley R. McCormick, son of Cyrus, hired him in 1898 only to do a facade and only at the request of his principal tenant, the Gage Brothers wholesale milliners, assigning the bulk of the three-structure complex to the firm of Holabird & Roche. The Bayard/Condict Building (1897–98) in New York was the sole Sullivan skyscraper erected for a new customer after publication of "The Tall Office Building," but even that commission was awarded to another architect, Lyndon P. Smith, who took Sullivan on as associate because he did not feel up to doing the job alone.[56]

Thus two of Sullivan's last three skyscraper clients selected him only after interested third parties intervened, and then not as chief of the works. And, as if to add insult to injury, when Carson Pirie Scott & Company purchased Schlesinger & Mayer's department store in 1905, it turned to Daniel H. Burnham rather than to Sullivan to expand his own (1898–1902) facilities. It is one of the great ironies of American architectural history that the famous essay that did no much to solidify Sullivan's posthumous reputation should have contributed during his lifetime to the destruction of his career.

Tragic as his situation may have been, however, Sullivan's was as representative as it was unique. In his book *The New Radicalism in America* (1965), cultural historian Christopher Lasch dissected a certain social type in a way that can help us understand Louis Sullivan's dilemma. Lasch defined "new radicals" as intellectuals who had "acquired a sense of being at odds with the rest of society" and who, in a particularly volatile moment in the United States around 1900, "understood the end of social and political reform to be the improvement of American culture as a whole, rather than simply a way of equalizing the opportunities for economic self-advancement." This, Lasch wrote, was "a confusion of politics and culture." Estranged from middle-class life, many new radicals identified "with other outcasts and tried to look at the world from their point of view"; equally estranged from the "dominant values of American culture" in general, they also came to distrust "intellect itself" to the extent of identifying "themselves with what they imagined to be the laws of historical necessity and the working out of the popular will." In the end, being powerless themselves, and themselves socially isolated, they became embittered by their own ineffectuality.[57]

In many ways Louis Sullivan resembled these new radicals. Certainly at odds with the rest of society, estranged from middle-class life and from dominant cultural values, he had little interest in equalizing economic opportunity. He too distrusted intellect, placing his faith in emotion revela-

tions that would assist the resurgence of popular will. He too confused politics and culture, believing that democracy–a political arrangement–could be brought about by cultural–in his case, artistic–effort. He also confused politics and culture by thinking that democracy could be achieved without political action. "The improvement of the quality of American culture as a whole" (Lasch's phrase) is certainly what Sullivan sought, like many poets and even a few architects, but he thought it would come about by developing new art forms. For all his talking about it, Louis Sullivan misunderstood the nature of power.

Sullivan never grasped the simple truth that the power he so much admired–of the individual's will to achieve–was but a benign form of the very same power–of the "modern feudal baron"–that destroyed him. He could never admit, perhaps even comprehend, that under capitalist social relations the will to achieve and the "lower and fiercer passions" he had described in 1896 were often one and the same. His insistence that democracy could be brought to life by art suggests that he grossly underestimated the extent to which the so-called American feudalism was entrenched. Perhaps he preferred to underestimate. The contention of his many contemporaries that the way to change power relations was to pit collective strength against collective strength in the political arena, at factory gates, or in the streets no doubt alarmed him. Cultural theory, not political action, was his métier.

When Sullivan told Harriet Monroe in 1905 that privilege and the trusts would need to be "overthrown" in order to achieve democracy, he came as close as he ever would to acknowledging an alternative course. But he instinctively backed away from political confrontation, preferring to think that unspecified acts of popular will would bring about "The New Way." His art, he believed, would help unleash that will. The vehicle through which he would arouse the people–commercial architecture–was in one sense an inspired choice, because tall urban buildings, certainly, and even small-town banks loomed large in their respective physical and cultural landscapes. But his vehicle was a tragic choice in another way, because Sullivan's architecture was intrinsically critical of the very people who had commissioned it. Every skyscraper and bank he designed and much of what he wrote beginning in the 1890s presupposed that other skyscrapers and banks, as well as their owners, were, by definition, evil.

So Sullivan and his clients worked at cross-purposes, they using him for social exploitation, he using them to improve the commonweal. Eventually, inevitably, urban business and financial leaders caught on and refused to hire him, leaving him dependent on a handful of small-town clients with minuscule budgets. The self-proclaimed architect of democracy was thus reduced to writing about it and to trying to build it in out-of-the-way places no one but their residents—and possibly Sullivan himself—cared anything about. But he kept his faith.

Sullivan's vision remains a vision only, on paper and in buildings still vibrant with purpose. He refused to give it up, believing to the end that his designs and writing—his poetry—would bring about democracy's garden. But his vision was com-promised from the beginning because he failed to appreciate the dangers involved in confronting power and, conversely, that he himself was powerless. So he never understood that if he turned on the class from which his clients came, if he opposed the interests of those upon whom his livelihood depended, he would be punished. Nor did he understand that if he ignored the most basic of rules, that success is more readily achieved by endorsing the ideology of those in power, he would be destroyed.

Because he was stubborn and naive, because he rounded on those he might better have cultivated, and did it noisily, Sullivan was indeed destroyed. His attack on the aesthetic effects rather than on the material causes of what he called neofeudalism was a strategy likely to fail in any case, but his confrontation with entrenched power from a position of no power made that failure inevitable. In the end, Louis Sullivan secured at least one victory, however, although he did not live to see it: even when misreading his intentions, no generation since his death has treated his work as archaeology, always as architecture, pulsating with life.

The Iconography of Architecture: Sullivan's View

NARCISO G. MENOCAL

Introduction

Louis Sullivan's concept of architectural and ornamental design was based on a belief that the universe was sustained by a cosmic rhythm. Change, flow, and one entity turning into another were effects of a universal becoming. Since he held that existence was rooted in rhythm, the mutability of phenomena was of greater consequence for him than any apparent physical stability things might seem to have. In that scheme, beauty emerged from a never-ending transformation of all things into new entities. Sensory knowledge was valid to him only for the instant it was acquired, for a different truth would exist by the next second—"For all is rhythm," he wrote.

The notion of a cosmic rhythm is then at the root of Sullivan's iconography, and I use the term with the meaning subscribed by the Spanish philosopher Xavier Zubiri (1898–1983). According to Zubiri, the Greek word *eikon* and the Latin term *imago* signify different things; *eikon* pertains to essence, *imago* to appearance.[1] Zubiri advanced that statement in a context of metaphysics, but one may extend it into aesthetics to argue that *iconography* pertains to the essential meaning of a work of art, to the very core of what it expresses, while *imagery* relates only to its appearance.

Sullivan's epistemological speculations were not results of systematic studies but of omnivorous autodidactic readings. It took him years to come to conclusions that became passionately held beliefs he made known through his numerous writings. But making architecture the medium for broadcasting his doctrines made his quest more difficult; buildings are obdurate about lending themselves as metaphors standing for the etherealness of permanent cosmic change. Their very essence is rooted in gravity, and (at least in Plato's mind) they express the basest aspect of matter.[2] It was Sullivan's task to turn the stability of buildings into a dynamic imagery revealing their iconographical essence. That is to say, the fundamental agreement of architecture with what he considered to be "The Universal Law" of rhythm. In a sense, more than as a designer of buildings, he considered himself to be the discoverer of the designs a sapient nature had determined for those particular buildings since the beginning of time.

Eventually, he meshed those ideas with French Beaux-Arts principles of design from the third quarter of the nineteenth century, principles he had acquired earlier during his professional training—as much at MIT as in the offices of architects for whom he worked in Philadelphia and Chicago and, later, at the Ecole des Beaux-Arts in Paris. According to Beaux-Arts teachings, each building, and even each part of a building, was to make evident its individuality—what it is for and what it is built of, as well as its particular relationship with gravity. But Sullivan never accepted Beaux-Arts theory as complete and much less final. To him, it was but a first, rational step toward the discovery of the architecture nature had prescribed at the moment when chaos became cosmos. That architecture had almost immediately become concealed under layers of history or, in other terms, by the arrogance of man unwilling to become subject to the dictates of nature.

In his mind, his buildings, collectively, established a medium, a language, or even better, a discourse that was not his because it belonged to nature, from which he had elicited it. He believed that he understood truth more clearly than others and wished to make truth known. In that sense, Sullivan considered himself a poet turning his work into a running statement on the intimate nature of buildings—and of architecture at large. As a poet interpreting the will of nature, he saw himself as completing Creation. In his dictum concerning the universal law that "form ever follows function," the function of the form was to express its own essence, to be an *eikon*, in Zubiri's terms.

Of themselves, those ideas were not original. Had he been only a writer, he would have been but one of the many intellectuals of the period who synthesized romanticism with transcendentalism at third hand. Yet his architecture gains full meaning only when understood as a consequence of his passionate ideology. Relating romantic transcendentalism to architecture was a process Sullivan developed slowly, through trial and error. His aim was to show mankind the way to communion with nature—that is to say, to the utopia—and he gained a sharper vision of his quest as his work unfolded. The evolution of that development—how he made the imagery fit the iconography—is one aspect of my study. Another is to understand the iconography in terms of the ideology; a third is to show how Sullivan's concentrated vision resulted in an exquisite architectural aesthetic, with the vision and the aesthetic mirroring his beliefs.

His aesthetic had a didactic function. It was to reinforce man's knowledge that he also was part of the universe and that as such he had to surrender his personal will to the universal will of nature. Sullivan shared with Emerson the ideal that each man was to disindividualize himself. "He is not to speak his own words or do his own works or think his own thoughts, but he is to be an organ through which the universal mind acts."[3] Given that condition, one understands why Sullivan's talent was best suited for raising to the level of high art commercial structures, office buildings, and one-room rural banks more than any other buildings he designed. The impersonality of those building types allowed him to do two things. One was to use the buildings to broadcast his ideas of

an architecture that would mediate between nature and an observer of architecture, in a relationship touching on the transcendent. The other was that those building types allowed him to create a fictive architectural observer who in fact was an archetypal abstraction.

That mechanism going from nature to building to man is another phenomenon I study in these pages. And that is the reason why I do not bring his residential work into my discussion. His buildings had an epiphanic universal function to fulfill, and therefore he had little interest in serving a client's private wishes. Moreover, he was not much interested in planning—by far the most important component in residential design. His houses are usually uninviting and formal, and lack the geometrical intensity and cohesion of the best Prairie work; neither did he attempt to correlate their exteriors with their interiors in any comprehensive fashion—any measure of domesticity in them was usually the result of George Grant Elmslie's hand.[4]

But when one explores Sullivan's thought to understand his commercial buildings, one is rewarded with an encounter with his superb passion. Important as his many accomplishments as an architect were, his fervor seeking release through architecture remains most astonishing about him. Acting like the creative principle of nature—or at least convincing himself that he did—exhilarated him. His mind assented fully to the belief that his work could raise humanity to a permanent manic godlike feeling, because to him the purpose of human consciousness was to attain to a constant and exquisite pleasure that in fulfillment became one with the erotic. In Sullivan's opinion, man's capacity for extending delight experientially once pleasure had ceased to operate physically raised humanity far above the rest of creation. His work, as a whole, was to offer us that quintessential experience.

I have used a linear, progressive argument for my discussion. In section 1 ("Normative Years: 1872–80"), I cover Sullivan's architectural education and emphasize the Francophile theory he received from teachers and employers. I also dwell on how Henry Hobson Richardson, Frank Furness, and others influenced him. In section 2 ("A Search for an Architecture: 1880−93"), I study his buildings of those years in context with his chosen architectural theory. In section 3 ("Genesis of an Iconography"), I present the sources of his iconography and the intellectual development that led him to it. In section 4 ("Birth of an Iconography: 1890−92"), I deal with the Getty and Wainwright tombs and the Transportation Building of the Chicago Columbian Exhibition, the three designs with which he first experimented with a mature notion of his iconography. In sections 5 and 6 ("Growth of an Iconography: The Skyscrapers of 1892−1903" and "Culmination of an Iconography: The Banks, 1906−24"), I analyze the progress of the imagery and iconography of the two building types with which he worked most in the 1890s and in the twentieth century, respectively, and I see the culmination of that process in his later banks. Finally, I reach conclusions in section 7 ("Meanings of an Iconography").

As one last prefatory remark, it is my pleasurable duty to state that in 1989 I was awarded a fellowship from the Temple Hoyne Buell Center for the Study of American Architecture, Columbia University, and in 1990 I received a fellowship from the John Simon Guggenheim Memorial Foundation. Both awards were earmarked for a study of the architecture of Frank Lloyd Wright. But my conversations in New York with Robert Twombly —already mentioned in the general introduction— excited me to revisit Sullivan and say about him what I had not said in 1980, in my book at the time. This is the result of that work, a task which would not have been possible without the generous support of the Buell Center and the Guggenheim Foundation. I acknowledge my deep gratitude to both institutions.

1: *Normative Years: 1872−80*

Richard Morris Hunt and Henry Hobson Richardson, the first American students at the Ecole des Beaux-Arts, brought back home—in 1855 and 1865 respectively—a method of design that soon became normative for a number of young American architects. Those young men either became Hunt's apprentices, worked as draftsmen in Richardson's office, read the French architectural press, or went themselves to study in Paris. Those French ideas, then new in the United States, had evolved from the romantic rationalist movement that Henri Labrouste and others had begun at the French Academy in Rome in the late 1820s and subsequently spread in Paris.[1] Although that movement had run its course in France by mid-century, its basic tenets lingered. For most of the rest of the century French architectural thought went on taking for granted that the elements of architecture were results of pragmatic solutions to discrete problems the profession had encountered throughout history. A building was to portray its individual essence instead of referring to an ideal, as neoclassical design did. That aim would be achieved by making the design reflect one or several things concurrently, such as the time and place it was built, the function it served, its relationship with gravity, or any combination of these the architect found suitable. Prescriptively, the architect was free to combine the elements of classical architecture in unclassical ways, and thus stretch standard notions of decorum.

Following that lead, by the 1870s American Francophile architects were trying hard to place in evidence how each portion of a design contributed to the overall scheme of a building. Those architects insisted as well on making manifest how efficiently each element of architecture responded to the stress or strain gravity exerted upon it. They also liked to make clear to a viewer how the compressive or tensile forces in each element affected adjacent elements within the structure. Another of their major concerns was to show how the building as a whole expressed the relationship between its architecture and gravity, as much as its own functional reality. In short, architects following the new trend relished in placing in evidence the "anatomy" and the "mechanical physiology" of buildings.

Those architects, however, constituted a minority. Most in the profession still favored the English views John Ruskin's writings had made popular in the United States since the 1850s. In "The Lamp of Obedience," Ruskin pointed out the four styles he considered as apposite antecedents to a development of a national English architecture and therefore to be favored over others: the Pisan Romanesque, the early Gothic of the western Italian republics ("advanced as far and as fast as our art would enable us to the Gothic of Giotto"), the Venetian Gothic ("in its purest development"), and the English earliest decorated.[2] But in the United States there were even fewer architects than in Britain willing to follow Ruskin's mimetic precepts to the letter. At best, American Ruskinian Gothic was a question of evoking–and most times merely alluding to–Ruskin's favorite styles, mixing their characteristics eclectically (even with classical detail), and achieving a picturesque effect based on the building's skyline, polychromy, and applied ornamentation. One result of such rampant eclecticism was that a young man seeking direction on how to become a designer found it hard to set a path for himself. Architectural choices were too numerous; the profession at large had little notion of a precisely defined architectural aesthetic; and architectural schools, then in infancy, were in no position to provide a nationwide focus on such matters.

In contrast with most young people his age, right from the start Louis Sullivan focused his architectural studies on a Franco-American architectural point of view then still circumscribed to an elite. He joined that minority through a number of decisions and incidents that took place early in life. In 1871, while yet fifteen, he decided to forgo the two years he still required for graduation from the Boston English High School, prepared himself for examinations for direct entrance to MIT, passed them with high marks, and became a student at the MIT department of architecture just after turning sixteen. There, instruction followed a definite French line established by William Ware, a direct disciple of Hunt's. Ware's assistant, Eugène Letang, was a recent arrival from the Ecole.[3]

When Sullivan entered the school in the fall of 1872, architecture had been taught for only four years at MIT. Located in Rogers Hall, at the corner of Boylston and Berkeley streets in the Back Bay area of Boston (a block away from the site where construction of Richardson's Trinity Church would start in April 1873), the school had been founded in October 1868 and would remain at that address until 1916.[4] MIT was also new. It had been established in 1861 through a charter granted William Barton Rogers by the Massachusetts General Court, although classes did not start until 1865, after the Civil War ended. That same year, William Robert Ware, just appointed professor of architecture by President Rogers, received a mandate to create the first architecture program in the nation since the days when Thomas Jefferson lectured at the University of Virginia. Ware (1832–1915), a partner in the Boston firm of Ware & Van Brunt, was a native of Cambridge and a graduate of both Harvard and its Lawrence Scientific School. As a former apprentice in Richard Morris Hunt's New York atelier, he chose the French Beaux-Arts system for the new program. Yet the curriculum at MIT was closer to French theory and technique of design than to French methods of instruction. Rather than having students divided into the two classes standard at the Ecole (second, or beginners, and first, or advanced), and earning *valeurs* (values, or points) from *concours* (competitions), instruction at MIT consisted of a four-year course leading to a Bachelor of Science in Architecture. There was also a special two-year professional program for pupils coming from architects' offices. Most students disregarded those options and attended courses for one or two years to continue later with their apprenticeship, as Sullivan did. Before the opening of the school, Ware had traveled extensively in England, Scotland, France, Italy, and the Low Countries, purchasing books, casts, models, and drawings. Nevertheless, textbooks were lacking when classes started. Teachers had to prepare whatever handbooks they needed, and Ware himself wrote two books, one on perspective and another on shades and shadows, which he published after he left MIT for New York to establish a school of architecture at Columbia College in 1881. He also compiled a series of illustrations on the orders that eventually became his *American Vignola*.[5]

In spite of efforts to establish a methodical system of instruction, architectural studies at MIT were less organized than Ware would have desired. Students found themselves having to help each other, a circumstance that, on the other hand, may have reinforced the illusion that they were at a French atelier. The arrival of Eugène Letang in 1871 brought MIT closer to the French system. Letang (1842–92), a former student of the first class attached to Emile Vaudremer's atelier, was hired to teach architectural design and remained teaching at MIT for the rest of his life, although he occasionally entered into competitions, such as the one for the Boston Public Library.[6]

Sullivan made a distinction between Ware and Letang in his *Autobiography of an Idea*. The thirty-year-old Letang

> had no professional air; he was a student escaped from the Beaux Arts, a transplanted massier as it were of the atélier, where the anciens, the older students, help the nouveaux, the younger set, along. He was admirably patient, and seemed to believe in the real value of the work he so candidly was doing. . . . So here was a student absorbed in teaching students, while Professor Ware conserved the worldly poise of the cultural Boston of the time,–creating and maintaining thus an air of the legitimate and approved.[7]

Letang's and Ware's differences in teaching puzzled Sullivan. Letang followed the *rationalisme classique* of Vaudremer's atelier. He insisted on coldly analytical plans in which the scale of parts placed in evidence a hierarchy of functions, efficiency counted as much as decorum, and locations of rooms and spaces depended on their impor-

tance, all set within a tight, precise, self-contained geometry that dictated axes delineated with pristine clarity. In elevation, crisp masonry volumes made evident their relationship with gravity. They also differed in height according to their functional significance, echoing the hierarchical conception expressed in the plan. Thus taught Letang.

Ware was different. Although a critic of design (he disliked "gimcrack roofs"),[8] he seems to have favored more his position as lecturer in the theory and history of architecture. Some of his lessons confused Sullivan. While Ware's idea of style came from romantic rationalism, he taught the orders from a strictly classical point of view, perhaps following uncritically some outmoded neoclassical handbook or other. He spoke of the orders and Greek architecture as if they were absolutes, embodiments of the immutability of academic perfection, "the goal of Platonic perfection of idea."[9] Yet, following a French bent, styles "were [to Ware] not sacrosanct but merely human," Sullivan commented.[10] But then, thought Sullivan, extending his new beliefs into the orders, if each design—as he was being taught—issued from a particular necessity (and therefore each was to be different from the rest), why would the orders constitute an ideal? And if so, why five and not one?[11]

Outside the school Sullivan found a different kind of architecture, one that did not require him to ask questions. Only three blocks away from the school rose the newly finished Brattle Square Church, "conceived and brought to light by the mighty Richardson, undoubtedly for Louis's special delight" (fig. 49).[12] Richardson became Sullivan's first major influence outside school because his work was exciting in ways that Sullivan had sought, but not found elsewhere. The design adhered to rules he understood. The volumes expressed the plan with clear-cut lucidity, the architect had shown a complete respect for the physical properties of materials and elements of construction, and their relationship with gravity was plainly evident. But this had been the basis for the design, not the goal of it, for the building

boasted of a freedom from prescription and stylistic decorum that made it fresh, exciting, and unique. The material was random ashlar rather than smooth stone, the composition was asymmetrical rather than symmetrical, and the style, instead of seeking a definite association with a moment in the past, was a magical mixture of masses that evoked the Romanesque only at large, with no attempt at a slavish imitation of any period of it. There was also a tower that was as Italian above as it was French or Spanish or whatever below. Moreover, there was the Renaissance-like explosion of Bartholdi's *Frieze of the Seven Sacraments*, a marvelous invention that pulled up the viewer's eye and made him realize the lightness of a design based on paradoxes, for while the materials were earthy, masculine, bold, and massive, the contours of the building spoke of a crisp, abstract geometry. The tower was also important in other ways. The structure was firmly anchored on the ground, yet the frieze and the delicate arcade

above it made it airy, proving that art could be based on ambiguity. Finally there was the outline of the building against the sky. It expressed itself as one thought, as one fact; monumental, yet not overbearing. This was a self-confident design, neither requesting nor requiring an association other than with itself.

Richardson had gone farther than any Frenchman or American the young Sullivan could think of. He had created his personal interpretation of what that church should be by transforming a cold, analytical French conception of design based on the relationship of the elements of architecture and gravity into something vital. He had fired French methods of design with emotionally charged forces that were as telluric as they were anthropomorphic, and brought the building alive in the quest of the sublime Ruskin extolled in his "Lamp of Power."[13] It was that highly personal as well as quintessentially American synthesis of reason and emotion coming together in a building, reinforcing each other, vibrating against each other, and rising together to create a whole larger than the sum of the parts that made Sullivan stand in awe before the Brattle Square Church, even if he could not understand why the building held such fascination for him, other than intuitively. It was a lesson only an American of Richardson's stature could offer him, an American standing on his own, free to disregard tradition in the European sense, and able to bring together that which elsewhere would have been exclusively French or exclusively English to create ultimately a vision of his own sense of beauty—hence a design as untrammeled by restrictions of decorum as if it had come forth from nature and not from the mind of man. In short, by expressing personal choices beyond any European limits, Richardson had Americanized the Beaux-Arts method of design.

But straight English influence was still strongly felt in the 1870s. Sullivan must have been aware of Sturgis and Brigham's Ruskinian Gothic Boston Museum of Fine Arts (1872–79), on Copley Square, two blocks away from the school of architecture he attended. There was also the equally Ruskinian new

Metropolitan Museum of Art in New York (1874–80), by Calvert Vaux and Jacob Wrey Mould, and innumerable churches in the English Neo-Gothic style. Richardson himself had not been immune to the notion that architecture should evoke, or even mimic, those styles Ruskin favored. The towers of his State Hospital in Buffalo (1872–78) were derived from the tower in the foreground of William Burges's project of 1866 for the Law Courts in London.[14] Also at that time, Russell Sturgis, one of the main supporters of Ruskin's doctrines in America, was designing his buildings on the Yale campus, and even Leopold Eidlitz, in spite of his explicit criticisms of Ruskin in his *Nature and Function of Art* (1881), showed strong English Neo-Gothic leanings in the 1870s, as for example in his 1875 Dry Dock Savings Bank in New York.

While Sullivan never wavered from a position set by French theory, he seems to have felt that the architecture he was learning at school was missing something that was terribly important to him, namely the passion that he had seen in Richardson's architecture. MIT, he thought, must be "but a pale reflection of the Ecole des Beaux-Arts."[15] Confusing Richardson's American traits for French-derived genius, he decided that he should go to France but felt that before going "it might be advisable to spend a year in the office of some architect of standing, that he might see . . . how an actual building was brought about."[16]

His decisions, in the end, were in no small degree marked by chance. Moreover, events may not have unfolded exactly as he recorded them in his *Autobiography*. He probably did not apply for work at Richardson's office in spite of his enthusiasm for the Brattle Square Church because he had no introduction to the architect he admired most. Ware, on the other hand, may have written on Sullivan's behalf to his old mentor, Hunt.[17] At Richard Morris Hunt's office in New York (where no work was available), Sidney Stratton, Hunt's assistant, suggested Frank Furness's office in Philadelphia, where, it so happened, Sullivan's grandfather and uncle lived. Arriving in Philadelphia in June 1873, he first roamed the streets looking at buildings,

until one caught his attention; it was Furness's Bloomfield Moore house, on South Broad Street.[18] Once at Furness & Hewitt, Sullivan discovered that "Frank Furness made buildings out of his head" but that his partner, George Watson Hewitt, who had trained in the office of John Notman, "did the Victorian Gothic in its pantalettes."[19]

Sullivan worked in Furness's office only from June to mid-November 1873, at which time he was dismissed as a result of the depression that began in September. Those five months were immensely important in his development. They coincided with the time Furness was defining his style after mastering geomorphism. Furness's buildings, although of brick and stone, must have seemed to Sullivan hewn out of primordial matter, in quest of the sublime—or at least of an evocation of it. They were kindled with the same fire he had seen in Richardson's work, in spite of the many differences between the two architects. The Pennsylvania Academy of Fine Arts, the Jewish Hospital, the Philadelphia Warehouse Company Building, and the Guaranty Trust and Safe Deposit Company Building were some of the projects on the boards, besides a number of houses and interior decoration commissions, including splendid ones for Fairlawn (the Fairman Rogers house in Newport) and Theodore Roosevelt Sr.'s house in New York.[20] But of all of Furness's work at the time, the one building Sullivan mentioned in his *Autobiography* was the Union Banking Company, the drawings of which he was told to retrace (fig. 50).[21] A three-bay, three-story structure on a high basement, the composition was quintessentially Furnessian.[22] It brings to mind a strange, almost primitive architecture in which plasticity builds up mass upon mass and the fenestration is exclusively defined by voids left hollow by the structure. A synthesis of French and American ideas, Furness's work showed Sullivan how to bring together theory, imagery, iconography, and typology. Collectively, those entities furnished him with a vibrant sense of transcendence he would eventually emulate.

But in the meantime, in the midst of a depres-

Figure 50.
Union Banking
Company Building,
Philadelphia, Frank
Furness (1873–74).
Historical Society of
Pennsylvania.

Figure 51.
Chicago City Hall–Cook
County Courthouse,
Chicago, James Egan
(1873–85).
Art Institute of Chicago.

Figure 52.
Palmer House Hotel,
Chicago, John Van Osdel
(1875).
Art Institute of Chicago.

Figure 53.
Honoré Block, Chicago,
Otis Wheelock (1871–72).
Art Institute of Chicago.

Figure 54.
Portland Block, Chicago,
William Le Baron
Jenney (1872).
Art Institute of Chicago.

Figure 55.
Lakeside Building,
Chicago,
William Le Baron
Jenney (1873).
Chicago Historical Society.

sion, and with no prospects of work in Philadelphia after being let go from Furness's office, the seventeen-year-old Sullivan moved on to Chicago, where his parents lived, arriving there on "the day before Thanksgiving in the year Eighteen Hundred Seventy-three."[23]

The depression had all but put a stop to the frenzied construction that had rebuilt Chicago in the years 1871–73, after the fire of 1870. Commissions then had been measured "by the mile," and while most of the new buildings were commonplace, some were done in the "grand manner" Sullivan abhorred. One of these was James Egan's Chicago City Hall–Cook County Courthouse (1873–85), a grand five-story pile in the English version of the Second Empire with a two-story base of cyclopean rustication, all walls above similarly rusticated, and giant Corinthian freestanding paired columns buttressing the building and supporting caryatids (fig. 51). Alfred B. Mullett's Chicago Federal Building seemed restrained by comparison. Eventually, there would also be John Van Osdel's Palmer House Hotel (1875), a huge seven-story pilastered, mansarded, pedimented piece of colossal architecture, complete with a rounded corner surmounted by a dome in the Parisian manner, and silver dollars imbedded in the floor of the barbershop, in the Midwestern mode (fig. 52). Commercial architecture was less ebullient. In 1871 and 1872, Otis Wheelock had designed the Honoré Block (fig. 53), Otto Matz the Nixon Building, and John Van Osdel the McCormick's Reaper Block.

When Sullivan arrived in Chicago, he walked around the city looking for a building he would like, as he had done in Philadelphia. William Le Baron Jenney's Portland Block stood out amid hundreds of facades made "genteel"—in Sullivan's opinion—by pedestrian treatment of detail and ornamentation. "A singularly sordid, vulgar vernacular in architectural speech" was his way of categorizing the style of the day.[24] In contrast, the beauty of the Portland Block did not depend on applied decoration but on the expression of the elements of construction. It showed no attempt at achieving monumentality through picturesqueness

(fig. 54).[25] Furthermore, the architect had had the courage to use pressed red brick, a material introduced in Chicago as recently as 1871 and which many considered "improper" for important buildings expected to exhibit the "nobility" of stone.[26] The Portland Block had been designed following the new Francophile aesthetic.

Shortly after his arrival in Chicago—perhaps even by December—Sullivan got his wish for a job in Jenney's office, where the Portland Block had been designed. But he soon became disillusioned with Jenney. He found out that "the Portland Block had been designed by a clever draftsman named Cudell,"[27] and that its bold use of pressed brick had been the wish not of the architect, but of the owner, the Boston investor Peter C. Brooks, later of Montauk and Monadnock buildings fame.[28] Yet Sullivan must have been aware that almost all architects (including himself later on) exploited the talents of their draftsmen and that the final result must have rested with Jenney.[29] The authorship of the Portland Block, therefore, was not at issue; Sullivan was angry possibly because the work he saw at the office was not consistent with the style of the Portland Block. While certainly Jenney was not turning out buildings in "a singularly sordid, vulgar vernacular," he was not working either in the romantic rationalist manner Sullivan had seen in the Portland Block. The office was busy with the last of the residential work at Riverside, where Jenney considered himself to be "Downing's heir,"[30] and his city work apparently did not appeal to Sullivan either. The Mason Building, for instance, had a delicate arcaded facade that crudely attempted to evoke Venetian architecture of the *quattrocento*. The Lakeside Building, another of Jenney's works of the period, was a mansarded five-story behemoth that brought together the basic Second Empire five-part composition with the most commonplace Victorian Gothic detailing, including a grand two-story applied Gothic archway marking the main entrance (fig. 55).

In his *Autobiography*, the sixty-seven-year-old Sullivan vented the anger of the seventeen-year-old Louis by writing that Jenney was "a free-and-easy cultured gentleman, but not an architect except by courtesy of terms."[31] That statement is often misinterpreted because it is usually taken in the context of an image of Jenney-as-functionalist-architect that historians like Sigfried Giedion and Carl Condit created later on the basis of buildings that Jenney had not yet designed in 1873.[32] Sullivan did not imply that Jenney was an engineer first and an architect second, and that his work was technically interesting but aesthetically mediocre, as most historians interpret Sullivan's opinion.[33] He was much harsher. Hedonism, not architecture, was at the center of Jenney's life.

> Louis soon found out that the Major was not, really, in his heart, an engineer at all, but by nature, and in toto, a bon vivant, a gourmet. . . . The major knew his vintages, every one, and his sauces, every one. . . . All in all the Major was effusive; a hale fellow well met, an officer of the Loyal Legion, a welcome guest anywhere, but by preference a host. He was also an excellent raconteur, with a lively sense of humor and a certain piquancy of fancy that seemed Gallic. . . . His stories were choice, and his voice, as one caught bits of it, was plastic, rich, and sweet.[34]

Sullivan's disappointment with Jenney reveals how set were his architectural convictions after less than two years of training, even though he had not even reached his eighteenth birthday. His architectural ideas remained centered in Paris. At the end of that summer of 1874, he was happy to leave for the Ecole des Beaux-Arts and Emile Vaudremer's atelier. Sullivan had worked at Jenney's for about six months, from about December 1873 until probably late June 1874, for on 11 July he sailed on the SS *Britannic*.[35]

In retrospect, Sullivan's Paris sojourn, while important to his development, was not indispensable. His French experiences broadened his horizon and reaffirmed his notions of architectural theory but did not enhance by much his professional development. He started his French education enthusiastically and passed the grueling entrance examination, for which Frenchmen took an average of two years to prepare.[36] But when he got to the atelier he found "little that he had not been acquainted with when he had left MIT fourteen months before. The sheets of paper were bigger, the plans more complicated, the drawing techniques more refined, but the ideas being applied were the same rationalist classicist ones with which he was familiar."[37] There was an even deeper problem. He did not find in France what he had come looking for, namely how to express an emotional force in design that would be more intense and more complete than the one Richardson's and Furness's work had made manifest to him—a vital means to give full vent to his passion for the lyrical without doing violence to the expression of structure and its relation with gravity.

In contrast to his wishes, he found in Vaudremer's work a clear and logical compartmentalization of functions. The logic of the plan translated into crisp volumes that often, but not exclusively, the architect would render in smooth ashlar, the untextured plain walls visually underpinning the abstract qualities of the design. Stylistically, Vaudremer showed a preference for highly personalized mixtures of Romanesque, Early Christian, and Byzantine elements for churches, a subdued classicism for public buildings (not devoid at times of a Gothic-like structural quality), and a highly simplified Tuscan manner for villas. Those choices allowed him to express the wall both as a surface and element of support and to define building types through a limited number of styles. Never arbitrary, his stylistic preferences always placed in evidence a consistency of expression related to function, as well as to mass and construction. Always logical, restrained, well structured, and above all clearly readable, Vaudremer's work, although dry at times, conveys in its better moments a feeling of controlled strength.[38] But that was not exactly what Sullivan was looking for; it did not fire his imagination in the ways he yearned for.

Disappointed, he all but walked away from the atelier, where he stayed for approximately three months only, from late October 1874 (when he was admitted to the Ecole) to late January 1875. During that time he began to work on a project due on 28 December,[39] but there is no record that he presented it and more than possibly he did not finish it. Making the physical conditions of the atelier the object (and symbol) of his professional dissatisfaction, he wrote: "The atelier is the damnedest pigsty I ever got into. . . . It is cold, and then when you light the fire it smokes so that it nearly puts your eyes out, and you have to open the windows, which makes a devil of a draft."[40] It is no surprise then that in his *Autobiography* he devoted little more than one page to describing life in Vaudremer's atelier and mistakenly credited the Church of the Sacré-Coeur to his *patron* rather than to Paul Abadie.[41] Even more to the point, in one of his sentences he suggests that he was more of an observer of atelier life than an actual student of architecture.[42] How different the situation would have been had he gone to Coquard's atelier instead of to Vaudremer's is entirely open to speculation, inasmuch as at the time Coquard was one of the most daring architects in France in color and ornamentation, albeit in terms that were typically French, relating mostly to antiquity and the Renaissance, but handled in an entirely personal manner.[43]

Since he had little interest in what the atelier had to offer, Sullivan passed his time in Paris in things that gave him pleasure, such as sharpening his skills in ornamental design. He copied plates from Ruprich-Robert's *Flore ornementale* (Catalogue, pls. 14–25) and possibly attended Ruprich-Robert's lectures at the Ecole des Arts-Décoratifs. Sullivan wanted to prepare himself to design the mural decorations for Moody's Tabernacle and the Sinai Synagogue his friend John Edelmann had assigned to him (Catalogue, pls. 7–9 and 11–13). He also read books on Beethoven and Mendelssohn, René Ménard's three-volume *Histoire de l'art*, and above all, Taine's *Philosophie de l'art* and *De l'idéal dans l'art*. Far more crucial, he had the time to acquire an understanding of French culture and to place in perspective all he had learned at MIT, Furness's, and Jenney's. He also traveled. He went to Italy and the South of France from approxi-

mately mid-January to mid-March 1875. What he discovered in Rome and Florence was eventually more important to his architecture than what he learned in Paris. The Sistine Chapel revealed to him that art could expand to heroic breadths in ways that could surpass Richardson's by far; Florentine *quattrocento* palaces taught him that volumetric abstraction could be a key factor to monumentality. Returning to Paris in mid to late March, he lingered there for five or six weeks, sailed back in early May, and arrived in New York on the 24th.[44]

After his return, Sullivan drifted from job to job for a few years. As a result of the depression, very few commercial buildings were erected in Chicago in the five years from 1874 through 1878.[45] He worked first for John Edelmann, who had left Jenney's office and, in partnership with Joseph S. Johnston, had secured the commissions for Moody's Tabernacle and the Sinai Synagogue. The buildings were finished early in the spring of 1876 in the standard red-brick-and-sandstone Gothic Revival of the day, but it was their ceiling decorations by Sullivan (the ones he had begun studying in Paris) that made them noteworthy. While we do not have a direct evidence of the entire work, and its use of color, three drawings of the Sinai Temple decorations, now in the Bentley Historical Library, University of Michigan, show that Sullivan was following the standard style of the day, based on renditions of flat, geometrized vegetal motifs (cf. pls. 40–42).[46]

Finding no subsequent work, Edelmann closed his office and went to Cleveland. Sullivan, now a freelance draftsman, turned despondent. In 1876–77 he toyed with the idea of abandoning architecture and becoming a bridge engineer. In *The Railway Gazette,* which his brother brought home each week, he had been following the construction of the Eads Bridge across the Mississippi in St. Louis and of the Cincinnati Southern Railway bridge across the Kentucky at Dixville, Kentucky.[47]

Work reappeared once the depression eased, and in 1879 Dankmar Adler hired Sullivan to design the organ grilles in the auditorium of the

Burnham & Root favored compositions resembling piles of red-brick building blocks that retained a remnant of Second Empire gentility, as in the Grannis and Montauk blocks, both of 1881. Edward Burling, Adler's former associate (now a partner of Francis Whitehouse), was more elegant with his First National Bank Building. It had a wide, six-story facade in the classical five-part composition, a sharply delineated masonry structure, and a fenestration of deeply incised, crisply rectangular windows. Jenney's First Leiter Building (1879) represented a third mode of structural rationalism that explored further the style initiated by the Portland Block seven years earlier.

The new Richardsonian mode of wide openings, robust piers, and increased "masculinity" became fashionable in the early 1880s. Burnham & Root's Burlington Office Building, while of 1882 and still of tall and thin rectangular windows, heralded the new type in Chicago with a self-asserting image of a ponderous mass bearing down on the soil. The following year, Clinton Warren's Dexter Building exhibited a full-fledged arcade. The style proliferated in 1884 and 1885 in buildings by Burnham & Root, such as the McCormick Harvesting Machine Company Building, the Insurance Exchange Building, the Art Institute, the Commerce Building, the Phoenix Building, and, more important in the series, the Rookery Building. Concurrently, Cobb & Frost designed a narrow, timid arcade for the Chicago Opera House, and, above all, Richardson designed his superb Marshall Field Wholesale Store (fig. 56). Such was the background in which Sullivan's work came into its own.

Central Music Hall, a commission Adler had secured after dissolving his partnership with Edward Burling. In his *Autobiography,* Sullivan presented an inaccurate chronology of his association with Adler.[48] He claimed that Edelmann, who worked for Burling & Adler, had introduced him to Adler;[49] that D. Adler & Company was established on 1 May 1880 with Sullivan as a one-third partner; and that the firm of Adler & Sullivan followed exactly one year later, with each an equal partner.[50] Sullivan's recollections were off by two years: the one-third partnership came in 1882 and the full partnership in 1883. From 1879 to 1882 he worked for Adler first as a freelance draftsman and then as a full-time employee; in 1880, while still freelancing, he was working as well for an architect named William Strippelman.[51]

During those years of the late 1870s and the early 1880s, Chicago architects began their experiments with new styles for commercial buildings.

2: A Search for an Architecture: 1880–93

During his early years with Adler, Sullivan, now a designer at last, searched for ways to expand what he had learned from Furness's work and Jenney's Portland Block. Above all, composition was for him a means to turn the constructive elements of a building into features of an aesthetic expression. He did this with a method that was closer to Francophile Néo-Grec America than to classical-

rationalist Paris. But he had little control over the plans, generally designed by Adler, who brought Sullivan first into the firm and then into a partnership because he recognized Sullivan's abilities for composition of facades and design of ornamentation. That was Sullivan's role in the firm, all but exclusively, an arrangement that defined his conception of architecture for life.[1]

Sullivan's design of the Borden Block (1880), one of his early buildings at the firm, depended on a novel structure Adler devised consisting of isolated stone foundations supporting masonry piers running the full height of the building, six stories plus an attic (fig. 57). To emphasize the piers—and their supporting function—Sullivan faced them with pilaster strips of red brick. He then corrected what could have been a spindly effect resulting from tall, narrow bays by creating a grid with the red brick pilasters and the horizontal sandstone elements the building featured. The latter comprised spandrels carrying decorative panels of dark terra-cotta (including the top row, with incised, dark, decorative lunettes) as well as string-courses that separated the floors into three groups of two stories each. The continued ascent of the piers beyond the top spandrels and up to the eaves reinforced the structural character of the design, especially since immediately under the eaves the spaces between piers were filled in with dark terra-cotta panels that expressed the nonbearing function of those surfaces. Applying a lesson in counterpoint he had learned from Furness, Sullivan turned the voids left by the structure into fenestration, thus emphasizing forcefully the structural character of the design.

In three subsequent commissions, the E. Rothschild & Brothers Store (1880–81), the Jewelers' Building (1881–82), and the Revell Building (1881–83), Sullivan explored a different type of relationship of structure and void. The structure was now a portal and the void was a multistory area filled in with a cast-iron-and-glass curtain wall. In the Rothschild Store, the spandrels and ornamental panels on the piers divided the composition into floors, the ornamentation became richer as the building rose, and the design profited from the plasticity of cast iron (fig. 58). The Jewelers' Building, the only extant Sullivan commercial design of this period, is a five-story structure of red brick and sandstone trim. The facade features a three-story cast-iron-and-glass front flanked by full side bays that act as piers. The whole rests on

a base of two differentiated floors with a cast-iron-and-glass front filling in the portal (fig. 59). The Revell Building was an elaboration of the Jewelers' Building type (fig. 60). It was also the firm's largest commission to date. At a cost of $321,112 it was more than three times as expensive as the $90,260 Jewelers' Building.[2] Placed on a corner lot, it had four three-story portals with cast-iron-and-glass curtain walls on one side and three on the other. These portals rested on two differentiated floors, as had been the case in the Jewelers' Building, but the Revell Building, being one story higher that the Jewelers' (to a total of six), carried an attic-like top floor with a highly ornamented skyline, a feature widely favored at the time.

That type of commercial building had its origins in France. While it is impossible to ascertain exactly which French designs Sullivan looked at, there are several possibilities. One was the *maison commerciale* at 3 rue d'Uzès that Edmond Guillaume designed in 1880 and César Daly published as Plate 30 of the 1880 issue of the *Revue générale de l'architecture* (fig. 61). The facade consisted of, first, a four-story metal-and-glass curtain wall framed at each side by a masonry bay. Above this was an attic of the same design of masonry and metal-and-glass. Finally, there was a receded sixth floor of standard masonry construction. Guillaume's *maison commerciale* has been suggested at least twice as the source of similar designs in the United States. Mardges Bacon proposed it as the antecedent to Ernest Flagg's Scribner buildings in New York (153–157 Fifth Avenue, 1893–94, and 597 Fifth Avenue, 1912–13) and saw it as a design issuing from Viollet-le-Duc's *hôtel de ville* in Plate XXIV of his *Atlas* (fig. 62).[3] More recently, Hans Frei proposed that the Guillaume building was the source for Sullivan's Borden Block.[4]

There were other buildings as well in this "portal style" that was closer to home and that Sullivan may have seen. Among them was the Roosevelt Building, New York (1874), by Richard Morris

Figure 61.
Maison commerciale,
*Paris, Edmond
Guillaume.*
Revue générale de l'architecture,
1880.

Figure 62.
Hôtel de ville, *Eugène
Viollet-le-Duc.*
Atlas, 1863.

Hunt—with a splendid cast-iron facade on 478–482 Broadway and a no less interesting rear at 40 Crosby Street (fig. 63).[5] The five-story front is comprised of three well-defined bays broken into a base, a three-story arcade, and an attic. Another possible source, albeit a remote one, could have been the studio building Richard Morris Hunt built at 51–55 West 10th Street in New York in 1857 (fig. 64). On the central portion of the facade, a self-asserting load-bearing brick structure, one bay wide, contained two large segmental-arch windows that almost, but not quite, established a transparent curtain wall, had it not been for the second-floor spandrel. (In that respect, neither did Viollet-le-Duc create a multistory metal-and-glass curtain wall in his *hôtel de ville.* On the other hand, typologically, both facades—which are only six years apart—share in a "family air" of well-defined masonry sides carrying balconies and framing an almost transparent center of segmental-arch windows. While historically each was undoubtedly a "milestone" in the architecture of the nation that produced it, on another level they were also specimens of an ongoing stylistic development.)

Yet another of Sullivan's sources could have been the *hôtel d'un peintre* Antoine-Anatole Jal designed in 1856 for the painter Pierre-Jules Jollivet and César Daly published in the 1858 issue of the *Revue générale de l'architecture* (fig. 65).[6] Jollivet (1794–1871), while also an engraver, devoted most of his time to painting history cycles on enameled lava (*lave emaillée*), a method the chemist Mortelèque developed in 1827. From 1833 to 1841 the architect Jacques-Ignace Hittorf made use of this technique to produce altar fronts, tabletops, and other similar items at Hachette et Compagnie, but soon thereafter ceramics supplanted lava as the supporting material for enameled surfaces.[7] Jollivet—best known today as the author of the ill-starred polychromatic exterior decoration of Hittorff's Church of Saint-Vincent-de-Paul that Baron Haussmann rejected after a trial piece had

been set in place—wished to use his own art to create a polychromatic facade on his house.

Jollivet's house was the first building ever to bear an enameled lava curtain wall. Although broken up into apartments, it still stands with its facade intact at 11 rue Malesherbes, a private one-block-long street in the Ninth Arrondissement, a short walk southeast of the Place Pigalle. The building has four floors. On the first, originally, were the vestibule, services, dining room, a small garden, and a studio beyond for painting on enameled lava. On the elevation, this floor reads as a rusticated base. On the second floor were the reception rooms and the library; the bedrooms were on the third. These two stories were combined on the elevation to appear as a giant two-story floor. Finally, a studio, six meters high, occupied the fourth floor, along with a mezzanine with two servants' rooms. The studio showed itself to the outside as high as the combined heights of the second

and third floors. Consequently, seen from the street, the building appeared to have two giant stories above a base. The composition was a standard French portico-like facade of load-bearing ends framing curtain walls, in this case with a clerestory of enameled lava on the second level (reception rooms and bedrooms) and a large, six-meter-high window facing north on the third level.

The question of which of these several buildings, if any, influenced Sullivan cannot be accurately answered. Only stylistic similarities—I dare not say affiliations—may be noted, inasmuch as the only evidence available is the knowledge that he owned the issues of the *Revue générale de l'architecture* corresponding to 1851–70 with the exception of the one for 1868.[8] That collection includes the Jal building of 1858 but not the Guillaume of 1880, yet one cannot assume that he had not seen the *maison commerciale* in an office copy of the *Revue générale*. On the other hand, it is impossible to

Figure 65.
Hôtel d'un peintre,
*Paris, Anatole Jal and
Pierre-Jules Jollivet
(1856–57).*
Revue générale de
l'architecture, 1858.

Figure 66.
Ryerson Building,
Chicago (1884).
American Architecture and Build-
ing News, 1885.

Figure 67.
Troescher Building,
Chicago (1884).
Inland Architect and
News Record, 1884.

establish an accurate stylistic chronology of the masonry-framed metal-and-glass building type, since so many of them were going up almost simultaneously. Therefore, using two buildings not as specific models that Sullivan may have followed but merely as arbitrary generic examples, one may say that the Rothschild Store was of the Roosevelt Building type and the Jewelers' and Revell buildings followed the type of Jal's Maison Jollivet.

In any case, that preliminary exploration of style ended in 1884, when Sullivan came under the influence of his friend John Edelmann (the architect who had commissioned him, then in Paris, to design frescoes for Moody's Tabernacle). Edelmann had just returned to Chicago, where he stayed through 1886. Sullivan always thought highly of Edelmann. "You can make up your mind that my reputation as an architect will always be inferior to his,"[9] Sullivan wrote his brother Albert in 1874, referring to Edelmann. Under Edelmann's influence, Sullivan's play of volumes became more three-dimensional than before and his style became suffused with a goodly dose of the English Queen Anne. The Ryerson Building (1884) looked like an excessively muscular, monstrously Gallicized ver-

sion of Norman Shaw's New Zealand Chambers, done by an American under the influence of Frank Furness (fig. 66). Other stylistic attempts foretold of things to come. In the Troescher Building, of that same year, a much-ornamented sixth floor with a rich skyline bore down on uninterrupted four-story-tall piers that in turn rested on a springy arcade of basket arches (fig. 67).

The facade for the remodeling of McVicker's Theater (1885) was Sullivan's worst design (fig. 68). The original building had a concave facade, semi-octagonal corner pavilions, and a two-story-high entrance arcade supported on spindly Corinthian columns—an architectural oxymoron prevalent for a few decades in the nineteenth century. Rather than bringing order to the composition, which Adler increased by two floors, Sullivan complicated it further. He made the semioctagonal pavilions more important than before by making them taller, placed a new semihexagonal central pavilion on the already meager entrance arcade, and perched the top floor across the building on stilts of uncertain balance. On no account did the composition create the portal effect Sullivan sought. It must have given the impression of unwieldy masses

upheld by a toothpick-like structure that might well topple with the first strong wind from the lake.

Success came the following year. The Chicago Auditorium Building was a result of the enthusiasm generated by the Chicago Opera Festival Auditorium, a temporary structure built by Adler & Sullivan in Grant Park in 1885 and demolished in 1892. Adler designed a superb building for the Chicago Auditorium, the largest structure in the city, with a budget running over $3 million. It combined into one structure a hotel, office block, and one of the best theaters in the nation, with acoustics and sightlines second to none. The elegance Adler achieved in the planning of the spaces and in their relationships to each other matched his success in inventing new methods of construction.[10] Sullivan's first task in the Auditorium was to

design the facades. If his design was approved, he was to proceed with the decoration of the building.

His first two facade designs were woefully inadequate. The first was a commonplace picturesque composition in red brick (fig. 69). It consisted of a two-story stone base, five-floor-high arcades with terra-cotta decorations, and an eighth floor running atticlike and supporting a gable roof with many dormers and complicated turrets. To mark the theater entrance, Sullivan made use of a broad tower of no great height. He capped it with a steep Late Gothic pitched roof and ended it with a gazebo-like lantern. To make the design even more picturesque, he rounded the corners of the building with small circular towers bearing conical roofs and capriciously broke the surface of the walls with large oriels.

The second design, two floors taller than the first, was better in some respects, worse in others (fig. 70). An attic supporting a full-floor cornice that made for a simpler, stronger skyline stood in place of the gable roof of the first design. The tower was also taller and now ended in a pyramidal roof. But as if compensating for the greater simplicity of the overall lines, the oriels, protrusions, and recessions on the walls were even more complicated than before. With his Beaux-Arts training eleven years behind and still under the influence of John Edelmann, Sullivan, very much the architect of the McVicker's Theater remodeling, created designs to be appreciated more as drawings than as architecture. Worse, in Paul Sprague's opinion, Edelmann "might even have made some early sketches for his friend Sullivan's Auditorium."[11] Fortunately for Sullivan, Edelmann, a political activist, left for New York to take part in Henry George's presidential campaign. With his career very much in jeopardy during that fall of 1886, Sullivan had no recourse but to think the problem through, alone, and the result is well known: one of the best buildings in American architecture (fig. 71).

An influence of Richardson's Marshall Field Wholesale Store is a matter of record, but what is not sufficiently emphasized is the fundamental difference between the two buildings, one a deep red

and the other a creamy white (cf. fig. 56). Sullivan decided to forgo the "muscularity" and "masculinity" of a dark, romanesquoid/early Renaissance massive fabric. Instead, he favored a design which while expressing great strength—as was fashionable at the time—did so with the greatest possible abstraction. The Auditorium ended Sullivan's Victorian polychromatic period and brought America and France together in new ways. Metaphorically speaking, the building was a fusion of Richardson and Vaudremer.

The Auditorium was a building such as America had never seen before. It called for neither polychromy nor ornamentation to make an iconographical statement, yet it was majestic and romantic, individual and characteristic. It was a building devoid of picturesqueness in a city that thrived on it. Furthermore, it sought no association with a historical past, identifying itself with nothing but itself, with its bones and muscles, sinews and skin. It was, in Sullivan's own words, "a building comely in the nude."

The Walker Warehouse (1888) was the best design to follow in the wake of the Auditorium (fig. 72). As for the design of the Auditorium, Sullivan based its composition on a section of Richardson's Marshall Field Wholesale Store,[12] but that dependence was but a superficial starting point. The building becomes more interesting when

Figure 71.
Auditorium Building,
Chicago (1886–90).
Photograph by Thomas A. Heinz.

Figure 72.
Walker Warehouse,
Chicago (1888).
Art Institute of Chicago.

one looks for Sullivan's artistic invention in it. To begin with, he based his rhythm on systems of fours, unobtrusively setting the tone with an arcade of four pairs of four-story-high arches with an attic above carrying four clusters of four rectangular windows each. A bold yet simple cornice topped the composition and created a unified rhythm across the building. Then, on ground level, two full Syrian-type arches took the center of a two-story-high base. With no polychromy and no ornamentation, the beauty of the building depended on simplicity of lines, mastery of proportion, absolute clarity on the relationship of structure and gravity, and a play of light and shadow highlighting moldings and seemingly incising even more a fenestration already well set into the wall. The Walker Warehouse was a child of Richardson's Brattle Square Church—a child that was simplified, abstracted, and turned into a cube carrying arcades.

The Walker Warehouse reveals how personal Sullivan's style was. He made use of only those principles of Beaux-Arts design relating to the expression of construction and its relation with gravity. In that, the building was superb. But the Walker Warehouse shows as well how little Sullivan cared for the critical Beaux-Arts relationship of elevation and plan, and the design was flawed in that respect. On first inspection, the two large arches, side by side, offered an ambiguous choice concerning how to enter the building, but worse, one eventually realized that neither marked an entry, since the doors were at the corners of the building. Sullivan's main concern had been the idiosyncratic rhythm of the elevation as a discrete shell, as the embodiment of an architecture of smooth, hard, well-defined surfaces of pristine abstraction. A return to first principles—as he understood them—was his way to restore to architecture what he called *power*. After the ordeal of designing the Auditorium (and subsequently understanding what he had achieved in it) he saw faults in many of the buildings around him. Although essentially virile, their masculinity was masked by layers of ornamentation and of excessive picturesque plasticity, like his own first Audi-

torium design. Using as a simile the story of Hercules dressed as a woman spinning at the feet of Omphale, he complained that in the architecture of the day, "[p]ower lament[ed] . . . at the feet of a modern Omphale . . . too much a matter of heart and fingers, and too little an offspring of brain and soul."[13] The Walker Warehouse was another of Sullivan's masculine forms "comely in the nude."

Sullivan's search for a new, unornamented architecture of power binds together his work of this period, in spite of typological differences and variations in size and budget, and sometimes, even, in treatment of surface. The Standard Club (1887) and the Victor A. Falkenau row houses (1888), for instance, shared in the texture of the Auditorium, while two 1890 works for Salt Lake City—the Hotel Ontario project and the Dooly Block—came close to the abstraction of the Walker Warehouse, a characteristic shared as well by an 1891–92 design for the Chattanooga Chamber of Commerce (fig. 73), Chattanooga, Tennessee, a six-story, U-shaped arcaded block with hip roofs and a superbly defined tenstory octagonal tower with a steep pyramidal roof placed at the center of the courtyard—often mistaken for the Victoria Hotel, Chicago Heights, Illinois, 1892–93. The Kehilath Anshe Ma'ariv Synagogue, Chicago (1890–91), on the other hand, was an abstraction of the tower of Richardson's Trinity Church (figs. 74–75).

With the Auditorium and its sequel of "buildings comely in the nude," Sullivan gained dominion over an arcuated, unornamented, simplified style, achieving sometimes a great deal of abstraction. His technique of design had matured to the point that he realized that a better composition would emerge from his own intuition than from analysis of architectural facts. Now he was in possession of an architectural language of his own; form and theory corresponded with each other at the same time that both were intensely personal; but in hindsight, whatever iconography existed was yet inchoate.

In 1890, Sullivan had to devise a new style. The office received the commission for the Wainwright Building in St. Louis, the firm's first metal-cage

skyscraper. Sullivan felt a need to accommodate its aesthetic needs, and that crisis unsettled his confidence. Four years after the Auditorium, and fifteen after Paris, the Néo-Grec had become for him—a Midwestern architect—more a general method to organize his thoughts than a repository of architectural theory. His cogitations about how a skyscraper facade should look finally resolved themselves as he walked down Michigan Avenue thinking the problem through.[14] That solution emerged from his American pragmatism as much as from his tempering its freedom and spontaneity with a logic he had learned from the Néo-Grec, and made his own.

The result of that walk was a decision to express the trabeated character of the steel frame as a colonnade. While no doubt in his mind the design pointed at American modernity, it was in fact a dissident descendant of the east facade of the Louvre and of the tradition of the French classical colonnade. The facade of the Wainwright consists of a seven-story-tall colonnade *in antis* supported on a two-story base, with a frieze taking up an attic carrying an ornamentation of *rinceaux* developing from portholes, following a type of attic decoration typical of the Italian Renaissance (fig. 76).[15]

Sullivan may have solved the Wainwright design in pragmatic terms, but there were limits he would not overstep. He may have considered those limits bound by architectural axioms, but in fact they resulted from his received Francophile

taste. In spite of his belief in architectural freedom, a colonnade still implied to him a rhythm sanctioned by classical canon. The two-window-wide bay of the steel structure Adler had designed might have seemed overly broad and awkward to Sullivan's sensibility, and he opted for a quicker rhythm. Of the five types of intercolumnations established by Vitruvius, the Wainwright's comes closest to the diastyle, that is, three diameters wide.[16] He may have chosen that rhythm over a eustyle one (two and a quarter diameters wide, and according to Vitruvius the one "specially to be approved, [having] proportions set out for convenience, beauty, and strength") not so much to mark the presence of a metallic structure instead of a masonry one but because he may have taken into consideration the height of the column—seven stories—as well as the scale of the capitals he had designed for it (and which contributed in no small

measure to the downbearing character of the structure). Following principles of romantic rationalism, he felt bound to express the characteristics of metallic construction, but without straying too far from canons of good taste handed down by classical tradition. Indeed, he may have gone too far in that direction. As early as 1896, Montgomery Schuyler pointed that "to crown a vertical post of coated steel with a pilaster-capital is . . . plainly a solecism."[17]

Being a romantic, Sullivan sought also a synthesis of opposites. The Wainwright synthesizes a classical colonnade with the spirit of the Gothic. Viollet-le-Duc's prestige as a theoretician was possibly higher in the United States than in France at the time, and Sullivan may have remembered Viollet-le-Duc's advice to draw lessons from the Gothic for modern work, to transform its principles of design into personal ones, and to avoid copying medieval styles verbatim. More to the point, Viollet-le-Duc established a link between a tall, multistory building supported on a metallic structure and Gothic construction. "A practical architect might not unnaturally conceive the idea of erecting a vast edifice whose frame should be entirely of iron, and clothing that frame, preserving it by means of a casing of stone," he had written in his Thirteenth Discourse.[18]

Two cathedrals Sullivan knew well from his French sojourn, Paris and Reims, furnish clues of Gothic influences on the Wainwright design.[19] The anomaly of the mullions and piers of the Wainwright looking alike to create a classical rhythm finds a source in the Cathedral of Paris, where a similar ambiguity of expression occurs (fig. 77). While sexpartite vaults called for an alternation of thicker and thinner piers on the nave elevation, the architect provided no such succession of major and minor supports, and made them look all alike. The rest of the facade may have come from a dormant memory of Reims. On the inside of the west wall of Reims, below the glazed triforium, a system of horizontal and vertical moldings determines alternating rows of vertical panels above and of smaller horizontal rectangles under

Figure 77.
Notre-Dame, Paris, nave
elevation.
Georg Dehio, *Die kirchliche*
Baukunst des Abendlandes,
1887–1901.

Figure 78.
Reims Cathedral, detail
of interior west wall.
Photograph by
Frank Horlbeck.

them (fig. 78). The large vertical panels frame cusped niches and the horizontal ones contain a decoration of naturalistically rendered foliage. If one imagines the large rectangles enclosing windows instead of niches, the similarities between Reims and the Wainwright facade become evident. The basis of the Wainwright design, then, consists of a classical colonnade that finds its dynamics in the Gothic, a fusion of opposites resulting from Sullivan's personal search for the characteristic solution for one particular building. It was a case of French romantic rationalism fully translated and co-opted into an American idiom.

The canonical position of the Wainwright in American architecture is well established, yet its early critics—Barr Ferree and Montgomery Schuyler—dealt with aspects of its composition, but never considered it as an archetype.[20] It was Sullivan himself who launched the myth of the

canonicity of the Wainwright Building. In the *Autobiography* he wrote: "In St. Louis, [the steel frame] was given first authentic recognition and expression in the exterior treatment of the Wainwright Building, a nine-story [*sic*] office structure, by Louis Sullivan's own hand."[21] That perception, stated thirty-four years after the building was designed, eventually turned into conventional wisdom, although it was slow in becoming so. Little was written about Sullivan's skyscrapers in the 1920s, much less about the Wainwright, other than in a few of Sullivan's eulogies, in 1924.[22] The first two histories of the skyscraper—Starrett's *Skyscrapers* (1928) and Mujica's *History of the Skyscraper* (1929)—do not even mention Sullivan, yet it is hard to think that his work was unknown to their authors.[23] Erich Mendelsohn's summarizing comment of 1928 explains why Sullivan's work was disregarded critically. At the height of the *Neue*

Sachlichkeit, Mendelsohn said about Sullivan's Schiller Building that "much as yet depends on tradition, but much is an honest attempt to develop the proper forms according to new conditions."[24] From Mendelsohn's point of view, the work was marred by a remnant of nineteenth-century historicism, especially, one would think, in what concerns ornamentation.

Only in the 1930s did the Wainwright Building emerge as an archetypal, canonical building. In his *An Autobiography*, from 1932, Frank Lloyd Wright stated:

> But—when he brought the drawing board with the motive for the *Wainwright Building* outlined in profile and in scheme upon it and threw it on my table, I was perfectly aware of what had happened.
>
> This was Louis Sullivan's great moment, his greatest effort. The skyscraper as a new thing beneath the sun, an entity imperfect, but with virtue, individuality, beauty all its own—was born.[25]

Three years later, in 1935, Hugh Morrison published *Louis Sullivan: Prophet of Modern Architecture*, a book that endorsed Sullivan's view of nine years earlier. "The Wainwright Building was the first successful solution of the architectural problem of the high building," Morrison wrote.[26] More important, Morrison was the one to link the Wainwright Building with Sullivan's essay "The Tall Office Building Artistically Considered."[27] That article was Sullivan's seminal statement on the skyscraper, where he presented his well-known dictum that "form ever follows function,"[28] as well as his often-quoted formula for the design of tall buildings:

> The practical conditions are, broadly speaking these:
> Wanted—1st, a story below-ground, containing boilers, engines of various sorts, etc.—in short, the plant for power, heating, lighting, etc. 2nd, a ground floor, so called, devoted to stores, banks, or other establishments requiring large area, ample spacing, ample light, and great freedom of access. 3rd, a second story readily accessible by stairways—this space usually in large subdivisions,

with corresponding liberality in structural spacing and expanse of glass and breadth of external openings. 4th, above this an indefinite number of stories of offices piled tier upon tier, one tier just like another tier, one office just like all the other offices—an office being similar to a cell in a honey-comb, merely a compartment, nothing more. 5th, and last, at the top of this pile is placed a space or story that, as related to the life and usefulness of the structure, is purely physiological in its nature—namely, the attic. In this the circulatory system completes itself and makes its grand turn, ascending and descending. The space is filled with tanks, pipes, valves, sheaves, and mechanical etcetera that supplement and complement the force-originating plant hidden below the cellar. [At the time, each large building had its own power plant in the cellar.] *Finally, or at the beginning rather, there must be on the ground floor a main aperture or entrance common to all the occupants or patrons of the building.*[29]

Quite accurately, Morrison said that "Sullivan probably wrote ['The Tall Office Building Artistically Considered,' first published in *Lippincott's Magazine* in March 1896] with the recently completed Guaranty Building in Buffalo [1894–95] more directly in mind than the Wainwright Building."[30] Yet, because superficially—and only superficially—the Wainwright and the Guaranty resemble each other, Morrison could not resist the temptation to offer the earlier Wainwright as the subject of Sullivan's article. In doing so, he made two errors of judgment. First, he disregarded Sullivan's experiments with form in the skyscrapers designed after the Wainwright and before the Guaranty; second, he opened the door for subsequent modernist critics to dismiss them completely. Moreover, by endorsing the Wainwright as the building best revealing Sullivan's theory of the skyscraper, he passed over two objections that had been made to its design, and of which he must have had knowledge. The first came from Irving K. Pond in 1924, only nine years before the publication of Morrison's book.[31] In his eulogy of Sullivan, after quoting his sentence about the

Wainwright Building being the first to reveal the reality of the metallic frame, Pond wrote:

> Now that sentence [by Sullivan] is susceptible of more than one interpretation; but what is intended to be conveyed is that Louis Sullivan solved in the Wainwright Building, in an authentic manner, the problem of covering architecturally the steel skeleton. That design is no more a solution of that problem than would be the application of a Palladian motif with a basement plinth, a classical colonnade extending through the height of two or more stories, and an entablature taking the attic story. There is in the Wainwright Building a two storied base or plinth; a series of columns all alike,–but every other one containing a steel core, though the exterior semblance is the same in all,–running through seven stories and having each a capital, and this feature is crowned with a frieze and cornice out of all proportion to the columns on which they rest–a horizontal, a vertical, and a horizontal, absolutely at variance with the movement within the frame.[32]

The second criticism Morrison disregarded was that of Montgomery Schuyler, who considered that placing capitals atop piers of encased steel on the Wainwright facade was an impropriety of expression.[33]

Morrison's was the only monograph on Sullivan for many years. Its position in the Sullivan historiography inextricably linked the Wainwright to "The Tall Office Building Artistically Considered." In spite of the six years and the host of different Sullivan skyscraper designs that separate the Wainwright from "The Tall Office Building Artistically Considered," the Wainwright became the building where form followed function. It was the kind of shibboleth functionalists cherished, including Pevsner and Giedion as well as the literally hundreds who echoed their views.

Concerning the Wainwright, Robert Twombly was the first to expand on a statement Sullivan made to his friend Claude Bragdon about "The Tulip," installment twenty-two of "Kindergarten Chats."[34] In 1903 Sullivan wrote to Bragdon:

> Those [among my buildings] that interest me date from the Wainwright building in St. Louis. . . . It was a sudden and volcanic design (made literally in three minutes) and marks the beginning of a logical and poetic expression of the metallic frame construction. . . . All my commercial buildings since the Wainwright are conceived in the same general spirit. . . . The structures prior to the Wainwright were in my "masonry" period [from which] the Auditorium Bldg. and the Walker [Warehouse], Chicago, are the best. . . . It was with the Wainwright "that I broke" (see K.G. Chat "The Tulip").[35]

Twombly, following Sullivan's lead, linked the last sentence in the quotation to Chat 22, where Sullivan used the metaphor of the tulip grower, who waits patiently year after year seeing the same kind of grayish, boring tulip come out until one year a miracle occurs, the tulip "breaks" and a magnificent, exciting new variety shoots forth. Such was the miracle of the Wainwright. It was a design that went much farther than any other Sullivan had designed before in his quest for a model for commercial buildings that would relate entirely to its structure. This effort was doubly important inasmuch as he was dealing with the skyscraper, the most important building type in the nation at the time. His "breaking out" was an unparalleled step leading from masonry buildings to metallic ones—yet that does not mean that the Wainwright was the culmination of his skyscraper efforts.

Along the same vein, one remembers that critics have written that "the Wainwright is not merely tall; it is *about* being tall; it is tall architecturally even more than it is physically."[36] While stylistically the statement is true, it is not so conceptually. The colonnade of the Wainwright could be cut down in height and one would obtain a very handsome building, not a tall one, but one extending horizontally and creating a modern interpretation of the standard model of the east facade of the Louvre, as for instance Sullivan himself did in 1892 in the first project for the Meyer Wholesale Store (fig. 79).

The Wainwright Building, then, has a double

Figure 79.
M. A. Meyer Wholesale
Store, Chicago, first
design (1892).
Inland Architect and News
Record, 1892.

importance: it was the first of a kind, and it was also, for Sullivan, a synthesis that was more efficient conceptually than aesthetically. On another level, the Wainwright reveals Sullivan's strong leanings in favor of French romantic rationalist theory as much as his desire to serve the aesthetic needs of what was to him a brand-new building type. The result, being the first, was riddled with problems, and yet it served him for other solutions for the skyscraper, such as for the commission of the Fraternity Temple, designed during the summer of 1891 to be the tallest structure in America (fig. 80). The ambiguity of the Wainwright design, where mullions looked like piers, might have bothered Sullivan. The ten-story masses of the Fraternity Temple looked like so many Wainwright Buildings where now all vertical elements were piers. The eighteen-story masses followed the same pattern except that their attics had two rows of portholes instead of one like the Wainwright. The central tower was to have an observation balcony surrounding the thirty-fourth floor. The building, the realty prospectus boasted, would have been "a landmark for the country within a radius of sixty miles . . . visible from Michigan City, La Porte, Aurora, Elgin, Waukegan, and intermediate points."[37] Reciprocally, that would have been the view from the thirty-fourth floor.

In the twelve-floor-plus-attic Portland Block

project (1892; a building different from Jenney's earlier Portland Block), Sullivan placed two uninterrupted corner piers holding together a facade that may be divided into four parts (fig. 81). There was first a ground floor with a three-bay storefront surrounded by a wide terra-cotta band and carrying the main door on center, framed by a similar band. Next, two rows of three windows combined the second and third floors into a unit of composition. Above came seven stories, each also three bays wide, but in this case the central bay had simple rectangular windows while the side bays were turned into uninterrupted clerestories, seven stories high. Above all this, and as a counterpoint to that forceful vertical movement, the building ended with a two-story colonnade where the horizontal rhythm of the three lower floors resonated in a higher key. As in a column, the profile of the capital projected more than that of the base. The Portland, in many ways, was Sullivan's translation of the Walker Warehouse into a building supported on a metal cage, and, as in the Walker Warehouse, the openings, because of the abstraction of the surfaces, were the outstanding features.

Two different projects for the Chemical National Bank building, St. Louis (c. 1894), and an unidentified design for a building also in St. Louis (c. 1893–95), are yet other examples of Sullivan's post-and-lintel architecture of this period. These three designs are similar in that besides having the standard Sullivanesque ornamented attic and cornice and differentiated one- or two-story base, their shafts are based on the same idea (figs. 82–84). On smooth, sharp, parallelepipeds, Sullivan established grids with incised windows, creating whole buildings out of the composition of the second and third floors of the Portland Building (cf. fig. 81). Another interpretation of these designs would be to say that in them the colonnade and spandrels of the Wainwright dissolved into a wall, and that the visual value of posts and lintels now depended on the shape of the windows, whether oblong or vertical rectangles.

That process of decomposition of the colonnade went further in the Chicago Stock Exchange

Figure 80.
Fraternity Temple,
Chicago (1891).
Industrial Chicago, 1892.

Figure 81.
Portland Block, Chicago
(1892).
Third Annual Exhibition of the
St. Louis Chapter of the Ameri-
can Institute of Architects, 1895.

Figure 82.
Chemical National Bank
Building, St. Louis,
second design (c. 1894).
Third Annual Exhibition of the
St. Louis Chapter of the Ameri-
can Institute of Architects, 1895.

Figure 83.
Chemical National Bank
Building, St. Louis,
first design (c. 1894).
Third Annual Exhibition of the
St. Louis Chapter of the Ameri-
can Institute of Architects, 1895.

Figure 84.
Unidentified office
building project,
St. Louis (c. 1897).
Art Institute of Chicago.

Building (1893–94) (fig. 85). A thirteen-story structure at a cost of $1,131,555, it was Adler & Sullivan's largest building after the Auditorium.[38] It was divided vertically into four zones. A low ground story acted as an elevated basement inasmuch as the second floor was the main one. A two-story-high arcade came next, with thirteen bays on LaSalle Street and seven on Washington Street. (This arcade indicated externally the location and height of the stock exchange room, rebuilt in the Art Institute after the building was demolished in 1972.) Above that two-story arcade came nine floors of alternating bays of Chicago windows and oriels—"in a variation on the Portland [Building] fenestration," Twombly has called it[39]—creating an undulating facade typical of many Chicago buildings of the 1880s and 1890s. At the top ran a colonnade. Finally, the entire composition was brought together by the corner piers and the top lintel combining into a huge portal, 180 feet wide and thirteen stories high.

Eclecticism was another step in Sullivan's process of trial and error in quest of an expression of the skyscraper type. Two buildings are important in this context: the project for the Mercantile Club (1891) and the St. Nicholas Hotel (1892–93), both in St. Louis (fig. 86). Each essentially consisted of a shaft supporting a cantilevered structure with a pitched roof housing reception rooms. The result, while not devoid of the hard-edged abstraction that had become typically Sullivan's, evokes late medieval–early Renaissance Northern European architecture.

To summarize Sullivan's first period, one sees first that his early commercial work, that of 1880–84, was an exploration into the Néo-Grec style he had admired in Jenney's Portland Block, a model he soon surpassed while still retaining the standard red-brick-and-sandstone-trim polychromy then in vogue. (Jenney's Portland Block, however, had not been so much a model as a precedent that helped Sullivan develop his own style, one that brought to it Furness's lessons without doing violence to Adler's notions of what a structure should look like.) Then, in the mid-1880s, he changed his style under the influence of John Edelmann. If Sullivan ever reached a nadir in his design it was in 1884–86, and it led to the two disappointing early studies for the Auditorium.

Sullivan seems to have worked best under stress, as the Borden Block, the Auditorium, and the Wainwright Building attest. While the Auditorium inaugurated a new style which he called his "masonry period," it was a one-of-a-kind building. Nowhere else do we find that kind of rugged look and cyclopean stereotomy in his buildings of 1887–90. Immediately after, Sullivan evolved into greater abstraction of volumes and surfaces, as if he were trying to divest himself of whatever remnant of picturesqueness the Auditorium retained. The Walker Warehouse was a refinement of what he achieved in the Auditorium, and served him far more than the Auditorium as a model of his own to follow—yet there were relapses into rustication that give an impression that he was not totally self-confident. Then came the skyscraper. However difficult the design of the Wainwright may have been, it was at the time but a solution to the problem of one building, not an attempt to invent an archetype. The stylistic variety of his work of 1880–94 witnesses his grasping for form as much as his brilliance as a designer, but he was also searching for something he did not find. His work had been the constant evolution of a crisis because he had not found a manner—a system, perhaps—with which to bring into a whole his style and the transcendentalist iconography on which his mind had been set since the mid-1880s.

3: Genesis of an Iconography

Sullivan's *The Autobiography of an Idea* reveals how his childhood aesthetic cravings determined the iconography he later favored, almost as a natural development.[1] Sherman Paul, in his assessment of Sullivan's position in American intellectual history, suggested that the *Autobiography* was inspired by Hippolyte Taine, who in his *Lectures on Art* "had written of the resemblance between seeds and ideas and of beneficence as the test of art."[2] Charles Whitaker, editor of the *Journal of the American Institute of Architects,* who commissioned the book, compared it to Henry Adams's *Education.*[3] But a closer source for the *Autobiography* would be Jean-Jacques Rousseau's *Émile* via Friedrich Froebel's *Education of Man.* Rousseau (1712–78) was concerned with the rearing of a child according to the laws of nature rather than to the artificial dictates of social decorum. Froebel (1782–1852), creator of the kindergarten system of education, opened the child's eye to the wonders of nature and most especially to the geometric understructure that sustained it and gave it order.

Sullivan's story of his life was a complement to his earlier "Kindergarten Chats." In the Chats, he showed how a student of architecture had to suffer through a process of unlearning and reconditioning before achieving communion with nature, because he had received an improper education. The *Autobiography*, on the other hand, was meant to serve as a case study showing how that young man should have been reared. A proper development of the instincts in childhood, Sullivan believed, would produce a correct attitude toward nature in adulthood. He considered himself fortunate that during childhood and youth many people helped him to develop his personality according to that view.[4] Three-quarters of the book was devoted to events that occurred before he went to work for Adler at the age of twenty-four.

Sullivan believed as strongly as Rousseau and Froebel did in the importance of childhood experiences as a grounding for a proper relationship between adults and nature. Hence his awareness of his own aesthetic preferences as a child is an important theme in the *Autobiography*. His childhood leanings and understanding of relationships between grown-ups and nature served him later as a basis for comprehending the beauty of nature, to him the model of all beauty. As an adult, he would come to hold that in the final democratic utopia elegant behavior would be proper to all at all times and that gorgeous architecture would be the background common to every life. Yet, while these thoughts may indeed have been a result of his persistent responsiveness to a beauty he had begun to experience in childhood, they may have been introduced by other causes as well. His desire to compensate with courtly deportment for his "Irish mongrel origins" was as important to his aesthetic desires as his peculiar romantic egalitarianism is central to the understanding of his notion that everyone should be equally refined. By the end of his life, when he wrote the story of his "Idea," Sullivan had perhaps learned from Emerson's essay "Compensation" that love of elegant manners was not the only "retribution" he had sought all of his life for having been a child of immigrants. Other problems of social adjustment complicated the issue. He had to contend not with one but with two different foreign traditions in his family. His father was Irish, his mother German-Swiss. Presumably, he felt that he had to make a choice, and he came to consider his mother's heritage as superior to his father's. He described his father as having "the eyes of a pig" and "an excessively Irish face," and he also recalled how in Boston, where he was born in 1856, his family name "was scorned by all but its owner."[5] Sullivan's contempt for his father's nationality may have originated with his mother. She attempted to pass as a Frenchwoman, struggling to disguise a German-Swiss parentage considered to be less refined than a French one at the time. But being Mrs. Patrick Sullivan made things worse for her. The name immediately conveyed the idea of an ignorant and rowdy "Paddy"— one of the "shanty Irish." She solved her problem, her son wrote, by Gallicizing *Sullivan* into *Tulive*

"as a general cover-name, and thus secured a happy, life-long escape."[6]

Sullivan's self-encysting within his own philosophical beliefs was partly a defense against the emotional vulnerability that colored his thought with vehemence and sought release in artistic activity. The intensity of his purpose led him to bind together the events of his *Autobiography* with three strands: (1) the realization of his own aesthetic emotions, (2) the development of his intellect, and (3) his turning a synthesis of these two into a conscious artistic intention. Later in life, he would bring together in his buildings symbols of the lyrical, the rational, and the heroic in ways that would parallel the three categories of the emotional, the intellectual, and the quest for knowledge of the absolute that colored his childhood and youth.

Concerning the first—the emotional or lyrical—and following the best tradition of Rousseau and Froebel, Sullivan stressed in the *Autobiography* how one of his childhood experiential urges fulfilled his adult life.[7] In his case, he developed his lyrical instincts through uninhibited contact with the land on his grandparents' farm in South Reading, near Boston, where he lived between the ages of five and fourteen. During those critical years he saw in nature analogs of his own physical sensations and made the surrounding world the object of his imagination. His grandmother, Anna Mattheus, and Julia, the Irish servant girl at the farm, were important figures in the story. The grandmother was the image of placid love, methodical in her ways and always calling on her all-embracing affection to bring down to earth a high-spirited family.[8] Julia, on the other hand, fired the child's imagination with her Irish folk tales spun around enchanted forests, giants, and denizens of the nether world, all of which allowed the child to transform the humdrum nature of the farm into a magical, transcendent world, especially "his domain," a small meadow crossed by a stream and bound by a grove and a marsh that satisfied his lyrical yearnings in ways no playmate could. "It was all his. No other boy could understand. Besides, he loved solitude as he loved activity, and the open."[9] That child felt "embryonic passions arising and shaping, ambitions vaguely stirring; while his sharp eyes saw everything."[10] When he encountered his "Great Friend," a gigantic, solitary ash, "he trembled strangely, he wished to cry."[11] But the most poignant moment of identification with nature came at the death of his grandmother when he was fourteen and his shock found soothing in a vision of the orchard in bloom on that April day. The contrast of the burgeoning flowers with a corpse that looked like "an ivory mask which repelled" made him "accept death as an evanishment . . . and Life as the power of powers."[12] He also understood that natural law extended beyond the visible and the tangible as he found solace in a realization of the rhythm of life and death that eventually would be central to his conception of the evolution of art.

Music was also an important lyrical factor from an early age. His father, a dancing master, must have possessed a sharp sense of rhythm. His mother, an accomplished pianist, opened to him the world of music. He tells how at the age of three he used to hide under the piano while she played and how at one point he felt so moved that he began to sob.[13] Others widened his appreciation of music later on. Mr. Tompson, the neighbor with whom he stayed after his grandmother's death, was musical also, and Louis got from him "some knowledge and some understanding and misunderstanding of the great oratorios," and sharpened his skills as a pianist.[14] Later he would play often, especially when a wider musical scope opened to him in Chicago and he became "an ardent Wagnerite."[15]

However important nature and music were in the development of his lyrical instincts, it was his mother, to whom he was very close, who possibly fostered them most. She had an intense personality and understood art in the Victorian feminine sense of an intense spiritual commitment that was to be revealed in expressions of deeply felt aesthetic emotions. And while emotionally bruised by the insensitivity of Bostonians toward immigrants,

she never became bitter, and thus could become a major influence on her son, pointing out to him, perhaps without realizing it, the characteristics he would recognize later as those of Whitman's "democratic man." Acknowledging his debt to his mother, in the *Autobiography* he ended a rhapsodical passage on her by calling himself "truly life of her life" and said, "If Louis is not his mother's spirit in the flesh, then words fail, and memory is vain."[16]

In true romantic fashion he felt that his intellectual development had been less important than his discovery of his own instincts, which he called "primordial,"[17] yet as a matter of course a number of people were important to the development of his mind. The first was Henri List, his grandfather, "a straight German of the Hanoverian type—six feet tall, well-proportioned, erect carriage, and topped by a domical head, full, clean-shaven face, thick lips, small gray eyes, beetling brows and bottle-nose. He was of the intellectual mold, and cynically amused at men, women, children and all else."[18] He took upon himself the education of his grandson, and more than likely knowingly followed a method Rousseau endorsed first and Froebel perfected later, for "he knew well enough that the child was living in the world of the senses."[19] An amateur astronomer, he brought order into Louis's strong but random conception of nature and broadened that conception into that of a well ordered, rational cosmos.

The lack of a bonding family religion was important to Sullivan's rationalism, the second strand shaping his professional life. With the exception of the grandmother, a conventional Methodist, the rest were rational agnostics in the mid-nineteenth-century sense. Yet the grandfather, it seems, had studied for the Catholic priesthood at some time. Sullivan's theory concerning the relations of man, inspiration, and what he later called the "Infinite Creative Spirit"—the all-knowing creative entity of nature—while rooted in romanticism, is also close to the Catholic dogma of salvation. The grandfather may have been the first to pass these ideas down to him, but already transmuted into a naturalist deism, since "Grandpa looked upon religion as a curious and amusing human weakness—a conclusive evidence of universal stupidity."[20] The mother, however, was far more romantic than her father. "Mother had a fixed idea that existence was continuous in a series of expanding becomings, life after life, in a spiral ascending and ever ascending until perfection was reached in a bodiless state of bliss."[21]

Sullivan's early schooling was typical of a small New England rural town at the time, neither exciting nor inspiring. At first he rebelled against it and felt that the out-of-doors had more to offer. Eventually he improved as a student and took conventional learning as a challenge, but it never fired him until he reached the English High School in Boston and encountered Moses Woolson, "a blend of wild man and poet . . . [who] had the art of teaching at his finger tips."[22] Woolson's method consisted of making his students observe, reflect, and discriminate. During that first year, Sullivan became "a mental athlete" and Woolson opened to him "the wonderland of Poetry."[23] Besides convincing Sullivan of the importance of an analytical intellectual method, Woolson also revealed to him the power of words and syntax in what must have been superb lessons on English literature. An admirer of elegant Gallic exactness, Woolson taught English literature using Taine's *History of English Literature* as a text. And not only did Woolson acquaint Sullivan with Taine—an event that was to have important repercussions later in Paris—but he also opened to him the world of botany, and Asa Gray, then teaching at Harvard, "would come occasionally to talk botany to the boys. He did this out of regard for Moses Woolson's love of science."[24] Later, Gray's *School and Field Book of Botany* would become Sullivan's constant companion and an important source in the development of his theory of ornamentation.

It is highly unlikely that, once in Philadelphia, the seventeen-year-old Sullivan became aware of the influence the Reverend William Henry Furness had on his son's architecture. Yet indirectly and unconsciously, those ideas—or at least the tenor of them—might well have had a bearing on Sullivan's thought during the five months he worked for Frank Furness.

A native Bostonian, William Furness (1802–96) was the lifelong friend of Ralph Waldo Emerson, his old schoolmate at the Latin School, and he delivered Emerson's funeral oration. A pastor for many years of the First Congregational Unitarian Church in Philadelphia (founded in 1796 by Joseph Priestly, Henry Hobson Richardson's great-grandfather), Furness had a long and distinguished career in the Philadelphia Unitarian Church until his retirement in 1875, finding time for writing extensively as well. Of his twenty-two books on the life of Christ and interpretations of the Gospels the most important was perhaps his first, *Remarks on the Four Gospels*, published in Philadelphia in 1836, the year of Emerson's "Nature." The book served as the foundation of his scholarly work. It was a celebration of nature as the substratum of all religion and an endorsement of Christianity only because Christ adhered to what Furness considered to be the universal teaching. Jesus had attuned Himself so perfectly with nature that His miracles were not suspensions of the natural order, but results of a higher understanding of the natural law. To Furness, Jesus was the archetypal utopian man, the man in perfect communion with nature, the Natural Genius.[25] It would not be farfetched to consider Frank Furness's work as his father's ideas turned into an architecture that, because it was intensely personal, was of itself also intensely American, based as it was on American transcendentalism. Such was Frank Furness's seminal contribution to American architecture in general and to Sullivan in particular, who followed in his wake in the adoption of a transcendentalist aesthetic.

Later, in Paris, more than Vaudremer or any of his teachers at the Ecole des Beaux-Arts, it was Christian-Victor Clopet who left the deepest imprint on Sullivan's intellect. Monsieur Clopet—as Sullivan called him in the *Autobiography*—was *répétiteur* in the *cours scientifiques* at the Ecole and also coached mathematics privately for students preparing for the Beaux-Arts entrance examination.[26] Upon his arrival at Clopet's academy, Sullivan—who had thought it prudent to review mathematics prior to his entrance examination at the Ecole—was told to throw out the books an American consular official in Paris had recommended to him. The books covered theorems and listed their exceptions, clearly an aberration in Monsieur Clopet's positivist mind; he proclaimed that *"here our demonstration shall be so broad as to admit of* NO EXCEPTION!"[27] That moment, Sullivan claimed, was like an epiphany, and he understood through Monsieur Clopet that without realizing it he had been seeking for the essence of architecture, that his wish was to find not a method of design, but *the* universal method of design, a zeal understandable in an eighteen-year-old and yet one that remained with him for the rest of his life.

The heroic is the third element of Sullivan's "Idea." It divides into two areas. The first stemmed from a belief that instinctive actions are ethically superior to rational ones, "[f]or Intellect is recent, and neuter, and unstable in itself, while Instinct is primordial and procreant."[28] The second area of the heroic concerned his identification of the male form as a symbol of transcendent constructive force.

Implied in the contest between an artist's acceptance of dogmas of social behavior and his urge for self-expression is the standard romantic struggle between a vertical corporate social conception and the individual who wishes to live according to a particular vision of the universe or of society. Within Sullivan's intellectual antecedents, that struggle began chronologically with Rousseau and ended with Nietzsche, with Emerson, Thoreau, and Whitman somewhere in the middle. In his terms, this was the contest between the "I will" and the "acceptance of tradition"; it was the clash between "Democracy" and "Feudalism," to use Whitman's terms that Sullivan made his own. But Sullivan's heroicism was based on a synthesis of a naturalistic lyricism and French rationalism, and this is an important clue to his

self-conception as a hero. Through his reason he had come to know the way that nature operated, the way it created, and through his romanticism he learned to create the illusion that his work was similar to that of nature. Yet, in the end, his architecture was unnatural because it was not the creation of a sapient nature but of a man who believed he had discovered the secret of nature and could create art in the image of nature. The heroic aspect lies within that paradox. Sullivan, the hero, saw himself as able to emulate the Yahweh of the Book of Genesis. His definition of "Man the Reality—Man the Doer"—i.e., the artist—is self-explanatory: "Container of self-powers: A moving center of radiant energy: Awaiting his time to create anew in his proper image."[29]

A number of passages in the *Autobiography* tell of the imposition of the will against unfavorable odds. One day, when Louis was about five, his father took him to the seashore. The elder Sullivan went rowing and left the child on the beach. There was a strong surf, and Patrick became smaller as he receded in the distance and waves concealed him from Louis's view from time to time. Louis was terrified, and "what he knew, all of himself, and beyond the knowledge of others, was that the sea was a monster, a huge monster that would have swallowed up his father, like one of the giants he had told his grandmamma about, if his father had not been such a strong man. He felt this with terror and pride. Thus arose in prophecy the rim of another world, a world of strife and power, on the horizon verge of a great sea."[30] Later, he encountered architects, like Furness, who "made buildings out of his head"; there was also "the mighty Richardson," and the engineers who built bridges across rivers, of whom he wrote: "Here was Romance, here again was man, the great adventurer . . . in his power to create beneficently."[31]

Eventually, Sullivan's intellectual development acted on his innate romanticism and made him fuse his concepts of the visible world and of self into one single sense of cosmic unity intimately apprehended. Only then did he consider himself ready to begin what he called his "I will" and see his creative work as a heroic assertion of ego in communion with the primal essence.

Such heroic fervor had moved Sullivan to see the male form as a symbol of power, as an image of ideal constructive force. In the *Autobiography* he claimed that in his youth "he came in a manner to worship man as a being, a presence containing wondrous powers, mysterious, hidden powers, powers so varied as to surprise and bewilder him. So that Man, the mysterious, became for him a sort of symbol of that which was deepest, most active in his heart."[32] Through accidental circumstances, in 1863, when he was almost seven, his father played an unconscious role in the development of his interest in the male form. Sullivan recalled that during a vacation in Newburyport, after a swimming lesson, "he took note of his father's hairy chest, his satiny white skin and quick flexible muscles over which the sunshine danced with each movement. He had never seen a man completely stripped, and was vastly proud to have such a father."[33] Shortly after this incident, during a Sunday-afternoon picnic, Louis strayed into a grove while his parents sketched. Suddenly he saw, half concealed by the trees, the towers and suspension chains of the Merrimac Bridge. Recording what was possibly his earliest anthropomorphic identification of a structure, he remembered thinking that the towers were mighty giants turned into stone. The child became frightened and began to cry. His father came, soothed him, took him by the hand, and both crossed the bridge. At that time Louis changed his fear of the structure into admiration for the men who had built it. His idea of power as a destructive giant was turned into one of a hero acting for the good of humanity. "On their way to rejoin Mamma, the child turned backward to gaze in awe and love upon the great suspension bridge. . . . And to think it was made by men! How great men must be, how wonderful; how powerful, that they could make such a bridge; and again he worshiped the worker."[34] A few days later his father took him to visit a shipyard: "Here were his beloved strong men, the workers—his idols. . . . He had his first

view of the power of concerted action. . . . What could men not do if they could do this, and if they could make a great bridge—suspended in the air over the Merrimac."[35]

However deeply Sullivan felt his yearnings, tastes, and even intellectual preferences, he nevertheless required a grounding on matters such as philosophy and social and architectural thought to turn his aspirations into a theory and an iconography for his work. This is not to say that Sullivan proceeded methodically in his education; he was never a scholar in the conventional sense of the word. Rather, he proceeded autodidactically, at random, choosing from here and there ideas that either coincided with his or, even better, expanded them.

Important in his development was the influence of John Edelmann (1852–1900). The twenty-one-year-old Edelmann was the foreman in Jenney's office when Sullivan, then seventeen, went to work there in 1873, right after arriving in Chicago.[36] The two struck a friendship that became stronger in the spring of 1874, when Edelmann co-opted Sullivan into the Lotos Club—an athletic association of young men who met in a boathouse by the Calumet River—to which Sullivan's brother, Albert, also belonged. Sullivan participated in club activities that spring, left for Paris in the summer, and became reinstated in the club upon his return to Chicago late in the spring of 1875. He remained an active member through the summer of 1877.[37]

At the Lotos Club, Sullivan's friendship with Edelmann grew into an informal master-disciple relationship that lasted for seven years, until Edelmann moved to Cleveland in 1881, that is to say, four years beyond Sullivan's resignation from the club. Of Edelmann, Frank Lloyd Wright said: "Louis H. Sullivan venerated none except Adler, Herbert Spencer, Richard Wagner, Walt Whitman, John Edelmann, and himself."[38] Edelmann—"brawny, twenty-four [in fact, he was twenty-one], bearded, unkempt, careless, his voice rich, sonorous, modulant, his vocabulary an overflowing reservoir"—became the self-appointed mentor of the seventeenyear-old Sullivan, who idolized him. Both in Jenney's office and in the Lotos Club, Edelmann constantly reiterated his rhetorical formula of "I myself . . . to the nth power of egoism."[39]

During their philosophical discussions, Edelmann, who spoke German from his childhood, introduced Louis to German transcendentalism, and his notions of heroic symbolism helped his pupil intellectualize his interest in the male form. To Sullivan, Edelmann was "a man of immense range of reading, [having] a brain of extraordinary keenness . . . that ranged in its operations from saturnine intelligence concerning men and their motives, to the highest transcendentalisms of German metaphysics." Sullivan also remembered that Edelmann "was as familiar with the great philosophers as with the daily newspapers . . . [and] knew all that the psychologists had written, and much, of his own discernment, that they but recently have begun to unveil."[40]

Such high praise was excessive; Edelmann was not the scholar Sullivan believed him to be. Recording more than anything else the joy he felt at the age of seventeen when Edelmann furnished him with an intellectual base that explained, reinforced, and sanctioned his emotions, Sullivan exaggerated his friend's accomplishments. There is no evidence of Edelmann's having ever received a systematic education in philosophy. This fact, as well as his actual age at the time, suggests that his apparent erudition in philosophy in general, and his knowledge of German transcendentalism in particular, had come from reading general textbooks on the subject. Only the most salient ideas of important transcendentalist philosophers—for the most part those one would expect a handbook to discuss—appear in Sullivan's writings. This was in all probability all of the information Edelmann had and passed down to him.

Thus, in Sullivan's "Essay on Inspiration" (1886) one sees Hegelian dialectics influencing a discussion of the contest between man and the awesome forces he is set to conquer. But typically of the 1880s in general, those ideas were couched

in a context different from Hegel's, as they were mixed with a goodly amount of romanticism. Like Edelmann, Sullivan had assimilated them at fifth or sixth hand rather than deriving them from their German sources. Yet, in spite of his eclectic attitude, Sullivan made direct use of several German transcendentalist concepts. (This is not to imply he had firsthand knowledge of them, but merely to state the possibility that he might have read secondhand sources, such as the general handbooks that Edelmann may have had.) The evidence appears in Sullivan's nomenclature—an aspect of philosophy a general survey invariably discusses. For instance, Sullivan's "Inscrutable Serenity" that appears in his "Essay on Inspiration"—or the "Infinite Creative Spirit," as he later called it—is close to Fichte's *allgemeinen Ich*—the Universal Ego or Self. This is the World-Creating Action, the Moral World Order, the *ordo ordinans*. According to Fichte (and also, incidentally, Schelling), man achieves true humanity when his sensuous nature enables him to act morally with no effort. Schiller expressed this idea in the concept of the *schöne Seele*—the beautiful or radiant soul. The *schöne Seele* is so closely identified with the will of nature that it fulfills the moral law through its own inclination. According to Schiller, only through aesthetic education, by apprehending the metaphysical essence of nature through sense and intuition, would man gain this nobility. Schiller's *schöne Seele* became Sullivan's *radiant soul*; the only appreciable difference between the two expressions was the language used to state them.[41]

Besides introducing Sullivan to philosophy, Edelmann also acquainted him with the notion of "suppressed functions." That idea appears time and again in Sullivan's writings as originating with Edelmann, who made it his own simply because he liked it. In point of fact, Rousseau expressed it first and Froebel expanded it. It had to do originally with how children should be brought up to become the kind of human beings nature intended them to be without having their "natural functions suppressed by social prescriptions."[42] Edelmann simply extended the idea into architecture and considered (as many others in the nineteenth century had) that each building should be designed as if nature had been the author, allowing its inner characteristic to be fully revealed by the composition rather than making it depend on a style imposed by historicist tradition.[43]

Sullivan's membership in Edelmann's intensely philhellenic Lotos Club was important to his developing an interest in the male form. Contemplating men in outdoor activities and comparing them with sources of heroic constructive power had been emotional and instinctive acts of his childhood and youth, but now, in the Lotos Club, he came to understand his inclinations rationally and aesthetically. Whenever they had an occasion, members lived in the boathouse, isolated from the community, engaging in athletic competition and exchanging ideas. Thomas Eakins's photographs of his disciples swimming and wrestling in the nude, outdoors, would furnish an image of some of the activities at the Lotos Club. Eakins's pictures are close in subject matter to drawings of nude men swimming and wrestling Sullivan and Edelmann made in the "Lotos Club Notebook," a sort of diary of events club members kept, presently in the Avery Library.[44] Sullivan enjoyed participating in the group and analyzed what he saw. "When in the sunlight [Bill Curtis, founder of the Club] walked the pier for a plunge, he was a sight for the Greeks, and Louis was enraptured at the play of light and shade."[45]

Edelmann's teachings and Sullivan's participation in activities at the Lotos Club probably served as a catalyst that channeled his interest in the male form into what later—when he wrote the *Autobiography* and recalled his reactions to Michelangelo's frescoes in the Sistine Chapel—had become a full acceptance of Nietzsche's concept of the *Übermensch*, or Superman. Once he read Nietzsche (probably by the turn of the century), Sullivan realized that what he had seen at the Sistine Chapel was the expression of an extraordinarily deep passion for, and the full range of, the symbolic capabilities of the male nude, as well as the extent of its iconographic and iconological possibilities, as a form.

Sullivan's enthusiasm for Michelangelo is natural. His romantic identification of the male form with the idea of power approximated the Renaissance Neoplatonic concept of earthly beauty as the image of the "divine idea." To Sullivan, the male body was the personification of the creative principle in a manner that was not dissimilar to Michelangelo's. It was a potential, immanent, and collected power that could produce, if called for, a forward-thrusting action capable of accomplishing feats of heroic proportions, such as, even, creating the universe. In the Sistine Chapel, Sullivan saw "[t]he man, the man of super-powers, the glorified man, of whom he had dreamed in his childhood . . . striding abroad in the open."[46] Also, "as he grew on through his boyhood, and through the passage through manhood, and to manhood itself, he began to see the powers of man coalesce in his vision into an IDEA of power."[47] His father, American bridge builders, Bill Curtis and John Edelmann at the Lotos Club, and finally Michelangelo had been men who, in an ascending order, could do, think, and imagine things.[48] In the *Autobiography* he says as much:

In childhood his idols had been the big strong men who did things. Later on he had begun to feel the great power of men who could think things; later the expansive power of men who could imagine things; and at last he began to recognize as dominant the will of the Creative Dreamer; he who possessed the power of vision to harness Imagination, to harness the intellect, to make science do his will, to make emotions serve him—for without emotion, nothing.[49]

Architecture, as Sullivan knew it in his youth, was not ample enough to allow him to expand existentially in pursuit of his "Idea." Only in a search for an understanding of the universal would his ill-defined but nevertheless powerful yearnings find relief in a quest for the ideal, or more correctly, for what he considered to be the ideal—within his paradoxically romantic terms. Under those conditions, he had no other psychological recourse except inventing his own architecture, and it took him years of adopting and synthesizing in his own intellect theories and styles of others to achieve that goal. Only then was he able to communicate his yearnings and ideals directly through design.

That "Idea" did not come to him all at once, and he was conscious, as he tells us in the *Autobiography*, that it had unfolded over the years:

Alas, what he [Louis] had assumed to be a single vast veil of mystery that might perhaps lift of a sudden, like a cloud, proved in experience to be a series of gossamer hangings that must slowly rise up, one by one. . . .[50] That IDEA which had its mystical beginning in so small thing as a child's heart, grew and nurtured itself . . . for it needs a long long time, and a rich soil of life-experience, to enable a simple, single idea to grow to maturity and solid strength. . . .[51] He was disturbed, however, by the elusive quality of the main thought he was pursuing, which seemed to recede and grow larger ever as he grew abler to deal with it.[52]

More to the point of his quest to uncover a technique of design that would reveal for all the arcanum of teleology, he wrote:

It is not to be supposed that Louis arrived directly at results as though by magic. Quite the contrary, he arrived slowly though boldly through the years, by means of incessant thought, self correction, hard work and dogged perseverance. For it was his fascinating task to build up a system of technique, a mastery of technique. And such a system could scarcely be expected to reach its fullness of development, short of maturity, assuming it would reach its fullness then, or could ever reach it; for the world of expression is limitless; the theory so deep in idea, so rich in content, as to preclude any ending of its beneficent, allinclusive power.[53]

To reach such "fullness of development" Sullivan continued to require sustenance from poets, thinkers, critics, theorists, and philosophers. Beyond those with whose work he had become acquainted in his youth, however indirectly, Walt Whitman, Hippolyte Taine, John Ruskin, Eugène Viollet-le-Duc, Leopold Eidlitz,

Immanuel Swedenborg, and Herbert Spencer stand out.

Whitman's poetry helped Sullivan translate into an American idiom many of the German concepts he may have learned from Edelmann. A letter he wrote to Whitman on 3 February 1887 documents his first reading of *Leaves of Grass* during the preceding year. "It is less than a year ago [hence 1886]," Sullivan wrote, "that I made your acquaintance so to speak, quite by accident, searching among the shelves of a book-store."[54] Sullivan first extensive quotation of Whitman was in "The Artistic Use of the Imagination," a paper he read to the Chicago Architectural Club on 7 October 1889.[55] *Leaves of Grass* reinforced his belief in the romantic truism that an artist is a creature of instinct rather than reason, and he announced—with even greater emphasis than Wordsworth and Victor Hugo did during the rising years of Romanticism—that "it is only when to the qualities of artist are added those of poet that reflection takes a powerful hand in shaping results." The poet was to him the man of vision, Whitman's "seer," the possessor of a "radiant soul," the "greater springtime." The artist was the "lesser springtime" following the poet's lead.

His conclusions in the "Essay on Inspiration" followed that trend. Communion with nature was to him man's highest achievement. The transcendent creative force he called the "Inscrutable Serenity" predetermined that art was to complete the natural order. In the essay he also told how he finally achieved peace at the moment he realized that his anguish had been caused by his arrogance in attempting to dictate to nature rather than hearing its voice. Approaching nature in humility, he discovered "the gladsome song of the soul at one with Inscrutable Serenity."[56] Communion with nature, however, "would not help him pierce the final mysteries," that is to say, coming to know the fundamental fact from which the cosmos derives. The closest he got to that stage was becoming aware of "the strangely complex thought of rhythm—for all is rhythm."[57] Nature's fundamental characteristic, therefore, is an eternal becoming with the present linked to the potential of the future. That all-sustaining rhythm revealed itself in every work of nature. He also learned that supreme joy lies for man in constructive work and that the production of art, when it follows the precepts of nature, falls into that category. Pleasure is man's reward for participating in a never-ending scheme of creation. In Sullivan's opinion, he could derive satisfaction from his work only through imitation of nature's behavior and manner of production, as foreordained; teaching his fellow men what he had learned was to be his life's work. When death would put an end to his efforts, he would return to nature. An architecture following nature's precepts would result in buildings that retained their identity as specimens, yet their overall designs would respond to unchanging typological principles. (The appearance of a species does not change in many generations, although each member of the group is recognizable as an individual.) The basis of a Hegelian historical becoming (and hence of dialectics) consisted for Sullivan in a progressive understanding of nature through art: "The vital purpose and significance of art is that of attuning its rhythmic song . . . to the rhythms of nature as these are interpreted by the sympathetic soul."[58]

Some of the arguments current in the 1880s in favor of expressing national values in architecture paralleled those ideals.[59] Although not clearly defined, one of the notions of national style was identified with a transcendentalist point of view that had percolated down to the level of popular culture. That attitude was evident in the symposium "What Are the Present Tendencies of Architectural Design in America?" held by the Illinois State Association of Architects on 5 March 1887.[60] In that meeting, Sullivan, along with John Root, Dankmar Adler, Clarence Styles, and William Boyington, attempted to identify a national style of architecture. Incongruities of argument reveal how much they underestimated the magnitude of their task, and how much they made up in self-confidence what they lacked in erudition and method. Root declared that there were four distinct and concurrent trends in American architecture: "catholicity, gravity modified by grace, utility, and splendor." Styles, on the other hand, pleaded for Yankee ingenuity to invent a national style of architecture that would be "an outgrowth of American thought and feeling, and the result of conditions under which that thought and feeling has been developed." Sullivan proposed an introspective method. "It seems to me," he said, "that the eventual outcome of our American architecture will be the emanation of what is going on inside of us at present, the character and quality of our thoughts and our observations, and above all, our reflections." To him, culture consisted of the way in which a nation sought the universal good through an amalgam of commonly shared human instincts. The main function of art was to make people conscious of those intuitive processes and speed up a nation's quest for perpetual happiness. To that end, in an earlier article ("Characteristics and Tendencies of American Architecture"), he had identified "a spirit of liberty" as the salient quality of American culture. He offered no explanation of how that "spirit of liberty" could be made manifest in buildings, and only mentioned two factors that in his opinion determined American love of freedom: no foreign domination had interrupted the development of national culture, and the country possessed the "fruitfulness . . . [of an] unexhausted soil."[61] The vastness of America, its self-sufficiency, and its spirit of egalitarianism were to Sullivan determinants of national identity.

Hippolyte Taine, who taught at the Ecole des Beaux-Arts from 1865 to 1883 (including, therefore, the period of Sullivan's attendance), had also explored notions of a relationship of art and society. The heightened interest in the expression of national values that the outcome of the Franco-Prussian War brought into Taine's thinking may have colored his lectures Sullivan may have attended as a student in Paris. Moreover, in Paris, Sullivan had been prone to accepting Taine's views. His high school teacher Moses Woolson, whom he revered, had introduced him to Taine through *A History of English Literature*. To Taine, a national art had to be fresh and new. In the "Conclusions" of his *Lectures on Art* (1864) he wrote: "The social medium of the present day, now in the course of formation, ought to produce its own works [of art] like the social mediums that have gone before it."[62] This book comprises both *The Philosophy of Art* and *The Ideal in Art*, which Sullivan read in Paris.[63] He found similar ideas when he returned home. Some of his American contemporaries were also reading Taine, available in British editions in 1865 and in American ones ten years later.

According to Taine's "final definition," the end of a work of art is "to reveal some essential or salient character, consequently some important idea, clearer and more completely than is attainable from real objects."[64] Taine believed in an ideal function of art, but he also considered that an observer could learn much about the society from which an artist originated by analyzing what "important ideas" he expressed in his art. A work of art was determined for Taine "[b]y an aggregate which is the general state of the mind and surrounding circumstances"; a national aesthetic was as autochthonous as vegetation;[65] and a modern aesthetic, while nondogmatic, would nevertheless conform to certain social, economic, and political laws.

Sullivan embraced those ideas which so closely matched his beliefs as general guidelines for determining national characteristics in art, but inasmuch as they were new (especially in America), he proceeded laboriously to make them evident in his work, there being no body of architecture to serve him as iconographical precedent. After defining his ideas during the second half of the 1880s, they remained in his mind for many years only at a theoretical level. He moved from theory to practice when he applied an eclectic method based on a number of widely held views on architecture he borrowed mainly from writings by John Ruskin, Eugène Viollet-le-Duc, and Leopold Eidlitz.

Ruskin's contentions that excellence in architecture depended not on planning and structure but on ornamentation and artistic composition, that decorative details are to copy the most common forms of vegetal and animal life, and that the design and application of ornamentation was to follow the organic principles of its models are all ideas close to Sullivan's own, yet there are fundamental differences between the two men.[66] To Ruskin, "as nature adorns earth so should man adorn buildings" to contribute "to his mental health, power, and pleasure,"[67] but unlike Sullivan, who was an agnostic, Ruskin saw a profoundly religious connotation in that way of linking the good, the true, and the beautiful. He held that imitating forms of nature in architecture was, more than a means of creating beautiful buildings, an act of thanksgiving to God for having created nature for the service of man.[68] To Ruskin man stood superior to and distinct from nature,[69] a notion Sullivan would never have agreed with.[70]

Sullivan did not believe he had invented a new architecture as much as he was certain he had discovered the method nature had prescribed for the creation of architecture since the beginning of time; he saw himself as a new Prometheus. But in spite of those intensely personal views, one must turn to Ruskin and Emerson for the theoretical basis of his ornamentation, which was to play two important expressive roles in his work. Ruskin had taught him to look at *Natura naturata* (or "created nature"); Emerson, at *Natura naturans* (the all-knowing creative principle of nature).

In his "Lamp of Beauty" Ruskin pointed out how architecture was to mirror the gorgeousness of nature. "All most lovely forms and thoughts are directly taken from natural objects," he wrote, and conversely, "forms which are *not* taken from natural objects *must* be ugly."[71] Those natural objects were to be lovely in themselves, and color was to Ruskin one of the sources of their loveliness. Rendering an organism beautiful through color was nature's way; architecture had no choice but to follow suit.[72] "I cannot consider architecture as in any wise perfect without colour," he stated,[73] since a building was "a kind of organised creature."[74]

Sullivan went beyond Ruskin's mimetism. Reflecting nature's gorgeousness in architecture had to him a reason beyond rendering a building lovely. By echoing the productions of nature he hoped to help humanity realize its vocation to become one with nature through the observation and use of architecture. The link of man and nature was not to be a result of moral duty, as Ruskin proposed, but a consequence of surrendering the self to beauty, which would be rewarded with a state of constant ecstasy, as Emerson had explained.[75]

Sullivan relied on the instincts nature had given him for designing like nature, or so he believed. He could not accept Ruskin's advice that imitation of specific historical periods would lead to imitation of nature.[76] To Sullivan that would imply substituting an imitation for nature, as a model. Ruskin's advice was historicist, dogmatic, and unfeeling; better to take instinctively from a myriad of sources whatever was needed at the moment and combine it best to promote gorgeousness. Thus it is we see Sullivan mixing in his ornamentation Islamic and Celtic motifs with naturalistic renditions of foliage and perhaps using as a background a pattern loosely derived from the Gothic.

In his work, combinations of motifs from different periods were not to be read taxonomically to identify the style of a building or of an ornamental piece, because *style*, to Sullivan, had nothing to do with evoking or imitating past periods of architecture. In a typically transcendentalist vein he identified *style* as the portrayal of essential character through outward appearance, and advised young architects to make note of the integrity of the *style* "of running water, of a pine tree, of a cow grazing in a meadow, of the sweeping eagle in his flight or [of] the open apple blossom, the toiling workhorse [or] the branching oak."[77] Like Viollet-le-Duc, Sullivan could have said, "Proceed as nature does in its productions and everything your brain may conceive will have style."[78] That notion of style as an unchanging entity existing beyond the reaches of taxonomy and archaeology was possibly the most important lesson Sullivan learned from Viollet-le-Duc. For Viollet-le-Duc, style was an intimate relationship of efficiency existing between a function, the form that serves it, the materials out of which the form is made, and the methods of construction with which it is built. As in nature, from which he took his model, such a relationship in design had to yield a *natural* beauty.[79]

Sullivan's concept of style—in spite of its close similarity with Viollet-le-Duc's—never went so far as accepting technology and the service of material needs as the bases of a new architecture, and its style. Neither would his American transcendentalist leanings allow him to approve of Viollet-le-Duc's attempts to formulate a style by applying Cartesian logic to understand the uses of past architectural forms. Out of a merging of logic, erudition, and engineering, Viollet-le-Duc believed, architects would derive a method similar to the empirical one French Positivists endorsed for the sciences, philosophy, and the arts.[80] Viollet's notion of *l'architecte savant* could not be further removed from the ideals of Sullivan. Neither had his ideas on architecture much in common with the more widespread nineteenth-century mechanicalist notion of functionalism, and of the proper way to express it in buildings. *"C'est notre maître, mon cher Sullivan, qui roulairait de gros yeux s'il te voyait commettre de telles hérésies, de pareils mensonges!"*[81] said Jacques Hermant, a former fellow student of Sullivan's at Emile Vaudremer's atelier in Paris, voicing his shock when he saw Sullivan had covered metallic structures with brick and terra-cotta, that he had clad his buildings internally in granite, onyx, plaster, or marble, but that their metal supports were nowhere visible.[82] Presumably both Hermant and his teacher Vaudremer accepted Viollet-le-Duc's precept that the first condition of good architecture was not to deceive,*"ni dans la composition de l'ensemble, ni dans celle des moindres détails de l'édifice à construire."*[83] Indeed, perhaps Viollet-le-Duc might have dismissed Sullivan as another gifted *architecte dessinateur* had he lived long enough to know his work.[84] Moreover, in one of their rare agreements, both Viollet-le-Duc and Ruskin rejected the notion that art may serve to express the metaphysical.[85] This issue, above all, separates Sullivan from both Ruskin and Viollet-le-Duc.

In that respect, Sullivan's ideas are much closer to Leopold Eidlitz's.[86] Born in Prague in 1823, Eidlitz arrived in New York twenty years later, finding that Emerson and his followers—Horatio Greenough among them—had created a sympathetic intellectual climate for beliefs he had acquired in Germany and Austria.[87] Eidlitz soon became prominent in architectural circles, was one of the founders of the American Institute of Architects in 1857, and published a series of articles in *The Crayon* around that time presenting his views on architecture. Those articles served him later as the basis for his book *The Nature and Function of Art, More Especially of Architecture*, of 1881.

I have found no evidence of Sullivan's owning a copy of Eidlitz's book, nor did he mention Eidlitz in any of his writings. But it is hard to imagine that he had not read Eidlitz's book carefully, as even some of his metaphors seem borrowed from it. Eidlitz, like Sullivan later, referred to nature as a means to establish a connection between a building and the transcendental idea from which its design emanated.[88] According to Eidlitz:

> *A work of art, like a work of nature, is a realized idea, and the ideal is the essence of architecture. It is the godlike attempt to create a new organism, which, because it is new, cannot be an imitation of any work of nature, and, because it is an organism, must be developed according to the methods of nature. It is this fact which places architecture . . . above all other arts. If a building can express no idea, as ideas are expressed in the works and through the laws of nature, then architecture never was an art.[89]*

The relation of form and function was also important to Eidlitz, but not as much as to Viollet-le-Duc. To Eidlitz, "natural organisms serve the purpose of teaching the relation of form to function, but the majority of men are by the process of so-called civilization removed from nature, and surrounded by creations of art." For Eidlitz, as well as for Sullivan, the word *art* had a pejorative

meaning, signifying sophistry in the handling of form, while poetry was to both "the expression of an idea in matter," or in other words, of the transcendent.[90] To Sullivan, and to Eidlitz, *style* was the characterization of a building's image. It depended more on a kinship of composition and decoration than on planning, construction, and structure, as Viollet-le-Duc had stated. (To Sullivan, Eidlitz, and also Viollet-le-Duc, the term *style* had the meaning that Zubiri—and I myself, by extension—ascribe to the word *iconography*.) As the student expressed it in Sullivan's "Kindergarten Chats," "a building, to be good architecture, must, first of all, clearly . . . be its image, as you would say."[91]

In relation to style—as he understood it—Eidlitz believed that the highest attainment of any art was to reproduce emotions, and noted how painting and sculpture achieved that aim by arresting motion.[92] Architecture was handicapped in that respect. It had a limited capacity to express emotion and lacked the representational range of painting or of sculpture. It could only hope to express emotions associated with stress and strain. Its expressive possibilities began and ended with the relationship of architectural masses and gravity. However, inasmuch as the human body is the noblest natural organism, architecture—according to Eidlitz—should resort to the human form to suggest feelings, as painting and sculpture do. He wrote:

> *The human frame does mechanical work, sometimes with the labor of a carrier of burdens, and then again with the ease of an athlete. It is these gradations of ease, grace, directness, and expression with which . . . mechanical work is done by the human frame, which furnish the architect the elements of art expressions in his structures. . . . Every structure, like the human body, that assumes to be a work of art, must also be possessed of a soul.[93]*

Eidlitz's main contribution to Sullivan was to make him aware of that kind of heroic architectural anthropomorphism, the best method—in Eidlitz's opinion—for representing the characteristic essence of a building, for giving it *style*. "It is the problem of the architect," he wrote, "to depict the emotions of the structure he deals with; to depict, as it were, the soul of the structure."[94] It was through Eidlitz that Sullivan finally came to consider buildings as paradigms of athletic virility. Describing Richardson's Marshall Field Wholesale Store in Chicago, Sullivan wrote in "Kindergarten Chats":

> Here is a man *for you to look at. A man that walks on two legs instead of four, has active muscles, lungs and other viscera; a man that lives and breathes, that has red blood; a real man, a manly man; a virile force–broad, vigorous and with a whelm of energy–an entire male. . . . I call it, in a world of barren pettiness, a male; for it sings the song of procreant power, as others have squalled of miscegenation.*[95]

This description served as one example of a general architectural principle, for in "Kindergarten Chats" Sullivan also stated:

> The architecture we *seek shall be as a man, active, alert, supple, strong, sane. A generative man. A man having five senses all awake; eyes that fully see, ears that are attuned to every sound; a man living in his present, knowing and feeling the vibrancy of that ever-moving movement, with heart to draw it in and mind to put it out. . . . To live, wholly to live, is the manifest consummation of existence.*[96]

Sullivan revealed much of his thought in this passage. "The vibrancy of that evermoving movement" refers to nature's constant recreation of the universe. "The heart to draw it in" stands for man's intuitive understanding of nature's process of creation, while "the mind to put it out" alludes to his intellectual ability to express it in art. This process of "drawing in" and "putting out" is but another expression of how man is part of nature, "for all [of nature] is rhythm,"[97] and man's creative force mirrors the creative force of nature. The result, "wholly to live," meant attaining the ultimate reward, a state of perpetual ecstasy.

Finally, the influences of Immanuel Swedenborg and Herbert Spencer on Sullivan need to be addressed. One of Sullivan's lifelong interests was

to master an architectural expression of Swedenborg's correspondences, with which he was acquainted; he referred to them in a symposium the Illinois Association of Architects held on 2 April 1887 on the subordination of details to mass in architectural design.[98] While *The Autobiography of an Idea* gives no information on how Sullivan learned about Swedenborg's theories, we know that there were people close to him who were interested in such philosophies. His mother, although belonging to no organized church, subscribed to religious convictions close to a Swedenborgian deism, and Sullivan claimed a strong affinity with his mother's beliefs.[99] His good friend John Wellborn Root held similar philosophical views, belonged to the Swedenborgian Church, and attempted to establish principles of design based on Swedenborg's correspondences.[100] Root's partner, Daniel Burnham, also belonged to that denomination.[101] John Edelmann is another possible source; at some time he may have been curious to know why transcendentalists were interested in Swedenborg. There was as well a large number of books and pamphlets on the subject that Sullivan might have come across.[102] An important one among them—and one he might have read—is Emerson's excellent monograph "Swedenborg or the Mystic," published in *Representative Men: Seven Lectures* (1850).

According to Swedenborg—the eighteenth-century Swedish mystic, philosopher, and scientist—love and wisdom are God's most important attributes, emanate from Him, and sustain the universe. He also believed that universal rationality, or wisdom, comes into harmony with the masculine principle of the cosmos, and emotion, or love, with the feminine. Since to Swedenborg the realms of the physical and the spiritual were the two halves of a transcendent totality, he posited that correspondences of wisdom-love, reason-emotion, and masculine-feminine existed between the two spheres.[103] From such concepts Sullivan finally learned that the heroism he sought as a result of becoming one with nature could be achieved only by accepting the dictates of the universal law, by striking a balance not so much of *sophia* and *agape*, but of reason and emotion, and expressing these in art as masculinity and femininity. In that scheme, the feminine was superior to the masculine, and Sullivan's great aspiration was to allow the feminine element in design—the gorgeousness of the building—to dominate the composition completely, and to conceal the masculine-rational sense of geometry that sustains and gives order to it. Nature behaved similarly: the leaves and flowers of a shrub conceal the branches that give it measure, order, and rhythm.

Transcendentalizing Herbert Spencer's mechanicist conception of the universe was another of Sullivan's iconographical goals. To Spencer, force, motion, and matter were the constants of a universe mechanically conceived. Force produced motion, motion determined the diffusion of matter, and conversely, concentration of matter slowed down motion. Fundamental cycles of evolution and dissolution grew out of each other, and that continuous creation of the universe was "the law that transcends proof."[104] Sullivan extolled

those concepts with fanatical zeal. He believed that they brought objective validity and scientific verification to ideas that in reality came from the transcendentalism that suffused his romanticism. To him, Spencer's philosophy sanctioned the belief that the subjective and the objective evolve into each other and are interchangeable because they are both reflections of the same transcendent rhythm. Lifting himself up to the level of *Natura naturans*, Sullivan sought to evoke ideas of mineral, plant, and animal through geomorphism, phytomorphism, and anthropomorphism in his architecture. He sought to express the three natural realms in his work in ways that seemed as if each evolved from the other two in rhythms that brought new dimensions to Spencer's conceptions. In his "Essay on Inspiration" Sullivan came to the conclusion that nature's secret lay beyond a progression of life to death to life again. The elemental rhythm sustaining the all in all led him to "the strangely complex thought of rhythm—for all is rhythm."[105]

4: *Birth of an Iconography: 1890–92*

In three designs of the period 1890–92—the Getty and Wainwright tombs and the Transportation Building of the Chicago Columbian Exhibition—Sullivan found that by using exterior ornamentation on a rectangular building he could create an architectural imagery subservient to his idealist iconography. The block-like shape of the building would represent the rational or masculine element in Swedenborg's terms, while decoration would stand for the emotional-feminine. In Sullivan's mind, a higher power of nature had determined that the geometric rational-masculine was to synthesize itself with the ornamental emotional-feminine to express the oneness of the good, the true, and the beautiful. His teleology, derived from his personal synthesis of ideas of Swedenborg and Spencer, also bound together the three strands that in one way or another had shaped his thinking since childhood. The rational was represented

by geometry, the emotional or lyrical by ornamentation, and their synthesis constituted the heroic. The realization of this third, synthetic strand would lead to the manic feelings any intelligent observer should experience when confronting creation. The heroic, in art, was a mimesis of the results of creation by *Natura naturans*.

The first full Sullivanesque iconographical statement appeared in the Carrie Eliza Getty Tomb (1890), Graceland Cemetery, Chicago, the first among his mature buildings to carry external ornamentation (fig. 87). Recognizing its importance, Wright called it "a great poem addressed to human sensibilities." More to the point, concerning the building's ability to express the basic, underlying rhythm of the universe, he added, "Outside the realm of music, what finer requiem?"[1] To paraphrase Sullivan, the "strong, athletic [Richardsonian] form" of the building carried with

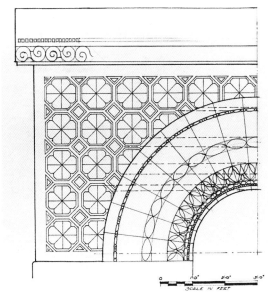

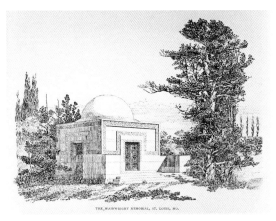

THE WAINWRIGHT MEMORIAL, ST. LOUIS, MO.

Figure 91.
*Wainwright Tomb, front
(1892–93).*
Photograph by
Narciso G. Menocal.

Figure 92.
*Wainwright Tomb, rear
(1892–93).*
Photograph by
Narciso G. Menocal.

ease its "raiment of poetic imagery . . . of which we dream."[2]

The Getty Tomb is an almost cubic block of gray Bedford limestone with a projecting cornice, a low stylobate, and three openings: an arcuated door at the front and a semicircular window at each of the sides. Each wall is divided into two areas: three ranges of smooth ashlar below and a pattern of octagons in relief above. Each octagon has a stylized, eight-pointed star within it, a Néo-Grec design adapted from pl. 129 of Ruprich-Robert's *Flore ornementale*, as David Van Zanten has shown.[3]

The Moorish appearance of the Getty Tomb was in line with an interest Sullivan had acquired through his ornamental work for synagogue commissions (which came to the office through Adler), since at least 1873.[4] (Because of Gottfried Semper's design for the Dresden Synagogue, from 1836, an Islamic style evoking the golden period of Jewish culture in medieval Spain had become standard for synagogues.)[5] More to the point, Sullivan had been engaged in the interior decoration of the Kehilath Anshe Ma'ariv Synagogue a few months before working on the tomb.[6]

Displaying an awareness that Moorish geometric patterns serve as sensuous textures, agents of aesthetic pleasure, and modules of design, Sullivan derived all the dimensions of the Getty Tomb from the octagons of the pattern. The front of the tomb is twelve octagons wide and the side sixteen, a ratio of 3:4. The door and the masonry at each side of it have equal widths, four octagons each. The dimensions of the archivolts around the door and windows also relate to the octagonal module,

and the crowns of the arches correspond in height to important points in the pattern (fig. 88).

Sullivan extended this Oriental trend into the Charlotte Dickson Wainwright Tomb, Bellefontaine Cemetery, St. Louis (1892–93), a building that resembles a North African funerary *qubba* (figs. 89–90).[7] The office rendering of the tomb shows an isolated white cube of a building surmounted by a low dome and flanked by parapets that extend forward to establish a front terrace, the whole placed in the midst of a romantic, abandoned North African orchard. Only beams of moonlight and poems by Hafiz are missing to complete the illusion. Reality is more prosaic. The Wainwright mausoleum is surrounded by many tombs of indifferent design in a parklike American cemetery in Missouri. Possibly searching for a greater harmony in his design in terms of the Islamic type that served as its inspiration, Sullivan placed an ornamental band along the top and side edges of the building and carried it across at the level of the parapets, to surround the openings (fig. 91). This ornament is repeated on all sides, but with different motifs in each. The shape and position of these bands suggest that the source of the design was an Islamic *pishtak*—the raised, square frame surrounding the entrance arch of important Muslim buildings. Indeed, the ornamented bands evoke the Koranic inscriptions that usually run along the edges of the *pishtak*. On another level, a comparison of front and back views of the building is useful to ascertain the roles of geometry, composition, and ornamentation in Sullivan's architecture. While from the

front the tomb has an air of dignified elegance and even of monumentality tempered by the human scale of the door, the parapets, and the terrace—as well as a definite Islamic flair—the back is different. The ornamental bands are not visually strong enough to dominate over the geometrical statement of a cube surmounted by a dome. The result is stark, dry, and academic—almost a bad imitation of Boullée that shows the limitations of Sullivan's style when the feminine element does not prevail (fig. 92).

The Oriental flair of the Getty and Wainwright tombs is also evident in the Transportation Building of the World's Columbian Exposition, designed a few months before the Wainwright Tomb. Its gate—the Golden Doorway—was a modified *pishtak* surrounded by *chatris*, the small pavilions surmounted with cupolas that generally flank the entrances of Indian mosques (fig. 93). More to the point, Sullivan introduced into the design that most characteristic of Islamic features, polychromy. But as had been the case of the pattern of stylized stars on the Getty Tomb, the polychromy of the Transportation Building was of French ascendancy, not Islamic. Externally—and excluding the Golden Doorway—the building consisted of a long red wall punctuated by arches (fig. 94). Sullivan established the design for the Transportation Building by turning inside out the arcaded courtyard of Félix Duban's Palais des Etudes of the Ecole des Beaux-Arts, from 1833–39, which Ernest-Georges Coquart ("one of the most violent of the young Néo-Grecs," in David Van Zanten's opinion)[8] had painted red in 1873, only a few months before Sullivan's arrival in Paris.

It is evident that Sullivan's use of Islamic features during these years was much more related to the Néo-Grec origins of his education than to any desire for an Islamic style revival. Pattern, for instance, was never the most prominent component of design in any of his Islamic-like buildings, in spite of its ordering role. Doors and windows were always far more conspicuous, their shape, ornamentation, material, and position making them stand out as the dominant features in the composition. That un-Islamic predominance of openings over pattern is peculiarly Western, as is evident, for instance, in Sa'adian mausolea erected in Marrakesh under Andalusian influence in the sixteenth century. Because of their indirect connection with Christian Europe, those buildings are among the few Islamic monuments to emphasize door openings more as means of entry than as structural arches. Sullivan favored that kind of North African style over other varieties of Islamic architecture (as Dimitri Tselos noted),[9] possibly for two reasons. It was closer to his own Western tradition, and since North Africa featured a more "primitive" kind of Islamic design than Spain, Egypt, or Persia, its architecture was closer to the Néo-Grec notion of archetype. Sullivan's choice of source, therefore, begins to explain why none of his designs can hope to match the algebraic subtlety of the best Islamic pavilions, like those of the Alhambra. Nevertheless, the Transportation Building was the first Sullivan design in which exterior plasticity took precedence over the expression of the mechanical functions of the elements of the facade. It was also the first to create an inversion of that standard rule of decorum that holds that the exterior appearance of a public building should be dignified and sedate, albeit urbane, while the interior might be as freely ornamented as the architect wished it to be.[10]

The experience Sullivan acquired in designing the Transportation Building contributed in no small measure to the success of subsequent iconography he sought in skyscraper design. For instance, at the corners of the second floor and on the main entrance spandrels of the Union Trust Building, St. Louis (1892), stood large terra-cotta winged heraldic lions, *sejant érectes*. This was the first instance of Sullivan's use of heraldic devices in commercial architecture. It seems to be a consequence not only of the Transportation Building, with its winged figures and its fountains with heads of lions gushing water, but more deeply an influence of the pervading atmosphere of the Columbian Exposition. The Exposition had opened the door for the City Beautiful Movement (and

Figure 96.
Fontaine des Innocents,
Paris, Jean Goujon
(1549), design altered in
1787.
Photograph by Narcio G. Menocal.

the Burnham Plan of Chicago, which literally transformed the city), as well as for a number of new governmental and educational buildings, and numerous banks, all in academic styles, the whole allowing for an image of classical urbanity Chicago had lacked in the 1880s. While it is well known that Sullivan fought the rising tide of academic classicism, one must be aware as well of the influence of the fair in his work. Typically, Sullivan metabolized that influence and transformed it into the energy he required to advance his quest for a style that would express his Swedenborgian conceptions. The "feminine," represented by a heightened interest in ornamentation and by symbols of urbanity, was an important element in the equation. Heraldic devices were part of the new language.

The most outstanding among those featured in the Transportation Building were the lion-head fountains by the secondary entrances and the winged figures on the exterior spandrels. The fountains were located in the small pavilions flanking the secondary entrances (fig. 95). They recall Jean Goujon's Fontaine des Innocents in Paris (fig. 96). Sullivan followed its second design, with which he was familiar. That is to say, his model was not the original fountain of 1549, consisting

of two bays on the rue aux Fers (present rue Berger) and one bay on the rue Saint-Denis, but the fountain on a freestanding square plan as redesigned in 1787 and subsequently moved by Davioud a few yards away from its original emplacement to give way to the building of Les Halles during the Second Empire.[11]

Important differences between the two designs are that Sullivan deleted the attic, the dome, and the Corinthian order, turned the *renommées* and the cartouches into nude male athletes, and changed Goujon's naiads into ordinary classical female nudes. He also blinded the arch and placed a tympanum on an order with foliated capitals that evoke, but do not mimic, the Corinthian order. The tympanum is entirely covered with vegetal ornamentation establishing a symmetrical composition about a central vertical foliated burst that resembles a heraldic *panache*. The lion-head fountain is inset immediately under the tympanum, and here he allowed his imagination the upper hand. While heads of lions conventionally issue from a more or less extended ornamented mane, he extended the mane far more than usual and turned it into a splendid vegetal frame around the well-defined head.

Another important feature of the Transportation Building was winged female figures, one painted above every other pier (fig. 97). A contemporary

description of them reads: "Above the pier of every other opening is a large figure, 14 ft. high, of a woman holding a screen in front between her hands, with the name of some famous inventor in regard to Transportation. The idea of Mr. Sullivan in these stiff and almost archaic figures was to get the idea of motion expressed without movement of the body, and for this reason the figures, which are all similar, have large outspread wings of white colour, which detaches them somewhat from the main colour scheme. The figures are painted on canvas, and afterwards applied to the facade."[12]

There is a considerable difference between the quasi-Byzantinesque geometrical abstraction of the figures, as executed, and the soft, naturalistic contours of a preliminary drawing in the Avery collection (fig. 98).[13] The drawing, in Paul Sprague's opinion, is not in Sullivan's hand, and he adds: "As it is of a relatively large size and on tracing paper, it was probably made by an assistant, perhaps Wright, for the purpose of combining several of Sullivan's designs into a single drawing preparatory to working it out in detail at a larger scale."[14] That drawing points to the fact that the idea of a figure in a frontal, hieratic position came later rather than sooner and that there might have been a consensus, possibly fostered by Sullivan himself, that the figures were to be idealized (albeit anatomically correct) renditions that in the late nineteenth century passed for evocations of the classical.[15]

It would be easy to argue that Sullivan was able to design the exterior of the Transportation Building as freely—and picturesquely—as he did because the composition was meant for a structure in a fair, and by right the design should have been as festive as possible. But that is not my argument. My position is that the tombs and the exhibition building allowed Sullivan to acquire a mastery over an ornamental exterior plasticity that was entirely personal, even more, idiosyncratic, and that he eventually applied to almost every building type he designed, with residential architecture—his weakest—being practically the only exception. By subverting the rules of decorum, Sullivan achieved his truly mature style, the one that completely matched his concept of architecture as a phenomenon derived from nature and in many ways equal to it, as it followed "rules of design" that he saw first in nature (and on which depended the gorgeousness of nature). At last, therefore, imagery and iconography (in Zubiri's terms) were parts of a whole in which Eastern and Western characteristics were integrated in a highly controlled technique; design was imbued with universality through a Swedenborgian balance of reason and emotion; and he was free to give vent to his lyricism while at the same time keeping it safe from excessive picturesqueness.

5: Growth of an Iconography: The Skyscrapers of 1892–1903

Sullivan's mature vision—which the Getty and Wainwright tombs and the Transportation Building had clarified for him—became too expansive to be fettered by considerations that would have been important to his teachers, or even to himself, a few years earlier. For instance, Vaudremer, his *patron* at the Ecole des Beaux-Arts, would never have accepted having architectural elements play subjective roles; much less would he have accepted that architecture should depend on a transcendentalist program. Vaudremer made evident his motto—*Ars in Vero* (art in truth)—in mechanistic terms of construction and in volumetric compositions that made the observer aware of the plan of a building from the outside.[1] Sullivan was not much interested in expressing the plans of tall office buildings, and neither was he interested in planning, which was mostly Adler's work. A majority were either U- or E-shaped, yet Adler makes us read them from the outside as rectangular parallelepipeds. Neither was Sullivan interested in a narrowly mechanical expression of function in the compositional and ornamental programs he established for Adler's designs. Quite the opposite—he used them to extend his method of architecture beyond limits acceptable to his peers, American and foreign. The intimation of organic life in architecture and the suggestion that certain structural elements were capable of movement became more important to him than the physical functions of buildings, their methods of construction, or the needs of clients, issues he considered as pedestrian problems easily solved by anyone of normal intelligence.[2]

Those ideas fit with Emerson's teachings. In his essay "On Art," Emerson proposed that the essence of each being was best symbolized by its external appearance. Correspondingly, in Sullivan's mind, planning and construction—depending as they do on the physical needs of society and on technological progress—were related not at all to nature, but only to the material development of civilization. Only through ornamentation would architecture echo the gorgeousness of nature and reach its true goal. A sensuous relationship between art and the observer was important to him. To achieve it, he had no qualms about concealing structure under ornamentation, or even about making mullions look like structural elements, as had been the case in the Wainwright Building. On the other hand, there is an undeniable French logic in his method of composition, and time and again he endorsed the Beaux-Arts system of design, of fixing the *parti* by an *esquisse* and subsequently developing it in the *rendu*. Yet at no point did he endorse a French aesthetic. In his *Autobiography* he maintained that the Ecole des Beaux-Arts concerned itself chiefly with method, "yielding results of extraordinary brilliancy, but which, after all, was not the reality he sought. . . . He felt that beneath the law of the School [that is, the basis of its methodology] lay a law [that of nature, or more accurately, *Natura naturans*] which it ignored unsuspectingly, or with fixed intention—the law he had seen set forth in the stillness of the Sistine Chapel, which he saw everywhere in the open of life."[3]

Because of his embracing Emersonian transcendentalism and Whitmanesque romanticism, Sullivan's attempts at embracing cosmic universality yielded solutions that were quintessentially American and even more, by the time he evolved them, Midwestern. But his method for designing skyscrapers reveals two main sources, one French and the other American. It shows influence from French romantic rationalism and Viollet-le-Duc's structuralism, but his iconography was largely determined by American transcendentalism and romanticism. Those two aspects (the French and the American) may be separated from each other only for purposes of art historical analysis. But then, yet at another level, he also used classical forms in unclassical ways, following French examples. Moreover, he also found useful Viollet-le-Duc's endorsement of the Gothic as a point of departure for a modern architecture devoid of historicist connotation.[4] Thus, in his skyscrapers of 1892 and beyond, he translated what he considered to be the essence of the Gothic as a system of forces in equilibrium into his own transcendentalist language. His new skyscraper type was to be like a new and organic Gothic cathedral jetting forth out of the earth like an exultant being, but now rising to remind man not of the bliss of life everlasting but of the joy of being one with nature in the here and now. In his own words, his tall buildings were to have an "element of loftiness, the suggestion of slenderness and aspiration, the soaring quality as of a thing rising from the earth as a unitary utterance, Dionysian in beauty."[5]

But the skyscraper performed two actions. One was subjective, it soared; the other was objective, it bore down on the soil. Sullivan solved this conflict by going to the original romantic simile and compared the pier to the trunk of a tree, to the primeval column that grew tall at the same time it was borne down by the weight of branches. That duality could not be transferred directly into construction; it created a paradox that Sullivan justified with transcendentalist arguments. In a pier, as in the trunk of a tree, there should be a constant rhythm of pulling up and pushing down. He identified the subjective component of growth (or upward pull) in the pier as the "Rhythm of Life" and characterized objective downbearing compression as the "Rhythm of Death." In an ambiguity he sought passionately, the objective became subjective and the subjective objective at the will of the observer, and according to his frame of mind. The capacity he granted architecture for being in a constant state of flux echoed the perpetual rhythmic becoming of the cosmos,[6] yet his metaphor went beyond a Spencerian model. In its downward pressure, in its recognition of gravity, the skyscraper was geomorphic; in its growth, like the trunk of a tree, it was phytomorphic; its gesture, its leaping aloft, was anthropomorphic. His tall office buildings became images of the unity of all that exists—mineral, vegetal, and animal—in the oneness of the cosmos. By making the images of the geomorphic, phytomorphic, and anthropomorphic interchangeable, they became like the facets of a crystal. In the end, all sang the same anthem. The result was a conception of subjective elasticity in structures that allowed for symbolizing the transcendent.

In 1892, Sullivan designed the first of two projects for the Trust and Savings Building, St. Louis.[7] This was his first tall building to respond to his transcendentalist program. The composition of the first project—perhaps even unconsciously—was a free translation of the Walker Warehouse into a metal-cage building, yet with differences between the two buildings standing out more prominently than the similarities (fig. 99). Among the differences, one notices that the base of the new building stood distinct from the rest of the structure, a feature not present in the Walker Warehouse. The base of the first Trust and Savings Building gave the impression of being load-bearing, when it actually was not. Sullivan's aim was to establish a programmatic contrast between the base and a frankly structural eleven-story arcade. The three bays of the base and the nine of the superstructure created a 1:3 rhythm that carried as well into the side elevation of what was to be a corner building. The arrangement turned the pier-mullion-pier of the Wainwright into a pier-mullion-mullion-pier system, accommodating the wide span of the arches at street level. Sullivan designed the superstructure differently from that of the Walker Warehouse (cf. fig. 72). The arcade of the warehouse seemed to be neatly punched out from a smooth wall with an almost abstract surface, and the overall composition of the building evoked an image of sharp, machine-tooled geometry, with the piers being what remained of the wall after the arches had been excised from it.

The superstructure of the St. Louis building, on the other hand, was a clearly defined structural system with each vertical feature equally articulated with sheaves of moldings encasing or not a metal support. Those moldings were the key to the new iconography. By creating a closed circuit, they established an expression of "the rhythms of Life and Death," of subjective upward elasticity and objective compression. Beginning at any point, one can follow the moldings down, then, with no interruption, across the second-floor sill, up the next pier, and finally, closing the cycle, across the top through the arch beneath the attic. As this circuit may be established clockwise or counterclockwise, neither the subjective expression of upward movement nor the objective statement of physical pressure is compromised. The piers seem to be giving the impression of carrying the weight down to the base while at the same time they are also capable of leaping, like limbs of a human frame. Sullivan reinforced his anthropo-

morphic scheme with two features. One was the opposing, frankly supporting character of the first-floor base, with its sweeping arches. The other was the way in which the lack of a mullion in the second-floor windows abstracted the opening, extending its width from pier to pier. That was an important feature in the design. It increased the buoyancy of the superstructure, making it spring, as it were, on the masonry base.

The second design for the Trust and Savings Building was for a larger structure than the first (fig. 100). It was sixteen floors high, against twelve, and had eight bays on the front and four on the side instead of the nine and three of the first project. Sullivan retained the design of the superstructure of the first design since it responded superbly to his desire for a transcendentalist iconography. But now he altered the base, and for the better. Instead of broad arches that created ambiguities of structural expression with the superstructure, he established for the base a post-

Figure 100.
Trust and Savings
Building, St. Louis,
second design (1893).
Hugh Morrison,
Louis Sullivan: Prophet of Mod-
ern Architecture, 1935.

Figure 101.
Guaranty Building,
Buffalo (1894–96).
Chicago Architectural
Photographing Company.

and-lintel system with a broad beam and stout columns that made evident the structural character of each of the vertical elements in the design. The new base did not compromise the iconographical program. On the contrary, the exaggerated lintel worked as a summer beam in its etymological sense of *sagma*, or pack saddle, carrying visually the superstructure. At the same time, the squat columns below it, with their broad capitals, translated into architecture the muscular strain of an Atlas-like feat, supporting the colossal weight of the building. The superstructure soared above, up to the height where Sullivan had poised a thin albeit broadly projecting cornice. A delicate lid, almost weightless, it gave the impression of floating, riding on the subjective upward forces of the structure. Its function seemed to contain them within the limits of the building, ever so lightly, at

the moment when those subjective, upward forces had spent themselves in their ascent and were about to fall into their objective descent. To reinforce that iconography, Sullivan placed a female figure with outspread wings on each of the corner piers, as if to symbolize the essence of their ascending character—of "the rhythm of Life." Above each of the other piers a tuft of vegetal ornamentation played a similar role.

The Guaranty Building, the last commission of the firm of Adler & Sullivan, came next among the buildings showing a transcendentalist iconography (fig. 101).[8] It is difficult to surmise why Sullivan abandoned here the scheme of the two Trust and Savings designs, but two thoughts come to mind. One is that he sometimes worked with a trial-and-error method. (For instance, the St. Nicholas Hotel and the Chicago Stock Exchange

Building–two designs which I do not see as carrying a transcendentalist iconography–stand chronologically between the second Trust and Savings project and the Guaranty Building.) A second thought is that Sullivan may not have been pleased with the harsh staccato vertical interruption the window mullions established in the upward rhythm of the Trust and Savings designs. Following his trial-and-error ways, he may have wished to experiment with a translation of the Wainwright design to a transcendentalist iconography. The advantages in this case would be that all the vertical elements would appear to be the same, window mullions would not appear to exist, and the success of the upward rhythm, on which so much of the iconography depended, was assured.

Because of their resemblance to each other, it is standard to pair the Guaranty and Wainwright buildings, yet they are only superficially similar, for they are fundamentally different. The Wainwright was based on classical precedent, while the Guaranty followed Sullivan's new Gothic-like style. Now his piers could indeed "seem to grow" with the "soaring Gothic" while at the same time they transferred loads down to the foundations.

The attics and cornices of the two buildings reveal how different the conceptions of the two designs were. In the Wainwright, the attic and cornice form together the top (and discrete) section of a classical tripartite composition (cf. fig. 76). In the Guaranty there is no such separation of parts–an elegant curve integrates the cornice and attic with the main section of the facade. The top row of windows immediately below the attic is also different in the two buildings. In the Wainwright they are rectangles sheltered by the frieze and are defined by the intercolumnation and the capitals of the piers. In the Guaranty the twelfth-floor windows are rounded, which establishes an arcade, not a colonnade. Each arch within that arcade is tall and thin–one window wide and ten stories high–a proportion that in no small measure contributes to an illusion of Gothic slenderness. To reinforce a perception that the building soars, Sullivan integrated the arcade and the thirteenth-floor

oculi by means of ornamental lines in a design reminiscent of William L. Johnston's Jayne Building, Philadelphia (1848), a structure he became familiar with during his stay in Frank Furness's office (fig. 102). But there was a major difference between the Jayne and the Guaranty. Johnston worked out the motif with standard Gothic Revival moldings on a flat plane. Sullivan, with an infinitely richer plasticity, developed the composition on a plane curving outward and used his own ornamentation rather than historicist forms.

There were further refinements in the Guaranty. The arches seem to be cut out from a flat surface that, as stated, curves outward at the top. The vertical elements (piers and mullions), as well as the attic and cornice, seem to be what is left of that surface after the excision of the arches took place. This effect is reinforced by the fact that

Figure 102.
Jayne Building,
Philadelphia, William L.
Johnston (1848).
Library Company, Philadelphia.

Sullivan bound together the vertical elements at the top of the building by means of decorative interlaces he placed around the arches and oculi and on the curving cornice. Thus, the interlaces become functional symbols that help us read the structure as if it were a fabric from which the arches had been cut off and then hung from the cornice and secured ten floors below, on the ledge of the two-story base. The spandrels, set in between the piers and mullions, seem to have no function other than keeping the vertical elements in place, preventing them from flapping in the wind and stiffening the building. So well did Sullivan integrate the vertical and horizontal elements of the structure that windows, rather than being primary elements of design, seem to be but the spaces left void between piers and spandrels. While Sullivan had experimented before with this feature of design, he had never been so successful with it as with the Guaranty.

An all-over pattern of ornamentation contributed immensely to the success of the design. The building is entirely clad in brown terra-cotta, and every square inch of it is ornamented. Much has been written about this condition, either accepting or lamenting it, but those views are so dated that they are already part of historiography. They were perhaps best summarized by Philip Johnson's review of the 1956 exhibition at the Art Institute of Chicago marking Sullivan's centennial. Johnson wrote about the lessons Sullivan's work could offer practicing architects, then thick in the midst of modernism. He noted that in the Guaranty Building "[e]ach square inch has [decorative] motifs enough for a whole building, but Sullivan mixes his patterns in a totally inexplicable manner. . . . It is hard to see what we architects of the mid-century can learn from such a strange profusion."[9] Almost fifty years later, and with a different historiographical perception, we see the ornamentation of the Guaranty as the factor that justifies the thinness and slenderness of the structure and bridges the gap between weakness and airiness.

The ornamentation works in other ways as well. As a texture, with sunlight playing on it, it grants the structure a life and a personality of its own. It also defines the volumes of the building not only physically, but more important, aesthetically; and because of its color creates a fundamental contrast with the glazing of the windows, which reads not as a covering of individual openings but as if there were a single ten-story sheet of glass behind the structure. Since the window frames are painted a color similar to that of the terra-cotta, the two materials are undistinguishable from a distance, a small detail that helps to increase the contrast between glass and terra-cotta. The glass, in the overall scheme, becomes the foil against which the structure and its ornamentation reveal themselves in all their richness.

Another function of the ornamentation was to support aesthetically the iconography of the "Rhythms of Life and Death." The main motif in the decoration of piers and mullions—two diagonal cross-axes holding foliage in the "cup" of a letter X—repeats itself, creating a quick rhythm that the observer may interpret as ascending or descending, according to his wish. The interlaces that help define the arches and oculi at the top of the building call to mind branches of trees intertwining high above the ground. To reinforce further the phytomorphic associations of the design, Sullivan framed the upper corners of the building with sprays of branches and leaves that spill over to embrace the top edge of the cornice. The ornamentation of the spandrels also contributes to the transcendentalist program. Contrary to the Wainwright, where the ornament of the spandrels changes on every floor and each panel gives the impression of being a discrete rectangular picture of vegetal motifs, all spandrels of the Guaranty carry the same design: three branches issuing from a bulbous shape placed on center at the bottom edge, the central branch rising vertically, and those to the sides at forty-five degrees. All three shoot out sinuous, interlacing foliage. The rest of the spandrel is taken up by a quiet background pattern, based mainly on circles. The top line of that pattern carries in addition a linear design from which dentil-like elements emerge; they curve forward to support the window ledge in a movement that echoes that of the building's cornice. But it is the three branches that dominate the composition. While of vegetal character, the contrast of their strict geometry with the free flow of their foliage reminds one of banners in rococo military art. With their festive, triumphant air, these ornaments lighten further the appearance of the building, and because they point upward, floor upon floor, they create a subtle but evident rhythm of ascension. Increasing the richness of the design, that upward movement plays with—at the same time that it contrasts against—the rhythms of the piers and mullions, in their ambiguity of ascent and descent.

Increasing the dialectical aspects of the design, the style of the two-story base is completely different from that of the superstructure above it, as had been the case in the Trust and Savings designs. The base is thick, sturdy, and downbearing, and its bays are double the size of those of the superstructure, thus revealing the true structure of the building. The two floors of the base are also different from each other. Fat columns with broad, foliated capitals dominate large shopfronts on the ground floor, there are oblong windows on the second floor, and *quattrocento*-like monumental portals allow access to the building. The texture, color, and overall ornamentation of the terra-cotta serve as a visual link between the bottom and top. Yet, even here, Sullivan established an elegant differentiation; the ornamentation of the base is wider and flatter than that of the superstructure, thus reinforcing the evidence of support of the base.

The Guaranty was a watershed in Sullivan's evolution. It was the first among his built tall commercial structures to establish an iconography that linked his Néo-Grec syntax with his transcendentalist aspirations. A prescriptive juxtaposition of a Renaissance-inspired design indicating the supportive character of the base in contraposition with the soaring aspects of a Gothic-derived superstructure and the pervasive insistence on the expression of the behavior of each element of con-

struction, individually as well as collectively, are all issues that point to the Néo-Grec. But the insistence on expressive ambiguity, with piers that ascend as much as they bear down, and the Swedenborgian emphasis on "feminine-emotional" ornamentation issuing from a "masculine-rational" geometrical structure are American elements of his aesthetic.

On the designs of all his subsequent skyscrapers Sullivan continued adding anthropomorphic meanings to the standard conception of the vegetal origins of the Gothic. There were no more waverings in his expression of his transcendentalist conception of the skyscraper, as there had been earlier in the designs of the St. Nicholas Hotel and the Chicago Stock Exchange Building. Now all his buildings would intimate the existence of organic life and suggest that certain structural elements were capable of movement.

His next step, the design for remodeling the Burnet House hotel, Cincinnati, developed further the idea he had first explored in the two designs for the Trust and Savings Building, which the 1893 depression prevented from being built. The Burnet House hotel remodeling, which was to take up a city block, was designed in July 1895, at the same time that much of the ornamentation of the Guaranty was still on the boards (fig. 103).[10] The building consisted of a symmetrical composition of

Figure 104.
Bayard Building,
New York (1897–99).
Museum of the
City of New York.

the Guaranty). Thus they harmonized with the columns of the base and established it as a classical load-bearing story contrasting with the Gothic-like soaring aspects of the superstructure. Secondly, in the ten-story-high corner pavilions, the window mullions ran uninterrupted from the cornice of the base to the top of each bay, instead of running interruptedly at each floor from sill to lintel. The Burnet House mullions were more visually prominent than the Trust and Savings ones. They increased the verticality of the composition at the expense of the importance of the horizontality of the spandrels, established a contrapuntal rhythm with the piers, and brought the whole design closer to a Gothic clerestory. Thirdly, and also on the corner pavilions, Sullivan placed a tympanum pierced by two small arches immediately below the main arch in each bay instead of the solid semi-circular tympanums of the two Trust and Savings designs. Their design, evoking the plate tracery of English Decorated Gothic, worked with the colonnette-like mullion to make clearer the contrast of the Gothic-like, airy superstructure and the Renaissance-inspired supporting base. Finally, Sullivan placed a winged female figure atop each pier rather than only on the corners. Each pier now had its own representation of the essence of its "rhythm of Life" emerging from it and marking its ascendant impulse.

While the Burnet House remodeling was not built, the Bayard Building, New York (1897–99), was the fourth and only built design in the group (fig. 104). The facade of the Bayard, which Sullivan considered to be his best,[11] shows how much he had refined an idea that he had first explored in 1892 in the first Trust and Savings design. He took the superstructure of the far-right corner block of the Burnet House hotel, with its five bays, raised it by two floors, and placed it on the base of the second design for the Savings and Trust Building. The juxtaposition altered the antecedents only in very minor ways. The main door (which remained on the right-hand side of the structure, as in the hotel) had a modified *quattrocento*-inspired design; the ornamentation—now for a building that was

three volumes: a central eight-story body ending on an arcade, and ten-story side pavilions, each with an attic and a projecting cornice. The corner ten-story-high pavilions were close to the designs for the Trust and Savings Building, with the same differentiation between a supporting base and an arcaded superstructure, and with moldings marking the soaring and downbearing "rhythms of Life and Death." A two-story base ran uninterruptedly from one end of the building to the other. The hotel extended behind these three volumes, taking up the whole block with a simple, utilitarian, fenestrated design.

For the design of the Burnet House, Sullivan changed four items from the Trust and Savings Building models. First, the entrances were in an Italian Renaissance style (as had been the case in

erected—was understandably better studied than in the preceding unbuilt projects; and the second-floor windows, contrary to their design in the hotel, went from pier to pier with no interruption of mullion, as in the second design of the Trust and Savings. The mullions on the Bayard facade, then, rested on the sill of the third-floor windows and ran uninterrupted up to the plate tracery immediately beneath the curves of the arches. Otherwise, as in the case of the Trust and Savings designs, and especially that of the Burnet House, the facades may be compared to an enormous Gothic clerestory, complete with plate tracery and elongated colonnettes.

The basic tenet of this new architecture appears in *The Autobiography of an Idea*, where Sullivan wrote that "the science of engineering is a science of *reaction*, while the science of architectural design—were such a science to be presupposed—must be a science of action."[12] The architect, in his role of engineer (or builder), was to express the dependence of the building on gravity, but as an artist, he was to challenge it. Architectural beauty would result from that dialectic. The two designs for the Savings and Trust Building, the Burnet House, and the Bayard Building, along with the Guaranty, reveal that dialectic by conjuring up images of "the rhythms of Life and Death" as well as by revealing a kinship with the organic through association with trees. The idea of an eternal becoming is evident in the polarities Sullivan ascribed to the symbolic rhythm of the piers: death supported life, evolution issued out of dissolution, and the objective and the subjective became interchangeable. Furthermore, in the Bayard, to create an even greater contrast between the supportive character of the base and the soaring ascension of the piers, Sullivan decreased the height of the floors as the building rises, establishing an optical correction that increases the vertical perspective.[13] As one looks up at the building, it appears to be taller than it actually is.

The Transportation Building figures are the antecedents to the winged female figures under the eaves of the second Trust and Savings design, the Burnet House remodeling, and the Bayard Building, but since only the Bayard was built—and is therefore the best-known among them—I will devote my attention only to the latter, and begin by considering a false legend surrounding the six figures floating beneath the cornice at the attic level.

It has been stated that "[t]he sextet of angels were added, over Sullivan's objections, but still by his hand, at the request of his client, Silas Alden Condict."[14] Apparently that contention first issued from Alden S. Condict, Silas's son, who passed it down to Meyer Berger, the architectural critic, who in turn published it in his "About New York" column in the *New York Times* of 15 May 1957. The column stated that according to Condict, he commissioned the building from Sullivan, and at the same time requested the architect to design "six angels with outspread pinions" because he wanted "every tenant and every visitor to the Condict Building to realize the true spirit of fair dealing among men can and should prevail during the six business days of the week, as well as on the Sabbath." This charming story is hard to believe, since the building was not commissioned by Condict but by the United Loan and Investment Company, and the person dealing with Sullivan was its president, Robert Avery. The design, according to documents in the files of the City of New York, was ready by 21 September 1897. Twenty-one months later, the mortgage on the building was recalled by the Bank for Savings in New York. It was from that institution, well after the design had been set, that Silas Condict and his wife Emmeline acquired a half interest. Moreover, Sullivan had been using similar figures in designs for about six years.

The figures perform a significant iconographic function (fig. 105). Although classical in appearance, they find their origins in medieval angels who support cornices and trusses on their wings to express an association between the roof of a church and the vault of Heaven (fig. 106). The Bayard Building figures translated that religious image into a transcendental one related to the sub-

Figure 105.
Bayard Building, pier
with winged figure
(1897–99).
Photograph by Richard Cleary.

Figure 106.
Reims Cathedral, angels of
apsidal chapel.
Photograph by Frank Horlbeck.

Figure 107.
Bayard Building,
winged figure (1897–99).
Brickbuilder, 1898.

Figure 108.
Salle des Sept Cheminées,
Louvre, Paris (1849–51),
frieze; Félix Duban,
architect; Francisque-
Joseph Duret, sculptor.
Avery Library,
Columbia University.

jective sense of upward tension, to the "rhythm of Life" that Sullivan wished to represent in his piers (fig. 107). The figures seem to have been directly inspired by the ones Félix Duban, the architect of the buildings of the Ecole des Beaux-Arts and one of the founders of the romantic rationalist movement, used in the decoration of the Salle des Sept Cheminées in the Louvre in 1849–51 (fig. 108). The room, which comprises the area of Louis XIV's former apartment in the Pavillon du Roi, today houses seventeenth-century Italian paintings. Duban, however, was charged to design it to display major works of the nineteenth-century French School, David's *Sacre de Napoléon* among them.[15] Following Percier's classical style—possibly to establish a reference to the First Empire that would meet with Louis Napoleon's approval—Duban designed a frieze with medallions in hexagonal frames portraying French artists active during the First Empire or shortly thereafter, such as David, Girodet, Prud'hon, Percier, Géricault, and Granet, who would, as it were, preside over their works shown in the room. Between the medallions, winged allegories of fame (*renommées*) extend palm fronds above the artists' heads. These figures, as well as the medallions, were executed by the sculptor Francisque-Joseph Duret (1804–65), also the author of the two bronze figures flanking the entrance to Napoleon's tomb in Les Invalides and of the St. Michael in the fountain at the foot of the Boulevard Saint-Michel.

The similarities of the Louvre figures with those on the facade of the Bayard are very close. The position of the bodies and the movement of the outstretched wings and arms are very much alike; the nervous, wavy drapery of Duret's figures finds an echo in the movement of the material around the breasts and waists of Sullivan's figures; and even the movements of the wrists are similar. There are differences, however. Duret's wing feathers are long, thin, and hard, creating a serrated outline, while Sullivan's are round and broad, forming a soft profile. Since Duret's figures were designed to be seen at closer range than Sullivan's, the face of each is different, as is the movement of the drapery. Sullivan's figures are all alike, cast from the same mold executed by the Perth-Amboy Company of New Jersey. A more important difference is that the feet of Duret's figures are visible and barely touch the consoles under them. The figures in the Louvre give the impression of having descended from Heaven and to be hovering in space while they honor the painters portrayed in the medallions. The feet of Sullivan's figures, by contrast, are concealed under the drapery and the foliage at the top of the piers. These figures are not alighting but slowly emerging from the piers of which they represent the ascensional spirit.

Sullivan was consistent also in his use of one motif throughout most of the vegetal ornamentation of the Bayard Building (cf. fig. 104), and, like the winged figures, it finds its source in classical design as well as in his decorative work in the Transportation Building. The motif consists of a central element, sometimes an antefix, sometimes a knot in a limb, and sometimes a lion's head (like the one in the Transportation Building fountains), out of which issues, left and right, a long sinuous branch that shoots out foliage spiraling inward. Variations of that motif produced the hexagonal cartouches on the second floor of the Bayard, the lower portions of the decorations of the spandrels of the third to the eleventh floor, the decorations of the spandrels on the top floor, and also the ornament on the lunette above the main door, although in this last case the design was modified to suit a semicircular contour. The movement of the vegetation atop the piers, as well as that of the capitals of the mullions and the first-floor columns, follows that pattern too, seeking in these cases a remote parentage with Ionic capitals.

Most of Sullivan's designs subsequent to the Guaranty and the Bayard display the same kind of nervous dynamism. A sketch of an elevation and plan of a country club jotted on the back of a business card on 26 June 1898 is one of them (fig 109).[16] The building, if erected, would have been a perfect cube. It was to stand isolated on the large grounds of a country club and to have four equal facades ("Open 4 sides," Sullivan inscribed on the card).

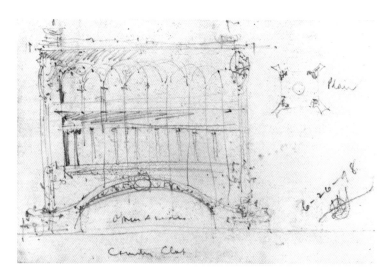

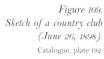

On each front, heavy corner buttresses, set at forty-five-degree angles, ascend and resolve into a broad, elegant, decorated segmental arch running from side to side at the first floor. Because of the angle of the stirrups and the flatness of the facade, one is to presume that the curve of the arch is three-dimensional. Set within a sturdy spandrel, the arch brings considerable buoyancy and springiness to the composition. Corner piers issue also from the stirrups. They are also at a forty-five-degree angle and end in a large efflorescence of ornamentation. Rather than sustaining the building, these corner piers seem to contain it after having shot up from the rootlike stirrups. As such, they establish a subjective-tensile balance with the objective compressive expression of the entrance arch. Another feature in this design is a thick beam that runs across approximately midway up the elevation to differentiate the second and third floors. This horizontal element gives scale to the design and prevents it from being excessively vertical. A colonnade, as visually in compression as it is actually supportive, holds up the beam and establishes the fenestration for the second story.

Sullivan's mastery at disguising compressive forces in structural elements is evident in the double alternate arcade of the third story. Extraordinarily thin piers (represented by single lines on the drawing) run practically the full height of the building, physically bringing the weight of the cor-

nice to the entrance arch. But exactly the opposite occurs visually. The arches seem to be in tension, as if jets of air were billowing them from below. The piers appear to be visually in tension and to anchor a series of balloonlike forms onto the powerful arch. (On the drawing, however, the first two piers on the left-hand side—the first two Sullivan would have drawn—rest on the thick beam running across between the second and third floors. Apparently he was not satisfied with that solution, possibly because it would not lend itself to the ambivalence he sought, and altered the design by bringing all other piers down to the arch.)

The counterpoint those piers establish with the first, alternating colonnade further emphasizes their character of "balloon strings," since the other piers are emphatically in compression, resting on the ledge of the beam. Sullivan thus underscored the ambiguity of tension-compression and objective-subjective to the point that two apparently equal juxtaposed arcades could vary in structural behavior and in their relationship with gravity. As in other buildings, he terminated the composition with a cornice and a decorated attic that in this case seems to float on the third-floor arcade. Again, as in most other cases, those features have an important aesthetic function to fulfill by acting as a lid containing the different systems of forces within the boundaries of the facade.

Sullivan's facade for the Gage Building belongs

in the same stylistic group as the country club design (fig. 110). In 1898, Stanley R. McCormick, the youngest child of Cyrus and Nettie Fowler McCormick, engaged the firm of Holabird & Roche to design three adjacent buildings facing Grant Park across Michigan Avenue in Chicago. The three structures were erected expressly for the millinery firms that were to occupy them. McCormick granted them extended leases before construction started, and the rent was to be based on a uniform percentage on the cost of each building. The southernmost of them was six stories high, the next seven, and the third, next to Henry I. Cobb's Athletic Club, was eight floors high. Gage Brothers & Company, formerly housed in Adler & Sullivan's Revell Building at Wabash Avenue at the corner of Adams Street (cf. fig. 60), offered to pay additional rent at a percentage equal to the increased cost of having Sullivan design a facade for their building. "They did so because they thought it would benefit their business in an equal degree. They put a commercial value on Mr. Sullivan's design, otherwise he would not have been called in."[17]

All three buildings are of steel skeletal construction. Besides their differences in height, they are also different in width. The middle and northernmost buildings are sixty-two feet wide and have three bays. The southernmost is narrower and only two bays wide. The two facades by Holabird & Roche are clad in molded brick and have large Chicago-type windows. Sullivan's front is in gray terra-cotta, and the first story was faced originally with ornamental cast iron. Sullivan's windows are also different from Holabird & Roche's transparent glass ones. He dropped a four-foot curtain of Luxfer Prisms from the top of the opening, reducing the transparent windows to continuous horizontal strips about four feet high. Sullivan's window design, according to Hugh Morrison, was meant to reduce glare.[18]

Sullivan continued his experiment with ambiguous design in the Gage commission. He made the two outside supports seem to be bearing down while the two inside ones seem to shoot up (fig.

111). The facade results in two equal torques moving in opposite directions. The two central piers have no capitals, but from each of them stems an acanthus decoration with an elegant upwardly sweeping movement. With these luscious tops, the central piers look like abstracted date palms, conveying a feeling of growth.[19] As in the Bayard Building, the decoration of the Gage Building is concentrated at spots, and can be read easily. At the ground level, the treatment is different, with the storefronts encased in a cast-iron frame that was completely covered with decoration.

Establishing a visual divorce between the cast-iron infrastructure and the terra-cotta superstructure was Sullivan's way to circumvent a major design problem Holabird & Roche's scheme had created. Since the central piers on the ground floor were behind the storefront, and therefore not visible from the street, he had no visual continuum from base to top. Neither did he have at the Gage the broad summer beam he had placed on the first floor of the Bayard Building and the country club. In short, he had no "saddle" on which to place his building. He sidestepped these handicaps by making the cast-iron frame act similarly to the entrance arch of the country club. By decreasing the importance of the side piers, practically depriving them of decoration, he increased the upward thrust of the central ones. He also struck a carefully studied balance between the acanthus decoration on the attic and the "legs" of the cast-iron frame and designed a simple cornice to decrease its visual weight.

A comparison of the Gage and Portland buildings, two designs by Sullivan of similar scale and structure, reveals the changes in the method of design for early and late skyscrapers (cf. fig. 81). In the 1892 example, fenestration dominated a composition that was exclusively downbearing in spite of the verticality the side windows established. In the 1898 building, the structure had a more intense nervous quality, dominated the composition, and established an anthropomorphic program that may be compared to an athlete with his feet firmly planted on the ground stretching up

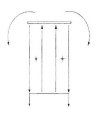

Figure 111.
Gage Building,
diagram of
visual forces.
Drawing by
Narciso G. Menocal.

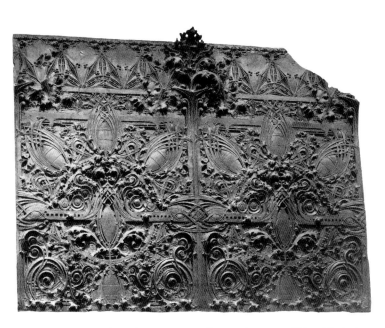

Figure 112.
Gage Building,
cast-iron relief.
Elvehjem Museum of Art,
University of Wisconsin.

Figure 113.
Schlesinger & Mayer
Store, Chicago
(1898–99; 1902–3).
Architectural Record, 1904.

his thoracic muscles and arms. (The *Hephaistos Striking the Anvil* in the Dumbarton Oaks collection comes to mind.) Unfortunately, that anthropomorphic program has been marred by two major changes to the building. In 1902, Holabird & Roche added four stories, making the building much too tall to express Sullivan's aesthetic intentions efficiently, although his design was preserved, and the attic, with its ornamentation and cornice, was reconstructed. Then, in 1955, the iron panels around the storefront were removed. Only five of the panels used on the building, each fifty by seventy-five inches, survive; a sixth, never used because it was broken before installation, is at the Elvehjem Museum of Art of the University of Wisconsin; the rest were sold as scrap (fig. 112).[20]

The story of the building for the Schlesinger & Mayer Store, now Carson Pirie Scott, is as complicated as it is well known. Essentially it was erected in two campaigns, one in 1898–99 and the other in 1902–3, with additions by D. H. Burnham & Company in 1906 (fig. 113).[21] In this design Sullivan went beyond his earlier work and involved two facades rather than one in an anthropomorphic

program, creating a volumetric composition instead of a planar one as heretofore. The result was a three-dimensional contrast between a well-defined vertical movement of piers on a corner circular tower and the receding-in-perspective horizontal lines of fenestration on the two walls issuing from the tower at right angles. The building's anthropomorphic counterpart in classical art could be the *Nike of Samothrace*, where one finds a similar dynamic relationship between the body and wings. As always, Sullivan applied in an expressive manner the law that form follows function and conveyed in this design the essence of how a corner tower anchors two equally important facades, proclaiming what he considered to be "the internal life" of a design.[22]

The Schlesinger & Mayer Store was to all intents and purposes Sullivan's last important commercial commission in Chicago. (The only multistory building he designed after it was the five-floor Crane Company Office Building in Chicago, built in 1904.) As his last skyscraper, the Schlesinger & Mayer building ended a line of tall commercial buildings that were phytomorphic at the same time that they were anthropomorphic and geomorphic. Their style seemed antiquated to his contemporaries because of its free-flowing botanical decorations and unacademic look. The source of that style—his transcendentalist and romantic ways—however popular it might have been in the Midwest of the 1880s, had been discarded almost a generation earlier on the Eastern Seaboard.[23] By the turn of the century Chicago had caught up with the Eastern Beaux-Arts style, aesthetically and intellectually.

Sullivan's bitterness at being ignored, especially at the moment of his maturity, when he had become fully capable of serving the needs of his iconography with his method of design, moved him to write in 1906 "What Is Architecture: A Study in the American People of Today." The piece reveals his disenchantment when he finally realized that the social and architectural trends of the day ran contrary to his ideals.[24] It also shows his disappointment with the architectural press, which ignored his work at the same time that it broadcast the cause of academic architecture. "Our architectural periodicals float along, aimlessly enough," he accused, "their pages filled with views of buildings, buildings, like 'words, words, words.'"[25] Three years later he complained again in "Is Our Art a Betrayal Rather Than an Expression of American Life?"[26] He saw himself as a new Elijah and wrote:

If I were asked to name the one salient, deeply characteristic social condition, which with us underlies everything else as an active factor in determining all other manifestations, I should say without the slightest hesitation betrayal. *It is so clear that no one can avoid seeing it who does not take express pains to shut his eyes. . . . The first and chief desire, drift, fashion, custom, willingness, or whatever you may choose to call it, of the American people, lies in this curiously passionate aptitude of betrayal.*

Sullivan was fifty-two when he wrote this article against a society that had left him behind. For the next fourteen years, until two years before his death, he encysted himself in his wrath but would not attempt to make it known in print. He well knew that few would publish that kind of material and even fewer would read it. In that same year, his friend and apologist Claude Bragdon summarized the situation when he lamented, "Outside of this little circle [of Prairie architects] Mr. Sullivan was either unknown, ignored, or discredited by those persons on whose opinions reputations in matters of art are supposed to rest."[27]

6: *Culmination of an Iconography: The Banks, 1906–24*

A need for a new building type, the rural bank, emerged in the Midwest in the late nineteenth century as a result of new economic relationships between "progressive" bankers and farmers.[1] Harvey Ellis's Security Bank Building, Minneapolis (1891), was the first among them. Frank Lloyd Wright's "A Village Bank," published in *The Brickbuilder* in 1901, and his two designs for the Frank L. Smith Bank in Dwight, Illinois (1904 and 1906), contributed also to the type, as well as Purcell & Feick's "City Bank," featured in the 1905 Chicago annual architectural exhibition (figs. 114–16).[2] Most of Sullivan's work from 1906 onward fell into this building type. As commissions trickled into his office, he refined by degrees a building type that, although having little in common with the tall office buildings he had been designing for more than twelve years, had nevertheless been well defined by other architects. (Elmslie kept a reproduction of Ellis's bank on his drafting table.)[3]

Because of the abrupt change, shifting from designing skyscrapers with freestanding structures to load-bearing one- and two-story brick buildings, it took Sullivan some time to bring to the banks what he had learned from the skyscrapers. As such, there is little in the design of his first bank, the National Farmers' Bank, Owatonna, Minnesota, 1906–8 (fig. 117), to remind one of the Gothic-derived aesthetic of the skyscrapers; its antecedent was the Golden Doorway of the Trans-

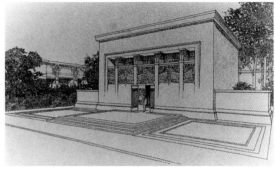

Figure 114.
Security Bank Building,
Minneapolis,
Harvey Ellis (1891).
Western Architect, 1912.

Figure 115.
"A Village Bank,"
Frank Lloyd Wright
(1901).
Brickbuilder, 1901.

Figure 116.
"City Bank," Purcell &
Feick (1905).
Northwest Architectural
Archives,
University of Minnesota.

Figure 117.
National Farmers' Bank,
Owatonna, Minnesota
(1906–8).
Northwest Architectural
Archives,
University of Minnesota.

portation Building of the Columbian Exposition (cf. fig. 93). In each case a monumental panel capped by a strong cornice framed a bold arch resting on a plinth. But since Sullivan was experimenting with a new aesthetic, there were fundamental differences between the two designs. For the Golden Doorway he had established a picturesque program associated with Islamic architecture, but he related the design of the Owatonna bank to the rhythms of Impressionist music and of French Symbolist poetry. At the same time, the bank was to evoke the colors of the Midwestern landscape of early spring or late autumn.[4] Neither the new aesthetic program nor the new type of construction allowed room for including the Gothic as he had reinterpreted it in his designs for skyscrapers. In time, however, and quite possibly subconsciously, his aesthetic passion for expressing a synthesis of French romantic rationalism and American transcendentalism asserted itself in dynamic, anthropomorphic designs that established a link with his earlier uses of the Gothic.

Another issue to consider is that until recently Sullivan's banks were universally accepted as major works of architecture yet consistently dismissed as an epilogue to his work, a paradox sustained by progressivist architectural historians. The banks never fit within the canonical progression of modern architecture as defined in the 1930s, 1940s, and 1950s. Giedion, Pevsner, and Zevi, for example, ignored them completely.[5] The banks, many thought, were the sad end of a once brilliant career that had given us nothing less than the modern skyscraper. Kenneth Frampton's statement that they were "the swan song of a culture that somehow never fully matured" would have diminished their importance half a century ago.[6] Today we accept Frampton's point in its true implication. We recognize that the banks are major works of art regardless of their remote location and modest function; in spite of their "relatively late date" in the history of the modern movement; and notwithstanding that they left no stylistic issue, except for Elmslie's banks and a few other buildings in the Midwest. Progressivist historians, including many Sullivan scholars (with the exception of John Szarkowski),[7] failed to see that the importance of Sullivan's banks is intrinsic, not relative.

My reassessment of them rests upon four considerations: (1) rejecting traditional assumptions about supposed exclusive stylistic links between the banks and Sullivan's earlier designs for tombs; (2) recognizing the heretofore neglected (and far more important) relationship between the banks and his skyscrapers of the 1890s; (3) understanding the relationship of the banks to a new conception of design that he enunciated in 1910 but had begun to practice before then; and, (4) appreciating the gender signification of the polychromy of the banks as an extension of his choice of colors for the skyscrapers. These considerations make it possible to discern a broadening of Sullivan's Swedenborgian metaphysics toward the end of his career. Concurrently, the architecture of his banks have meanings richer than those of his previous work. This growth was nonlinear. It developed by trial and error, success and lapse. My appraisal of it will show the banks as they truly are: products of an increased awareness of Sullivan's conception of architecture that enabled him to surpass his earlier goals and achievements.

My argument requires challenging the conventional wisdom that Sullivan's banks are stylistic variations of his tombs and other works of 1886–92—of which the Wainwright Tomb may be cited as a generic example. Consider two of the common characteristics among Sullivan's buildings from those years. First, they are rendered mostly in smooth ashlar, which establishes a degree of planar abstraction on their surfaces. Second, their decorations are usually constructed out of the same materials as their walls. This treatment reinforces homogeneity and allows for stronger relationships between ornamentation and walls than between ornamentation and voids (such as doors and windows). The banks are different. Instead of a monochromatic treatment, there is a rich polychromy; instead of a smooth surface, a rich texture; instead of a geometric abstraction, a lyrical evocation of the landscape; instead of a homogenized relationship between wall and ornament, a contrast in colors and materials that produces a richer plasticity; instead of ornamentation related to the compositional masses, decoration that focuses attention on the doors and windows and serves as a framing element regardless of its location; and instead of ornamentation that works to create an exclusively downward tectonic effect, ornamentation that helps to establish compositions in which symbolic, upward pulls seemingly defy gravity. In particular, this last suggests that, in time, Sullivan's bank style became close to that of his skyscrapers, in meaning as much as in ties to the Gothic.

In the process of working with a building type new to him, Sullivan extended his ideas on architecture, making his new opinions public in 1910 in *Suggestions in Artistic Brick*.[8] After holding for many years that plan and function were secondary elements of architecture, he now gave them new emphasis, probably impressed by the new definition of architecture advanced by the Prairie movement. But that change of mind constituted no full embrace of the new Midwestern ideas. Drawing upon the rationalism he had learned at the Ecole des Beaux-Arts, he argued that the new architecture was an adjustment to new possibilities of construction. Thanks to the "modern mechanically pressed brick [or tapestry brick, the architect] began to feel more sensible of the true nature of a building as an organism or whole."[9] He also suggested that "this new material, brick, has led to a new development, namely that in which all the functions of a given building are allowed to find their expression in natural and appropriate forms—each form and the total shape evidencing, instead of hiding, the working conditions of the building as exhibited in its plan."[10] More economically and efficiently than before, the plan of a building could serve as the basis for designing its masses. A new organic unity could be brought into composition by rendering all exterior surfaces of a building in tapestry brick, a material that brought with it the added advantages of a rich texture and a splendid polychromy. Sullivan's new conception may have been influenced by Gottfried Semper's ideas on the textile origins of the wall and its ornamentation, of which he may have been aware since the late 1880s; it was only now, when he was using a new material, that he found an application for those theories.[11] In *Artistic Brick* he wrote of the new wall: "Manufacturers, by grinding the clay of the shale coarse and by use of cutting wires, produced on its face a new and most interesting texture, a texture with a nap-like effect, suggesting somewhat an Anatolian rug; a texture giving innumerable highlights and shadows, and a moss-like softness of appearance."[12]

Sullivan adapted his new beliefs to his standard transcendentalist pattern of thought. He anthropomorphized buildings and spoke of their yearning, resulting from a fundamental law of nature, to have their plans revealed by their volumes. "The building plan," he wrote, "clamors for expression and freedom . . . in a way that will satisfy its desires, and thus, in so doing, express them unmistakably. This is, in essence, the natural basis of the anatomy and physiology of design."[13]

Some of these new convictions were based on ideas of Viollet-le-Duc. In *Suggestions*, Sullivan wrote, "This law is not only comprehensive, but universal. It applies to the crystal as well as to the plant, each seeking and finding its form by virtue of its working plan, or purpose, or utility."[14] Similarly, Viollet-le-Duc had written in his Sixth Discourse:

> Nature, in all her works, has style, because, however varied her productions may be, they are always submitted to laws and invariable principles. The lilies of the field, the leaves of the trees, the insects, have style, because they grow, develop, and exist according to essentially logical laws. We can spare nothing from a flower, because, in its organization, every part has its function and is formed to carry out that function in the most beautiful manner. Style resides in the true and well-understood expression of a principle; therefore, as nothing exists in nature without a principle, everything in nature must have style.[15]

After reassessing Viollet-le-Duc's ideas, as well as other principles of French architectural theory he had learned as a student in Europe and America, Sullivan accepted implicitly (albeit never overtly) the Prairie School tenet that the new architecture should insist on an intimate relationship between plan, volume, and function. His reappraisal of his definition of architecture reinforced some of his old opinions while bringing new notions to the fore. The idea that each element of a design was a discrete entity that nobly expressed its own mechanical and, therefore, functional reality was consistent both with his French training and his transcendentalist interests, but bringing floor plans into prominence was new for him. In the past he had considered the design of plans a "pedestrian" activity and even had difficulty devising them efficiently. (One notes especially his problems with residential floor plans.)[16] Earlier, Adler had designed the floor plans of the office buildings commissioned to the firm. After the dissolution of the partnership, Sullivan had few problems designing the plans of the tall buildings of the late 1890s. They were mostly of the "loft" or warehouse type, requiring no great study.

Turning a past weakness into a salient feature of design was no great struggle for Sullivan. Wim de Wit has shown how Sullivan's plans for banks derived from six solutions for "progressive bank floor plans" published in the February 1905 issue of *The Architectural Review* (which antedates Sullivan's first bank design by a year).[17] De Wit's discovery explains why Sullivan once stated that "the requirements [for the banks were] given, and it only remained to jot them down on paper." He was as free of complicated decisions about planning as he had been for skyscrapers. He could devote as much attention to composition and ornamentation for the banks as he had for the tall office buildings of the 1890s; he was making their designs evolve from plans he did not have to invent. This may account in large part for his successes with rural banks, especially in the light of his failures with residential work in the same period.

The National Farmers' Bank, Owatonna, Minnesota (1906–8), his first, was perhaps the most difficult to design for him, for two reasons. Not only was he dealing with a new building type, but also he was devising a new aesthetic (cf. fig. 117).[18] Central among his new artistic ideas was his appreciation of French Symbolist poetry and Impressionist music. Since the 1880s such poets as Mallarmé, Rimbaud, and Verlaine in France and Maeterlinck in Belgium, expanding ideas first explored by the Parnassians and Baudelaire before them, had used the material universe to express the immaterial realities of thought and feeling through correspondences, allegories, and consciously invented symbols. Behind every incident, behind almost every phrase in this literature, lay a concealed universality, the adumbration of greater things. To Maeterlinck, for instance, the supreme mission of art was to reveal the infinite as well as the grandeur and secret beauty of man. He believed that artists were imbued with a special sensitivity to the universal, and that it was their task, through art, to give lesser beings a glimpse of that vision. Art, to Maeterlinck, was a metaphor, because artists were unable to express directly the breadth and intensity of their intuition, and even if they could, the people would not understand it. Symbolist poets also sought to represent the unity of all feeling and integrated into poetry effects from other arts. Their verses evoke the colors of the painter and the rhythms of the musician. These are all aesthetic objectives that Sullivan recognized as close to his own, and his awareness of this movement is more than likely. These comments on Symbolism are but a restatement of Richard Hovey's introduction to his two-volume translation of Maeterlinck's plays, of which Sullivan kept a copy in his summer cottage in Mississippi.[19]

Musical associations were also important to Sullivan's new style. Debussy, Satie, Ravel, and other Impressionist composers summoned to music what the Symbolist poets sought in words. Debussy's pieces evoking color are well known; he based his only opera, *Pelléas et Mélisande*, on Maeterlinck's play and translated into music Mallarmé's *L'après-midi d'un faune*. Sullivan's awareness of such links among color, rhythm, and allegory is manifest in an often quoted letter he wrote to Carl Bennett, the vice-president of the Owatonna bank, in which he stated that he wished to create "a color symphony." Bennett, who was highly sensitive to music (during his student days he had conducted the Pierian Sodality, the Harvard symphony orchestra), presumably encouraged Sullivan to create an architectural composition that would symbolize a harmony with poetry and music through color and light. On December 7, 1911, he wrote Sullivan a highly complimentary letter in which he said, "I have often likened your work to that of the great musicians or poets, and have thought of ourselves as though we possessed exclusively . . . one of the symphonies of Beethoven."[20]

Polychromy and composition played fundamental roles in Sullivan's associating his banks with French Symbolist poetry and Impressionist music. Differences in style, meaning, and purpose between the imagery of the new buildings and that of earlier designs is striking, thus there are more differences than similarities between the Owatonna bank and the Golden Doorway of the Transportation Building in the Columbian Exhibition, 1891–93 (cf. fig. 93). Consider, for instance, that the coloristic effects of the Golden Doorway depended on applied plaster ornamentation and paint, while those of the Owatonna bank are integral with the materials. The buildings, moreover, also differed in function and scale, but more important to our discussion, in degree of picturesqueness. The rich polychromy of the Golden Doorway—a golden hue highlighted by "no less than forty tints of colours" seen against the red background of the rest of the building—must have created effects that the black-and-white photographs through which we know the building cannot hope to capture.[21] Other features increased its sumptuousness. Important among them were the telescoping arches, the inwardly turning plinths, the sculptural decorations, and the reliefs on the tympanum that the surrounding architecture framed. Large deco-

Figure 118.
National Park Bank,
New York, Donn Barber
(1905).
Architectural Record, 1905.

rative motifs on the archivolts and exuberant ornamentation along the outer perimeter and on the
cornice elaborated further the picturesqueness of
the Golden Doorway.

Nothing so lavish appears in the Owatonna
bank. True to his new conception of style, Sullivan
allowed the materials to speak for themselves and
kept applied decoration to a minimum. The plinth
is stone, the spandrel brick, and the cornice, raked
this time as befits its material, is also brick. Only
a small band of terra-cotta and two imposing cast-
iron ornaments frame the large window on each
street facade and establish a chromatic affinity
between the tapestry brick and the stained glass.
The proportions of the design are equally simple.
Sullivan divided each facade horizontally into four
approximately equal parts, each about the length
of the radius of the window. The vertical module
is more or less half the horizontal, and he used it
five times: once to the sill of the window (the
height of the stone base), twice more to the crown
of the arch, another to the top of the incised terra-
cotta band, and the fifth to the top of the cornice.
Sullivan's goal was a "rich box in which to keep

money and valuables."[22] The bottom of the box
was identified by the stone plinth, and the lid was
represented by the corniced tapestry-brick spandrel. The latter, in spite of its sturdiness, conveyed
a sense of lightness because of the ample window
it defined. Each part played its role efficiently. The
historicist allusions of the Golden Doorway and its
exotic associations with the Islamic world had no
place in the Owatonna design.

Sullivan arrived at this design by a process of
trial and error, as is well known. He first considered a facade with three narrow arched windows,
but following the suggestion of his assistant,
George Grant Elmslie, he changed them into the
one sweeping arch of the final design.[23] It is generally accepted that Donn Barber's National Park
Bank in New York, published by Montgomery
Schuyler in the April 1905 *Architectural Record*, was
a possible source for many features of the Owatonna bank, including the large semicircular window, albeit translated from an academic Beaux-Arts
idiom into a progressive one (fig. 118).[24] Perhaps
Sullivan or Elmslie noted Schuyler's closing
remark about the National Park Bank's central
room being "a noble apartment, much in advance
of anything for the same purpose we have hither-
to had to show."[25]

Sullivan may have looked for still other sources
to guide him, a statement that may seem at odds
with his dictum that "he made buildings out of his
head." But considerable evidence suggests that
whenever he confronted a new architectural problem, he usually looked for an existing design to
serve as a foundation on which to build a new conception. Such cases usually ended in a transformation of the source into something completely
different from what it was originally.[26]

For the first design of the Owatonna bank he
may well have turned to the library of the Law
School in Paris, designed by Louis-Ernest
Lheureux in 1876–78 and enlarged in 1892–97 (fig.
119). It is more than likely that Sullivan knew this
building through photographs Russell Sturgis published in 1898 in "Good Things in Modern Architecture," an article in *The Architectural Record*. There

Sturgis praised as well Sullivan's Bayard Building, and published a view of it.[27] If, indeed, Sullivan used the Law Library as a source for the Owatonna bank, he chose a model that was not new but twenty years old. Sturgis's article may have misled him into thinking that the Law Library was a brand-new building, for the text confuses the 1892–97 extension with the entire building.

Until the 1950s, when it was torn down, the Law Library stood on the rue Cujas as an extension of an earlier building by Soufflot across the square in front of his better-known Pantheon, and catercorner from Henri Labrouste's Bibliothèque Sainte-Geneviève, to which Lheureux's building was stylistically related—Lheureux had been a student in Labrouste's atelier. The facade of the Law Library was in accord with its internal structure, in which metal struts transferred stresses from a metal-and-glass roof to corner masonry piers in a system that Hautecoeur characterized as a derivation from Viollet-le-Duc.[28] Exterior corner piers framed the composition and revealed that the masonry at the corners withstood the thrust of the metal struts holding up the roof. At the center of the facade a recessed screen of three arches rested on a robust sill. That sill, in turn, carried an inscription dating the foundation of the building. This epigraphic function reinforced the nonstructural character of the panel, which recalls the curtain walls under the windows of the Bibliothèque Sainte-Geneviève, across the street. But there the similarities ended. Unlike the arches of the Bibliothèque Sainte-Geneviève, those of the Law Library did not support the structure. A recessed panel above them revealed that the masonry between the piers was nonsupporting. Following his teacher's example, Lheureux kept ornamentation to a minimum. Besides some standard carving on the imposts and other similar moldings, the most conspicuous ornaments were the arms of the City of Paris placed high on each of the corner piers.

The analytical quality of Lheureux's design matched Sullivan's new conception of an architectural composition issuing out of planning and construction. Sullivan may have thought that he

Figure 119.
Law Library, Paris,
Louis-Ernest Lheureux
(1876–78).
Architectural Record, 1898.

was looking at a design of 1897, but the appeal of Lheureux's composition may have come not from its alleged modernity, but from its reflection of the lessons he had learned in Paris at the time this building was being designed.[29] From the three windows of the Law Library he may have gone to the three windows of the first design of the Owatonna bank; from the shields at each of the upper corners of the Law Library facade, to the quasi-heraldic cast-iron ornaments on the upper corners of the Owatonna facade; and from Lheureux's structural system, to a load-bearing one. Regardless of how extensive Elmslie's collaboration on the Owatonna bank may have been, it remains Sullivan's work. By possibly fusing into his own vision elements from Lheureux and Barber—as well as from the plans De Wit discovered in *The Architectural Review*—Sullivan came to synthesize a new idea for a building type.

Sullivan's new method of architecture was also similar to that of Ernest Flagg, another former student at the Ecole des Beaux-Arts. According to Mardges Bacon, Flagg "showed respect for building process and legible parts—the very qualities inherent in the French models."[30] Assessing the development of Flagg's commercial buildings, Bacon points out characteristics that also appear

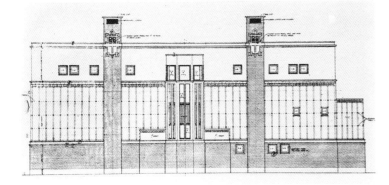

in Sullivan's banks, especially that "corners were closed and emphasized, allowing the middle to be opened up."[31] This typical French trait of considering a facade as a portal was to appear time and again in Sullivan's rural banks, as it did in his first commercial structures, such as the Jewelers' Building (cf. fig. 59).

Sullivan's second bank, the Peoples Savings Bank in Cedar Rapids, Iowa (1910–11), is the most rational and least lyrical in the series (fig. 120). It has a minimum of ornamentation and comes closest to his conception of the Prairie style, in which the volumetric expression of the plan, rendered in tapestry brick, played a very important role. The building consists of a narrow, oblong, two-story central banking room reinforced on the outside with corner pylons and surrounded by a single-story rectangle of offices, all in tapestry brick. Observing its stark appearance, Montgomery Schuyler identified the main characteristics of Sullivan's new style in a passing remark that pointed out how the Cedar Rapids bank had been "clearly designed from within outward," and how "Mr. Sullivan had denied himself all the opportunities of doing what he can do so much better than any other living architect," namely creating "fantastic decoration."[32]

Personal tragedy may have partly accounted for Sullivan's change of style. In 1909, in the wake of the 1907 depression, he was ridden with debt and was compelled to sell his summer cottage on Biloxi Bay, Mississippi. Moreover, he was constrained to move his office from the Auditorium Tower to cheaper rooms below; lost Elmslie's services (Elmslie had long worked on half pay); filed for bankruptcy; and sold at auction his books and works of art to retain only $100.[33] In a letter to Bennett he complained that insomnia, poverty, worry, the auction, and the loss of George Elmslie had driven him as if on a whirlwind "to the very verge of insanity or suicide, or nervous collapse."[34] He recuperated thanks to the care of a friend, Dr. George Arndt, and declared that he was ready to start "a new life," although he was "living hand to mouth, on the bounty of a few warm friends who can ill afford the small advances they have made."[35] It was also in 1909 that he was first approached by the officers of the Cedar Rapids bank, only to have his design rejected because it was much too expensive to build.[36] Desperately in need of work, he simplified the design in 1910, to the point that Montgomery Schuyler could characterize the final result as "a highly specialized machine."[37]

Perhaps he considered that his new style—which he developed out of necessity—was more in keeping with current ideas of progressive architecture, and reached new conclusions on design. St. Paul's Methodist Episcopal Church, Cedar Rapids, and the Carl K. Bennett House project, Owatonna, two of his most austere designs, followed in the wake of the Cedar Rapids bank (figs. 121–22). Sullivan's new emphasis on volume at the expense of decoration accords with his statements in *Artistic Brick*, from 1910. These were not to be followed by new theoretical statements until 1918, when he revised "Kindergarten Chats" and subsequently published his *Autobiography of an Idea* and his *System of Architectural Ornament*. Other than *Artistic Brick*, no written evidence is available concerning Sullivan's ideas on design during most of his bank period. One must turn from its pages to the buildings to glean more about his intentions and preferences.

He did not maintain such a severe, stark style for long. In 1913 he had a change of heart and restored lyrical ornamentation to his aesthetic. At the same time, he attempted to recapture the anthropomorphic quality of his turn-of-the-century skyscrapers, which owed so much to his conception of the Gothic as a paradigm of forces in equilibrium. At first he had difficulties recapturing in the banks the anthropomorphism of the skyscraper period because he allowed lyrical sentimentality to take the upper hand in their design. In the John D. Van Allen & Son Store, Clinton, Iowa (1913–15), he applied three thin, pierlike decorations to only one facade of a corner building, giving the impression of an incomplete program (fig. 123). These vertical decorations were derived from the central piers of the Gage Building facade

Figure 123.
John D. Van Allen &
Son Store, Clinton,
Iowa (1913–15).
State Historical Society
of Iowa.

(cf. fig. 110) but resulted in different expressions of structure and iconography from those at their source. In the Gage Building, the palm-tree-like central piers responded to a need that was both physical (encasing a metallic support) and anthropomorphic (creating an upward visual thrust that contrasted with the downward visual movement of the outside piers), whereas the analogous elements in the Van Allen Store were reduced to unnecessary decorative staffs, since they were placed at the mid-bays and therefore had nothing to do with structural iconography. Although the Clinton building is one of Sullivan's less inspired efforts, its historical importance is assured; it was his first attempt to apply his skyscraper style to a small building.

Sullivan proceeded to give a new dimension to what he had previously learned from the Gothic in the Merchants National Bank, Grinnell, Iowa (1913–14), his first load-bearing construction to show a mastery over a dynamic composition of upward thrusting and downward-bearing forces, symbolic and real (fig. 124). Cautious at expressing anthropomorphism in load-bearing construction, he concentrated his dynamic effects exclusively on the ornamentation around the door and the rose window above it, creating an effect that was appropriate to the characteristics of terra-cotta and

establishing a clear distinction between construction and ornamentation. His new use of terra-cotta ornamentation made his small buildings rich with an anthropomorphic program that linked them to the aesthetic of the skyscrapers, yet did no violence to their load-bearing construction. The sharply defined, box-like shape of the banks accommodated his desire to express construction and to reveal the plan of a building in its volumetric composition. The use of tapestry brick allowed him to develop his new interest in exterior polychromy. In short, he achieved the synthesis of his mature bank style.

The facade of the Grinnell bank is masterly. For a wall of tapestry brick pierced by a door, a rose window, and two rectangular windows, Sullivan developed an extraordinary terra-cotta ornamentation based on a sketch for ornament he designed in April 1902 (Catalogue, pl. 202). Concentric squares, diamonds (squares rotated forty-five degrees), and circles surrounding the rose window seem to be supported by two piers framing the door. Beside each pier Sullivan placed a heraldic winged lion *sejant érecte* holding up a

shield. Gothic-like finials stand atop the cornice above each pier.

The extraordinary elegance of the solution depended on Sullivan's command of geometry and proportion. What had been an approximation to a system in Owatonna became exact in Grinnell, where his design conformed to a module he made evident in the width of the ornaments that make up the cornice.

By way of example, one notices that the facade is a rectangle twenty-one modules wide and nineteen modules high. The diameter of the circular window is four modules and that of the outer terra-cotta circle is nine. The distance from end to end of the efflorescences at the sides of the rose window is eleven modules. The door opening is four modules high, and that is the same dimension from center to center of the engaged columns flanking the door. The height of the portal is six modules to the cornice. The side windows are four and a half modules wide by two and a half modules high (including the lintel ornamented with circles, which is half a module thick). Finally, and as a last example of modularity, the heraldic lions may be inscribed in rectangles that are three and a half modules high (from the pavement to the tip of the wing) and one module wide. A result of the modular system is that the proportions of the perimeter of the building and those of the terra-cotta ornamentation harmonize with each other and with the rest of the composition in ways that, because they are geometrical, are also musical. What had been a fairly simple exercise for the Owatonna bank came to fruition in Grinnell.

A good proof of Sullivan's success in the design of the Grinnell bank is that no one has remarked about its geometry, in spite of how much this building has been studied; the gorgeousness of the building (the feminine-emotional element in Swedenborgian terms) dominates over the rational-masculine geometry. The observer is captivated by the way in which the tapestry-brick wall becomes a subtle background for the terra-cotta ornamentation surrounding the door and the rose window, and by the chromatic contrast between one material and the other. One also notices how much of the ornamentation derives from the Gothic via the skyscrapers. This becomes evident not only in the motifs, but more importantly in the anthropomorphic buoyancy with which the geometrical ornamentation surrounding the window seems to float above the piers and cornice surrounding the door, while, at the same time, being visually supported by them. In the Grinnell bank, furthermore, one encounters the synthesis of Sullivan's studies of Islamic architecture. One admires how beautifully he concentrated the ornamentation around the entrance and window above it, as a medieval Moorish architect would have, controlling fully the observer's attention and not allowing it to wander except to realize the harmony between what is highlighted and its background. Then, there is the final softening touch. The ornamented cornice, like those in the best Islamic buildings, somehow seems to tie everything together. It establishes a nervous skyline that echoes the vibrancy of the terra-cotta below and harmonizes in color with the tapestry brick. Yet it is not overly assertive. It slightly diffuses the importance of the rose window so that one admires the entire building as a work of art and not exclusively its central ornamentation.

In his Grinnell building Sullivan brought his bank style up to a new level by incorporating into his method of design the anthropomorphism he had mastered in designing skyscrapers and by working out complex proportional relationships. Yet the evidence suggests that he did not immediately realize that he had found the best solution to the problem of the rural bank, for with his next such structure he experimented in a different vein. In the Home Building Association Building, Newark, Ohio (1914–15), he investigated further the stylistic possibilities he had first explored in the Van Allen Store and reinterpreted ideas from his late-nineteenth-century skyscrapers—the Gage, Bayard, and Schlesinger & Mayer buildings—on the scale of a two-story structure (fig. 125). On the two street facades Sullivan developed an anthropomorphic program in which the subjective and

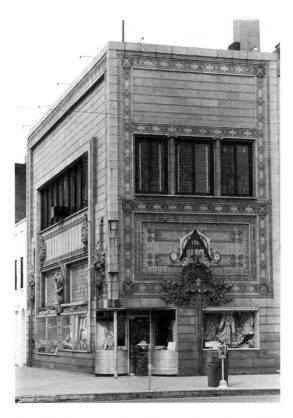

the objective struggle to become interchangeable in ways that are even less successful than in the Van Allen Store. Still obsessed with the idea of a literal adaptation of his skyscraper style onto his banks (in spite of the aesthetic success of Grinnell), Sullivan compressed together too many things: one of his winged lions, a mosaic, a terracotta staff that blossoms profusely in front of the mosaic for no apparent reason, decorative borders that divide the front into four rectangles, more ornamentation on the side, and all kinds of moldings. The Gage facade could not be squeezed onto so small a building.

The Newark bank is also different from all the others in that it is completely clad in greenish-gray terra-cotta. Such a departure from the norm is important as a means of gender identification, an idea rooted in Sullivan's mind by the time he designed the Owatonna bank in 1906. Its browns expressed the idea that banking was a masculine activity as much as they evoked aspects of the Midwestern landscape. At the same time, the design established a link with music through association with French Symbolist poetry, as had been the case with the Owatonna bank.

In establishing chromatic gender differences between dark, anthropomorphic, brown terra-cotta buildings and light, cream or greenish-gray gynecomorphic designs, Sullivan may have remembered that such differentiations were standard in polychromatic sculpture and painting. By way of a few random examples within a tradition more than four thousand years old, one thinks of the painted limestone Egyptian statue *Prince Rahotep and His Wife Nofret*, from c. 2610 B.C. (Egyptian Museum, Cairo); the Roman frescoes in the House of the Vetii, in Pompeii, from before A.D. 79; Peter-Paul Rubens's *The Rape of the Daughters of Leucippus*, from 1617 (Alte Pinakothek, Munich); and Guillaume-Adolphe Bouguereau's *Birth of Venus*, from 1879 (Musée des Beaux-Arts, Nantes). In these examples, and in literally hundreds of others anyone could recall, the male complexion is rendered dark and the female creamy white.

The iconographic assignation of gender through color in the banks was an extension of an earlier, similar attribution in the skyscrapers. Along with the color of the Gage and Schlesinger & Mayer buildings, the cream-white hue of the Bayard established a chromatic contrast with the light terra-cotta brown of the earlier Wainwright and Guaranty buildings. In all probability the shift from brown to cream-white was related to a more pronounced emphasis on the building as an ornament to the city, a context that sought an association with gorgeousness, and hence femininity. So central was that idea in Sullivan's mind that in a description of the Bayard he characterized the building as "cream-white, maidenlike and slender."[38] Taking Sullivan's anthropomorphic and gynecomorphic interests as a parallel of architecture and nature, one may establish a three-part progression in his skyscrapers, based on the relationship of ornamentation and color. In the Wainwright, structure and color dominated visually over the ornamentation; that skyscraper is chronologically the closest to the earlier Auditori-

um style of "male buildings comely in the nude." In the Guaranty, of 1894, he repeated the brown—and hence male—terra-cotta color of the Wainwright, but also increased the feminine or gorgeous element by covering the entire building with ornamentation, which he considered to be more important than the masculine or structural aspect. Thus, the Guaranty stands as an intermediate stage, with masculine and feminine elements having equal importance. Finally, in the Bayard, with its cream-white complexion, he allowed the feminine to dominate through color as much as through ornamentation (as he did as well in his two subsequent tall buildings, the Gage Building and the Schlesinger & Mayer Store). It was in that sense that Sullivan considered the Bayard a "cream-white . . . and slender" gynecomorphic building.

There is another point to consider in this argument: whether Sullivan's use of light-colored materials in the Auditorium Building and its progeny of 1887–92 represents an attempt at gynecomorphism. I do not believe so. His main aim at that time was simplification and abstraction of form—and hence an avoidance of polychromy—and not an expression of a transcendentalist iconography. Transcendentalism first appeared through ornamentation in his work in 1890 with the design of the Getty Tomb and extended into his commercial architecture in 1892 with the first design for the Trust and Savings Building. Furthermore, one also notices the lack of exterior ornamentation (the main gynecomorphic element) in the Auditorium Building and its sequel.

The World's Columbian Exposition may have had an influence on his shift to cream-white buildings. The exhibition had made Chicagoans hungry for urban harmony and cohesion. Sullivan's heightened interest in gorgeousness, lightness, and femininity may have been his answer, his offering of new possibilities, to a society bent on "urbanizing" itself through an academic language that understood architectural elegance in terms of a revival of French seventeenth- and eighteenth-century forms. While his deep hatred for such architecture is a matter of record, he advanced with the times, recognizing, along with academic architects, that buildings should no longer be designed as entities standing in a self-imposed isolation. Rather than disregarding their surroundings, buildings were to respond to the aesthetic needs of the city. In Sullivan's mind this was to be done without loss of individuality in the design. The Bayard, Gage, and Schlesinger & Mayer buildings should be read as parts of a statement of a new and intensely personal urban architectural style as well as fiercely individual specimens of architecture.

In the banks, Sullivan went further than in his late skyscrapers, where he had shown the masculine and the feminine coupled, yet severally distinct. Now sexual signification became interchangeable through his use of color. The large areas of mosaic, of terra-cotta ornamentation, and of art-glass windows softened—gynecomorphized—the brown masculine boxiness of the banks, themselves already softened by the polychromy of the tapestry brick. Without denying the masculinity of banking, the buildings became extensions of the ornamentation. An ambiguous interchange of opposites (masculine-feminine in this instance) became complete and involved whole buildings rather than only parts of them (as had been the case with the piers of the Bayard Building).

In his two last executed banks, Sullivan took the final, logical step beyond his achievements in Grinnell. He involved whole facades in anthropomorphic programs instead of depending exclusively on ornamentation, but prudently limited himself to the tectonic possibilities of load-bearing construction.

This is evident in the Peoples' Savings and Loan Association Building, Sidney, Ohio (1916–18) (fig. 126). There the great arch seems to carry the weight of the spandrels to nothing more substantial than a pair of windows, an imaginative exercise in ambiguity that makes ornamentation above an opening appear to support one of the most ponderous masses of the facade. The mechanical reality is different, however. At each of the lower sides of the elevation a marble base and the

Figure 126.
Peoples' Savings and Loan Association, Sidney, Ohio (1916–18).
Ohio Historical Society.

Figure 127.
Saint-Augustin, Paris, Victor Baltard (1860–71), detail of portal.
Photograph by Narciso G. Menocal.

masonry flanking the windows receive the downward thrust of the arch. To paraphrase Sullivan's statement, "the subjective becomes the objective" and both are interchangeable in this composition, which, at the same time, calls attention to the entrance to the building, the focus of the facade.[39] To emphasize that effect, pillars flanking the door rise to support heraldic winged lions that become symbolic buttresses, propping up visually, though not supporting physically, the mosaic of the tympanum. They recall the four symbols of the evangelists Victor Baltard placed against the tympanum of his Church of Saint-Augustin in Paris (1860–71), a building of recent construction when Sullivan was in Paris (fig. 127).

The hexagons on the cornice of the Sidney bank work as a module in a system similar to that of Grinnell. The great arch, including the terra-cotta archivolt, is nine modules wide, and the brick at each side two and a half. The distance from the crown of the extrados of the terra-cotta archivolt to the top of the staff decorating the cornice is five modules, and it is also five modules from the pavement to the tip of the wings of each lion. The distance from the center of one lion to the other is half that, two and a half modules. Thus on this facade (a total of fourteen modules across and thirteen modules high) Sullivan continued the experi-

ments in geometry that he had refined in Grinnell.

The anthropomorphic program of the Farmers' & Merchants' Union Bank, Columbus, Wisconsin (1919–20), is even richer (fig. 128). Its success depends on its economy of means, good proportions, and the dynamic qualities of its composition. The facade consists of three principal elements: a set of three piers, one huge lintel, and a tapestry-brick panel framing a telescoping arch decorated with terra-cotta archivolts. The openings—windows and door—are less important visually and read like spaces left between these motifs. The loveliness of the facade depends in no small measure on symmetry and balance enriched by harmonious proportions among the parts. By way of example, the top of the lintel divides the facade in half; the radius of the window equals one-sixth of the height of the building, and this is also the height of both the rectangular window and the marble panel of the lintel; the lintel itself may be divided into four squares; and the terra-cotta archivolt rises from the central axes of the two outer lintel squares. All the parts are proportional to

each other and to the whole in a modular system.

A mannered treatment of form prepares the architectural elements for their anthropomorphic roles. The thickness of the lintel is exaggerated, the visual affinity between the arch and the lintel is more important than the relationship between the arch and the window, and the piers hold up the lintel at the ends, rather than at the points supporting the arch. Needless to say, had Sullivan chosen to support the lintel at the springs of the arch, there would have been no need for a central pier, the door would have been on-center, the lintel could have been thinner, and the facade would have been static, academic, and banal.

Finally, there is the anthropomorphic program itself. The observer comes away with the impression that the building resulted from masses surging from below while others pressed from above. What one witnesses as architecture is the final dramatic moment of equipoise on the all-important lintel, which now justifies its thickness. One also realizes that the anthropomorphism of the Columbus bank springs from the essential tectonic characteristics of its load-bearing construction, while finding consonance with the Gothic-derived anthropomorphic and phytomorphic effects of the skyscrapers of the 1890s. Having the richest anthropomorphic program, the bank in Columbus reveals how Sullivan synthesized into one conception his lifelong architectural quest. His French training is evident in the manner in which he used academic forms to underscore an anti-academic idea. The design also makes manifest two other important features: how his later banks and his later skyscrapers are like two different facets of the same crystal, and how his concept of the Gothic, which had to do more with the behavior of form in dynamic composition than with style, is central to the relationship between the two building types.

His architecture of 1906–22 unfolded, then, through trial and error, success and lapse, in a discrete, yet nonlinear development. He traveled a long road from the early banks, which turned away from the designs of the skyscrapers, to the later works, which were based on their lessons, and surpassed them. The 1906 commission from Owatonna opened a new chapter in his career. From memories of the Golden Door of the Transportation Building, and perhaps through his awareness of the Law Library in Paris, he constructed in Owatonna a magnificent box that brought his architecture to a new level of kinship with music, color, and nature in a synthesis similar to that achieved by Impressionist composers and French Symbolist poets. In the Owatonna bank he became the American architectural counterpart of Mallarmé, Rimbaud, Debussy, and above all Maeterlinck, whose work he greatly admired.

That *tour de force* bore no immediate fruit. After Owatonna, he completed only two commissions between mid-1907 and May 1910, the Henry Babson House in Riverside, and the Harold and Josephine Crane Bradley House in Madison, Wisconsin. In those designs he chose to explore the Midwestern progressive style his clients expected of him in residential work. Even more important, he may have decided to use those commissions to broadcast his ability to design houses in the new style, and thus secure more work, since he was in desperate need of money.[40] Those designs helped him reach new conclusions, which he published in 1910 in *Suggestions in Artistic Brick*. Concurrently, he designed his most austere buildings: the Peoples Savings Bank, Cedar Rapids (1910); the St. Paul's Methodist Episcopal Church, Cedar Rapids (1910); and the Bennett House project (1912).[41] The Purdue State Bank, West Lafayette, Indiana, designed in 1913, at almost the same time as the Grinnell bank, falls also into this type of severe architecture, but because it is so small (and had such a small budget) its simplicity may have been the result of financial considerations rather than of a specific aesthetic desire.

Tired of a stern geometry, and possibly missing his characteristically luxuriant ornamentation, for the H. C. Adams & Co. Land and Loan Offices, Algona, Iowa (1913), one of his minor works, he quoted the facade of the Wainwright Tomb in three dimensions rather than two (fig. 129).[42] That incursion into plasticity seems to have whetted his

Figure 129.
H. C. Adams & Co.
Land and Loan Offices,
Algona, Iowa (1913).
Northwest Architectural
Archives,
University of Minnesota.

Figure 130.
Krause Music Store
facade, Chicago (1922);
building by William C.
Presto.
Photograph by
Thomas A. Heinz.

appetite for ornamentation, and he fell into the facile lyricism of the Van Allen Store and of the building in Newark, Ohio, both separated in chronology curiously enough by the superb design of the bank in Grinnell.

While that bank set the style for those in Sidney and Columbus, the Newark building, which was different from them because of its cladding of greenish-gray terra-cotta, later found issue in the Krause Music Store Facade, Chicago (1922), his last executed design, for a building by William Presto (fig. 130).[43] The composition, also faced with greenish-gray terra-cotta, reveals how adeptly Sullivan simplified his excesses in Newark to establish a portal in ways that are proper, because they create a lavish frame.

Aside from the efforts in Newark and Chicago, three among the later banks—the ones in Grinnell, Sidney, and Columbus—show how Sullivan arrived at an extraordinary conception of architecture that in no small measure was in debt to his mastery of geometry and that turned into a synthesis of his philosophical ideas, theory of architecture, and method of design.

In the banks Sullivan created a new architecture out of an amalgam. His new desire to express the plans of buildings volumetrically was part of it, as much as the lessons in anthropomorphism he had learned from the skyscrapers. His new use of color to express poetry, music, and gender and the maturation and extension of virtually every idea he had entertained since the beginning of his career were also part of his new architecture. The process became complete when he matched that iconography with the style, scale, function, and method of construction of his new buildings. His method evolved laboriously as it came to include images of dark and light, of action and reaction, of the subjective and the objective, of the ambiguous and the concrete, and of life and death. It was the portrait of a lyrically rural landscape that also expressed the awesome universality of the cosmos.

One of Sullivan's lifelong interests was to master the architectural expression of Swedenborg's correspondences. His great aspiration had always been to allow the feminine element—the gorgeousness of the building—to dominate the composition completely, and to conceal the masculine-rational sense of geometry that sustains it and gives it order, as for example, the leaves and flowers of a shrub conceal the branches that give it order and rhythm. He achieved this goal first in his ornamental designs of the late 1880s, and later in his skyscraper designs of the 1890s, but he went much further in the banks. In one of the most consciously ambiguous architectural iconographies ever devised, he forced elements of architecture to express their objectively functional character at the same time that they are symbols of opposing subjective meanings at much more profound levels than ever before in his work. Because the sig-nification of the elements of architecture in his banks shifts constantly from one meaning to another, the observer's understanding of each element swings back and forth from one meaning to its opposite, from the objective to the subjective, from the real to the imagined, from the ponderous to the soaring. All this may be the result of analyzing only one element in a building at a time.

The system is even richer than I have heretofore explained. On one level, ambiguities of meaning may be shifting from the objective to the subjective. At the same time, the subjective signification may be changing of meaning on another iconographical level. Such may be the case, for example, of a pier. Its meaning may fluctuate between the objective and the subjective, as it may express compression at the same time that it seems to soar. Yet, while that pier is acting simultaneously in both categories of the objective and the subjective, it may be expressing as well two other opposite subjective meanings. Its dominant color, brown, may express masculinity; the gorgeousness of the polychromy of its different hues, femininity. Making the iconographic ambiguity even richer, the browns of that pier also accord with a subjective representation of the Midwestern landscape. The observer does not realize all these meanings at the same time, but one after another. Thus, appreciation of the banks becomes as rhythmic as Sullivan's transcendentalizing of Herbert Spencer's theories. One thing becomes another to turn into yet a third and even a fourth. Imbedding symbol within symbol and change within change, Sullivan's banks stand for the essential rhythm that supports the cosmos; they rush toward "the mind's native land," as Mallarmé put it. It is perhaps no coincidence that his two last banks, in Sidney and Columbus, in which he best expressed his aesthetic conception of a bank as a building type, roughly coincide with the rewriting of the "Kindergarten Chats," a task that required him to rethink his ideas on architecture. One endeavor reinforced the other, and after a period of search spanning the years from Owatonna to Grinnell, he returned, renewed, to his basic concept of architecture, one that he now expressed in a new style. *The Autobiography of an Idea* and *A System of Ornament According with a Philosophy of Man's Powers*, which appeared after the banks, reaffirmed the implicit statements he had made through the design of his late buildings. His banks were the last and most complete expression of that vision. Far from being a sad epilogue to a once brilliant career, they were its magnificent culmination.

7: Meanings of an Iconography

At the end of his life, Sullivan may have considered that among the approximately 250 drawings he had kept, some represented the highest expression of his poetry. Frank Lloyd Wright, who in many ways understood him best (and to whom Sullivan gave most of the drawings), called him "a lyric poet-philosopher evolving a language of his own—his ornament—in which to utter himself: unique among mankind."[1] Sullivan would have agreed with Wright. A poet, in his definition, was "a man of VISION." Not necessarily a writer of verse, the poet was "the man who sees things rhyme; for rhyme is but the suggestion of harmony; and harmony is but the suggestion of rhythm; and rhythm is but the suggestion of the superb moving equilibrium of all things."[2] The statement leads to the center of his beliefs, to the dictum that "all is rhythm."

Only a "democratic man" could be a poet in Sullivan's terms, an idea he borrowed from Whitman. In *Democratic Vistas* (1871), Whitman established an opposition between *democratic* and *feudal* not in reference to political systems, but to denote characteristics of men who were or were not in communion with nature.[3] He denied that any nation had reached a democratic system, but the United States was on the way to being the first. The salvation of civilization hinged on the maturing of American democracy, a process that would come through a series of emotional, intellectual, and social developments. "The United States," Whitman wrote, "are destined to surmount the gorgeous history of feudalism, or else prove the most tremendous failure of time."[4] But since American political institutions—as they then existed—were democratic only in name, they were unable to bring about the millennium, that is, true

democracy. Only the poet (whom Whitman defined as "the aesthetic worker in any field"),[5] could create a democratic climate by taking "possession of the more important fields."[6] The poet alone understood that "democracy can never prove itself beyond cavil, until . . . it luxuriantly grows its own forms of art, poems, schools, theology, displacing all that exists."[7] These new forms, created by "new races" (that is, by the new man),[8] were to be grounded on nature, seen as both a transcendent force and a cultural reality.

Sullivan expanded the thesis of Whitman's *Democratic Vistas* in his own *Democracy: A Man-Search*, a book he wrote in 1907–8.[9] The work is divided into six "Groups" (each of several chapters) in which he considered the development of man's quest for enlightenment. "Group I: Parting of the Ways" presents man at the crossroads of feudalism and democracy. Groups II, III, and IV, "Face to Face," "The Man of the Past," and "Dreams," look at the past mainly for three reasons: to examine the evils born of misuse of power in the feudalization of money and property, to indict the tyranny of feudal aristocracy, and to make evident man's persistent search for God and for a definition of his own spirit. "Group V: The Man of Today" presents the struggle of the feudal power of money against the democratic power of the artist, each fighting for the soul of modern man. "Group VI: The New Way" describes the future. Peace will come when democracy, nature's ally, destroys feudalism. Man will then understand that what he thought of as "God" was just a rudimentary conception of nature. Relating to a deity through liturgy will finally be perceived as a misunderstanding of man's aspiration to integrate himself with nature through art.

The influence of Hegel's *Philosophy of History* is apparent in Sullivan's assumption that events follow a law of becoming, which he described as follows:

> *The Man of the Past, in his way, sought Justice. The path was tortuous, obscurely lighted. He could not detach right from might, nor right from cunning. He dreamed, aspired, and fell. Again aspired, again to fall. But at each recurring crisis he aspired higher, and fell perhaps not quite so far. For, somehow, somewhere in his heart sang the small voice of Democracy. He heard it now and then in flitting moments. When not too busy at his engrossing feudal tasks, he heard its song—and was cheered, he knew not quite how or why.*[10]

The teachings of Christ offered a glimpse of democracy,[11] but Christianity lives in dread of Christ's gospel out of cowardice. "So western thought . . . in its fanatical resolve to deny the great life and exist boastfully madly apart from it— has reared a Church and many churches wherein to imprison the Christ, that His real voice may not be heard abroad. . . . Indeed it requires the power of a great hierarchy and an army of priests to keep the little voice duly muffled." Western man, Sullivan thought, "has the same love of man on Easter morn that the wolf has for sheep on Easter morn."[12]

Responsibility for this immorality rested with everyone, not exclusively with an abusive minority. Universal reformation was imperative for the establishment of democracy, and universal cowardice was the principal obstacle to progress. Fear makes a man dishonest. It prevents him from following his instincts to make his life a continuous proclamation of the truth he carries within him. Everyone is to blame for the evil in the world: "Poor and rich, the broken, the demented, outcast, criminal are [responsible for evil] just like you and me! There is something interchangeable in us that fits exactly with them all; . . . the *Feudal Thought*; the axle-thought of all civilization of the past and of today."[13]

Feudalism, Sullivan explained, depends on man's inability to grasp his relation with nature.

This inability is the product of man's "singular perversion of his intellect, called vanity, and that singular intellectual repression of his heart, called hypocrisy, [which] have obscured his sanity of vision. So, to fortify himself in his vanity and hypocrisy, to 'prove' that his vision is clear, he has invented philosophies, doctrines, religions, dogmas galore—vain and hypocritical as himself."[14] Recasting earlier ideas, Sullivan stressed that feudal thinking did not issue from the desire of a privileged few to dominate the masses, but from

> *an unadulterated conception of self-preservation in the individual and the mass which evoked the spirit of might . . . as right. . . . Thus the dream of absolutism, as an ambition and a goal, came boldly and bodily imagined forth of the multitudes to lure on prince and priest. And thus, in the dream of the lowly, came the ferment of man's intellectual madness. For the dream of force and cunning, of glory and power, of dominion and servitude, of master and man, made his world unreal.*[15]

While feudalism makes man debase himself while searching for a false security, the situation has improved in the course of history, and "property, vested rights, the law, the constitution, the government, the army and navy . . . [will be seen in the end] as fictions."[16] "It is not because men are essentially vicious that they are feudal," Sullivan insisted, "it is merely because they do not clearly understand the essential and concrete nature of their relationship to their fellows, to the earth, and to the spirit of integrity."[17] Curiosity shows how there is hope for man. It pushes him to circumvent his fears in his search for the meaning of life. "But in his ignorance man has thought that science is the ultimate means for comprehending the cosmos, of which he vaguely understands himself to be a part."[18] As his search for the meaning of life continues, he will realize that trying to understand nature through reason alone is foolish, and therefore vain and feudal. It is then that democracy will become the fulfillment of history. Only in this last stage will every man realize that his true vocation consists of a full existential comprehension of self and that his essence and nature's are one and the same. Democracy, Sullivan defined, "is but the ancient and primordial urge within us of integrity or oneness. . . . For Democracy and the oneness of all things are one."[19] Such oneness moved him to say that "[t]he universe and all therein may be expressed by the word Ego." Since Yahweh defined Himself as "I am," Ego, to Sullivan, "is therefore the I AM of things. . . . Life sings its song:–It is the song of Ego. . . . Man has not believed in Integrity; hence his anguish. . . . Man sings the song of death–the song of fear, the song of distrust–for he knows not Ego. He will not believe that Ego is I AM–and that there is but one I AM, universal, and himself."[20] *Democracy: A Man-Search* is but Whitman modified by Nietzsche. The final outcome will be a race of supermen for whom life will be a constant ecstasy because of a fully realized insight into the essence of the cosmos.

Only such men would be able to understand the full import of his message, of the message he conveyed in the poetry of his buildings and of his ornamentation, or so Sullivan thought in his romantic rapture. In his mind, that poetry was not of his invention. It was a revelation, as much as a shadow, of the universal rhythm: of the cycles of life, death, and regeneration; of the passing of the seasons; and of the way the art of an era emerged, matured, and died, to reappear, transmuted, in the next period, a process Sullivan turned into the subject of his "Etude sur l'inspiration," a long poem in prose of which we have the text in French translation, in longhand, on forty-nine leaves, dated September 1893.[21]

He wrote the poem in connection with his new friendship with André Bouilhet, a *délégué rapporteur*, that is, a member of the jury sent by the Union Centrale des Arts Décoratifs to award prizes at (and pass judgment on) the World's Columbian Exposition. Reviewing Sullivan's relationship with Bouilhet is useful on two accounts. It sheds light on Sullivan's desire for recognition in France and it reveals how a Frenchman of advanced ideas like Bouilhet (who linked Sullivan's work with Art Nouveau because of stylistic similarities in the use of organic decoration) discriminated between Sullivan's writings and his architecture, admiring the latter and all but dismissing the former.

One of Bouilhet's duties in America was to prepare a report on both the Exposition in particular and the state of the arts in the New World, at large. Bouilhet, a metalsmith, wrote his report with the subtitle *Notes de voyages d'un orfèvre*, and used for his text a long letter he wrote to his father from Chicago in July 1893.[22] The date is important in relation to that of Sullivan's "Etude" because Bouilhet quoted from it in July while its date in the Art Institute manuscript is September. Bouilhet told his father in July that Sullivan had given him "[a] small brochure . . . a sort of dithyramb in honor of his art, [in which] one finds an exposition of his ideas in a way that is somewhat clouded, but most certainly very poetic."[23] It is odd, therefore, that Sullivan would go to the trouble of making a new copy, in French, in September. The only speculation I can offer is that in September Sullivan did not know that a letter Bouilhet had written to his father in July would become his report, and might have thought that Bouilhet would publish his "Etude" in the *Revue des arts décoratifs*. On the other hand, as we have seen, Bouilhet thought that Sullivan's poem was interesting but "somewhat cloudy" in style, "a dithyramb," and thus excessively impassioned, and opted only for a few quotations and paraphrases to give the gist of it in his report.

Bouilhet liked Sullivan as an architect and a person, and said of him that "he is an artist, a poet, a dreamer doubling as a practical man; it is delightful to follow the development of his artistic theories, and he does it with such fire in his exposition that he brings you into it and convinces you."[24] Sullivan was the only architect he mentioned by name, and in his report he covered at length the Transportation Building and the Auditorium. He also made a passing complimentary remark on the Fisheries Building, but did not mention the name of its architect, Henry Ives Cobb. The rest of the report, while covering some

art glass, is mostly about American silver, mainly Tiffany's and Gorham's, an understandable choice for a silversmith.

Bouilhet seems to have been a *fin-de-siècle* aesthete. He devoted the first three pages of his report to San Francisco's Chinatown (then different from today) and lamented that he had to return to Chicago when his wish would have been to push on to the Orient and return to France from the East by way of Marseille. He saw America as a young, potent nation creating a fresh new art, one completely different from that of Europe.

In his estimation, while Sullivan was a former student at the Beaux-Arts, he remained *bien Américain*, and his work had "not at all the air of a submission to the Rome Prize."[25] He went on then to say that the Transportation Building was the most original design in Jackson Park. The Auditorium left him with a similar impression: "The decoration was completely original and new for us. . . . M. Sullivan has been careful to give a personal character to his ornamentation and borrowed nothing from the known styles."[26] To make this new work known in France, Bouilhet took with him casts of Sullivan's ornament to Paris, and a galvanoplastic cast of the door of the Getty Tomb remains to this day in the basement of the Musée des Arts Décoratifs in the Louvre (fig. 131).

In his summation, Bouilhet concluded that Americans, and most particularly the silversmiths, were creating an art for their nation and for their time. While he mentioned no names at the end, he may have been thinking of Sullivan as much as of other American artists when he pointed out that in their opinion a new country required a new art. In Bouilhet's view, the style they had created "was a composite—somewhat barbarous, somewhat savage perhaps—which I would gladly call the American style, which is neither Hindu, nor Arab, nor Japanese, but a mixture of little of each, and is renewed by a curiously pointed study of plants and made young by a frank conception of nature, which they admire."[27]

Sullivan's "Etude sur l'inspiration" stands parallel to the earlier and much better known "Inspiration" of 1886. The "Etude" shows how Sullivan's thought had evolved in the seven years between the two works and how his vision of artistic creation and stylistic evolution as homologues of the universal rhythm was clearer than in 1886. The 1886 work had been a frenzied rhapsody proclaiming his understanding of the universal rhythm as the fundamental characteristic of an ever-changing nature. The artist (i.e., the poet) was to translate that universal rhythm into the internal, characteristic rhythms each of his creations demanded. In 1893, after designing the tombs, the Transportation

Building, and a few of the skyscrapers that led to the Bayard design, he was able to explain better than before the relationship of the artist with nature—and the process of creation itself. The new romantic poem in prose was far more sedate in tone than its predecessor.

Probably following Monsieur Clopet's method (with which he had become acquainted when preparing his mathematics entrance examination at the Ecole des Beaux-Arts), Sullivan divided the "Etude" into the standard parts of a theorem. There is a Preface, a Proposition, a Demonstration of the Proposition, and a Conclusion.

The Preface is a summary of the work, as Sullivan says, and considers the evolution of art in five phases, yet only four are stated; the fifth is implied. In the first, art exists as a potentiality dormant in nature. In the second, the artist appears with a yearning for creating, for discovering art within the bosom of nature; this desire, which Sullivan called "inspiration," also comes from nature. In the third phase, the artist, under the dominion of inspiration, puts his desire into action: "At this moment art finds its fulfillment and the culmination of its existence."[28] At the fourth phase Sullivan made a leap from the artist to the art production of an age. Apparently, he had used the word "artist" as a metonymy in the first three phases, standing for a period as much as for a person. In any case, decadence sets in in the fourth phase. Sullivan made no mention of a fifth phase, but later in the text the reader is led to understand that it consists of the death of a period, of its return to nature, whence a new image of inspiration will rescue it, renewed and changed into the new art of a new age.

Sullivan also considered the role of the critic. The critic's task was to ascertain the degree of inspiration the artist has drawn from nature and to judge how well he has been able to express his relationship with it in his art. The critic was also to tell his public whether the work under observation was part of an "ascending or descending period," a notion Sullivan derived from Taine. The position of the critic became parallel to that of the

artist in what Sullivan called in the preface the "second phase." Because they are both human beings, both understand the potentiality for art in nature. Sullivan wrote: "In short, whether creative act, or enjoyment and analysis of art, the fundamental base is always the same, that is, the *spiritualization of the sentiment of nature*."[29]

The first section after the Preface is titled "Artistic Theories of the Author." Sullivan divided it into two subsections, "Sources of Inspiration" and "Artistic Evolution." In "Sources of Inspiration" he explained how art exists as an inert entity in nature and how the human soul can only reach "a hazy Idealism" by itself. Extending his notions of Swedenborgian correspondences, he considered that "[t]rue art is the result of the fertilization of the human soul by the soul of nature," a sexual metaphor that to him had the force of a straight statement of fact.[30] In "Artistic Evolution" he explained that the fertilization, gestation, and birth of art was a process governed by "the law of unity that governs the worlds of bodies and spirits. . . . The evolution of art is the faithful shadow of the evolution of nature, and of its reproduction." It is born, matures, degenerates, and dies. Possibly considering much of the architecture of his day and of the need to regenerate it into something else, he added: "Art that has completed its cycle must be allowed to disappear." Then, and because "death is only temporary . . . a new era arises." As in nature, where new plants, though issuing from new combinations and effects, always resemble the species from which they emerged, "each school of art establishes a harmony with the period that witnessed its birth and composes an original symphony with the idea that gives it shape."[31] And he reiterated, "It seems that today we are coming to the end of a long artistic interregnum and that we shall witness the blossoming of a young school."[32]

In the second section, "Proposition," the subsection titles make evident the sexual metaphor involving man and nature: "Nature in Isolation Is a Lost Force" and "Fertility of the Soul of Man in Communion with the Soul of Nature."

The third section, "Demonstration of the Proposition," subtitled "The Voices of Nature," is the longest in the work, and the most repetitive. It explains how the birth and growth of art are similar to daybreak and dawn, as well as to the rise of spring, which turns into summer. Inexorably, art will degenerate, as nature does in autumn, and the artist will despair. Sullivan became exuberantly romantic in this section: "And thus a great soul disappears forevermore into the deep darkness, never to live again. It gives up the struggle, unable to retain a life that flees, and embraces death, which drags it into nothingness."[33] But then (and continuing in his romantic vein), "If death is unavoidable, resurrection is certain," and the cycle begins again with the "Appearance of a New Artistic Evolution."[34] Paraphrasing Taine, Sullivan concluded: "Thus, in a generation that blossoms and grows under the same sun flows a common life, the soul of an era; the impulse of a common spirit pushes all its members to a unique labor, the incarnation of a dream of art that will stamp them with its heraldic seal."[35]

The "Etude" ends with Sullivan's "Conclusions," in which he presented a number of dicta he called "Thoughts" that he had stated as well in the 1886 "Inspiration," also as conclusions. These "Thoughts" point to the existence of what Sullivan called earlier the "Inscrutable Serenity" and to his belief that everything in the cosmos, whether physical, spiritual, or intellectual, owes its existence to the superior rhythm from which everything, including time, generates.

A few themes link together the sections of the "Etude." One is that the existence of the sublime in nature depends on the existence of human sensitivity. ("Only the heart of man . . . that brings forth the marvelous, makes the forest powerful and astonishing.")[36] Another is the sexual metaphor in which Sullivan presented the creative force issuing from the alliance of nature and the human soul wooing each other.[37] A third theme is the extension of Swedenborgian correspondences into the creative process, with nature being the feminine-intuitive element and the "soul of man" the mas-

culine-rational. Finally, there is the typical Sullivanesque notion that without death there is no regeneration, a result of the universal rhythm.

While most of Sullivan's writings deal with the fundamental idea of the universal rhythm, nowhere did he depict it better than in his ornamental work, which developed more concisely than his architecture. Also, it matured earlier because it was not complicated by issues of typology and referred to only one criterion: his vision of nature. His ornamentation, the core of his iconography, developed in several stages. First, in the 1870s, there was a calligraphic, abstracted, symmetrical style that was no different from the standards of the day (Catalogue, pl. 7). By the early 1880s there is evidence of a new language Sullivan established with vegetal forms. Although retaining symmetry, these new forms were fleshier and more convincingly organic, less English, and closer to the style of Ruprich-Robert (Catalogue, pl. 87). Soon thereafter the rhythms became more sensuous, ascending flamelike, and leaves and stems seemed to sway, as in a breeze (Catalogue, pl. 108). Also, superposition of elements and complex interlaces appeared, as well as juxtaposition of different motifs (Catalogue, pl. 125). From that time on, around 1890, his stylistic language was set in vocabulary as much as in grammar and syntax, and he was free to develop its poetic content to whatever levels his aesthetic aspirations required.[38]

Other than botanical and geometrical forms, he used other figures as ornamental motifs. There were winged females below the eaves of a number of tall buildings and, in different form, on the facade of the Transportation Building. In addition, he used a small repertory of heraldic beasts, including griffins, lion heads, lions *sejants érectes*, and American eagles. Except for the eagle and the lion, frequent symbols in nineteenth-century American banking and finance, he used those motifs only ornamentally, in ways unrelated to standard late-medieval iconography. Yet the central staff of the Krause Music Store facade carries a letter K surrounded by a wreath in ways that suggest heraldry, and the cast-iron ornaments on the upper corners of the facades of the Owatonna bank remind one of scutcheons surmounted by helmets (fig. 132). Finally, on the tower of the first design for St. Paul's Methodist Episcopal Church, Cedar Rapids, Iowa (1910), he placed angels playing trumpets, a clear homage to the *Frieze of the Seven Sacraments* in the Brattle Square Church of his youth, although Bartholdi put them at the corners and Sullivan in the middle of the wall (cf. figs. 120 and 49).[39]

The best explanation of Sullivan's ornamentation came at the end of his life, in his *A System of Architectural Ornament According with a Philosophy of Man's Powers*, which completes for us his image as a poet.[40] He presented in it a system of iconography which he believed to be universal because he saw it as a reflection of nature.

The story of how the work developed is well known. A group of Chicago architects, Sullivan's fellow members at the Cliff Dwellers Club, "conceived the idea that he should perpetuate his name and philosophy in some enduring form."[41] The Burnham Library of the Art Institute was brought into the project, as well as Charles Whitaker, editor of the Press of the American Institute of Architects. The result was the publication of *A System*, a book illustrated with twenty plates of prodigious artistry in which Sullivan synthesized his ideas on ornamentation. The reproductions for the original edition were to be in halftone, but because of technical difficulties, not to say cost, Whitaker, who was in charge of the project, chose a line-cut process printed in gray ink. Sullivan came to detest the plates, finding them dull and dead rather than alive and breathing in their own atmosphere. All subsequent editions of *A System* reproduced the plates of the original edition except for the 1990 edition of the Art Institute of Chicago, for which a system of reproduction better than the one Sullivan intended was chosen, with each nuance of Sullivan's pencil and each slight foxing of the paper becoming amazingly clear. What is more important, this edition is the first to present all the text and titles that Sullivan

Figure 132. Owatonna bank, cast-iron ornament. Photograph by Thomas A. Heinz.

rightly considered to be of capital importance, and that had been expunged from all previous editions, including the first.

Sullivan linked his system to an aesthetic theory of the creative process as he thought nature intended it to be. He developed his assumptions in three phases: the sensory, the spiritual, and the practical. In each the inorganic became organic, the ideal real, and the subjective objective. The drawings translated the dialectics of the synthesis of the objective and the subjective into visual symbols in which organic efflorescence issued from systems of lines, straight or curved. The method synthesized Swedenborg's and Spencer's ideas. In a parallel with Swedenborgian correspondences, vegetal motifs, representing the feminine-emotional, dominated visually, while the underlying linear system, standing for the masculine-rational, sustained the design as a structure. The Spencerian analogy was related to an expression of the eternal becoming. Any shape could turn itself into a decorative motif by generating ornamentation, theoretically of itself. Any item of ornamentation contained, and eventually could give birth to, new motifs, a process that could repeat itself even an infinite number of times.

The manner in which complex forms may generate from inorganic and organic matrixes is the subject of Plates 1 and 2. Plate 1, titled "The Inorganic," begins with a square, an inorganic form (Catalogue, pl. 252). By means of increasingly complex ornamental lines, Sullivan developed the shape into a decorative motif in which the gorgeousness of the efflorescence (which could never become totally organic, since it issued from a square) dominates over the geometrical system.

Plate 2, "Manipulation of the Organic," is the obvious counterpart to Plate 1. It begins with two rows of fourteen simple and compound leaf forms (Catalogue, pl. 253). The purpose now is to show how one natural form could become another and how, in turn, that second form may produce infinite morphological variations that depend exclusively on the inventiveness of the artist, or, as Sullivan would have it, on his inspiration, which was always dependent on his embracing nature and losing himself in her. On a third row of drawings Sullivan changed the shape of one simple leaf form into a compound one. Then he took two different stages in that development and turned them each into an ornament at the bottom of the page. The principle Sullivan is explaining on this plate is symbolized by the figure on the center of the sheet. A seed germ with two cotyledons stands for the universal beginning from which nature created the entire vegetal kingdom, in all its variety.

Sullivan developed his ideas on the inorganic-organic duality further in Plates 3 and 4, and now, in the new edition of *A System*, we come to know his intentions fully. Inasmuch as this edition published for the first time all the different blocks of Sullivan's text that had been deleted previously, we finally have Sullivan's all-important definition of morphology, "a process whereby an original form gradually changes into another form."[42] Plate 3 shows how the elemental shapes of the circle, the square, and the triangle are capable of generating all polygons, and from them creating myriad combinations of axes and subaxes (Catalogue, pl. 254). Following Sullivan's conception of morphology, those lines are capable of releasing something akin to aesthetic energy and therefore develop designs. Since Sullivan was dealing here only with inorganic form, the compositions, perforce, depend on axial symmetry. In Plate 4, "Fluent Geometry," he showed how axial, symmetrical design may become progressively dynamic by allowing the lines to become increasingly plastic (Catalogue, pl. 255).

The previously deleted titles of Plates 5 and 6 tell us much. Five is "The Value of Axes [Life is Infinite]" and 6 is "Manipulation of Variants in a Given Axial Theme"—theory and practice, as it were. Now that Sullivan's definition of morphology is available to us, his statement on Plate 5 gains new life through a fuller meaning. Sullivan wrote: "Any line straight or curved, may be considered an axis, and therefore a container of energy, and directrix of power. There is no limit to variations or combinations, or to the morphology possible" (Catalogue, pl. 256).[43] That is to say, in ornamental design, axes are the determinants of morphology. They are like evergrowing branches shooting out leaves and blossoms as well as new branches that become new axes by themselves. Plate 6 develops further the subject of Plate 2 and shows how those combinations are all but limitless (Catalogue, pl. 257). Sullivan began at the top of the sheet with a simple design of three curvilinear lines labeled A, B, and C. The four ornaments that complete the plate demonstrate how each line can dominate as an axis over the other two, and how, as well, all three axes can reach a state of compositional equilibrium.

The third step in Sullivan's program (after showing the duality of the organic and the inorganic and the morphological importance of axes) was to devote the rest of the treatise, beginning with Plate 7, to what he called "the doctrine of parallelism" (Catalogue, pl. 258).[44] Parallelism, to Sullivan, was far more than a geometrical device to establish rhythm and measure—although it was that as well. He considered it to be "mystical." Man becomes co-creator by what Sullivan saw as "the powers of the imaginative will. . . . His creations are but parallels of himself," as well as expressions of "the parallelism between man and nature."[45] In architecture, parallelism was to be expressed geometrically, and more profoundly so, in curvaceous rhythms of ornamentation. Moreover, by stressing the importance of parallelism through word and drawing, and by insisting on the existence—and even mystery—of hidden morphological rhythms of growth, dissolution, and new growth, Sullivan, without so stating, brought *A System* full circle in his theory and returned to the beginning, to the "Essay on Inspiration," to "the complex thought of rhythm—for all is rhythm." Through the doctrine of parallelism he turned ornament into an entity with universal iconographical value, for it stood as metaphor, simile, and symbol of the essence of anything in the cosmos, and as such of the cosmos itself.

Through parallelism, ornamentation fulfilled a social role. It was to be, collectively, an object lesson demonstrating the creative possibilities of man in communion with nature. It was meant to help create an enlightened citizenry by making man live in a "naturally" gorgeous environment. Sullivan's aim was to create through his work—or better, through the observer's recognition of his work—a community equal to that which nature would have created, had the community been a natural product. His was the standard dream of all utopians to recreate the Garden of Eden. But in that Garden of Eden the individual (as the "democratic" unit) was to retain his own personality. Each ornament in a Sullivan building calls for our attention as well as serving a purpose within a program. It is only within the whole that individuality—and the purpose of individuality—can be seen, as is the case, for instance, of a flower in nature, or more to the point, of the tone of a single brick within a tapestry wall.

Sullivan believed that what he called democracy was the ultimate realization of the oneness of all things. The true was implied for him in the realization of the oneness of all in a transcendent cosmos. The good depended on the realization of one's place in that transcendent totality. The good

and the true, leading into the beautiful, would also bring humanity into an aesthetic vision similar to the Christian beatific vision, or to Emerson's ecstasy. Like *caritas* in Christianity, democracy was to bring beauty to everyday intercourse, and his ornamentation expresses his message better than his buildings because of its succinctness and intensity. In his opinion, "ornament should appear, when completed, as though by the outworking of some beneficent agency it had come forth from the very substance of the material and was thereby the same right that a flower appears amid the leaves of its parent plant."[46]

Sullivan considered himself a poet first and an architect second, a statement that brings up the romantic issue of the divinely inspired poet. That divinity was embodied in a transcendent nature; it was the "creative spirit," as he called it. He saw himself as a prophet, and, as architect, he believed himself to be an agent of nature. His buildings make evident that vision because of their two different functions. One is the obviously typological: the building is a bank, an office building, a church, or a residence. But differently from other architects, while he developed forms corresponding with the use of the building, he portrayed the relationship between form and use in a transcendental manner. A building should express what it is in the same way that a pine, for instance, expresses "pineness."

Ornamentation played a singularly important role in the expression of the essence of a building, as it touched on the transcendent, and George Hersey's comment that the Latin verb *ornare* (to ornament) means "to prepare" as well as "to beautify" comes to mind.[47] Hersey gave as example the crucial segment within a sentence in one of Hyginus's fables, but a translation of the entire statement clarifies further the meaning. According to Hyginus, "*Ibi Aeneas patris ornavit exequias, ludicroque certamine honores debitos manibus solvit.*"[48] My translation: "There [in Sicily], Aeneas made ready his father's funeral rites by fulfilling the honors owed the souls of the dead with contests and games." Extending, then, the signification of the verb, if one considers that a Roman architect orna-mented a temple to prepare it for the deity, one might ponder to what end Sullivan used orna-mentation. In other words, what was he preparing his buildings for?

The answer brings us to the second function of Sullivan's architecture—arguably the most important. He prepared the building—or the space—for us; for reinforcing in our minds the notion that each of us, like each of his architec-tural forms, has a pre-established function to per-form in nature, or to call it differently, a natural vocation. His buildings may be called in that respect "temple-like" because he ornamented them with our reception of his democratic vision in mind—his vision of the all in all. As a temple, each becomes an image of cosmogony, a "sacred space," as opposed to a "profane space," to quote Mircea Eliade's terms.[49] He established ambiguous rhythms in the service of that didactic function, evoking the plant-like and the mineral-like and the human-like, and turning those metaphors into facets of the same crystal. As perhaps he would have liked to think, all his metaphors stood for the same truth. Each pointed to the functions nature intended for his buildings since the beginning of time. There is, furthermore, the issue of the all in all. Each entity in nature partakes of the cosmos, is an image of the cosmos, and the cosmos partakes of it. On the other hand, each entity is itself and no other. That ambiguity was also part of Sullivan's vision. Each of his buildings, individually, turns into a witness to a transcendent nature, and we are back, once more, to his idea of parallelism.

His conception of democracy explains his buildings and allows us to enjoy them all the more because we realize that the building, as an aes-thetic fact of extraordinary quality, matches the aesthetic vision of Sullivan the artist. The state-ment that "all is rhythm" was for Sullivan the embodiment of the godhead who reflected his image in all that is. He took that image and turned it into architecture. To the last he evoked what he understood to be the rhythm of nature by using compositional contrasts of ornamentation and plasticity. His writings and his buildings are the two sides of a single coin. In both he always returned to an ideal archetype pulsating with the tension of opposites, and he stood his teleological idea of architecture at the center of his work.

INTRODUCTION TO

Study on Inspiration

"Etude sur l'Inspiration," Louis Sullivan's revision of his 1886 "Essay on Inspiration," is a forty-nine-leaf document (including a cover sheet and four title pages), handwritten in French, dated "Sept. 1893" and initialed "JE." The manuscript is in poor condition. Beginning with leaf 3, what appears to be water staining becomes progressively more intrusive as the text proceeds, making portions of the "Conclusion" starting on leaf 40 virtually unreadable. The translators have therefore enclosed with brackets the words they have supplied when context dictates, including the word "illegible."

Acquisition records indicate that George Elmslie donated the "Etude," along with other Sullivan material, to the Art Institute of Chicago in June 1947. (A photocopy of the original was made available for research in October 1980.) On a typed inventory of those gifts Elmslie wrote that the "Etude" was "translated by a friend of L. Sullivan's," meaning that it was originally written in English.

According to historian Lauren Weingarden, that friend may have been John Edelmann, because the "JE" on the lower-right corner of the "Etude" cover sheet closely resembles the "JE" with which Edelmann initialed one of his few surviving architectural drawings.[1] Sullivan met Edelmann in 1873 when both were employed by Chicago architect William Le Baron Jenney, remaining friendly through Edelmann's various relocations that culminated in his late 1880s move to New York, where he died in 1900. It may be that the cast of ornament Sullivan designed for the 1891 Charlotte Dickson Wainwright Tomb in St. Louis that Edelmann installed as a living-room frieze in his 1894 Kearney, New Jersey, residence was a belated wedding present, as his chroniclers have suggested,[2] or even a house-warming gift. But, according to Weingarden, it might also have been a thank-you for the recent "Etude" translation, or

possibly all three rolled into one. On the other hand, since there is no evidence that Edelmann knew French, it could be that Sullivan gave him a copy already translated by a third party, and that Edelmann initialed the manuscript to indicate ownership, should he lend it to someone else.

The "Etude" may have been translated, perhaps even written, to strengthen what Weingarden calls Sullivan's "second French connection," the first being his student stay at the Ecole des Beaux-Arts in Paris in 1874–75. Of the many commentators on the 1893 World's Columbian Exposition in Chicago, only André Bouilhet made it a point to interview Sullivan, so impressed was he with the decorative and color programs of the Transportation Building. Bouilhet's essay in the September 1893 issue of the *Revue des arts décoratifs,* organ of the Union Centrale des Arts Décoratifs, praised Sullivan effusively, paraphrasing some passages and directly quoting others from a little brochure that Sullivan gave him,[3] that is, the "Etude," also dated that month. Weingarden proposes that Sullivan gave Bouilhet a rough draft of the manuscript to inform his *Revue* essay. But this would not preclude another possibility: that he later sent Bouilhet a finished copy—hoping for French publication—to accompany an exhibition of ornamental pieces Sullivan donated to the Musée des Arts Décoratifs, André Bouilhet serving as "intermediary," in 1894.[4]

Just as Bouilhet took certain liberties with portions of the "Etude" text—he "summarized the tenets, made corrections of the grammar, and eliminated the passages he thought were unessential," Weingarden writes[5]—so too have the present translators, but in different ways for different reasons. That version of "Inspiration" was never published in its original English form and presumably never will be, Sullivan's text apparently having been lost. And only the fragments Bouilhet transcribed have appeared in French. Bearing in mind that Sullivan's extensive writings still in print enable readers to savor his unique manner of expression, and that his prose was informed by late-nineteenth-century literary conventions not our own, the translators have chosen to render "Etude sur l'Inspiration" in a style more appropriate for the era in which it is for the first time published in its entirety than for the era in which it was originally conceived.

Study on Inspiration

LOUIS H. SULLIVAN

Preface

Let me summarize briefly the essential ideas of this essay.

The evolution of art develops in five phases:

First phase. Art appears first in nature as the potential of an inert power awaiting a moving force, a seed ready to bring life to the human soul.

Second phase. The artist is the moving force; his soul is the virgin soil where that seed will germinate. By linking himself to nature, the artist incorporates the seed into himself, giving art a concrete and individual form.

At the height of this phase, impelled by *inspiration*, the artist feels the desire to act born within him.

Third phase. Now the artist moves beyond desire to *action*; he executes the work that inspiration has given him the desire to create. At this moment art finds its fulfillment and the summit of its existence.

Fourth phase. Decadence begins. The artist lives in a dwindling twilight; his ideal blurs; his artistic sensibility dulls. Degeneration increases to the point at which his intellectual spark leaves him once and for all. Degeneration has plunged the artist into the deepest shades of forgetfulness, and he is like a corpse deprived of a soul.

♣

Having sketched the artist's role and odyssey, let us turn to the observer, to the critic who confronts the artist and his work.

The critic seeks to determine the phase to which the work of art he sees belongs, of which ascending or descending period it bears the mark. He assesses the personality of the artist; he weighs the significance of the artist's inspiration, which will have been drawn from contemplation of nature as well as from the examination and even more vital perception of the sentiments of the human soul. The critic measures the power of the artist's inspiration, fountainhead of all artistic expression, discerning the importance and the aim of the artist's work, and the value of his achievements.

As a result the critic develops an intelligence as sharp and complete as the limits of his own artistic sensibility, and as his capacity to empathize with the object of his study, will allow.

In short, whether creative act, or enjoyment and analysis of art, the fundamental base is always the same, that is, the *spiritualization of the sentiment of nature.*

Spirituality by itself is nothing but aimless and weak abstraction because one has lost sight of physical nature.

Sensuality by itself ends in a sterile and narrow materialism, since it is devoid of any idealization! Only the fusion of soul and senses, their communion with nature and humanity under the aegis of ardent empathy, can give birth to a true art.

♣

Since art exists in nature as veiled and latent power,

Since perception of that power and possession of that mysterious force by the human soul is the true source of inspiration,

I wanted to attempt a celebration of that never-ending hymn of the human soul as it searches for and is joined to the soul of nature.

A. Theories
Artistic Theories of the Author
♣
I. Sources of Inspiration
♣

The soul of things is in itself an inert power. Its slavish imitation is nothing more than gross materialism.

The human soul, by itself, can only give form to a hazy Idealism and create weak abstractions without foundation.

True art is the result of the fertilization of the human soul by the soul of nature.

❧

Such a fertilization proceeds through six phases:

(I) The human soul, plunging into the depths of nature's manifestations, listens to the voices that come forth: the voice of spring: blossoms' freshness; the voice of summer: triumph's full bloom; the voice of fall: decadence's sadness; the voice of death: nothingness; the voice of the sea: infinity.

(II) Filled with these manifestations, having heard these various languages, the human soul *retreats into itself* to seize their spirit and soul, and then assimilates them.

(III) In contact with the soul of things, human *imagination* awakens.

(IV) Then come conception and gestation, from which springs *inspiration*.

(V) Inspiration begets the *desire* to express [nature's manifestations] in visible form.

(VI) The *incarnation* of that desire is a *work of Art*; the incarnator, is the *Artist*.

II. Artistic Evolution

❧

By virtue of the law of unity that governs the worlds of bodies and spirits, the evolution of art is the faithful shadow of the evolution of nature, and of its reproduction. Art proceeds in its development through three phases that follow each other according to an inexorable law, as in nature: the burst of spring, the triumph of summer, and the decadence of fall. Then, inevitably, decrepitude and the extinction of the artistic era come. No effort may cancel its demise, any attempt is useless. There is life no longer, only reminiscences without originality, false conceptions, whimsies in bad taste. The spirit that kept that artistic era alive is no more. Art that has completed its cycle must be allowed to disappear. Then comes a period of transition, comparable

to the death of winter in nature.

But that death is only temporary.

❧

Dormancy, then a new era arises, its point of departure is what remains of the preceding school, just as renewal is based on the compost and the seeds of the preceding year.

The new school, in turn, must find its inspiration in the sources of nature, and follow the same phases as its predecessor.

❧

Each successive artistic epoch, however, has its own traits, its specific physiognomy, even though it uses identical material, follows an identical evolution.

As with nature, whose plants, always the same, create arrangements and combinations resulting in effects that are always different, always new, so also each school of art establishes a harmony with the period that witnessed its birth and composes an original symphony with the idea that gives it shape and personifies it.

Each artist in that school makes a contribution at once personal and part of a whole, itself representing a unique edifice, since all artists' work springs from the same spirit which gives life to the epoch, all share the same faith, follow the some ideal.

It seems that today we are coming to the end of a long artistic interregnum and that we shall witness the blossoming of a new school.

B. Proposition
Nature in Isolation Is a Lost Force

❧

Look at the forest, laborious creation of the ages! Is it not, by itself, but a plaything of the storm? Look at it—raising itself powerfully!

The tocsin of the onward rushing tempest has tolled. The destroyer comes forth, with its awesome fury!

The giant [trees], bent by its blast, howl together in a frenzied choir. Teeth chatter at the sound of their infernal music! In the storm's occasional flickers of light, the eye catches glimpses of the enormous mass resisting. —A blinding bolt of lightning! —A deafening thunder! —A stark odor of pitch! —Then, silence! —A great groaning! And the work of centuries falls, smashed to pieces; the might of centuries lies reduced to nothing. Is the forest worth more than a spark, than a furtive smile, than a straw?

Only the heart of man, his powerful heart, his heart that brings forth the marvelous, makes the forest powerful and astonishing. His soul envelops it with sympathy, holding it close. Man alone creates its grandeur, weaving it into his joys and his tragedies.

Fertility of the Soul of Man in Communion with the Soul of Nature

When the soul of nature and the soul of man sing in cadence they give voice to ravishing expressions, unforgettable ecstasies; they ring forth in extraordinary raptures!

In their rich, varied tongue they tell a thousand charming stories in which themes of life and death mingle with our smiles and tears.

Creative force is born of this alliance of two infinites, nature's boundless reality, the heart's boundless illusion. As they mingle they reveal Idealization of Reality, Incarnation of the Ideal. The soul of nature becomes a hymn to life as it emanates from the human soul.

C. Demonstration of the Proposition

The Voices of Nature

The Voices of Spring

Daybreak

In nature—The daybreak of the new year, gliding amidst thick clouds, shines dimly on a drowsy world. Wild grasses, the first to be awakened, venture to sprout and cover with a downy velvet the damp rock and the empty plain.

At the same time, a timid murmur arises from the shrubs, the first flare of harmony announcing the coming of spring.

In man—The benumbed heart awakens with the cool breeze. The winter snows that imprisoned it melt and flee like a stream flowing quickly down the mountain.

Opening the door to the new day, the heart hears the newborn world's hesitant dawnsong!

Dawn

In nature—Stolid vistas break into movement everywhere.

The sun rises through pink mists.

The limpid light increases, revealing silhouettes in the distance against a pearly horizon.

The breeze, leaping across the four corners of the earth, murmurs with its cool voice to each in turn the signal of the grand awakening.

Nature, on the watch, comes forth joyously, arranging her spring attire on the way. —In the silken folds of her green robe, she places slender blossoms of soft coloring; with each step she places new ones, their fragile life soon spent next to her breast. —Then, discarding those ephemeral adornments, she covers herself with a thousand hardy, vivacious flowers that dazzle the eye with their bright colors.

Man—Man walks in the purified air, quivering with the joy of life. Spontaneous thoughts burst from his soul, as fountains gush from snowy rocks. His imagination expands like a river in the misty valley. Pulsating with hope, rich with desires, his heart listens to the marvelous symphony that rises from everything that grows and mounts to the heavens.

The Voices of Summer

In Nature—

Deep greens terraced *en masse* glistening in the summer sun!

Sparkling colors, ravishing the eye!

Invisible clouds of perfumes floating over the

plain and hovering underneath the foliage! Visible breath of the earth, dancing in the heated air to the strident sound of the cricket. Nature spreads out her glories; it is the triumph of life.

On every branch sounds the lusty fanfare of the birds: love, love, long live love!

In man—Thus the various elements turn in rhythmic cadence around man, the center and sun of nature.

They go forth in joy to fulfill their destiny, now at its noon hour, from whence they will proceed submissively to the inevitable conclusion, ever-recurring destruction.

It is the human being who attracts, harmonizes, and illuminates them, and breathing in their essence, gives them his creative soul in exchange. Flood my heart, waves of growing nature! Ebb and flow in its vast estuary! Spread on its shores the swelling flow of your immensity!

I know you now, oh Nature! My deepest sight has fathomed the secrets of your life: it reaches, across your changing expressions, to the distant fountain from which comes all Joy!

The Union
♣

Amidst the tender grasses and the prairies covered with flowers, the lark conceals itself, hops, runs, retraces its steps, imbibing the odors that surround and intoxicate it.—

It opens its wings, soars, and quickly rises toward the sky; its eye always fixed on the distant earth.

It flies, its heart throbs, its songs grow more joyful as it sees now at a glance immense tapestries of grass, undulating groves.

It spins among the images, at last embracing the fairyland of nature, possessing it.

And, satisfied, it throws itself to the wind, which softly places it on its nest.
♣

Thus man, roaming the countryside all day, has drunk the sap [of nature] and fills his heart with the plenitude of life.

Light dims, and the reddening of the dusk guides me toward the fresh and calm haven of night. *But* in the depths of darkness, the beloved memory of the day's visions accompanies me. Under the caress of the serene light of the moon my senses slumber as my spirit awakens. In the delicious isolation into which my soul withdraws, its dream resonates with the suggestive impulses of its remembrances.

[The soul of man] seeks the fertilizing soul of nature through the visions that have charmed it, until he sees it, waits for it, and embraces it. Inspiration comes forth, my heart overflows, my tongue loosens, my breath bursts forth in melodious song, a creative cry that echoes in the very stars.

The Voices of Autumn
The Voices of Winter
♣

Artistic Evolution
♣

I. Old Age and Death of Nature
♣

In the gray light of autumn days, darkened leaves swirl in the air and fall one by one to join their dead companions while the giant [trees] sing the adagio of funereal lamentations.

The richly adorned robe of nature falls in tatters. Trees, like fleshless specters, brutally crash their dead limbs against each other. A shroud of mists extends over an anemic nature that lies down to sleep.

The birds are gone: the forests are silent.

The withered hills, cracked by long droughts, bristling with leafless bushes, seem like a group of old women squatting side by side wrinkled by the years and by the torments [of life], whistling a lugubrious elegy through their broken teeth.

It is summer that is gone; a summer that will not return; a grand existence has been laid to rest in the tomb where it awaits the requiem of the winter snows.

The savage winds howl in the darkness, like forsaken dogs.

Night, in black velvet robes, its finger circled by the crescent of the moon like a jewel, royally presides over the sleep of nature.

Stalactites of ice reflect light furtively in the shade.

Smashed oak trees, cracked, weathered rocks, impure air of damned days, monstrous shocks of waves, cinders of destroyed cities, broken bridges, interrupted commerce, fortunes destroyed, ruin and desolation everywhere!

II. Decrepitude and Death of an Artistic Era

♣

And we, who held nature in our arms in her flowering youth, share in the agony of her withered old age: a common empathy makes us follow her phases and suffer the fate of her evolution.

From the first to the last, do not our creations issue from the union of the soul of things with the human soul? The same inexorable law commands these two souls, rules over their common birth, their common growth, and their common decay.

When an art that has grown old faces decrepitude, vain it is to want to halt the course of destiny that drags it into the tomb.

Instead, let our sympathy follow the dying [art] on its way to the sepulchre. The inexorable hour has struck.

At that moment the long litany of unfulfilled promises passes before our weeping eyes. —The heart grows anguished and sinks into despair. —Benumbed by submission, man wanders into the valley of negation in quest of unseizable phantoms.

A muffled voice issues from that half-open tomb where lies a consummated life. It slowly strings together the memories of the past: the pure joy of now so remote a childhood, the ardors of youth that have faded away; the illusions that wilted without having blossomed.—And then, what?— It instructs us to look kindly on the slow decay of that beautiful life, once so spontaneous, fresh, and vivid. It instructs us to be sympathetic toward those loves killed by desires that were not fulfilled.

This is the time when erroneous judgments, aborted projects, and failings of all sorts float in the air.

Seeds have only sterile soil in which to germinate, just as ideas have bloomed, later on to fade.

The rotten [tree] trunks are sapless; why waste belated cares on them?

The last breath of the Spirit that animated that age escapes slowly, the ultimate sigh of the dying. The body, bereft of a soul, lies inert, as a leaf floating to Nirvana.

And thus a great soul disappears forevermore into the deep darkness, never to live again. It gives up the struggle, unable to retain a life that flees, and embraces death, which drags it into nothingness.

In the storm of death, what is the weight of our feeble hopes and of our childish fears? They are like a spark from a chimney on a stormy night, that shines for an instant and disappears into black forgetfulness.

Resurrection of Nature
Appearance of a New Artistic Evolution

♣

But the death that levels is at the same time the source of life.

Eternal and sublime companion of all existence, it destroys to create.

If death is unavoidable, resurrection is certain. It is not the eternal end of things; it is the end of a worn out world; it is the incubation of a regenerated world.

When in the cycle of evolutions the predestined hour will shine in another spring equinox, nature will raise herself from her dark dwelling place, throwing away the sheets of black topsoil, sole vestige of foliage from long ago. Fresh, vigorous, full-blown, greeting the clear day and the warm sun, [nature] will bestow its produce and its perfume.

♣

Similar to flowers born in the dust of flowers, a new artistic era comes forth from the cinders of a vanished art, with insatiable desires for as yet undiscovered marvels. Then, progressively, like a plant, it grows, it develops; also, in time, it will accomplish its predetermined work.

And in the same way that a plant grows and fades lacking the sense of the death that awaits it, thus the life of art must gravitate with a sure step toward the highest summit it can attain, then fall in resignation down the slope that leads to the culmination of its destiny.

Distinctions of Ideal Variation of Form in Artistic Periods

This new life, rooted in the remains of an extinct existence, nourished by the same old sources, will nevertheless be guided by a new star: the faith that will animate it will be a personal faith; growing in its own atmosphere, it will have its own color; in a word, it will have a distinct and specific individuality.

In the new concert, each will assume a rhythmic role assigned to him. We will receive the pitch from a new maestro conducting the symphony. The same sap that flows underground and gives roots the power to grasp the earth and absorb its juices also climbs to the summit of branches, allowing the princely head of the oak tree to wave in the breeze and fight against the storm or soar in the stillness of silent nights.

Thus in a generation that blossoms and grows under the same sun flows a common life, the soul of an era; the impulse of a common spirit brings all its members to a unique labor, the incarnation of a dream of art that will stamp them with its heraldic seal.

Voices of the Sea

Legions of thought lie dormant in the bosoms of your waves. —The immense sea exchanges her secrets with the passing winds. —Her breast, day and night, ebbs and flows, but who will under-stand her language? Her lips are sealed to the man infatuated with his own thought. —Only to the man privileged to be as impetuous as she, at times calm and deep, does she speak frankly and unveil herself freely.

Oh, sea! From the depths of your unfathomable throat allow your mysterious song to come forth [with] discreet rustling, rhythmic boiling, [your] triumphal entrance hymn of the Great Spirit. Sitting in front of you with ready ear, my heart open full to receive you. Introspective, I listen to you.

The morning sun, in the ardor of its youth, extends itself over you, embracing your immen-sity—an ocean of flames over an ocean of water—; each wave on which its rays shatter reflects its image.

Oh, sea! Over you hovers another force, my feverish soul—who seeks to see its image in your mirror. Speak at last, speak to it, bent toward you listening to the song of the deep.

The breeze, caressing you, saturates itself with the salts of your breath. But my thought wanders and turns toward you without sating its hunger. Like a traveler coming to the end of his journey, exhausted, begging shelter, I bring my lips to the drink, transformed.

Elohim, Elohim! I am at the bottom of the abyss, give me your hand! Alas! Inaccessible, how far you remain from me!

And yet, of all that this immense universe con-tains, it is you (the sea) who are closest to the human soul!

My sister, I greet you! Greetings, companion of my soul, beloved shadow! On your reflecting sur-face, in your dark abysses, in your ever-moving waves, in your ever-changing currents, in your sensitive nature—unreachable, inexplicable—I see right beside me, there, before my very eyes, the true image of my soul that I have been seeking. Do not deny me, oh sea!

Awaken in me an echo of your voice, deep voice of your abyss; strident voice of your foam made turbulent by the whip of the wind; calm and serene voice of pure days, caressing voice of sunny days.

Having found refuge in the silence of night under the benevolent gaze of the moon—sweet companion of my dreams—I begin to sing an inspired hymn.

D. *Conclusion*
Conclusion of the Poem
♣
Formulas & Metaphors Containing the Author's Theory
♣
Integral Translation

My voice has reached its limit and my song is now complete. Under the calm of the heavens I rest, while my thought, like an echo extending my voice, still resonates and reflects—[like] a full moon—the vanished sun of my songs.

Thought: that blossoming succeeds itself as inevitably as noon and twilight, harnessed to the chariot of the sun: that [illegible] tomorrow follows [illegible] on the heels of today and soon comes forth, bringing the dawn of a new day.

Thought: That thus Action follows the course of Intention step by step, [which] is the sun of souls, [their] life and creative source. That with [Intention, Action] rises ceaselessly and without pause toward the zenith of Desire.

Thought: That without sun, there is no dawn; so without sustained desire there is no effective action nor fertile birth.

Thought: That from desire comes Art, made manifest in a work.

Thought: That the Art of a nation is the twin to that innate desire, boundless like space, arising spontaneously, dispatching darkness suddenly with its abrupt dawn. With that new dawn modest works gradually appear, emerging in their naive grace and youthful gaiety, akin to the earth's downy green at the [renewal?] of the seasons

Thought: That at the end of the year weakened plants fade and disappear while in the forest the autumn wind makes only trembling and confusing noises.

Thought: That seasons flee and soon come to an end. Pursuing one another, they pass on without stopping, carried in the maelstrom of the eternal rotation of growth and decay.

Thought: That in the midst of calm and tumult there resides a hidden Power, mysterious, impenetrable, eternally serene.

It is this that stamps growth and decay with a distinctive seal by elusive gradations of successive nuances, this that carries both, that sustains and nourishes them, concerned equally for both. — And, nevertheless, the tide of destiny, ebbing and flowing in mysterious waves, carries spring in its folds, makes it advance in an enchanting rhythm to the heights of its vocation, then advances obediently down the fatal slope of decay, gliding into the tomb, where it falls into the sweet oblivion of death.

A strangely complex rhythm, for all is rhythm.

Thought: That the [illegible] alliance of artistic and natural rhythm—created by the sympathetic interpretation of the human soul—determines the vitality and the specific expressiveness of the art that represents them.

Thought: That to perceive and to give material form to the harmoniously correlated rhythms of nature and humanity—rhythms sustained, nourished by an unfathomable, inaccessible, unreachable Essence yet evident in all its representations; an Essence at times changing and deceptive, at times serene and restful—is the mark of the highest inspiration and the most sublime degree that Art, in its supreme power, may attain.

Thought: That [to understand?] the [mark?] of that [elusive?] Essence on material works, to recognize its [primacy and?] its omnipotence in all growth and in all decline, the senses must first [be awakened?] and transported to the highest spheres of the ideal through the versatile, serene, and strengthening influences of the human soul.

Thought: That to attempt in cynical pride to grasp that Essence using shrewdness as if it were a delicate instrument, to attempt to discover it by strategic manipulations of a cleverly conducted method, is vain folly.

Thought: That a respectful attitude toward the spirit would have no greater success.

Thought: That this Essence has nothing in common with human intelligence and has no relation to it whatever; that it can be approached and understood only by the heart that surrenders to the influence of an exquisite and ardent sympathy.

Thought: That intelligence speaks the language of logic, unquestionably a vital language, but a language of reflection and of *ex post facto* thinking; while the language of the soul is impenetrable intuition, a language that is eminently vital, spontaneous and primordial.

Therefore I conclude: That the greatest art is that which incorporates at once the greatest and the smallest amount of thought; that is to say, within which logic and intuition blend in miraculous union.

That the moments in which the soul loses consciousness of its individuality and [thus freed?], struggles toward infinity, are moments of inspiration.

In the quiet of meditation the soul unites with nature.

As the drops of rain become one with the sea, under the warm and splendid sun of inspired imagination vapors evaporate. They rise through the atmosphere of sublime attempts and transform themselves into lovely images carried by the imponderable winds of projects. Then they condense and fall at last in the guise of tangible realities, sometimes sweet smiling swells, sometimes somber furies, following the needs of the changing seasons. There they nourish and refresh, and through a thousand vicissitudes and metamorphoses, return at last to the great sea of Nature. From this the essential and profound thought [follows?] that a spontaneous and truly vital art must come from nature in all the freshness of youth, and has no other mother.

That the specters of decadent artistic eras which have lost their character of spontaneity—specters that come out of their tombs and wander haphazardly dressed in tawdry, ill-assorted finery, mendacious ghosts and illusions—must disappear in the dawning light of the new artistic life.

That such a dawn is about to rise over this nation is an indisputable fact. In the night that is ending, ghosts come from everywhere, restless and uneasy, and their shapes are erased [illegible]. The sky lightens with the gleam of new desire, and, it [illegible]. It lifts me toward the heavens [illegible] to seize a ray of sunlight which [illegible], and I sing this prophetic hymn of spring.

Catalogue of the Drawings
1867–1923

This catalogue lists all drawings known to us that Louis Sullivan made in his own hand still existing in one of two possible forms: actual drawings held in public or private collections, and those available only in published or unpublished reproduction. (We have excluded drawings by employees of the firm of Adler & Sullivan, and of Louis H. Sullivan, Architect.)[1]

The catalogue is divided into two parts, each arranged chronologically. The first records the 273 extant drawings in Sullivan's hand. Each entry includes title or subject matter, date, inscriptions (if any), medium, size, present location, provenance, and major sources of illustration. The second section, with twenty-four entries, lists those drawings which, while lost, are known through publication, photographs, and blueprint or black-line copies.

This material has a tangled history. On 27 May 1918, Sullivan placed his office drawings and other records in storage and gave three boxes of negatives to Chicago photographer Henry Fuerman for safekeeping. Four days later he closed his architectural office in the Chicago Auditorium Building.[2] What happened to the stored material is anyone's guess, although some of it has surfaced from time to time.[3] Not everything was packed away, however. The evidence suggests that Sullivan kept 230 drawings in his possession: 215 of his own, and fifteen others by draftsmen.

More than half the drawings Sullivan kept came down to us through Frank Lloyd Wright. On 13 April 1924 (the eve of Sullivan's death), Wright visited his mentor, leaving with a sheaf of 132 drawings. Of these 117 were by Sullivan, fifteen by others (six by George Grant Elmslie, two by Wright, and seven by unknown draftsmen).[4] No one knows if Sullivan chose them for Wright or permitted his former disciple to make his own

selection, but they include some of the very best.

Eventually, Wright gave nine away as gifts: one, by Sullivan to Douglas Haskell, editor of *Architectural Forum*, and eight to Richard Nickel in recognition of his assistance with the 1956 Sullivan retrospective at the Art Institute of Chicago. Of the eight Nickel drawings, seven were by Sullivan and one by an unknown employee in the Adler & Sullivan office.

These nine Wright gifts found their way into various repositories. Haskell's widow, Helen, donated her husband's (No. 171), along with his papers, to the Avery Library, Columbia University. Nickel gave away six of his eight as follows: two by Sullivan (Nos. 146 and 184) to the Art Institute; one (No. 227) to the Avery Library; and three (Nos. 127, 188, and 189) to Tim Samuelson. The seventh (No. 137) remains with the Richard Nickel Committee. The eighth, a perspective rendering for a double house (1883), Chicago (ink on paper, 46 x 55 cm.), which he also gave to the Art Institute, is not in Sullivan's hand.[5]

In 1949, before parting with anything Sullivan had given him, Wright selected thirty-nine drawings to illustrate *Genius and the Mobocracy*, his tribute to his "lieber meister." This fulfilled the promise Sullivan had extracted from Wright to publish what he, Wright, referring to Sullivan, called "the dearest treasure of his heart."[6] Wright kept his collection largely intact for thirty-five years, but in 1965, six years after his death, his widow sold it to the Avery Library, which acquired it with funds provided by Edgar Kaufmann Jr. The sale encompassed the 123 drawings remaining from the original 132 (minus the nine that Wright had given away, listed above), which is to say that the Avery acquired 109 Sullivan drawings plus fourteen not in his hand.[7] Subsequently, eight of the Sullivan drawings (Nos. 275 and 278–84) were stolen, reducing the Avery collection to 101 by him plus fourteen by assistants.

George Grant Elmslie, Sullivan's testamentary executor, dispersed among four recipients the ninety-eight drawings in Sullivan's possession at his death. Elmslie gave sixty-two to the Art Institute in three installments (forty-four in 1931, one in 1932, sixteen in 1933, and one at a date unknown);[8] two to William Martin, c. 1931–32;[9] twenty to the School of Architecture at the University of Michigan c. 1936 (via its dean, Emil Lorch, Elmslie's brother-in-law);[10] and fourteen to the Avery Library in 1936.[11]

Sixty-one other drawings were not part of Sullivan's estate. The Art Institute owned the twenty plates (nineteen of drawings and one—No. 9—of text) of *A System of Architectural Ornament According with a Philosophy of Man's Powers* (1924) as well as the thirty-six leaves of its first draft, sixteen of which carry sketches. There were eleven drawings the architect had given to his niece, Andrienne Sullivan (who donated them to the Art Institute);[12] three given to J. Russell Wheeler, president of Sullivan's Farmers' & Merchants' Union Bank, Columbus, Wisconsin (1919), who gave them to the Art Institute;[13] one to Earl H. Reed, who also gave it to the Art Institute;[14] and seven to William Presto, Sullivan's associate for the 1922 Krause Music Store commission, Chicago (1922).[15]

Four other drawings have a curious provenance. Numbers 88 and 134–36 in the collection of Ruth Guyer, Chicago, were found by a man named John Moulton inside a book he purchased at the 1909 auction of Sullivan's property. Moulton gave them to a nurse who took care of him in old age. She gave them to Joseph A. Guyer's aunt, who gave them in turn to her nephew (Ruth Guyer's late husband) sometime before 1940.

Finally, four drawings (Nos. 121, 199, 209, and 234) lack an early provenance.

By way of summary, the following list gives the present location of Sullivan's drawings. A question mark next to a donor's name indicates that the date of the gift is unknown.

1. The Art Institute of Chicago

123 drawings

a)	From Sullivan, *System of Ornament* draft	16
b)	From Sullivan, *System of Ornament* plates	19[16]
c)	From George Elmslie (1931)	44
d)	From George Elmslie (1932)	1
e)	From George Elmslie (1933)	16
f)	From George Elmslie (?)	1
g)	From Andrienne Sullivan (?)	11
h)	From Earl H. Reed (1956)	1
i)	From Richard Nickel (1957)	2
j)	From J. Russell Wheeler (1957)	3
k)	From Robert Keuny (1980)	2
l)	From Robert Keuny (1992)	1
m)	From Wilbert and Marilyn Hasbrouck (1993)	6

2. Avery Library, Columbia University

117 drawings

a)	From George Elmslie (1936)	14
b)	From Richard Nickel (?)	1
c)	From Olgivanna Wright (1965)	101
d)	From Helen Haskell (1983)	1

3. University of Michigan, Ann Arbor

20 drawings

(These came to the School of Architecture from George Grant Elmslie via Emil Lorch, c. 1936. In 1972 they were transferred to two University of Michigan institutions)

a)	At the Bentley Historical Library	16
b)	At the University Museum	4

4. Chicago Architectural Foundation

1 drawing

5. Private collections   12 drawings

Total: 273 drawings

Concerning provenance, a listing is as follows:

1. LHS to The Art Institute .... 35 drawings
2. LHS to Frank Lloyd Wright .... 109[17]
3. LHS to George Grant Elmslie 98
4. LHS to Andrienne Sullivan 11
5. LHS to William C. Presto 7
6. LHS to J. Russell Wheeler 3
7. LHS to Earl. H. Reed 1
8. LHS to George Mann Niedecken 1
9. Drawings found in book owned by LHS 4
10. Early provenance unknown 4

Total: .... 273 drawings

Thematically, the collection may be divided into three main groups. First are the drawings from Sullivan's youth, perhaps kept as mementos. These include student exercises from the Massachusetts Institute of Technology and from Paris, his erotic sketches of 1875 (when he was a footloose eighteen-year-old in Europe), and his academic nudes, beginning with the muscle studies of December 1877 and running through the seated female of February 1881.

A second group consists of thirty drawings of eight buildings and one monument, but if one discounts the seventeen drawings for the Columbus, Wisconsin, bank (1919) and three for the National Terra Cotta Society Monument (1921 and 1923)—that is to say, those drawings made after 1918, when he placed his archives in storage—there remain only ten sketches for seven buildings, each one the recording of a first idea. These drawings are the site plan for his own house and that of his friends, the Charnleys, on adjacent lots in Ocean Springs, Mississippi (c. 1890, one sheet of office stationery, No. 127);[18] the facade for the 1892 Victoria Hotel project (one sheet of tracing paper, No. 146); the facade for the Eliel Building project (1894, one sheet of office stationery, No. 167); the plan and elevation of the First Church of Christ Scientist project, Chicago (c. 1895, on two three-by-five-inch cards, Nos. 188 and 189); a sketch for a country club (1895, on the back of his business card, No. 192); a preliminary plan and two elevations of the

Babson House, Riverside, Illinois (1907, No. 203); and the plan and elevations of the Grinnell, Iowa, bank (1913, on three sheets of the local Storm Pharmacy stationery, Nos. 205–7).

The third group of drawings, by far the majority, consists mostly of sheet after sheet of studies for ornamentation and of depictions of ornaments for buildings and projects. So compelling was this aspect of his work that at times Sullivan would instinctively make ornament out of what was not. In a rendering of the interior of the McVickers Theater, for example, he made the boxes look like ornamental items (No. 89).

Sullivan's drawings are as illuminating of him as a man as they are of his artistry. In this regard, the question arises as to why he chose to keep only a few select drawings with him after 1918, carting them around from one apartment and office to another. The answer may include a confluence of factors. One was likely personal: to create a kind of reassuring self-portrait as his career continued to decline. A second may have been public: to keep a record of what posterity might otherwise forget (hence his insistence that Wright publish his "treasure"). A third factor could have been professional: to have a library for future designs, architectural and ornamental. His use of a sketch from 2 April 1902 as the source for the principal feature of the 1914 Grinnell bank facade substantiates his *modus operandi*, at least in one instance (Nos. 202 and 206).

If these 297 drawings (including the twenty-four known only through reproductions) were all that remained of Sullivan's work, it would be tempting to label him an ornamentalist who only occasionally ventured into architectural design. Witness one peculiarity of the collection. It entirely lacks those comprehensive studies of buildings by others and of other periods that are the stock-in-trade of most architects' sketchbooks from Villard de Honnecourt clear down to Le Corbusier, Alver Aalto, and Louis Kahn. We know Sullivan held most American architecture in contempt, but he certainly approved of—even admired—buildings by John Root and Henry Hobson Richardson, in particular. Yet he appears never to have drawn a single line even from buildings he liked. This omission is particularly striking with regard to Paris, and perhaps even more so for Florence, which he loved so much that "he did not know how he came to break the golden chains that bound him there, a too willing captive."[19]

Why are there no depictions of cathedrals, squares, palaces, or even tiny details that certainly caught his eye during his ten months on the Continent in 1874–75? That such drawings once existed, were put in storage in 1918, and then were lost seems improbable, since he took pains to keep close at hand those of which he was especially fond, that spoke to him personally—almost viscerally, one might say—which would have meant drawing such as those.

Another peculiarity of the collection is the paucity of drawings of his own buildings, especially the large and quite visible commissions that made him famous. Where are the facade and myriad other sketches he must surely have made for the Chicago Auditorium, the Guaranty Building, or the Schlesinger & Mayer Store? Where is the "sudden and volcanic design" for his first skyscraper, the Wainwright Building in St. Louis, over which, he stated, he "broke," meaning that his creative effort catapulted him to a higher stage of artistic consciousness, to an epiphany, to the true beginning of his career?[20] Was Sullivan compressing time and events for dramatic purposes when he penned that account in 1903, and "broke" only gradually (if at all) during a long series of sketches? The collection has no answers for these questions.

Sullivan's seeming lack of interest in retaining his architectural drawings is of a piece with the fact that seldom—hardly at all—did he discuss his own buildings (although he wrote relentlessly about the nature and development of architecture), a practice standing in marked contrast to what has been routine since the sixteenth century: the publication by architects of illustrated treatises featuring their own work. For Sullivan, buildings were almost too mundane for such exalted treatment, because, in a sense, he saw them as lit-tle more than necessary accidents of design. Architecture could not exist without them, but they were not essential to its nature. In his transcendental scheme of things, the essence of architecture existed on a higher, more exalted level, well above that of mere structure. "Architecture-as-an-absolute"—to give it a name—percolated down to buildings as a matter of course, turning construction into art, but architecture always remained part of *Natura naturans*; buildings of *Natura naturata*.

Nevertheless, these drawings complement both his writings and his buildings and round out his thought for us. The writings reveal his determined investigation into the consequences for contemporary practice of architecture's timeless meanings, while the buildings embody the exquisitely beautiful as well as the eminently practical results of that investigation. But the drawings proclaim more eloquently than anything else—and perhaps more succinctly—the implications of two of his work's fundaments: that the process of drawing was more revelatory for him than its subject matter, or even the finished product, graphic or built, and that in his conception of architecture ornamentation was seminal.

For Sullivan, ornamentation conveyed more directly than buildings—more "intensely" was his word—the characteristics of design a transcendent nature expected humanity to discover. Such a notion clearly belongs within the scope of romanticism's fascination with the particular as a means of discovering and revealing the absolute. And here one encounters a paradox. It is an ancient convention of architecture to consider ornaments as phenomena of immanence, and therefore characteristic entities; in their particularity dwells the meaning of the whole. Yet their role is usually subservient to the architectural scheme, which reduces their potential to proclaim the absolute. But in Sullivan's scheme of things, ornamentation was closer to the absolute than buildings were, and the process of drawing it the means by which the absolute—that is to say, "nature's way"—was rendered comprehensible.

So the age-old architectural paradox weighed

heavily on Sullivan, because as time passed he found himself increasingly reversing the relationship between structure and ornament, the former becoming visually subservient to the latter. Toward the end of his life this became apparent in two major ways: in the prominence given to ornament on his last building facades—on his final four banks beginning at Grinnell in 1914, for example, and on the 1922 Krause Music Store, Chicago (a prominence anticipated as early as 1894–95 at the Guaranty Building)—and in 1924 when he encapsulated his most fiercely held notions in a single work, calling it *A System of Architectural Ornament,* emphasis on ornament.

These drawings, as a collection, bring to mind John Ruskin's illustrations for *The Seven Lamps of Architecture,* a comparison that may seem gratuitous if not facetious, given Sullivan's scorn for Ruskin. But except for the central issue of Ruskin's love for the architecture of the past as opposed to Sullivan's determined call for a new architecture for the future (a difference not pertinent here), there are strong similarities. Like Ruskin's drawings of ornamentation, most of Sullivan's are also the result of isolated, spontaneous

flashes of imagination jotted down in order not to lose them. Even when he knew exactly where a piece of ornament was to be placed, Sullivan's drawing usually appeared alone on a sheet, with no indication of its location in a room or on a facade. A quick notation, such as "Plaster Cap[ital] in Waiting Room" (No. 152), was all he required. The relationship of ornament to architecture remained in his head, as *A System* also suggests.

Wright knew Sullivan best. In his review of Hugh Morrison's *Louis Sullivan: Prophet of Modern Architecture,* he wrote: "Sullivan was essentially a lyric poet-philosopher interested in the sensuous experience of expressing inner rhythms evolving [into] a language of his own—ornament—in which to utter himself: unique among mankind."[21] Wright's statement resonates in the following illustrations.

Part I of the catalogue, "Drawings," limits the sources of illustrations to those publications in which Sullivan's extant drawings are the main subject, directly or indirectly, and their listing follows. In Part II, "Lost Drawings," each entry carries a full record of the earliest source of illustration.

Key to Source Abbreviations

FLLW/LHS (followed by a number): Refers to the cataloguing system at the Avery Library, Columbia University, for drawings purchased in 1965 from the Frank Lloyd Wright Foundation.

H: Indicates Louis H. Sullivan*, A System of Architectural Ornament According with a Philosophy of Man's Powers*, ed. Ada Louise Huxtable (New York: Eakins Press, 1967), unpaginated.

M (followed by a number): Indicates a page number in Sarah C. Mollman, *Louis Sullivan in the Art Institute of Chicago: The Illustrated Catalogue of Collections* (New York: Garland, 1989).

S (followed by a number): Refers to the classifications system developed by Paul E. Sprague for *The Drawings of Louis Henry Sullivan: A Catalogue of the Frank Lloyd Wright Collection at the Avery Archi-

tectural Library* (Princeton, N.J.: Princeton University Press, 1979).

Su: refers to Louis H. Sullivan, *A System of Architectural Ornament According with a Philosophy of Man's Powers* (New York: Press of the American Institute of Architects, 1924), 12 pp. + 20 plates.

W: Refers to Frank Lloyd Wright, *Genius and the Mobocracy* (New York: Duell, Sloan and Pearce, 1949; enlarged edition, New York: Horizon Press, 1971). This work contains thirty-nine unnumbered drawings as an unpaginated portfolio.

Z (followed by a number): Indicates a page number in Louis H. Sullivan, *A System of Architectural Ornament According with a Philosophy of Man's Powers*, ed. John Zukowsky (New York: Rizzoli, 1990).[22]

I. Drawings

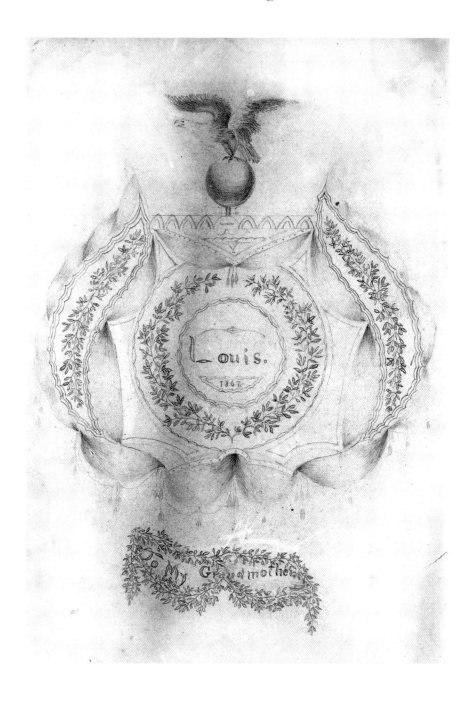

1. *To my Grandmother*, 1867. Dated and inscribed *Louis* on the design.

Pencil on paper, mounted and matted (22.5 x 15.5 cm.).
Art Institute of Chicago; gift of George Grant Elmslie, 1931. M. 228.

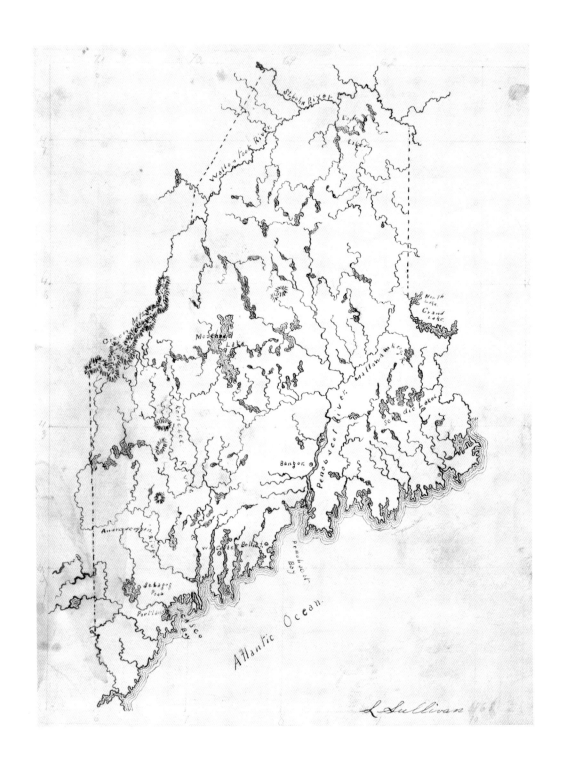

2. Map of Maine, 1868. Dated and signed *L Sullivan*.

Ink on paper, ruled out in pencil (25 x 19.5 cm.).
Art Institute of Chicago; gift of George Grant Elmslie, 1931. M. 228.

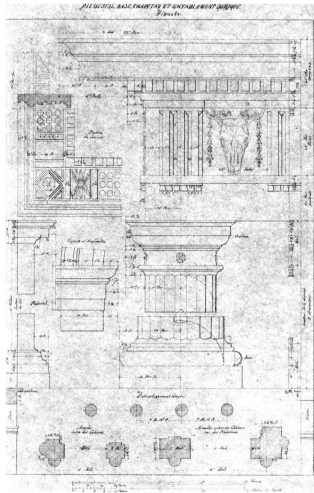

3. Study of a variant of the Doric order [c. 1871–72?].
Inscribed *ORDRE DORIQUE MUTULAIRE/
de J. Barrozzio de Vignole* [sic]; identifications of features
on drawing and dimensions in modules.

Ink on tracing paper (30.5 x 20.3 cm.);
mounted on board (45.7 x 35.5 cm.).
Art Institute of Chicago; gift of George Grant Elmslie, 1933. M. 206.

4. Study of a Roman Doric Order [c. 1871–72?].
Inscribed *PIEDESTAL, BASE, CHAPITEAU ET
ENTABLEMENT DORIQUE./Vignole;* identifications of fea-
tures on drawing and dimensions in modules.

Ink on tracing paper (30.5 x 20.3 cm.);
mounted on board (45.7 x 35.5 cm.).
Art Institute of Chicago; gift of George Grant Elmslie, 1933. M. 207.

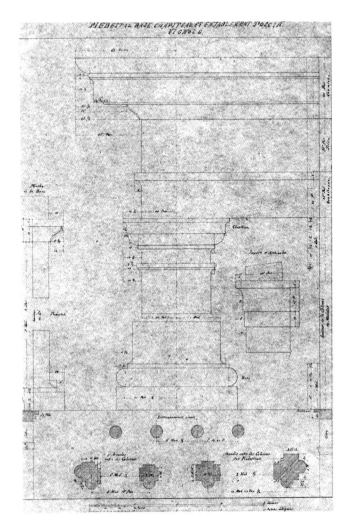

5. Study of a Tuscan order [c. 1871–72?].
Inscribed *PIEDESTAL, BASE ET ENTEMBLEMENT TOSCAN/VIGNOLE;* identification of features on drawing and dimensions in modules.

Ink on tracing paper (30.5 x 20.3 cm.); mounted on board (45.7 x 35.5 cm.).
Art Institute of Chicago; gift of George Grant Elmslie, 1933. M. 207.

6. Study of entablature of composite order [c. 1871–72?].

Pencil on tracing paper (20.5 x 19.7 cm.); mounted on board (45.7 x 35.5 cm.).
Art Institute of Chicago; gift of George Grant Elmslie, 1933. M. 208

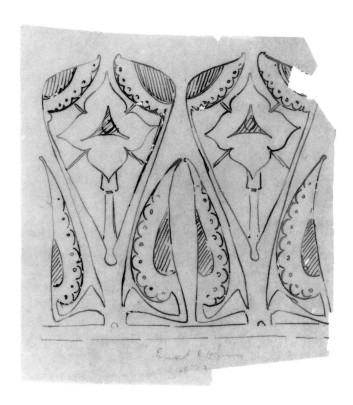

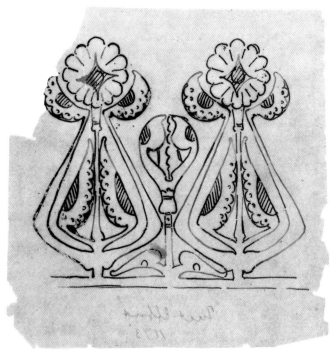

7. Design for fresco (?) [1873]. Inscribed in pencil by
Frank Lloyd Wright: *First Effort/1873*.

Purple ink on tracing paper (21 x 19 cm.).
Avery Library, Columbia University, FLLW/LHS 93;
purchased from Frank Lloyd Wright Foundation, 1965. S. 2.

8. Design for Fresco (?), [1873]. Inscribed in pencil by
Frank Lloyd Wright, on verso: *First Effort/1873*
(appears on illustration as written backward).

Purple ink on tracing paper (17.2 x 16.5 cm.).
Avery Library, Columbia University, FLLW/LHS 11;
purchased from Frank Lloyd Wright Foundation, 1965. S. 3.

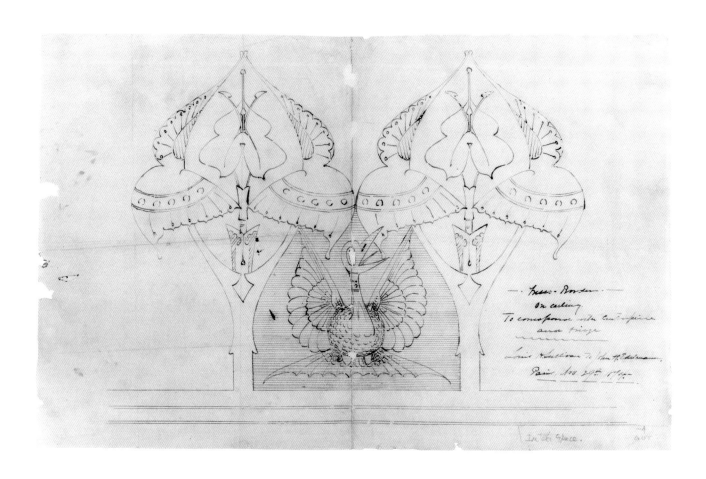

9. Design for fresco. Inscribed *Fresco Border/On Ceiling/
To Correspond with Centerpiece/and Frieze/Louis H. Sullivan to
John H. Edelman* [sic]*/Paris, Nov. 29th 1874*; cropping marks in
pencil by Frank Lloyd Wright, for publication in
Genius and the Mobocracy (1949).

Purple ink on tracing paper (26.3 x 41.3.).
Avery Library, Columbia University, FLLH/LHS 18; purchased from
Frank Lloyd Wright Foundation, 1965. W. (right half only); S. 4.

10. Landscape and cartoonlike head studies (7 December 1874).

Signed *Louis H. Sullivan* and dated.

Pen on paper (27 x 21 cm.).
Art Institute of Chicago; gift of Andrienne Sullivan (Louis Sullivan's niece),
date of gift unknown. M. *229*.

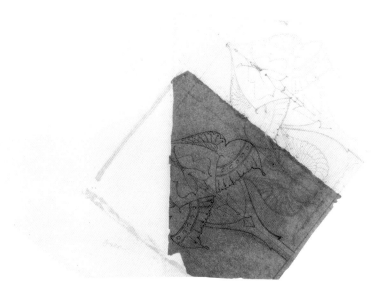

11. Design for a ceiling fresco for John Edelmann [late 1874].

Pencil on wove card stock (29.2 x 47 cm.).
Bentley Historical Library, University of Michigan; gift of George Grant
Elmslie, c. 1936, to Emil Lorch, for College of Architecture and Design,
University of Michigan; transferred to Bentley Historical Library, 1972.

12. Design for ceiling fresco for John Edelmann [late 1874].

Pencil on wove card stock (26 x 41 cm.).
Bentley Historical Library, University of Michigan; gift of George Grant
Elmslie, c. 1936, to Emil Lorch, for College of Architecture and Design,
University of Michigan; transferred to Bentley Historical Library, 1972.

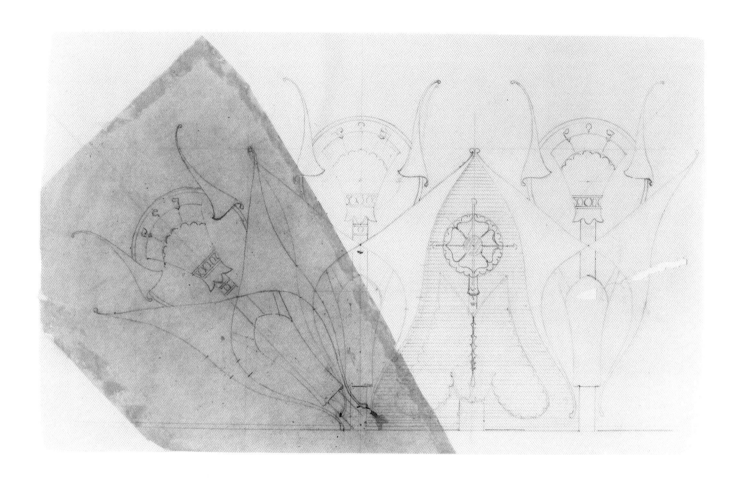

13. Design for border of fresco for John Edelmann [early 1875].

Pencil on wove card stock (26 x 41 cm.).
Bentley Historical Library, University of Michigan; gift of George Grant
Elmslie, c. 1936, to Emil Lorch, for College of Architecture and Design,
University of Michigan; transferred to Bentley Historical Library, 1972.

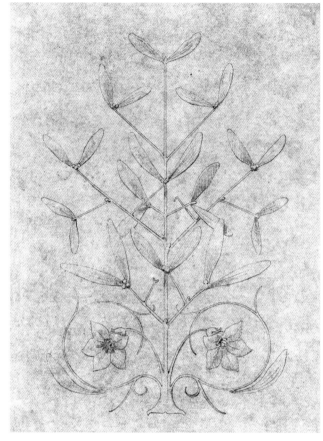

14. Study after Victor-Marie Ruprich-Robert, *Flore ornamentale* (Paris, 1866–76), Plate 93: *Fleurs: 1. Liriodendron tulipifera, 2. Mahonia aquifolium* [c. 1875].

Pencil on tracing paper (26.8 x 20.2 cm.).
Art Institute of Chicago; gift of George Grant Elmslie, 1933. M. 210.

15. Study after Victor-Marie Ruprich-Robert, *Flore ornamentale* (Paris, 1866–76), Plate 105: *Compositions, Ajustement: 1. Viscum album, 2. Platycodon grandiflorum* [c. 1875].

Pencil on tracing paper (26.9 x 20.2 cm.).
Art Institute of Chicago; gift of George Grant Elmslie, 1933. M. 210.

16. Study after Victor-Marie Ruprich-Robert, *Flore ornamentale* (Paris, 1866–76), Plate 108: *Compositions, Ajustement: 1. Oenothera macrocarpa, 2. Cinchona calysaya* [c. 1875].

Pencil on tracing paper (26.9 x 20 cm.).

Art Institute of Chicago; gift of George Grant Elmslie, 1933. M. 211.

17. Study after Victor-Marie Ruprich-Robert, *Flore ornamentale* (Paris, 1866–76), Plate 111: *Compositions, Ajustement: 1. Fuchsia hybrida, 2. Gentiana lutea, 3. Sciadophyllum pulchrum* [c. 1875].

Pencil on tracing paper (26.5 x 20 cm.).

Art Institute of Chicago; gift of George Grant Elmslie, 1933. M. 212.

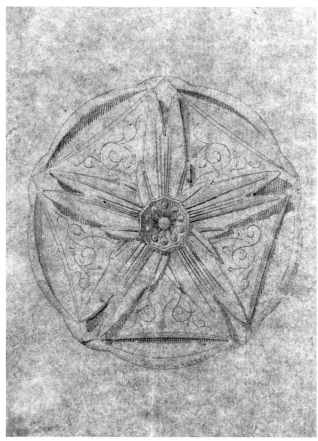

18. Study after Victor-Marie Ruprich-Robert, *Flore ornamentale* (Paris, 1866–76), Plate 117: *Compositions, Rosace: Sedum acre* [c. 1875].

Pencil on tracing paper (26.8 x 20.4 cm.).
Art Institute of Chicago; gift of George Grant Elmslie, 1933. M. 213.

19. Study after Victor-Marie Ruprich-Robert, *Flore ornamentale* (Paris, 1866–76), Plate 118: *Compositions, Rosace: Lychnis sylvestris* [c. 1875].

Pencil on tracing paper (26.7 x 19.9 cm.).
Art Institute of Chicago; gift of George Grant Elmslie, 1933. M. 214.

20. Study after Victor-Marie Ruprich-Robert, *Flore ornamentale*
(Paris, 1866–76), Plate 119: *Compositions, Rosace:*
1. Solanum tuberosum, 2. Liriodendron tulipifera [c. 1875].

Pencil on tracing paper (26.8 x 20.2 cm.).
Art Institute of Chicago; gift of George Grant Elmslie, 1933. M. 215.

21. Study after Victor-Marie Ruprich-Robert, *Flore ornamentale*
(Paris, 1866–76), Plate 124: *Compositions: 1. Bas-Relief; Myristica
moschata, 2. Ajustement; Petunia nyctaginiflora* [c. 1875].

Pencil on tracing paper (26.8 x 20.2 cm.).
Art Institute of Chicago; gift of George Grant Elmslie, 1933. M. 216.

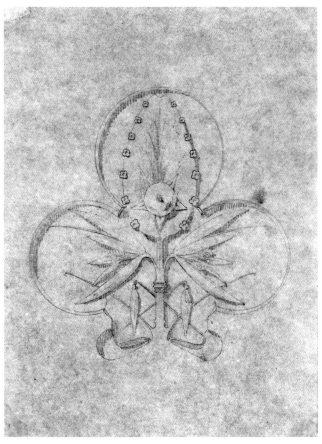

22. Study after Victor-Marie Ruprich-Robert, *Flore ornamentale* (Paris, 1866–76), Plate 125: *Compositions, Bas-Relief: Tropoeolum majus* [c. 1875].

Pencil on tracing paper (27 x 20.2 cm.).

Art Institute of Chicago; gift of George Grant Elmslie, 1933. M. 217.

23. Study after Victor-Marie Ruprich-Robert, *Flore ornamentale* (Paris, 1866–76), Plate 126: *Compositions, Bas-Relief: 1. Aventa sativa (Avoine cultivée), 2. Bryophyllum calycinum, 3. Alsine media* [c. 1875].

Pencil on tracing paper (26.7 x 20.1 cm.).

Art Institute of Chicago; gift of George Grant Elmslie, 1933. M. 218.

24. Study after Victor-Marie Ruprich-Robert, *Flore ornamentale* (Paris, 1866–76), Plate 139: *Compositions: Entablement* [c. 1875].

Pencil on tracing paper (27 x 20.4 cm.).
Art Institute of Chicago; gift of George Grant Elmslie, 1933. M. 219.

25. Study after Victor-Marie Ruprich-Robert, *Flore ornamentale* (Paris, 1866–76), drawing inspired by Plates 74, 78, and 88 [c. 1875].

Pencil on tracing paper (27.5 x 20 cm.).
Art Institute of Chicago; gift of George Grant Elmslie, 1933. M. 220.

26. *Nouvelle Année,* after a drawing by Alfred Grévin published in
Le Journal Amusant (9 January 1975). Inscribed: *Et bien, oui, là! J'ai eu envers toi des
torts . . . excessifs; mais ça m'est égal, à partir d'aujourd'hui veux-tu que tout soit oublié?
Dis, voyons, Théodore, veux-tu passer l'éponge?/Nouvelle Année;*
initialed *L. H. S.* and dated 15 March 1875.

Ink on tracing paper (30.5 x 20.9 cm.). Bentley Historical Library, University of Michigan;
gift of George Grant Elmslie, c. 1936, to Emil Lorch, for College of Architecture and Design,
University of Michigan; transferred to Bentley Historical Library, 1972.

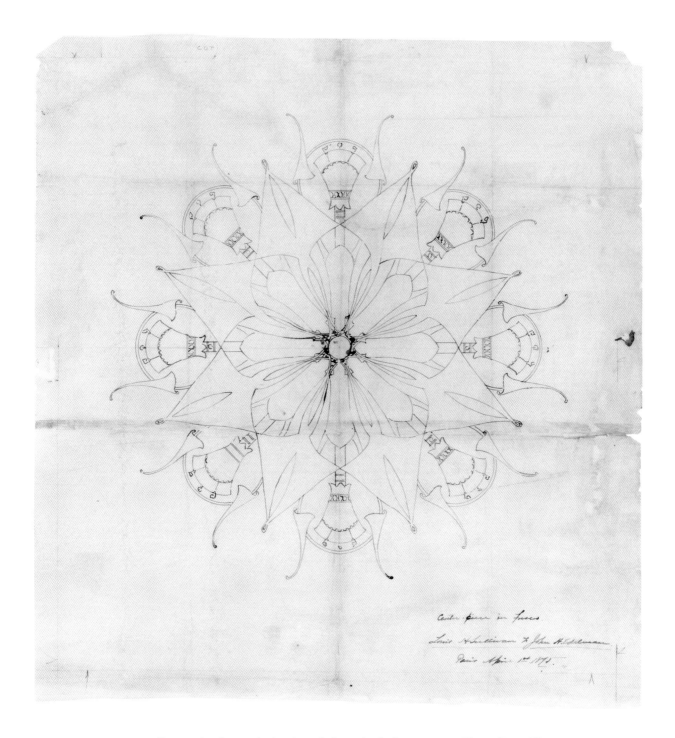

27. Design for fresco (1. April 1875). Inscribed: *Center-piece in Fresco/Louis H. Sullivan to John H. Edelman* [sic]*/Paris, April 1st 1875*; cropping marks in pencil by Frank Lloyd Wright, for publication in *Genius and the Mobocracy* (1949).

Ink on tracing paper (50 x 41.5 cm.). Avery Library, Columbia University, FLLW/LHS 33; purchased from Frank Lloyd Wright Foundation, 1965. W., S. 5.

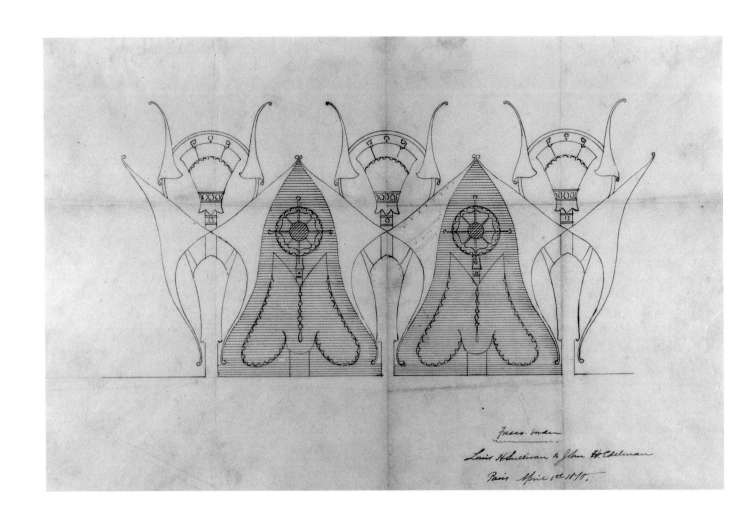

28. Design for border of fresco. Inscribed: *Fresco Border/Louis H.
Sullivan to John H. Edelman* [sic]/*Paris April 1st 1875.*

Ink on tracing paper (26.3 x 41.3 cm.). Avery Library, Columbia University,
FLLW/LHS 17; purchased from Frank Lloyd Wright Foundation, 1965. W., S. 6.

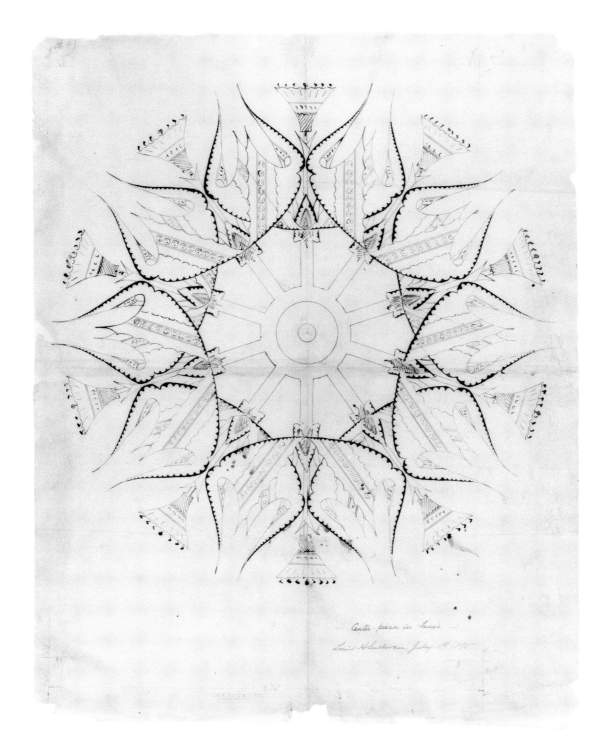

29. Design for fresco (11 July 1875).
Inscribed *Center-piece in Fresco./Louis H. Sullivan/July 11th, 1875.*

Ink on tracing paper (51.2 x 41.3 cm.). Avery Library, Columbia University,
FLLW/LHS 32; purchased from Frank Lloyd Wright Foundation, 1965. W., S. 7.

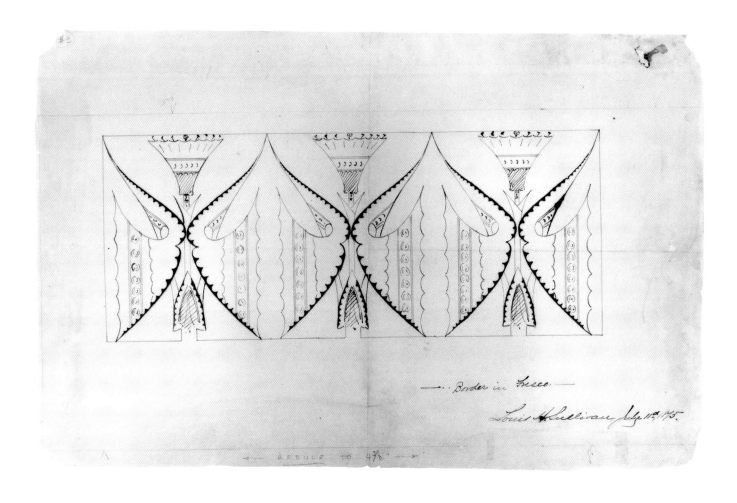

30. Design for border of fresco (11 July 1875).
Inscribed *Border in Fresco./Louis H. Sullivan/July 11th, 1875.*

Ink on tracing paper (26.3 x 41.3 cm.). Avery Library, Columbia University,
FLLW/LHS 19; purchased from Frank Lloyd Wright Foundation, 1965. W., S. 8.

31. Design for a stair railing [c. 1875–80].
Copied from the *Moniteur des architectes* (1870),
Plate 27: *Une rampe en fer forgé–M. Magne, Architecte.*

Pencil on tracing paper, mounted and matted (21 x 13.6 cm.).
Art Institute of Chicago; gift of George Grant Elmslie, 1931. M. 242.

32. Brothel scene (February 1875).
Initialed *L. H. S.* and dated.

Ink on paper (27 x 21 cm.). Art Institute of Chicago;
gift of Andrienne Sullivan, date of gift unknown. M. 229.

33. Sexual fantasy [c. 1875].

Ink on paper (19.5 x 18 cm.). Art Institute of Chicago;
gift of George Grant Elmslie, 1931. M. 253.

34. Fashonable woman with male observers (27 February 1875). Initialed *L. H. S.* and dated.

Ink on paper (23.5 x 16 cm.). Art Institute of Chicago; gift of George Grant Elmslie, 1931. M. 230.

35. Two street musicians (28 February 1875). Inscribed: *Déjà le violoneux commence à râceler son instrument;* initialed *L. H. S.* and dated.

Pen on paper (27 x 21 cm.). Art Institute of Chicago; gift of George Grant Elmslie, 1931. M. 231.

36. Woman in profile lighting a cigarette (6 March 1875).
Initialed *L. H. S.* and dated.

Ink on paper (29.5 x 19 cm.). Art Institute of Chicago;
gift of George Grant Elmslie, 1931. M. 230.

37. Woman wiping a dish (8 March 1875). Dated. Inscribed:
La mère Corbinet gémit un peu de cette grosse dépense.
Mais comme il s'agit d'un voeu, elle se résigne.

Ink on paper (19 x 16.5 cm.). Art Institute of Chicago;
gift of George Grant Elmslie, 1931. M. 231.

38. A painter and his model (29 March 1875).
Initialed *L. H. S.* and dated.

Pen on paper (33.7 x 25.6 cm.). Art Institute of Chicago;
gift of George Grant Elmslie, 1931. M. 232.

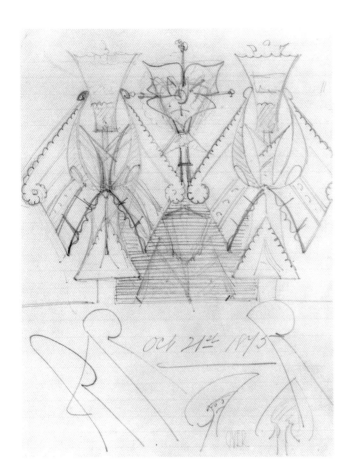

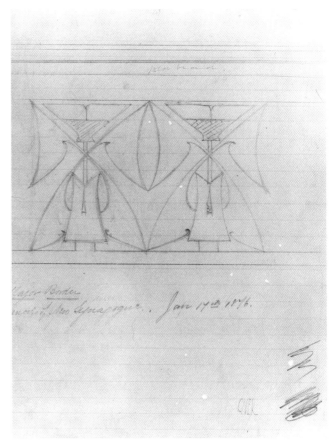

39. Design for ornament (21 October 1875). Dated.

Pencil on notebook paper with blue lines (12.7 x 15.2 cm.).
Bentley Historical Library, University of Michigan; gift of George Grant
Elmslie, c. 1936, to Emil Lorch, for College of Architecture and Design,
University of Michigan; transferred to Bentley Historical Library, 1972.

40. Study of fresco, Sinai Synagogue, Chicago. Dated.
Inscribed *Major Border/[Ch]ancel of* [illegible]
Synagogue. Jan. 17th 1876.

Pencil on notebook paper with blue lines (12.7 x 15.2 cm.). Bentley
Historical Library, University of Michigan; gift of George Grant
Elmslie, c. 1936, to Emil Lorch, for College of Architecture and Design,
University of Michigan; transferred to Bentley Historical Library, 1972.

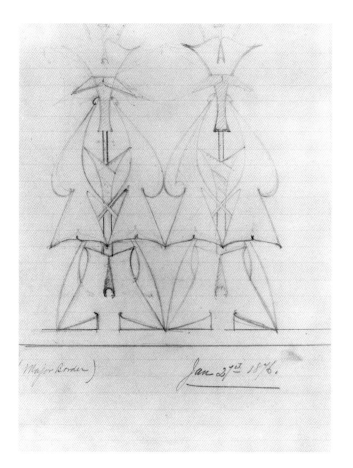

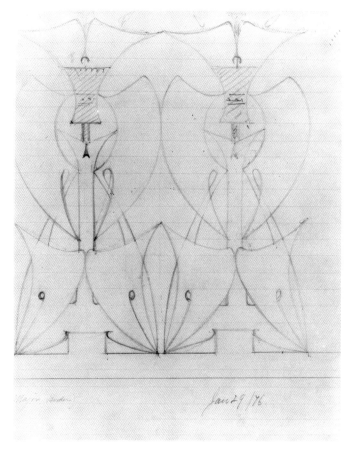

41. Study of fresco, Sinai Synagogue, Chicago. Dated.
Inscribed *(Major Border)* Jan 27th 1876.

Pencil on notebook paper with blue lines (12.7 x 15.2 cm.). Bentley
Historical Library, University of Michigan; gift of George Grant
Elmslie, c. 1936, to Emil Lorch, for College of Architecture and Design,
University of Michigan; transferred to Bentley Historical Library, 1972.

42. Study of fresco, Sinai Synagogue, Chicago. Dated.
Inscribed *(Major Border)* Jan 29 \76.

Pencil on notebook paper with blue lines (12.7 x 15.2 cm.). Bentley
Historical Library, University of Michigan; gift of George Grant
Elmslie, c. 1936, to Emil Lorch, for College of Architecture and Design,
University of Michigan; transferred to Bentley Historical Library, 1972.

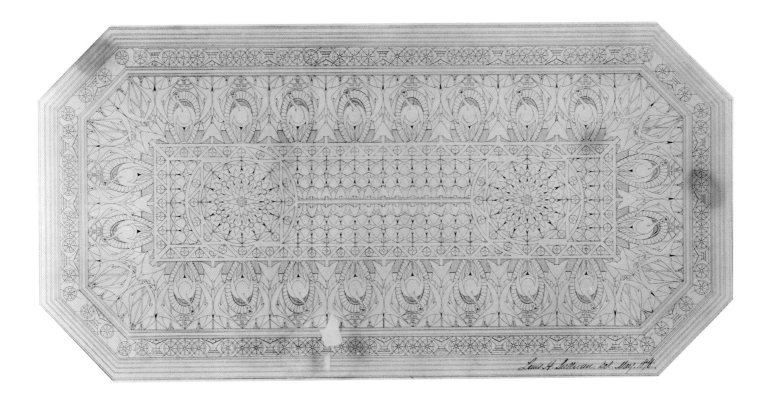

43. Design for a fresco (May 1876). Signed *Louis H. Sullivan,*
Del[*ineator*] and dated.

Ink on paper, mounted and matted (40 x 73.5 cm.). Art institute of Chicago;
gift of George Grant Elmslie, 1931. M. 2.

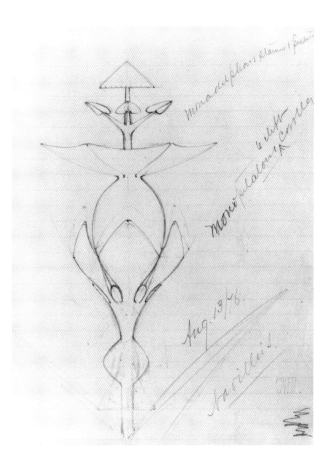

44. Woman's head in profile (16 June 1876). Dated.

Pencil on ruled notebook paper (19 x 13 cm.). Art institute of Chicago;
gift of George Grant Elmslie, 1931. M. 232.

45. Plant (13 August 1876). Dated. Inscribed with botanical terms.

Pencil on notebook paper with blue lines (12.7 x 15.2 cm.). Bentley Historical
Library, University of Michigan; gift of George Grant Elmslie, c. 1936,
to Emil Lorch, for College of Architecture and Design, University of Michigan;
transferred to Bentley Historical Library, 1972.

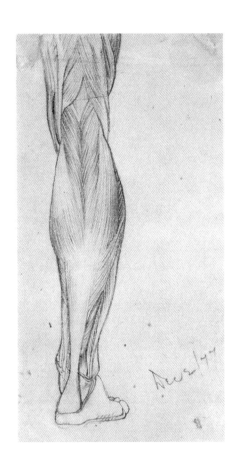
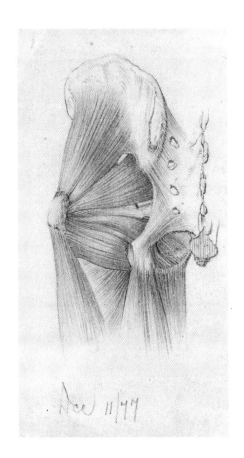

46. Studies of muscles (2 and 11 December 1877). Dated.

Pencil on paper, matted and mounted together (13 x 6 cm. each).
Art Institute of Chicago; gift of George Grant Elmslie, 1931. M. 233.

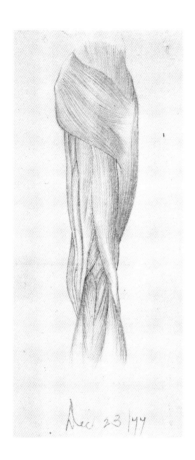
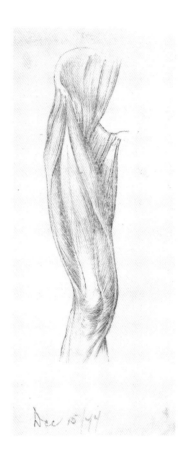

47. Studies of muscles (15 and 23 December 1877). Dated.

Pencil on paper, matted and mounted together (13 x 6 cm. each).
Art Institute of Chicago; gift of George Grant Elmslie, 1931. M. 233.

48. Grotesque head in profile (25 December 1877). Dated.

Pencil on paper (11.5 x 7 cm.). Art Institute of Chicago;
gift of George Grant Elmslie, 1931. M. 234.

49. Nude woman; tree sketch (26 December 1877). Dated.

Pencil on paper (14.5 x 13.5 cm.). Art Institute of Chicago;
gift of George Grant Elmslie, 1931. M. 234.

50. Grotesque head (26 January 1878). Dated.

Pencil on paper (19.5 x 10.4 cm.). Art Institute of Chicago;
gift of Andrienne Sullivan, date of gift unknown. M. 221.

51. Grotesque head (28 January 1878). Dated.

Pencil on paper (19.5 x 10.4 cm.). Art Institute of Chicago;
gift of Andrienne Sullivan, date of gift unknown. M. 222.

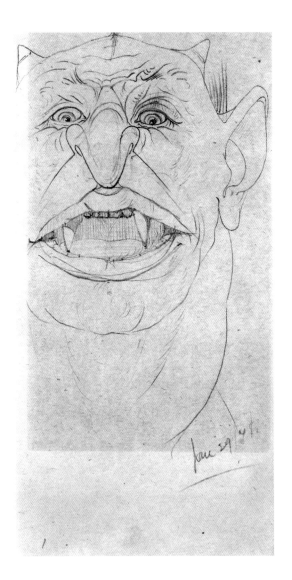

52. Grotesque head (29 January 1878). Dated.

Pencil on paper (19.5 x 10.4 cm.). Art Institute of Chicago; gift of Andrienne Sullivan, date of gift unknown. M. 222.

53. Grotesque head (30 January 1878). Dated.

Pencil on paper (19.5 x 10.4 cm.). Art Institute of Chicago; gift of Andrienne Sullivan, date of gift unknown. M. 223.

54. Grotesque head (6 February 1878). Dated.

Pencil on paper (19.5 x 10.4 cm.). Art Institute of Chicago; gift of Andrienne Sullivan, date of gift unknown. M. 223.

55. Head of an imaginary animal (24 February 1878). Dated.

Pencil on vellum (13 x 9.5 cm.). Art Institute of Chicago; gift of Andrienne Sullivan, date of gift unknown. M. 235.

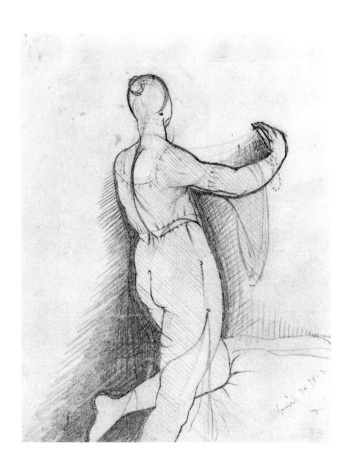

56. Woman from rear, kneeling on a cushion (7 April
1878). Dated. Verso: class notes on saturation, trimmed.

Pencil on paper (13 x 10.5 cm.). Art Institute of Chicago;
gift of George Grant Elmslie, 1931. M. 255.

57. Nude woman twisting her hair (10 April 1878). Dated.

Pencil on paper (31.5 x 18.5 cm.). Art Institute of Chicago;
gift of George Grant Elmslie, 1931. M. 235.

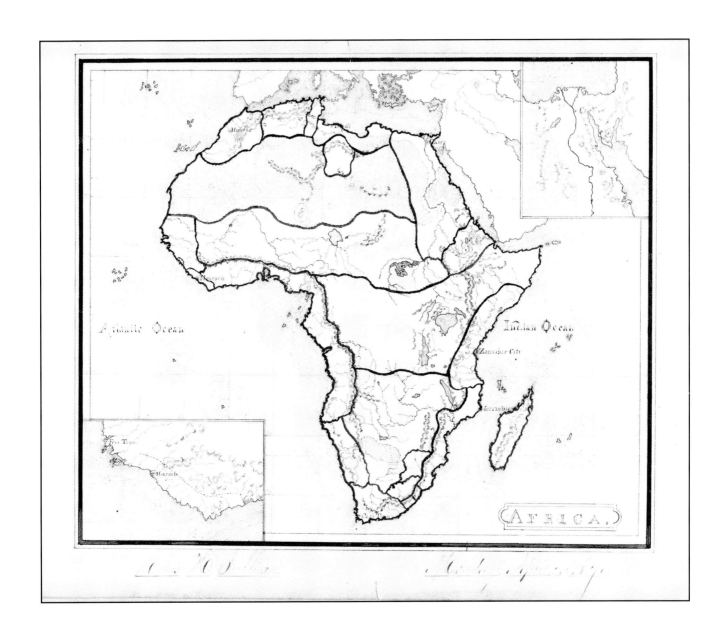

58. Map of Africa (25 April 1878).
Signed *Louis H. Sullivan* and dated.

Black and green ink on paper (25.9 x 32.3 cm.). Art Institute of Chicago;
probable gift of George Grant Elmslie, date of gift unknown. M. 272 (noted).

59. Man's face in profile (2 November 1878).
Initialed *L. H. S.* and dated.

Pencil on paper (22 x 14.2 cm.). Art Institute of Chicago;
gift of George Grant Elmslie, 1931. M. 236.

60. Male nude, kneeling (20 January 1879). Dated.

Pencil on paper (6.7 x 5 cm.). Art Institute of Chicago;
gift of George Grant Elmslie, 1931. M. 236.

61. Head in three-quarter profile, wearing a cap
(24 February 1879). Dated.

Pencil on paper (19 x 19.5 cm.). Art Institute of Chicago;
gift of George Grant Elmslie, 1931. M. 237.

62. Male nude seated on block, and a study of a head and
geometrical figures (3 April 1879). Initialed *L. H. S.* and
dated. Inscribed: *A philosopher meditating upon the
"unconditionally unlimited."*

Pencil on paper (34.7 x 21.3 cm.). Art Institute of Chicago;
gift of George Grant Elmslie, 1931. M. 238.

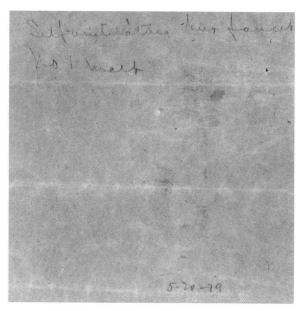

63. Male nude seated on block (20 April 1879). Dated.

Pencil on paper (17 x 13.5 cm.). Art Institute of Chicago;
gift of George Grant Elmslie, 1931. M. 238.

64. Three-quarter profile (20 May 1879). Dated. Sketch on a
note inscribed: *Self-ventilating* [illegible] *faucet/No 1 matt.*

Pencil on paper (10 x 10 cm.). Art Institute of Chicago;
gift of George Grant Elmslie, 1931. M. 239.

65. Male nude sitting on steps, gesturing with left hand and
looking over left shoulder (28 September 1879). Dated.

Pencil on paper (26.5 x 21 cm.). Art Institute of Chicago;
gift of George Grant Elmslie, 1931. M. 239.

66. Male nude, with arms wrapped around head
(19 October 1879). Dated.

Pencil on paper (30.5 x 21 cm.). Art Institute of Chicago;
gift of George Grant Elmslie, 1931. M. 240.

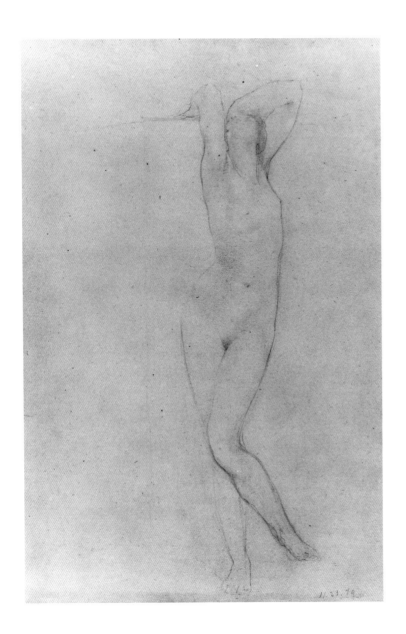

67. Female nude (23 November 1879). Dated.

Pencil on paper (32.4 x 20.9 cm.). Bentley Historical Library,
University of Michigan; gift of George Grant Elmslie, c. 1936, to Emil Lorch,
for College of Architecture and Design, University of Michigan;
transferred to Bentley Historical Library, 1972.

68. Female nude, leaning on a pedestal
(22 December 1879). Dated.

Pencil on paper (14 x 9.5 cm.). Art Institute of Chicago;
gift of George Grant Elmslie, 1931. M. 240.

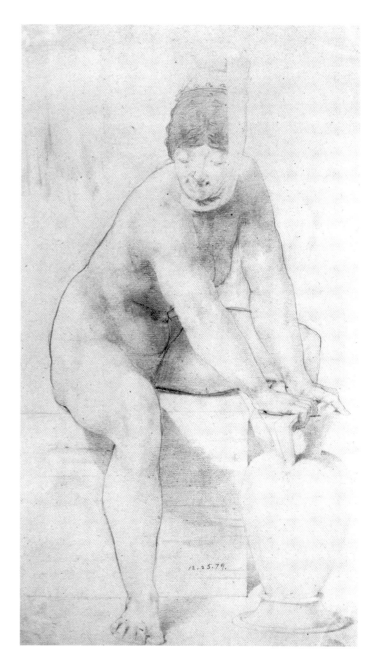

69. Female nude on a step (23 December 1879). Dated.

Pencil on paper (19 x 10.5 cm.). Art Institute of Chicago;
gift of George Grant Elmslie, 1931. M. 241.

70. Seated female nude, with chin supported by a strap,
leaning on an urn (25 December 1879). Dated.

Pencil on paper (33.5 x 19.5 cm.). Art Institute of Chicago;
gift of George Grant Elmslie, 1931. M. 241.

71. Nude female figure, with Spanish comb in hair,
seated next to a baluster [c. 1879–80].

Pencil on paper (29 x 19 cm.). Art Institute of Chicago;
gift of George Grant Elmslie, 1931. M. 255.

72. Nude female figure, with left foot on a step,
right hand on a baluster [c. 1879–80].

Pencil on paper (33 x 20.5 cm.). Art Institute of Chicago;
gift of George Grant Elmslie, 1931. M. 256.

73. Female nude, seated on stairs next to a head of a monster on a pedestal; study for No. 74 (8 February 1880). Dated.

Pencil on paper (34 x 21 cm.). Art Institute of Chicago; gift of George Grant Elmslie, 1931. M. 243.

74. Female nude, seated on stairs next to a head of a monster on a pedestal (10 March 1880). Dated. Inscribed: *A. F. S.*

Pencil on paper (35 x 21.5 cm.). Art Institute of Chicago; gift of Andrienne Sullivan, date of gift unknown. M. 243.

 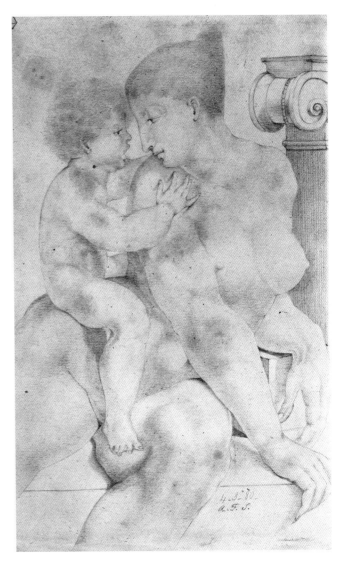

75. Female nude and child; study for No. 76
(14 March 1880). Dated.

Pencil on paper (32.3 x 21 cm.). Art Institute of Chicago;
gift of George Grant Elmslie, 1931. M. 244.

76. Female nude and child (3 April 1880). Dated.
Inscribed: *A. F. S.*

Pencil on paper (35 x 21.5 cm.). Art Institute of Chicago;
gift of Andrienne Sullivan, date of gift unknown. M. 244.

77. Nude female figure (1 April 1880). Dated. Cropping marks
in pencil by Frank Lloyd Wright, for publication in
Genius and the Mobocracy (1949).

Pencil on paper (12.6 x 9.9 cm.). Avery Library, Columbia University, FLLW/LHS
36; purchased from Frank Lloyd Wright Foundation, 1965. W., S. 9.

78. Nude youth, with urn (7 April 1880). Dated.

Red ink with traces of pencil on paper (14.5 x 9 cm.).
Art Institute of Chicago;
gift of George Grant Elmslie, 1931. M. 245.

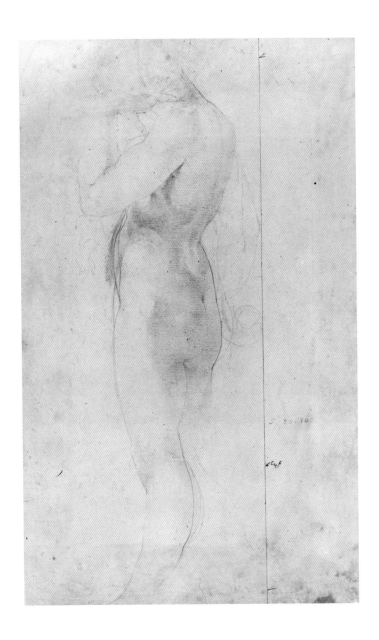

79. Female nude (30 May 1880). Dated. Cropping marks in
pencil by Frank Lloyd Wright, for publication in
Genius and the Mobocracy (1949).

Pencil (34.2 x 21.2 cm.). Avery Library, Columbia University, FLLW/LHS 38;
purchased from Frank Lloyd Wright Foundation, 1965. W., S. 10.

80. Portrait of John Edelmann (17 November 1880).
Initialed *L. H. S.* and dated, in ink. Inscribed in pencil:
Portrait of John H. Edelmann.

Pencil on paper (19.9 x 12.8 cm.). Art Institute of Chicago;
gift of George Grant Elmslie, 1932. M. 245.

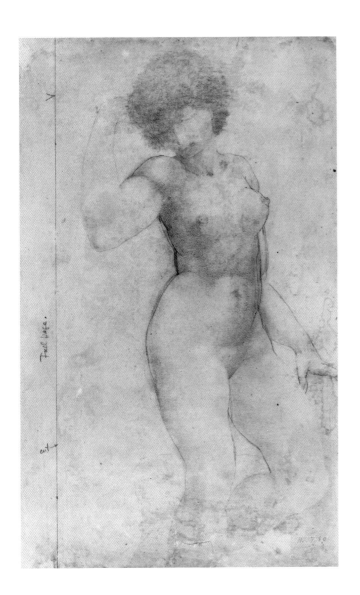

81. Female nude (17 November 1880). Dated. Cropping marks
in pencil by Frank Lloyd Wright, for publication in
Genius and the Mobocracy (1949).

Pencil on tracing paper (34.2 x 21.1 cm.). Avery Library, Columbia University,
FLLW/LHS 37; purchased from Frank Lloyd Wright Foundation, 1965. W., S. 11.

82. Profile of a bearded man (29 November 1880).
Dated. Inscribed: *Louis H. Sullivan/*
To Earl H. Reed/Sept. 18–'13.

Pencil on paper (26 x 21 cm.). Art Institute of Chicago;
gift of Earl H. Reed, 1956. M. 246.

83. Seated female nude with Spanish comb in hair
(27 february 1881). Dated.

Pencil on paper (31 x 20.5 cm.). Art Institute of Chicago;
gift of George Grant Elmslie, 1931. M. 248.

84. Sheet of sketches (23 March 1881). Dated.
Recto of No. 85.

Pencil on paper (16 x 11 cm.). Art Institute of Chicago;
gift of George Grant Elmslie, 1931. M. 247.

85. Doodles and sketches. Undated.
Verso of No. 84.

Pencil on paper (16 x 11 cm.). Art Institute of Chicago;
gift of George Grant Elmslie, 1931.

86. Design for ornament (16 April 1881). Dated.

Pencil on paper (30.5 x 20.9 cm.). Bentley Historical Library,
University of Michigan; gift of George Grant Elmslie, c. 1936, to Emil Lorch,
for College of Architecture and Design, University of Michigan;
transferred to Bentley Historical Library, 1972.

87. Design for capital of column on porch of M. Wineman residence,
Chicago, Illinois [c. July 1882]. Inscribed on upper left-hand side:
Capital for Porch Columns/Residence for
M. Wineman, Esq. D. Adler and Co[.], Archts.

Pencil on paper (63.1 x 70.9 cm.). Avery Library, Columbia University, FLLW/LHS 34;
purchased from Frank Lloyd Wright Foundation, 1965. W., S. 12.

88. Design for Adler & Sullivan office door light [1883].
Inscribed: *SCALE 3" = 1 FOOT. (1/4" = 1 INCH)/(2) Two lights like this: Sand
blast pattern on best quality French polished plate glass*
[followed by two illegible words within a parenthesis].

Blue-line drawing tinted with blue and gold watercolor wash on paper (30.2 x 18.7 cm.).
Collection Ruth Guyer, Chicago; drawing found by John Moulton inside a book he purchased
at the 1909 auction of Sullivan's property; given by Moulton to a nurse who gave it to Joseph
A. Guyer's aunt, who gave it to Joseph A. and Ruth Guyer sometime before 1940.

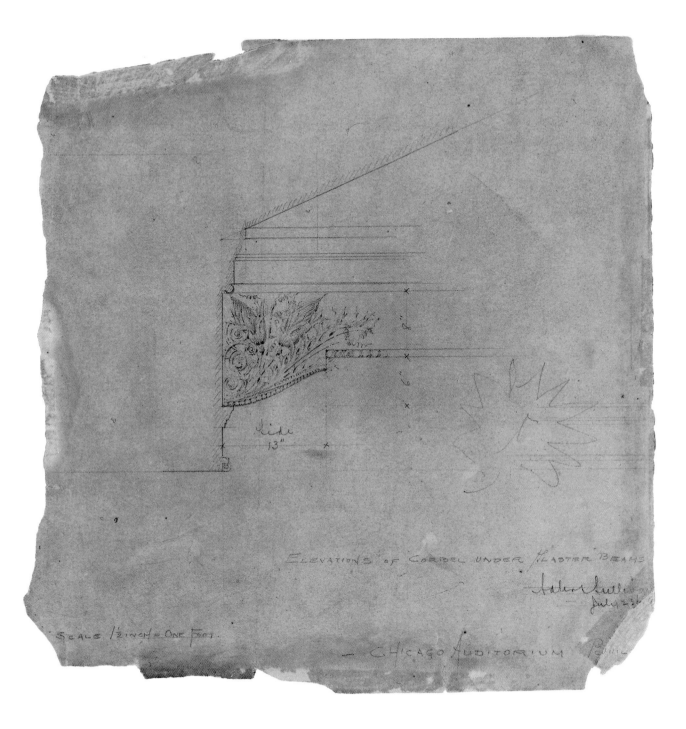

89. Boxes, McVicker's Theater, Chicago, Illinois (9 January 1883).
Dated. Cropping marks in pencil by Frank Lloyd Wright,
for publication in *Genius and the Mobocracy* (1949).

Pencil on drawing paper (34.2 x 21.2 cm.). Avery Library, Columbia University,
FLLW/LHS 49; purchased from Frank Lloyd Wright Foundation, 1965. W., S. 13.

90. Design for ornament, McVicker's Theater, Chicago, Illinois
(6 May 1884). Dated. Cropping marks in pencil by Frank Lloyd
Wright, for publication in *Genius and the Mobocracy* (1949).

Pencil (34.7 x 21.2 cm.). Avery Library, Columbia University, FLLW/LHS 15;
purchased from Frank Lloyd Wright Foundation, 1965. W., S. 14.

91. Man's head in profile (6 August 1884). Dated.
Inscribed: *Latham.*

Pencil on paper (21.5 x 14 cm.). Art Institute of Chicago;
gift of George Grant Elmslie, 1931. M. 248.

92. Design for ornament (13 April 1885). Dated. Inscribed by
Sullivan: *alphabet*; inscribed by Frank Lloyd Wright: *The begginig* [sic]
of the plastic period–85-G; cropping marks in pencil by Frank Lloyd Wright,
for publication in *Genius and the Mobocracy* (1949).

Pencil on paper torn from a pad (27.5 x 17.6 cm.). Avery Library, Columbia University,
FLLW/LHS 21; purchased from Frank Lloyd Wright Foundation, 1965. W., S. 15.

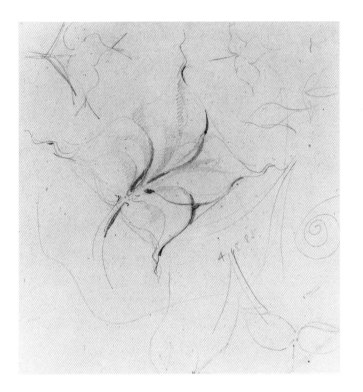

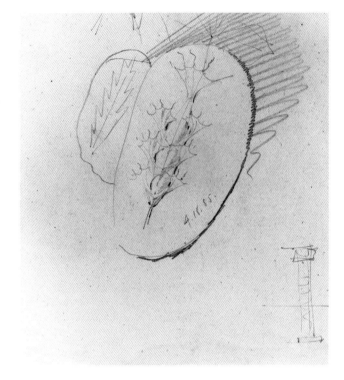

93. Sketch for ornament (18 April 1885). Dated.
Recto of No. 94.

Pencil on paper (17.4 x 17.1 cm.). Avery Library,
Columbia University, FLLW/LHS 14; purchased from
Frank Lloyd Wright Foundation, 1965. S. 17-A.

94. Sketch for ornament (18 April 1885). Dated.
Verso of No. 93.

Pencil on paper (17.4 x 17.1 cm.) Avery Library, Columbia University,
FLLW/LHS 14; purchased from
Frank Lloyd Wright Foundation, 1965. S. 17-B.

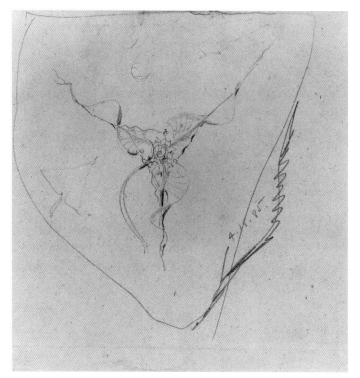

95. Sketch for ornament (18 April 1885). Dated. Inscribed in pencil by Frank Lloyd Wright: *chapter end*; cropping marks in pencil by Frank Lloyd Wright, for publication in *Genius and the Mobocracy* (1949).

Pencil on paper torn from a pad (7.6 x 17.7 cm.). Avery Library, Columbia University, FLLW/LHS 125; purchased from Frank Lloyd Wright Foundation, 1965. W., S. 18.

96. Sketch for ornament (18 April 1885). Dated.

Pencil on paper (17 x 16.4 cm.). Avery Library, Columbia University, FLLW/LHS 13; purchased from Frank Lloyd Wright Foundation, 1965. W., S. 16.

97. Design for ornament (17 May 1885). Dated.
Inscribed in pencil by Frank Lloyd Wright: *Combined L and S. L motive*
[sic]; cropping marks in pencil by Frank Lloyd Wright for
publication in *Genius and the Mobocracy* (1949).

Pencil on paper torn from a pad (27 x 17.7 cm.). Avery Library,
Columbia University, FLLW/LHS 40; purchased from
Frank Lloyd Wright Foundation, 1965. W., S. 19.

98. Hand with a leaf (20 July 1885). Initialed *L. H. S.* and dated.

Pencil on paper (25 x 20.3 cm.). Art Institute of Chicago;
gift of Andrienne Sullivan, date of gift unknown. M. 249.

99. Standing female nude from the rear, against a backdrop
of greenery (30 August 1885). Dated.

Pencil on paper (19.5 x 18 cm.). Art Institute of Chicago;
gift of George Grant Elmslie, 1931. M. 250.

100. Man's head in profile, smoking a cigar (20 September 1885). Dated. Inscribed in pencil: *Webster*.

Pencil on paper (20 x 16.5 cm.). Art Institute of Chicago; gift of George Grant Elmslie, 1931. M. 251.

101. Three-quarter profile of a woman wearing a hat (20 September 1885). Dated.

Pencil on paper (17.5 x 14 cm.). Art Institute of Chicago; gift of George Grant Elmslie, 1931. M. 251.

102. Design for ornament, McVicker's Theater, Chicago, Illinois
(30 September 1885). Dated.

Pencil on paper (26.6 x 16.7 cm.). Avery Library, Columbia University, FLLW/LHS 20;
purchased from Frank Lloyd Wright Foundation, 1965. W., S. 24.

103. Design for ornament (19 October 1885). Dated.
Inscribed in pencil: *To Earl H. Reed/Louis H. Sullivan/Sept 18—'13.*

Pencil on paper (19.8 x 14 cm.). Art Institute of Chicago;
gift of George Grant Elmslie, 1931. M. 252.

104. Man's head in profile, with ponytail
(6 December 1885). Dated.

Pencil on paper (15.5 x 13.5 cm.). Art Institute of Chicago;
gift of George Grant Elmslie, 1931. M. 252.

105. Design for ornament (18 December 1885). Dated.
Cropping marks in pencil by Frank Lloyd Wright for publication
in *Genius and the Mobocracy* (1949). Recto of No. 113.

Pencil on paper torn from a pad (27.3 x 17.6 cm.). Avery Library,
Columbia University, FLLW/LHS 22; purchased from
Frank Lloyd Wright Foundation, 1965. W., S. 23.

106. Female nude grasping a tree limb [c. 1885].

Pencil on paper (17 x 13 cm.). Art Institute of Chicago;
gift of George Grant Elmslie, 1931. M. 253.

107. Studies of heads [c. 1885].

Pencil on paper (20 x 17.5 cm.). Art Institute of Chicago;
gift of George Grant Elmslie, 1931. M. 254.

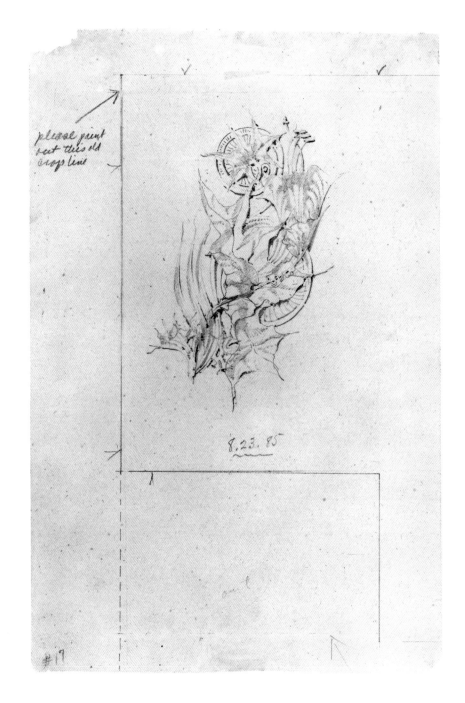

108. Design for ornament (23 August 1885). Dated.
Cropping marks in pencil by Frank Lloyd Wright for publication in
Genius and the Mobocracy (1949).

Pencil on paper torn from a pad (26.8 x 17.7 cm.). Avery Library,
Columbia University, FLLW/LHS 4; purchased from
Frank Lloyd Wright Foundation, 1965. W., S. 20.

109. Designs for ornament (23 August 1885). Dated.
Inscribed in pencil by Sullivan: *Tribute*; inscribed in pencil
by Frank Lloyd Wright: *Chapter ends* [but not illustrated
in *Genius and the Mobocracy*].

Pencil on paper (17.7 x 26.7 cm.). Avery Library, Columbia University,
FLLW/LHS 89; purchased from Frank Lloyd Wright Foundation, 1965. S. 21.

110. Design for ornament (28 August 1885). Dated.
Cropping marks in pencil by Frank Lloyd Wright for
publication in *Genius and the Mobocracy* (1949).

Pencil on paper (13.6 x 9.9 cm.). Avery Library,
Columbia University, FLLW/LHS 5; purchased from Frank Lloyd
Wright Foundation, 1965. W., S. 22.

111. Head of woman (22 September 1885). Dated.

Pencil on paper (26.7 x 17.8 cm.). Bentley Historical Library,
University of Michigan; gift of George Grant Elmslie, c. 1936,
to Emil Lorch, for College of Architecture and Design,
University of Michigan;
transferred to Bentley Historical Library, 1972.

112. Sketch for cover of a catalogue for Robert Stevenson
& Co., Wholesale Druggists [January 1887].
Inscribed in pencil: *Robert S . . . Co.*

Pencil on paper torn from a pad (27.3 x 17.6 cm.). Avery Library,
Columbia University, FLLW/LHS 92; purchased from
Frank Lloyd Wright Foundation, 1965. S. 25-A.

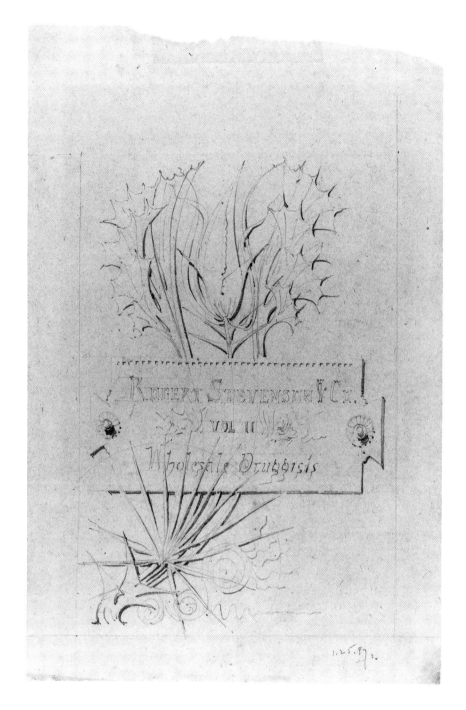

113. Design for cover of a catalogue for Robert Stevenson
& Co. Vol. II. Wholesale Druggists (25 January 1887).
Dated. Verso of No. 105.

Pencil (27.1 x 17.7 cm.). Avery Library, Columbia University,
FLLW/LHS 92; purchased from
Frank Lloyd Wright Foundation, 1965. S. 25-B.

114. Design for corbel, Auditorium Building, Chicago, Illinois (23 July 1888). Dated.
Inscribed in pencil: *ELEVATIONS OF CORBEL UNDER PLASTER BEAMS/Adler &
Sullivan/July 23/88/SCALE 1 1/2 INCH = ONE FOOT/CHICAGO AUDITORIUM.*

Pencil on paper (25.3 x 25.1 cm.). Avery Library, Columbia University, FLLW/LHS 5;
purchased from Frank Lloyd Wright Foundation, 1965. S. 26.

115. Design for corbel, Auditorium Building,
Chicago, Illinois [c. 1888–89].

Pencil on paper (20 x 10.1 cm.). Avery Library, Columbia University,
FLLW/LHS 9; purchased from Frank Lloyd Wright Foundation, 1965. W., S. 27.

116. Design for mosaic on stair landing in hotel, Auditorium
Building, Chicago, Illinois [c. 1888–89]. Inscribed: *Hotel Landing*.

Pencil on paper torn from a pad (8.3 x 19.7 cm.).
Avery Library, Columbia University, FLLW/LHS 64; purchased from
Frank Lloyd Wright Foundation, 1965. S. 28.

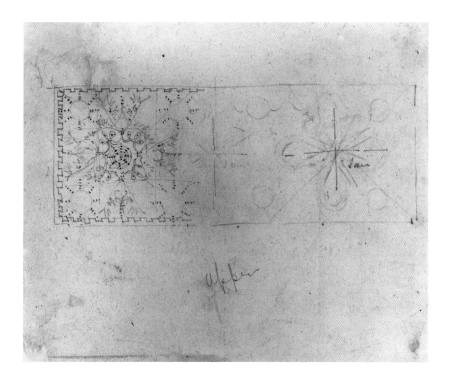

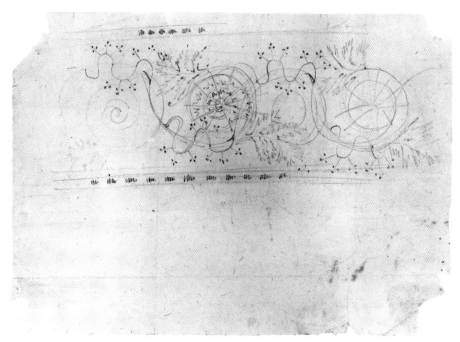

117. Design for mosaic on stair landing, Auditorium
Building, Chicago, Illinois [c. 1888–89]. Inscribed: *upper*.

Pencil on paper torn from a pad (13.9 x 17.6 cm.).
Avery Library, Columbia University, FLLW/LHS 121; purchased from
Frank Lloyd Wright Foundation, 1965. S. 29.

118. Design for mosaic, Auditorium Building, Chicago,
Illinois [c. 1888–89]. Recto of No. 119.

Pencil on paper (13.9 x 19.6 cm.).
Avery Library, Columbia University, FLLW/LHS 91; purchased from
Frank Lloyd Wright Foundation, 1965. S. 30-A.

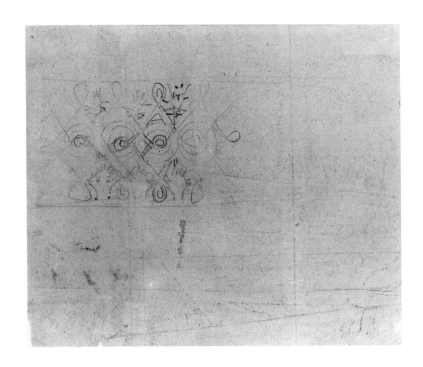

119. Design for mosaic, Auditorium Building,
Chicago, Illinois [c. 1888–89]. Verso of No. 118.

Pencil on paper (13.9 x 19.6 cm.).
Avery Library, Columbia University, FLLW/LHS 91; purchased from
Frank Lloyd Wright Foundation, 1965. S. 30-B.

120. Design for capital, banquet hall, Auditorium Building,
Chicago, Illinois (15 April 1890). Dated. Inscribed:
Banquet Hall Cap/A & S. 4\15\90.

Pencil on paper (13.7 x 20.6 cm.).
Avery Library, Columbia University, FLLW/LHS 88; purchased from
Frank Lloyd Wright Foundation, 1965. W., S. 32.

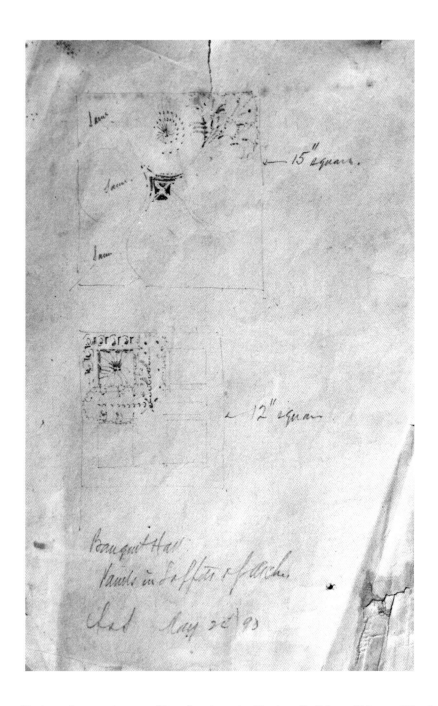

121. Designs for panels on soffits of arches, Auditorium Building, Chicago, Illinois
(24 May 1890). Inscribed, on upper design: *same* (three times); next to upper design:
15" square; next to lower design: *12" square*; on lower left-hand corner of sheet:
Banquet Hall/Panels in Soffit of Arches/LHS May 24\90.

Pencil on paper (21 x 13.4 cm.). Collection Peter Howard, Berkeley, California; purchased by Mr. Howard
from Toby Holtzman, Southfield, Michigan, 1992; purchased by Mr. Holtzman from the Max Protetch
Gallery, New York, 1986; former collection Crombie Taylor, Los Angeles; early provenance unknown.

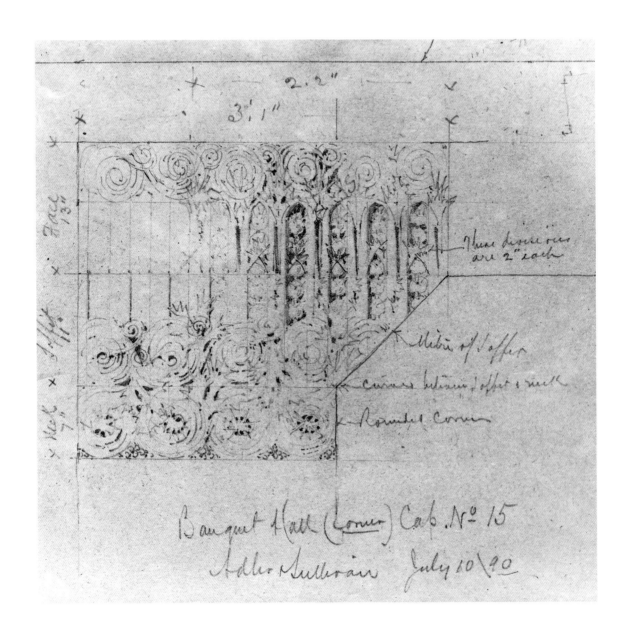

122. Design for capital, banquet hall, Auditorium Building, Chicago, Illinois
(10 July 1890). Inscribed, on right-hand side: *These divisions/are 2" each,
Mitre of soffit, curve between soffit and neck, Rounded corner;* at bottom:
Banquet Hall (corner) Cap. No. 15/Adler & Sullivan July 10\90.

Pencil on paper (18.1 x 18.5 cm.). Avery Library, Columbia University, FLLW/LHS 50;
purchased from Frank Lloyd Wright Foundation, 1965. W., S. 33.

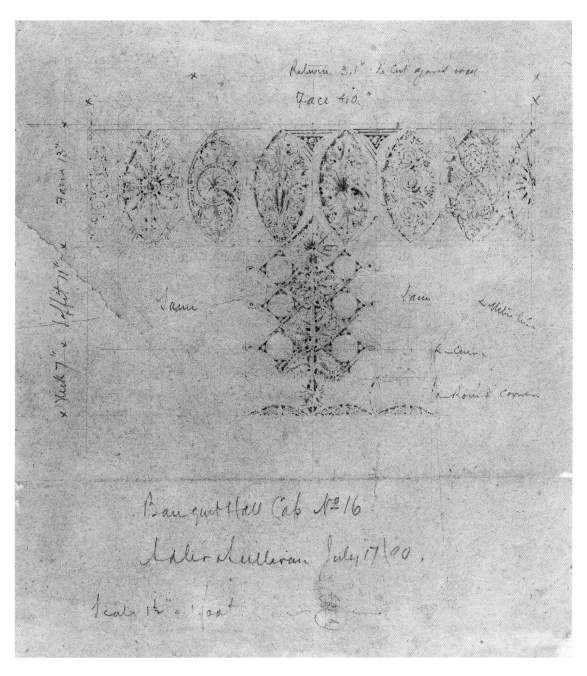

123. Design for capital, banquet hall, Auditorium Building, Chicago, Illinois
(17 July 1890). Inscribed, on left-hand side: *Neck 7", Soffit 11", Facia 13";* at top:
Return 3.1" to cut against wall/ Face 4'0"; on right-hand side: *Mitre line, Curve, Round
corner;* left and right of drawing: *Same;* at bottom: *Banquet Hall Cap No. 16/Adler and
Sullivan July 17\90/Scale 1 1/2" = 1 foot* [followed by Sullivan's initials in a monogram].

Pencil on paper (21.6 x 19.4 cm.). Avery Library, Columbia University, FLLW/LHS 53;
purchased from Frank Lloyd Wright Foundation, 1965. S. 34.

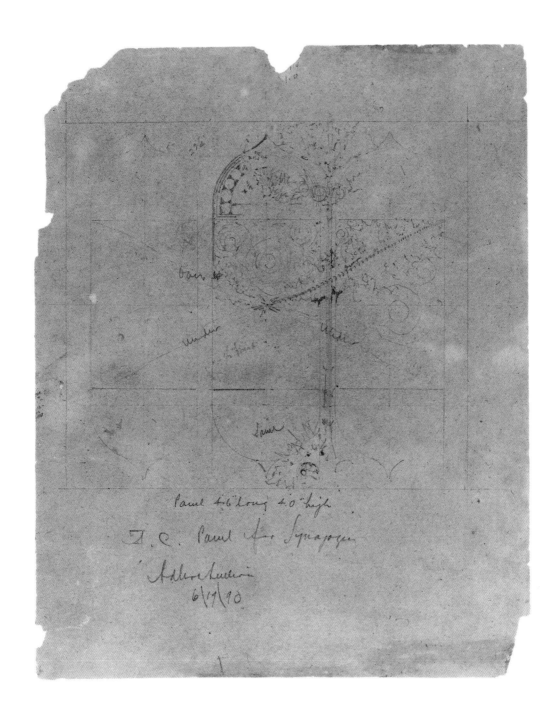

124. Design for ornament, Kehilath Anshe Ma'ariv Synagogue, Chicago, Illinois
(19 June 1890). Inscribed, on design: *over, under, 1/2" break*; below design: *Panel 4'6" long
4'0" high*; at bottom: *T. C.* [terra-cotta] *Panel for Synagogue/Adler and Sullivan/6\19\90.*

Pencil on paper (26 x 21 cm.). Avery Library, Columbia University, FLLW/LHS 52;
purchased from Frank Lloyd Wright Foundation, 1965. S. 35.

125. Design for frame and a mural [c. 1890].

Pencil on tracing paper (52.8 x 50 cm.). Avery Library, Columbia University,
FLLW/LHS 31; purchased from Frank Lloyd Wright Foundation, 1965. S. 37.

126. Design for cornice, Getty Tomb, Chicago, Illinois
(16 October 1890). Dated. Cropping marks in pencil by Frank Lloyd
Wright for publication in *Genius and the Mobocracy* (1949).

Pencil on the back of Adler & Sullivan imprinted stationery on the left side,
and this attached on the right side to a piece of plain paper (21.1 x 43.9 cm.).
Avery Library, Columbia University, FLLW/LHS 25;
purchased from Frank Lloyd Wright Foundation, 1965. W., S. 38.

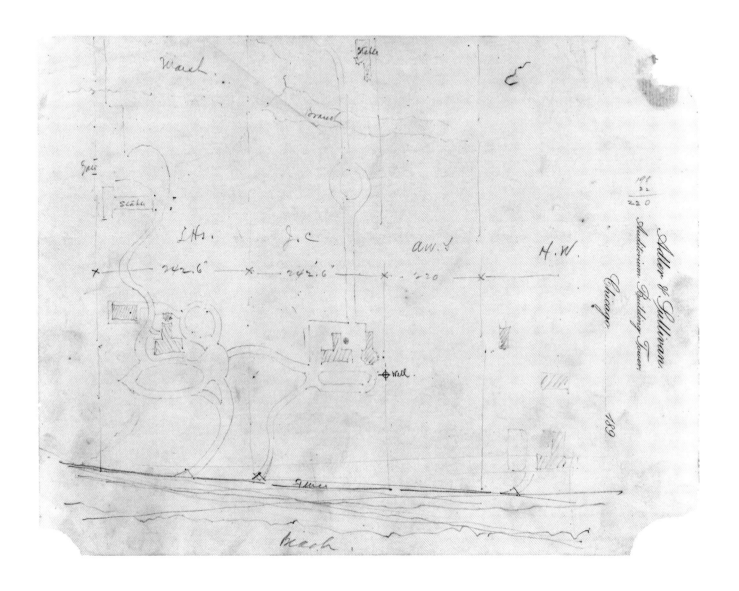

127. Site plan for properties of Louis Sullivan, James Charnley, Albert Sullivan,
and Horace Williston, Ocean Springs, Mississippi [c. 1890].
Inscribed, on upper left and center of sheet: *Marsh*[,] *Branch* [and] *Stable*;
on center of sheet: *L.H.S.*[,] *J.C.*[,] *A.W.S.*[, and] *H.W.*; string of dimensions:
242[']*.6"*[,] *242*[']*.6"*[,] *and 220*[']; on lower center of sheet: *well*; at bottom of
sheet: *fence/Beach*; on left-hand side of sheet: *Gate/stables.*

Pencil on Adler & Sullivan imprinted stationery (21.6 x 28 cm.).
Collection Tim Samuelson, Chicago; gift of Edgar Kaufmann jr. to Richard Nickel on behalf of
Frank Lloyd Wright, 1956; gift of Richard Nickel to Tim Samuelson, 1971.

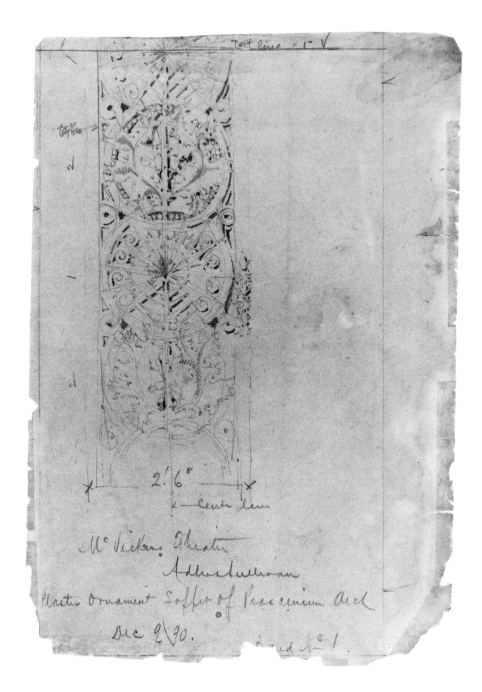

128. Design for soffit, McVicker's Theater remodeling, Chicago, Illinois,
(9 December 1890). Inscribed, on design: *2'6", Center line;* below: *McVickers
Theater/Auditorium/Plaster Ornament*[,] *Soffit of Proscenium Arch/Dec. 9 90;*
cropping marks in pencil by Frank Lloyd Wright, for publication in
Genius and the Mobocracy (1949).

Pencil on paper (30 x 21 cm.). Avery Library, Columbia University, FLLW/LHS 46;
purchased from Frank Lloyd Wright Foundation, 1965. W., S. 40.

129. Design for plaster ornamentation, balcony front, McVicker's Theater remodeling, Chicago, Illinois (25 December 1890). Pencil on paper (19 x 29.1 cm.).
Inscribed with dimension; at bottom: *McVicker's Theatre/Adler and Sullivan Archts/Plaster Ornamentation of Balcony Front*[,] *Scale 1/8" = 1'/Dec. 25\90*; cropping marks in pencil by Frank Lloyd Wright, for publication in *Genius and the Mobocracy* (1949).

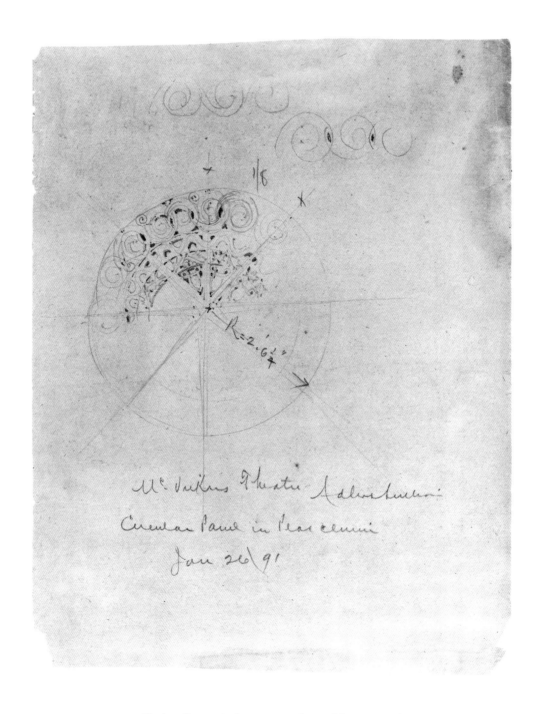

130. Design for central ornamental panel in proscenium,
McVicker's Theater remodeling, Chicago, Illinois (26 January 1891).
Inscribed, on design: *R = 2'.6 1/4"*; at bottom: *McVicker's
Theatre/Adler & Sullivan/Circular Panel in Proscenium/Jan 26\91.*

Pencil on paper (26.5 x 21 cm.). Avery Library, Columbia University, FLLW/LHS 54;
purchased from Frank Lloyd Wright Foundation, 1965. S. 42.

131. Design for ornament, McVicker's Theater remodeling,
Chicago, Illinois (2 February 1891). Inscribed with dimension;
at bottom: *Band No/McVickers Theatre – Adler and Sull* [rest of signature
torn out]/*Feb 2\91*; cropping marks in pencil by Frank Lloyd Wright,
for publication in *Genius and the Mobocracy* (1949).

Pencil on paper (25.5 x 21.2 cm.). Avery Library, Columbia University, FLLW/LHS 45;
purchased from Frank Lloyd Wright Foundation, 1965. W., S. 44.

132. Design for ornament, McVicker's Theater remodeling, Chicago, Illinois
[c. 1890–91]. Inscribed *McVicker's Theatre/Adler & Sullivan Archts/Plaster
Ornament in Sounding Board/Band No. 4*; cropping marks in pencil by Frank
Lloyd Wright, for publication in *Genius and the Mobocracy* (1949).

Pencil on paper (31 x 13.6 cm.). Avery Library, Columbia University, FLLW/LHS 47;
purchased from Frank Lloyd Wright Foundation, 1965. W., S. 45.

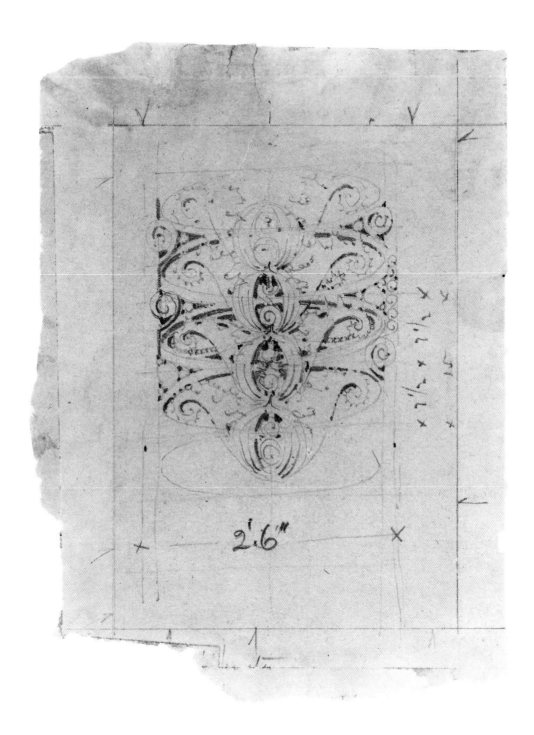

133. Design for ornament, McVicker's Theater remodeling, Chicago,
Illinois [c. 1890–91]. Inscribed with dimensions; cropping marks in pencil by
Frank Lloyd Wright, for publication in *Genius and the Mobocracy* (1949).

Pencil on paper (18.7 x 14 cm.). Avery Library, Columbia University, FLLW/LHS 6;
purchased from Frank Lloyd Wright Foundation, 1965. W., S. 46.

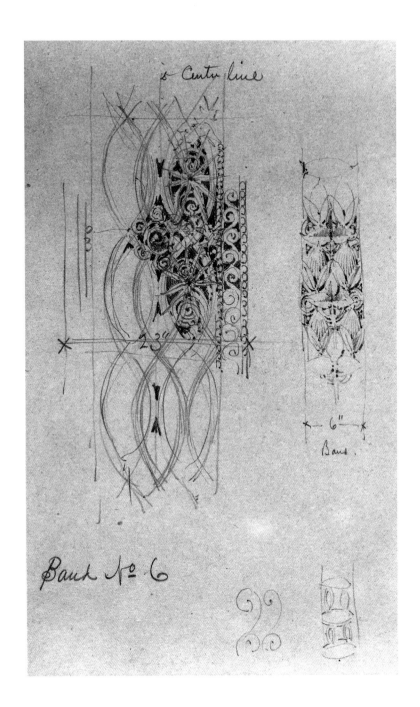

134. Design for two ornaments, McVicker's Theater remodeling,
Chicago, Illinois [c. 1890–91]. Inscribed with dimension on design; beneath
left-hand figure: *Band No. 6*; beneath right-hand side figure: *Band*.

Pencil on paper (34.9 x 21.6 cm.). Collection of Ruth Guyer, Chicago; drawing found by
John Moulton inside a book he purchased at the 1909 auction of Sullivan's property;
given by Moulton to a nurse who gave it to Joseph A. Guyer's aunt, who gave it to
Joseph A. and Ruth Guyer sometime before 1940.

135. Design for ornament, McVicker's Theater remodeling,
Chicago, Illinois [c. 1890–91]. Inscribed with dimensions on design;
at bottom: *Band no 8 (Face of Frame)*.

Pencil on paper (34.7 x 21.6 cm.). Collection of Ruth Guyer; Chicago; drawing found by
John Moulton inside a book he purchased at the 1909 auction of Sullivan's property;
given by Moulton to a nurse who gave it to Joseph A. Guyer's aunt, who gave it to
Joseph A. and Ruth Guyer sometime before 1940.

136. Design for ornament, McVicker's Theater remodeling, Chicago, Illinois [c. 1890–91]. Inscribed with dimension on design.

Pencil on paper (34.7 x 21.6 cm.). Collection of Ruth Guyer, Chicago; drawing found by
John Moulton inside a book he purchased at the 1909 auction of Sullivan's property;
given by Moulton to a nurse who gave it to Joseph A. Guyer's aunt, who gave it to
Joseph A. and Ruth Guyer sometime before 1940.

137. Design for ornament, McVicker's Theater remodeling,
Chicago, Illinois [c. 1890–91]. Inscribed with dimensions on design;
cropping marks in pencil by Frank Lloyd Wright, for publication in
Genius and the Mobocracy (1949).

Pencil on paper (19.6 x 16.5 cm.). Richard Nickel Committee Collection, Chicago
(drawing currently in the hands of Nickel's heirs); gift of Edgar Kaufmann jr.
to Richard Nickel on behalf of Frank Lloyd Wright, 1956. W.

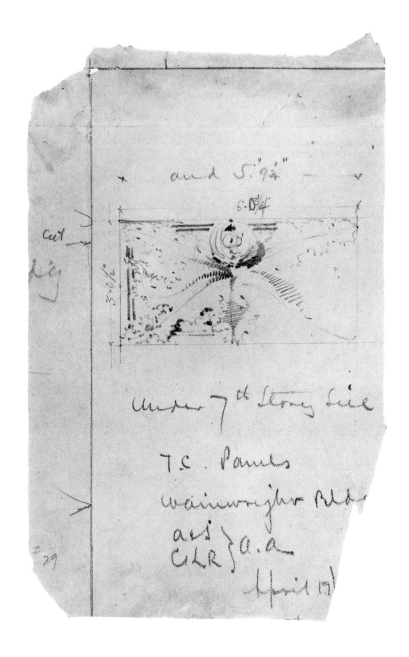

138. Design for ornamental panel, Wainwright Building, St. Louis, Missouri (19 April [1891]). Inscribed with dimensions; at bottom: *Under 7th Story Sill/T.C.* [terra-cotta] *Panels/Wainwright Bldg./A & S/CLR/a.a* [Adler & Sullivan, Charles L. Ramsey, Associated Architects]*/April 19*\[year torn off]; cropping marks in pencil by Frank Lloyd Wright, for publication in *Genius and the Mobocracy* (1949).

Pencil on paper (18.5 x 11.5 cm.). Avery Library, Columbia University, FLLW/LHS 122; purchased from Frank Lloyd Wright Foundation, 1965. W., S. 51.

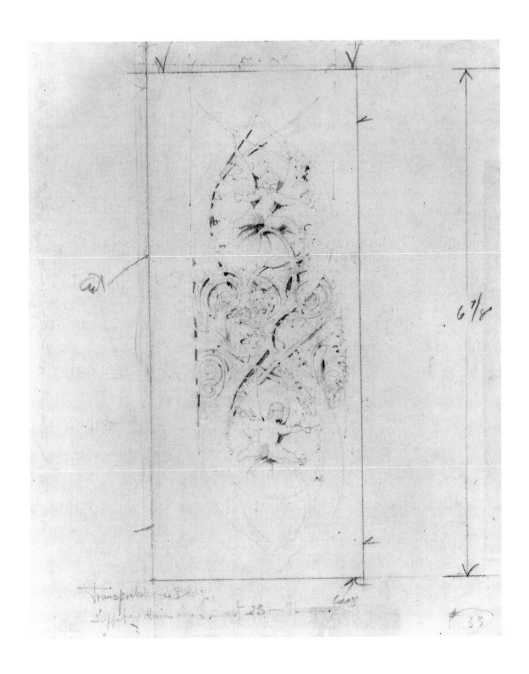

139. Design for soffit of main arch, Transportation Building, World's
Columbian Exposition, Chicago, Illinois (23 September 1891). Inscribed
with dimensions; at bottom: *Transportation Bldg./Soffit of Main Arch. Sept.
23–91*; cropping marks in pencil by Frank Lloyd Wright, for publication in
Genius and the Mobocracy (1949).

Pencil on paper (17.3 x 10.6 cm.). Avery Library, Columbia University, FLLW/LHS 7;
purchased from Frank Lloyd Wright Foundation, 1965. W., S. 52.

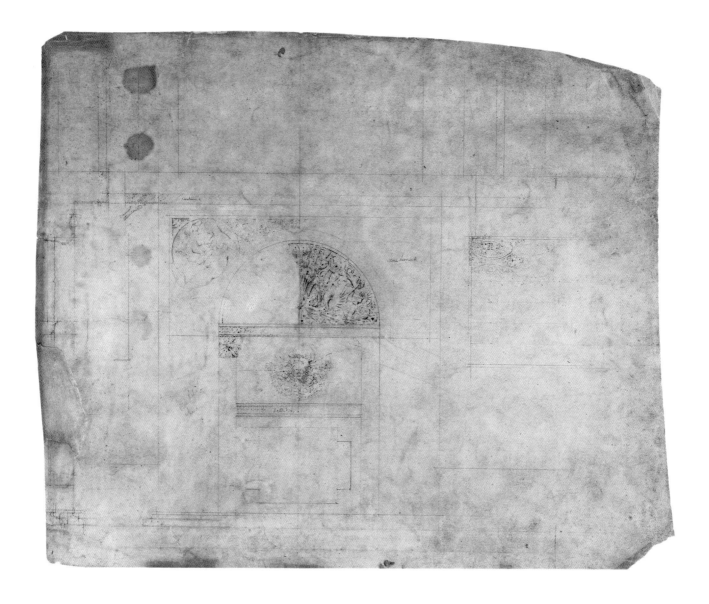

140. Design for fountain, Transportation Building, World's Columbian
Exposition, Chicago, Illinois [1891]. Inscribed, on upper left-hand side
of design: *ornament returned on soffit, continued*; on right-hand side: *same
Reversed*; on lower left-hand side of design:
Bas Relief here; below lion's head: *dentils*.

Pencil on paper (50.3 x 60.8 cm.). Avery Library, Columbia University, FLLW/LHS 27;
purchased from Frank Lloyd Wright Foundation, 1965. S. 53.

141. Design for doorframe, Wainwright Tomb,
St. Louis, Missouri [1892].

Pencil on paper (20.2 x 24.3 cm.). Avery Library, Columbia University,
FLLW/LHS 2; purchased from Frank Lloyd Wright Foundation, 1965. S. 55.

142. Design for frieze, Wainwright Tomb, St. Louis, Missouri;
incorrectly dated by Sullivan 30 January 1890 [1892].

Pencil on brown paper (39.9 x 63 cm.). University of Michigan Museum of Art, Ann Arbor;
gift of George Grant Elmslie, c. 1936, to Emil Lorch, for College of Architecture and Design,
University of Michigan; transferred to University of Michigan Museum of Art, 1972.

143. Design for frienze, Wainwright Tomb,
St. Louis, Missouri [1892].

Pencil on brown paper (39.9 x 63.2 cm.). University of Michigan Museum of Art, Ann Arbor;
gift of George Grant Elmslie, c. 1936, to Emil Lorch, for College of Architecture and Design,
University of Michigan; transferred to University of Michigan Museum of Art, 1972.

144. Design for frieze, Wainwright Tomb,
St. Louis, Missouri [1892].

Pencil on brown paper (40 x 62.8 cm.). University of Michigan Museum of Art, Ann Arbor;
gift of George Grant Elmslie, c. 1936, to Emil Lorch, for College of Architecture and Design,
University of Michigan; transferred to University of Michigan Museum of Art, 1972.

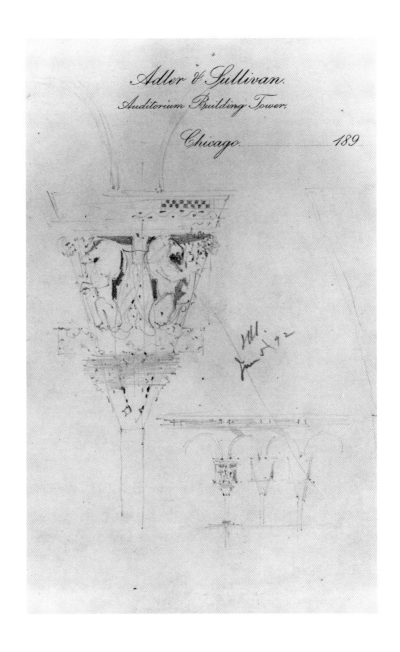

145. Design for capital of an arcade and sketch of arcade
(5 June 1892). Initialed *LHS* and dated.

Pencil on Adler & Sullivan imprinted stationery (21.3 x 13.6 cm.).
Avery Library, Columbia University, FLLW/LHS 98;
purchased from Frank Lloyd Wright Foundation, 1965. S. 57.

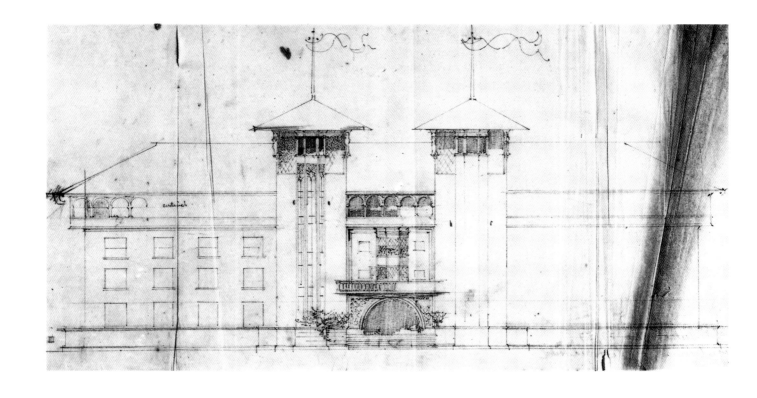

146. Design for Victoria Hotel, Chicago Heights, Illinois [1892].

Pencil on tracing paper (22 x 45.5 cm.). Art Institute of Chicago;
gift of Richard Nickel, c. 1957; gift of Edgar Kaufmann jr. to Richard Nickel
on behalf of Frank Lloyd Wright, 1956. M. 67.

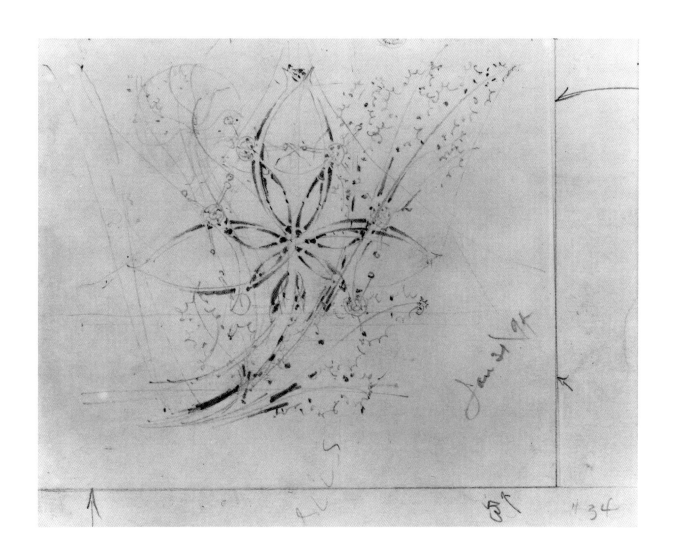

147. Design for ornament (31 January 1894). Dated.
Cropping marks in pencil by Frank Lloyd Wright, for
publication in *Genius and the Mobocracy* (1949).

Pencil on paper (11.9 x 14.9 cm.). Avery Library, Columbia University, FLLW/LHS 8;
purchased from Frank Lloyd Wright Foundation, 1965. W., S. 59.

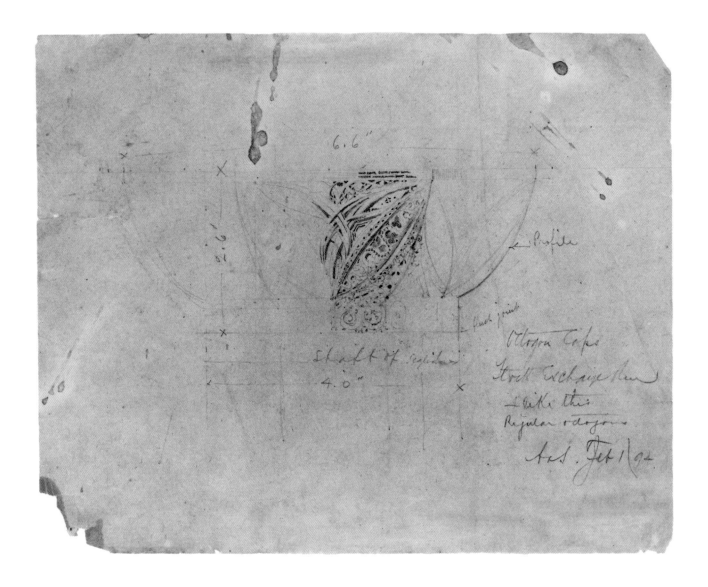

148. Design for capitals, stock exchange room, Chicago Stock Exchange
Building, Chicago, Illinois (1 February 1894). Inscribed with dimensions;
at bottom of design: *Shaft of Scagliola*; on right-hand side of design:
Profile/flush joint; on right-hand side of sheet: *Octagon Caps/Stock Exchange
Room/4 like this/Regular octagons/ A & S. Feb. 1\94.*

Pencil on paper (20.2 x 25.4 cm.). Avery Library, Columbia University, FLLW/LHS 57;
purchased from Frank Lloyd Wright Foundation, 1965. S. 60.

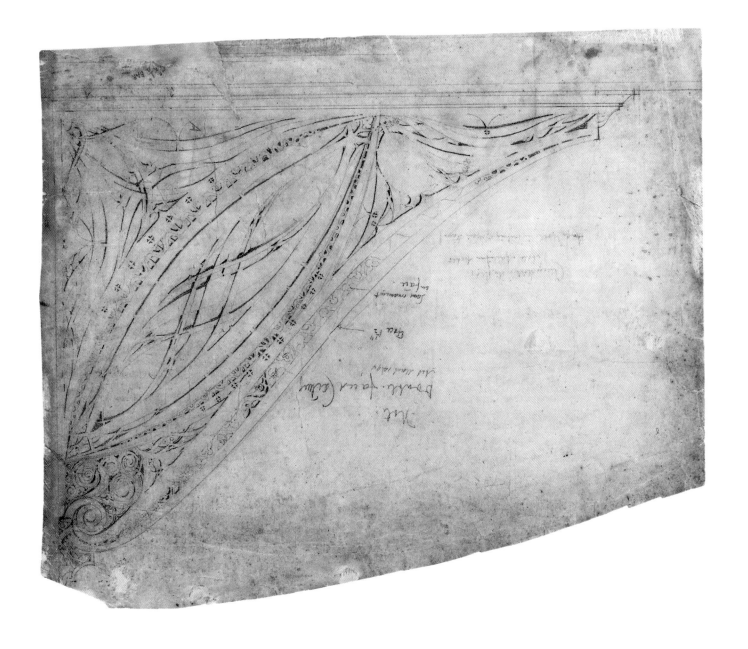

149. Design for angle block in railing of main stairs, Chicago Stock Exchange
Building, Chicago, Illinois (14 March 1894). Inscribed upside down:
*Note:/Double-faced Casting/A & S[.] March 14 94/Face 1 1/2"/Same ornament/on
face/Chicago Stock Exchg. Bldg/Adler & Sullivan, Archts/Angle block in
railing of Main Stairs.*

Pencil on paper (46.2 x 55.7 cm.). Avery Library, Columbia University, FLLW/LHS 30;
purchased from Frank Lloyd Wright Foundation, 1965. S. 61.

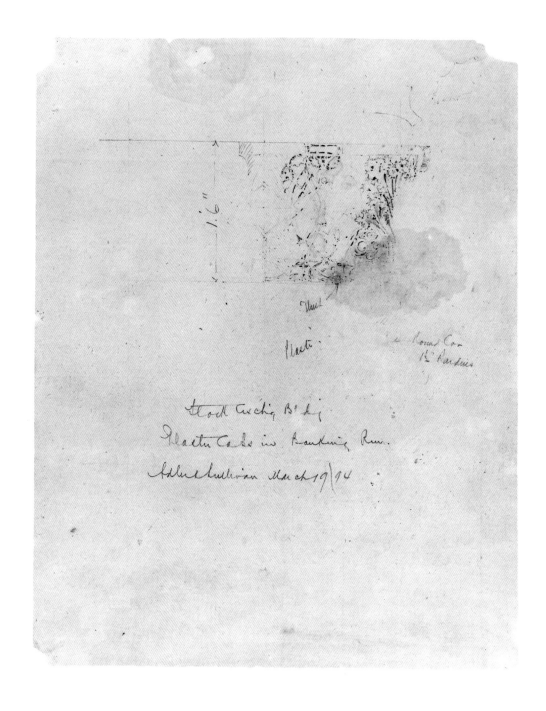

150. Design for capital, stock exchange room, Chicago Stock Exchange
Building, Chicago, Illinois (19 March 1894). Dated. Inscribed with
dimensions; below capital: *Flush/Plaster/Round cor/1 1/2" Radius*;
below drawing: *Stock Exchg Bldg/Plaster Caps in Banking Room/
Adler & Sullivan March 19\94.*

Pencil on paper (25.3 x 20.2 cm.). Avery Library, Columbia University, FLLW/LHS 58;
purchased from Frank Lloyd Wright Foundation, 1965. S. 62.

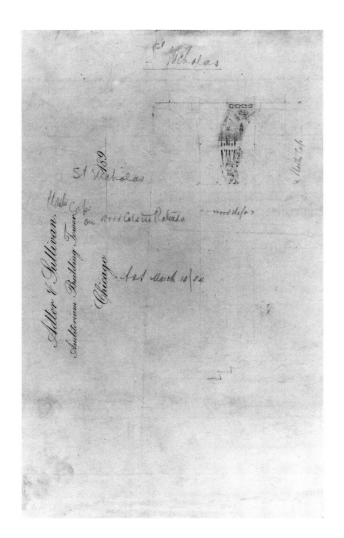

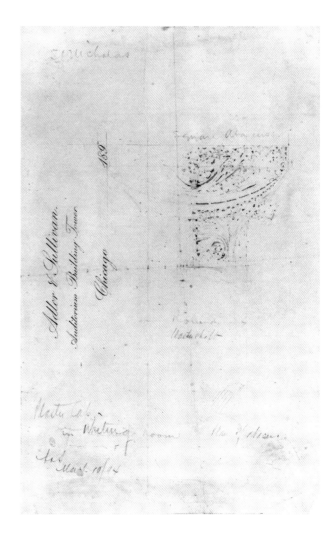

151. Design for capital, St. Nicholas Hotel, St. Louis, Missouri
(10 March 1894). Inscribed with dimensions; above drawing:
St. Nicholas; on right-hand side of design: *Plaster caps*;
at bottom of design: *wood shaft*; on left-hand side of sheet:
St Nicholas/Plaster Caps/on Wood Cols. in Rotunda/A & S[.]
March 10/94.

Pencil on Adler & Sullivan imprinted stationery (21.1 x 13.5 cm.).
Avery Library, Columbia University, FLLW/LHS 62; purchased from
Frank Lloyd Wright Foundation, 1965. S. 63.

152. Design for capital, St. Nicholas Hotel, St. Louis,
Missouri, elevation and plan (10 March 1894). Inscribed on
upper left-hand corner of sheet: *St Nicholas*; above elevation:
Square Abacus; below elevation: *Round/Plaster shaft*; below
plan: *Plan of Abacus*; on lower left-hand corner of sheet:
Plaster Cap/in Waiting Room/A & S/March 10/94.

Pencil on Adler & Sullivan imprinted stationery (21.1 x 13.6 cm.).
Avery Library, Columbia University, FLLW/LHS 63; purchased from
Frank Lloyd Wright Foundation, 1965. S. 64.

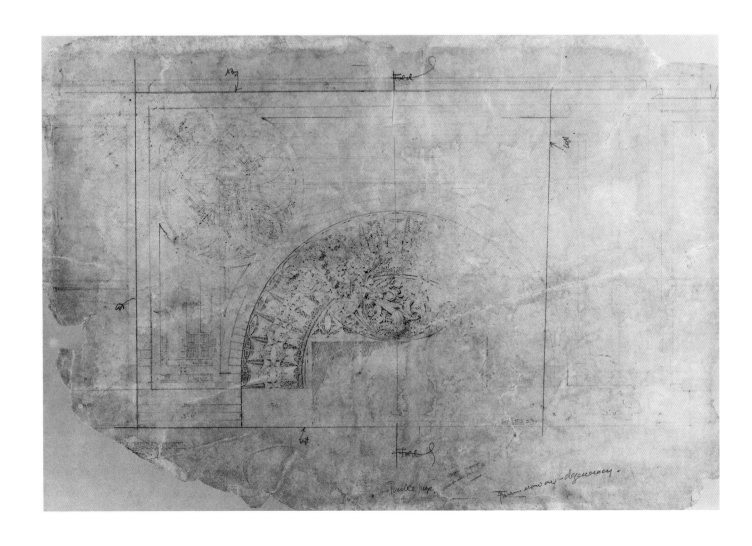

153. Design for fireplace, St. Nicholas Hotel, St. Louis, Missouri (May 1894).
Dated and initialed *LHS*. Inscribed in pencil by Frank Lloyd Wright:
From now on–degeneracy; cropping marks in pencil by Frank Lloyd Wright,
for publication in *Genius and the Mobocracy* (1949).

Pencil on paper (34.2 x 49.3 cm.). Avery Library, Columbia University, FLLW/LHS 26;
purchased from Frank Lloyd Wright Foundation, 1965. W., S. 65.

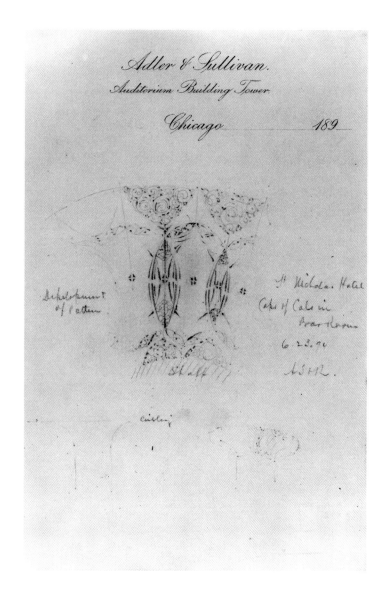

154. Sketches of ornamentation, elevation, and perspective of bar room
capital, St. Nicholas Hotel, St. Louis, Missouri (23 June 1894). Inscribed on
left-hand side of sheet: *Development of Pattern*; below ornamental design: *Staff*;
on right-hand side of sheet: *St Nicholas Hotel/Caps of Cols. in Bar Room/
6.23.94/A[dler]* *S[ullivan]* & *[Charles L.]* *R[amsey]*; above elevation: *ceiling*.

Pencil on paper (27.4 x 20 cm.). Avery Library, Columbia University, FLLW/LHS 41;
purchased from Frank Lloyd Wright Foundation, 1965. S. 66.

155. Three designs for stencils, St. Nicholas Hotel, St. Louis, Missouri (27 July 1894).
Inscribed on upper left-hand corner: *Gentlemen's Restaurant*; on left-hand side of
sheet: *(Drawn full size)/St Nicholas Hotel/A*[dler,] *S*[ullivan] *& *[Charles L.] *R*[amsey]
July 27\94; on upper center of sheet: *Restaurant*; above third stencil design: *Café*.

Pencil on paper (20.8 x 27.5 cm). Avery Library, Columbia University, FLLW/LHS 69;
purchased from Frank Lloyd Wright Foundation, 1965. S. 67.

156. Design for stencil, St. Nicholas Hotel, St. Louis, Missouri
(28 July 1894). Inscribed *(Drawn full size)/St Nicholas Hotel/July 28\94.*
A[dler,] S[ullivan] & [Charles L.] R[amsey].

Pencil on paper (11.9 x 11.5 cm.). Avery Library, Columbia University, FLLW/LHS 60;
purchased from Frank Lloyd Wright Foundation, 1965. S. 68.

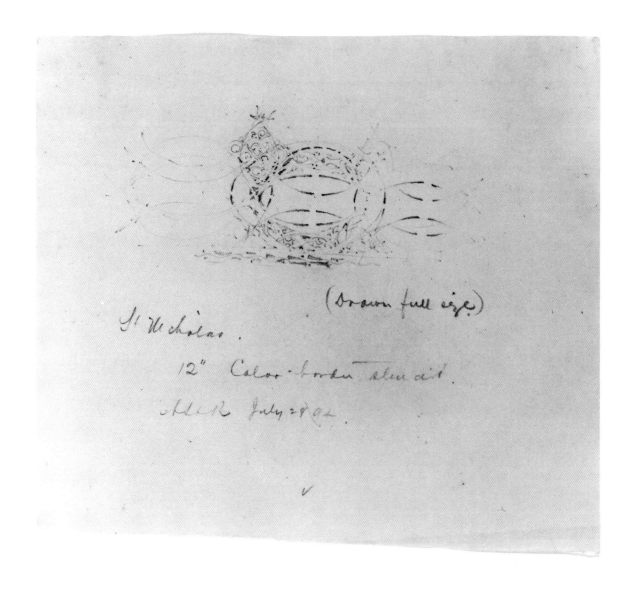

157. Design for stencil, St. Nicholas Hotel, St. Louis, Missouri (28 July 1894).
Inscribed *(Drawn full size)/St Nicholas/12" Color-border stencil/A[dler,]
S[ullivan] & [Charles L.] R[amsey] July 28\94.*

Pencil on paper (12.1 x 13.7 cm.). Avery Library, Columbia University, FLLW/LHS 70;
purchased from Frank Lloyd Wright Foundation, 1965. S. 69.

158. Design for stencil, St. Nicholas Hotel, St. Louis, Missouri
(28 July 1894). Inscribed *St Nicholas/Stencils for Color decoration/A[dler,]
S[ullivan] & [Charles L.] R[amsey] July 28\94 (drawn full size)*.

Pencil on paper (12.4 x 13.9 cm.). Avery Library, Columbia University, FLLW/LHS 71;
purchased from Frank Lloyd Wright Foundation, 1965. S. 70.

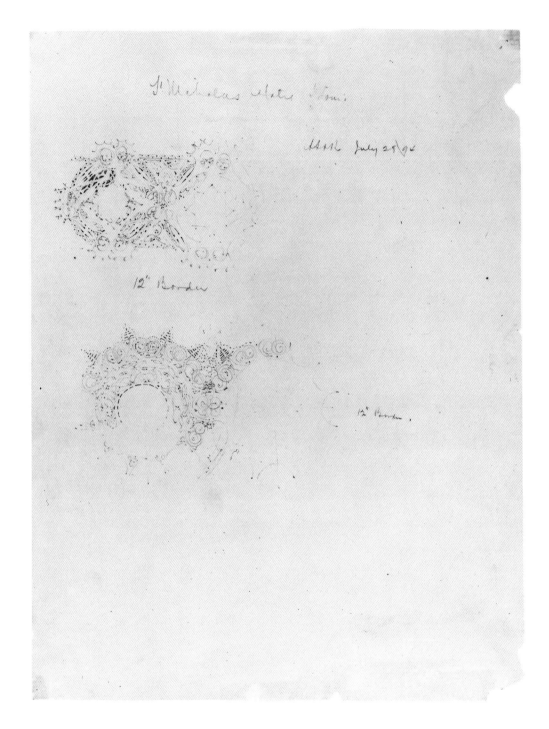

159. Two designs for stencils, St. Nicholas Hotel, St. Louis, Missouri (28 July 1894).
Inscribed on top: *St Nicholas Hotel*[,] *St Louis/A*[*dler,*] *S*[*ullivan*] *&* [*Charles L.*] *R*[*amsey*]
July 28\94; next to each design: *12" Border.*

Pencil on paper (27.6 x 20.9 cm.). Avery Library, Columbia University, FLLW/LHS 67;
purchased from Frank Lloyd Wright Foundation, 1965. S. 71.

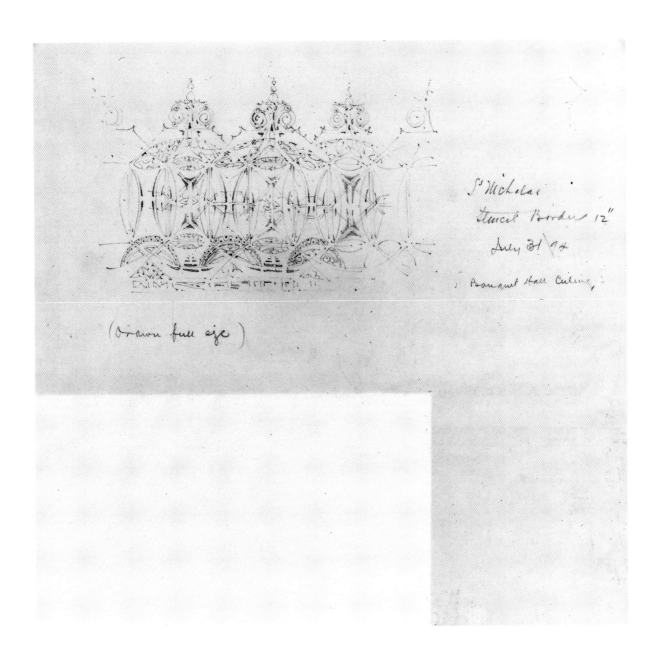

160. Design for stencil on ceiling of banquet hall, St. Nicholas Hotel,
St. Louis, Missouri (31 July 1894). Inscribed on right-hand side of sheet:
St. Nicholas/Stencil Border 12"/July 31\94/
Banquet Hall Ceiling; under design, not in Sullivan's hand: *(Drawn full size).*
Pencil on paper (20.1 x 20.8 cm.). Avery Library, Columbia University, FLLW/LHS 65;
purchased from Frank Lloyd Wright Foundation, 1965. S. 72

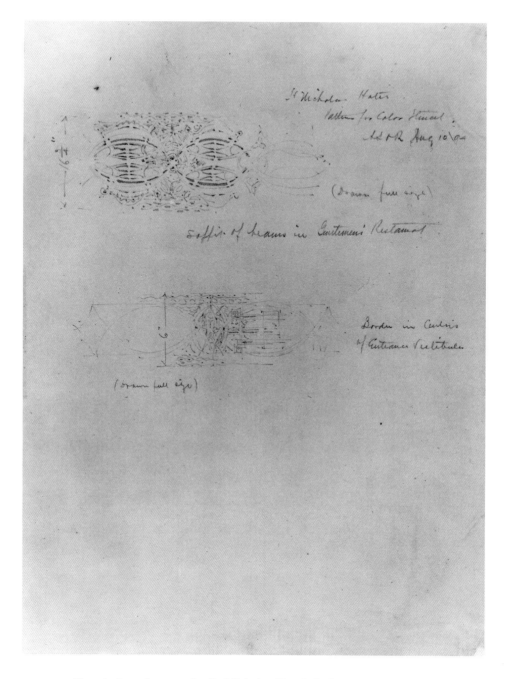

161. Two designs for stencils, St. Nicholas Hotel, St. Louis (10 August 1894).
Inscribed with dimensions; to the right-hand side of the uppermost design:
St Nicholas Hotel/Pattern for Color Stencil/A[dler,] S[ullivan] & [Charles L.] R[amsey]
Aug. 10\94/(Drawn full size) [not in Sullivan's hand]/*Soffit of beams in Gentlemen's
Restaurant*; next to the lower design: *Border in Ceiling/of Entrance Vestibule/
(Drawn full size)* [not in Sullivan's hand].

Pencil on paper (27.5 x 20.6 cm.). Avery Library, Columbia University, FLLW/LHS 68;
purchased from Frank Lloyd Wright Foundation, 1965. S. 73.

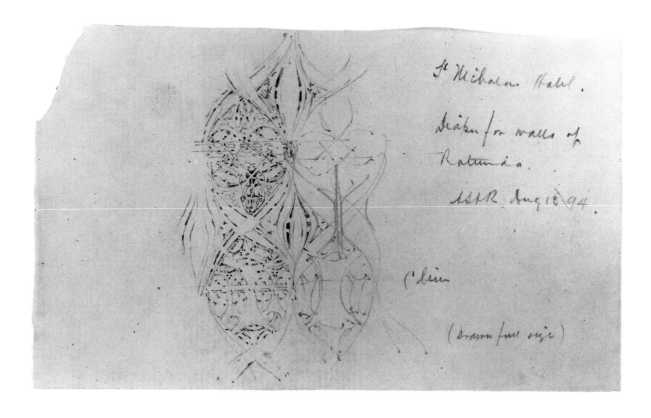

162. Design for stencil for rotunda, St. Nicholas Hotel, St. Louis, Missouri (18 August 1894). Inscribed *St Nicholas Hotel/Diaper for walls of/Rotunda/ A[dler,] S[ullivan] & [Charles L.] R[amsey] Aug 18\94/C[enter] line/ (Drawn full size)* [not in Sullivan's hand].

Pencil on paper (9.9 x 16.5 cm.) Avery Library, Columbia University, FLLW/LHS 72; purchased from Frank Lloyd Wright Foundation, 1965. S. 74.

163. Design for stencil in gentlemen's restaurant, St. Nicholas Hotel,
St. Louis, Missouri (20 September 1894). Inscribed
St Nicholas Hotel/12" Border in Ceiling/Gentlemen's Restaurant /Sept 20\94.

Pencil on paper (16.7 x 20.9 cm.). Avery Library, Columbia University, FLLW/LHS 66;
purchased from Frank Lloyd Wright Foundation, 1965. S. 75.

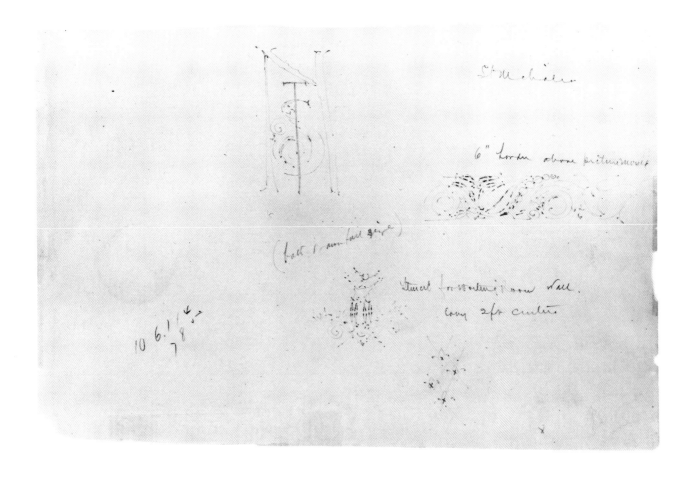

164. Two designs for stencils, one monogram, and one sketch for stencil (?),
St. Nicholas Hotel, St. Louis, Missouri [1894]. Inscribed on upper right-hand corner
of sheet: *St Nicholas/6" border above picture mould*[*ing*]; on a slant, not in Sullivan's
hand: *(Both drawn full size)*; next to lower design: *Stencil for Waiting Room Wall/*
Every 2 ft [*on*] *center*; on the lower left-hand side, unrelated numbers, on a slant.

Pencil on paper (14.1 x 20.9 cm.). Avery Library, Columbia University, FLLW/LHS 61;
purchased from Frank Lloyd Wright Foundation, 1965. S. 76.

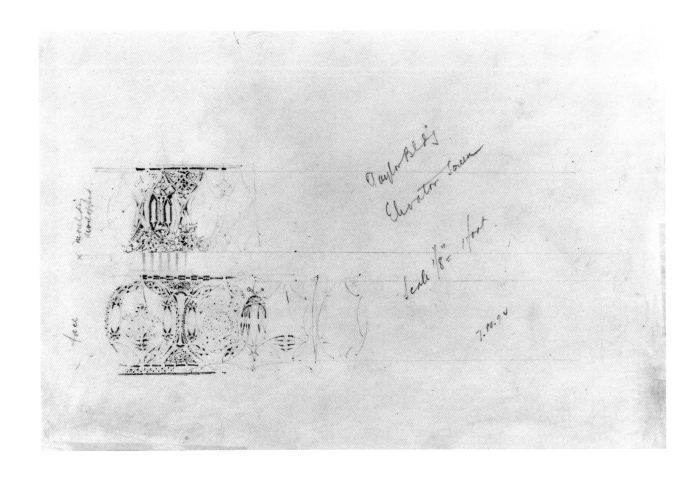

165. Design for elevator screen, Taylor Building remodeling,
Chicago, Illinois (10 July 1894). Inscribed with dimensions on left-
hand side; on right-hand side: *Taylor Building/Elevator
Screen/Scale 1/8" = 1 foot/7.10.94.*

Pencil on paper (13.7 x 20.9 cm.). Avery Library, Columbia University,
FLLW/LHS 12; purchased from Frank Lloyd Wright Foundation, 1965. S. 77.

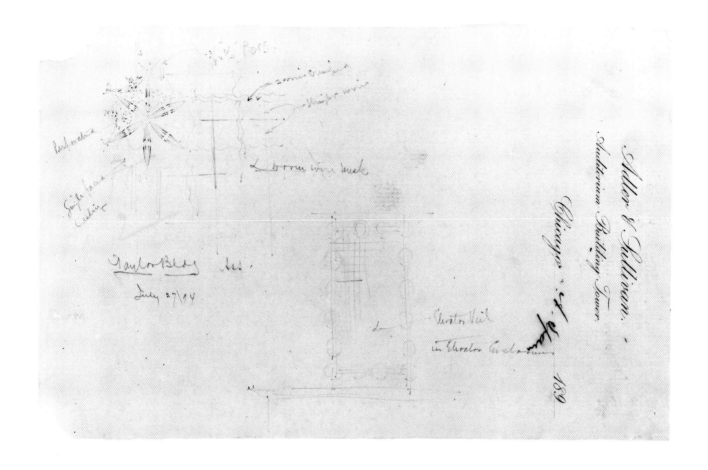

166. Detail and general sketch for elevator screen, Taylor Building remodeling, Chicago, Illinois (27 July 1894). Inscribed on left-hand side of detail: *Perforated/Single faced/Casting*; on right-hand side of detail: *3/8" x 3/4" Bars/2 wires crimped/Straight wires/woven wire mesh*; under detail: *Taylor Bldg. A&S/ July 27\94*; on right-hand side of sketch: *Elevator Veil/in Elevator Enclosure*.

Pencil on Adler & Sullivan imprinted stationery (13.4 x 21.2 cm.).
Avery Library, Columbia University, FLLW/LHS 59;
purchased from Frank Lloyd Wright Foundation, 1965. S. 78.

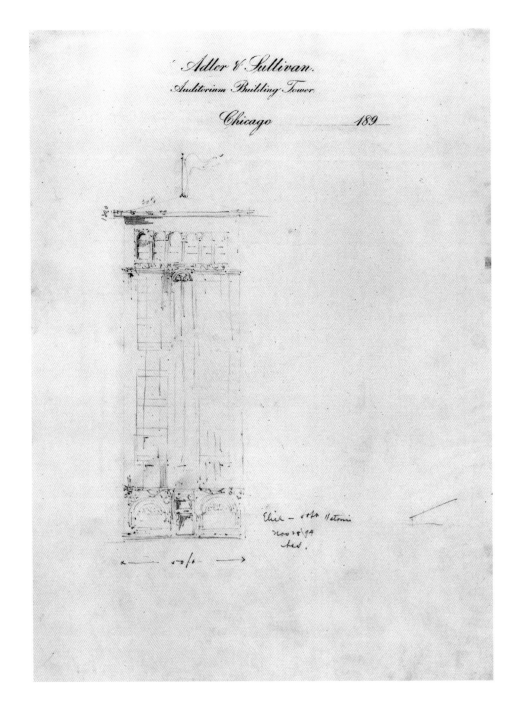

167. Eliel Apartment Building project, Chicago, Illinois (28 November 1894).
Inscribed *Eliel—50 ft 11 stories/Nov. 28\94/A&S*;
50 ft. dimension inscribed below design.

Pencil on Adler & Sullivan imprinted stationery (27.4 x 20 cm.).
Avery Library, Columbia University, FLLW/LHS 23;
purchased from Frank Lloyd Wright Foundation, 1965. S. 79.

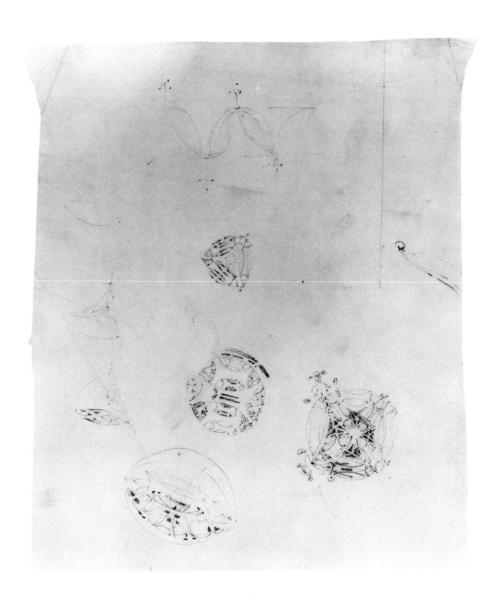

168. Designs for ornament [c. 1894].

Pencil on paper (20.8 x 17.1 cm.). Avery Library, Columbia University,
FLLW/LHS 81; purchased from Frank Lloyd Wright Foundation, 1965. S. 80.

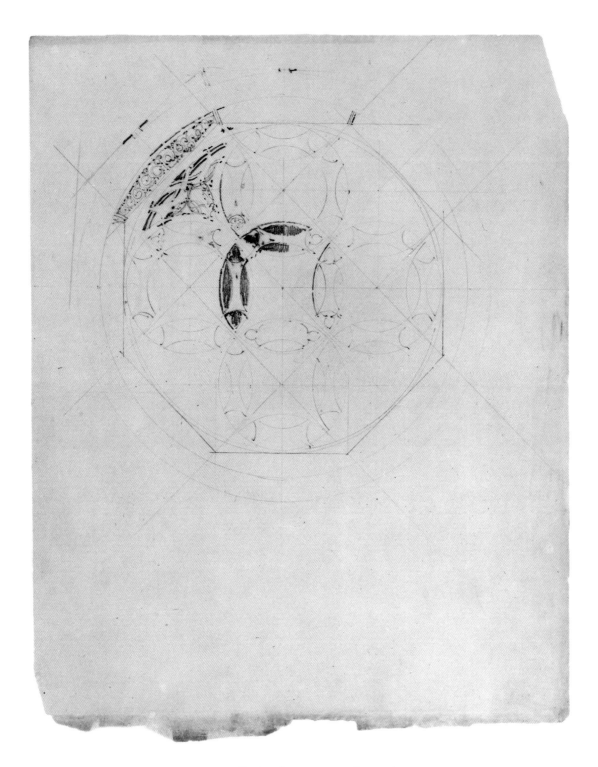

169. Design for ornament [c. 1894].

Pencil on paper (27 x 21.2 cm.). Avery Library, Columbia University,
FLLW/LHS 96; purchased from Frank Lloyd Wright Foundation, 1965. S. 81.

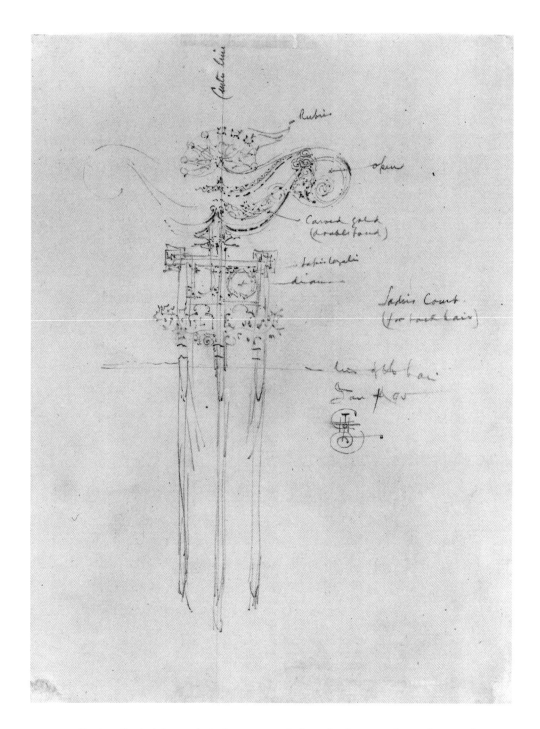

170. Design for lady's comb (4 January 1895). Inscribed at top: *Center line*; on the
right-hand side: *Rubies/Open/Carved gold/(double band)/Lapis Lazuli/diamond/Ladies
Comb/(for back hair)/line of the hair/Jan 4 95*; initialed with *LHS* monogram.

Pencil on paper (26.6 x 21.7 cm.). Avery Library, Columbia University, FLLW/LHS 99;
purchased from Frank Lloyd Wright Foundation, 1965. S. 87.

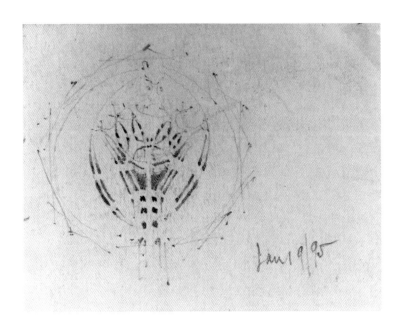

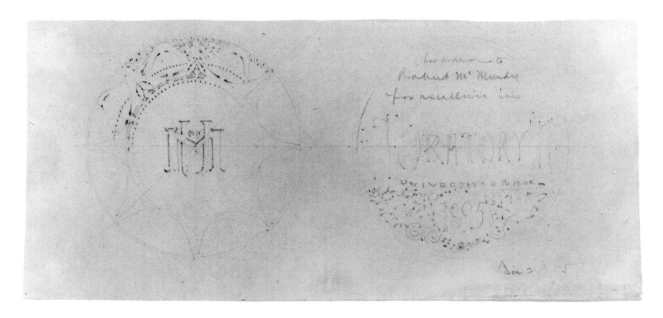

171. Sketch for ornament (19 January 1895). Dated.

Pencil on paper (6.7 x 8.2 cm.). Avery Library, Columbia University, Douglas Haskell Collection; drawing taped, presumably by Frank Lloyd Wright, to inside cover of a copy of his *Modern Architecture: Being the Kahn Lectures for 1930* (Princeton, N. J.: Princeton University Press, 1931); book and drawing given by Wright as a gift to Douglas Haskell; book and drawing given by Helen Haskell to Avery Library, 1983.

172. Design for recto and verso of oratory medal for the University of Michigan (29 January 1895). Inscribed with UM monogram on recto; on verso: *Awarded to/Robert McMurdy/for excellence in/ORATORY/University of Michigan/1895.*

Pencil on paper (8.1 x 18.2 cm.). Avery Library, Columbia University, FLLW/LHS 55; purchased from Frank Lloyd Wright Foundation, 1965. S. 90.

173. Design for recto of oratory medal for the University of Michigan
(30 January 1895). Dated and initialed *LHS*; inscribed with UM monogram
on design; below design: *Actual size 2 1/2" diam.*

Pencil on paper (27.2 x 21.5 cm.). Avery Library, Columbia University, FLLW/LHS 56;
purchased from Frank Lloyd Wright Foundation, 1965. S. 91.

174. Design for title page of *Inspiration* (5 March 1895).
Dated and initialed with *LHS* monogram.

Pencil on paper (13.7 x 20.3 cm.). Avery Library, Columbia University, FLLW/LHS 85;
purchased from Frank Lloyd Wright Foundation, 1965. S. 92.

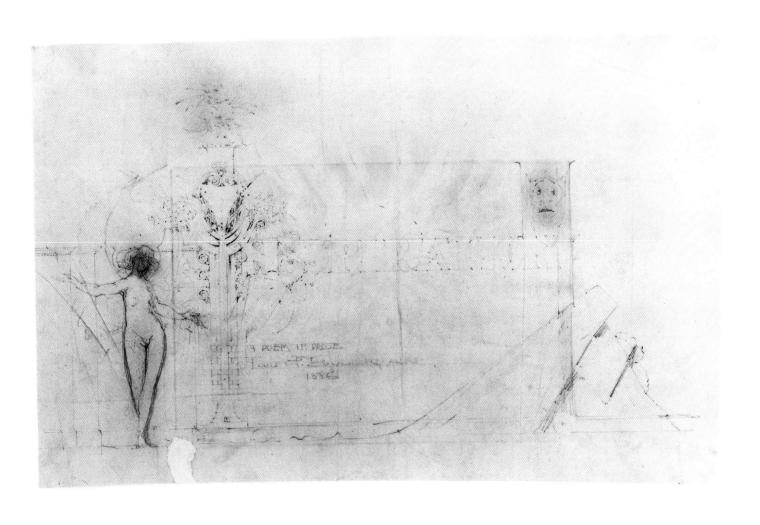

175. Design for title page of *Inspiration. A Poem in Prose,
Louis H. Sullivan, 1886* [c. March 1895].

Pencil on paper (21.9 x 34.5 cm.). Avery Library, Columbia University, FLLW/LHS 16;
purchased from Frank Lloyd Wright Foundation, 1965. S. 93.

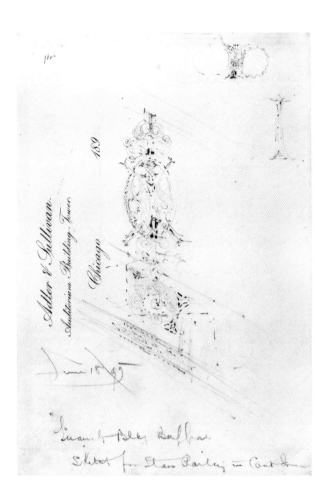

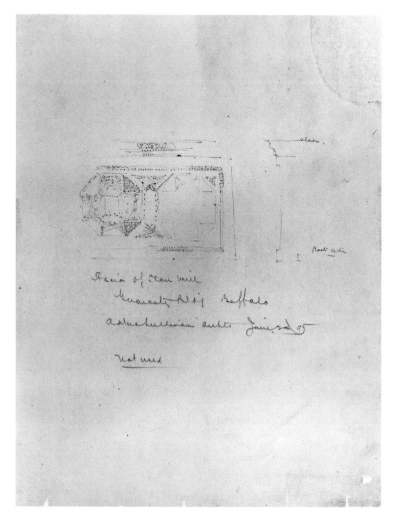

176. Design for stair railing for Guaranty Building, Buffalo, New York (18 June 1895). Inscribed *June 18\95/Guaranty Bldg Buffalo/Sketch for Stair Railing in Cast Iron.*

Pencil on Adler & Sullivan imprinted stationery (20.2 x 13.6 cm.).
Avery Library, Columbia University, FLLW/LHS 73;
purchased from Frank Lloyd Wright Foundation, 1965. S. 94.

177. Design for fascia of stairwell, Guaranty Building, Buffalo, New York (24 June 1895). Inscribed *Fascia of Stair Well/Guaranty Bldg Buffalo/Adler & Sullivan Archts June 24\95/Not used.*

Pencil on paper (27.5 x 21.2 cm.).
Avery Library, Columbia University, FLLW/LHS 74;
purchased from Frank Lloyd Wright Foundation, 1965. S. 95.

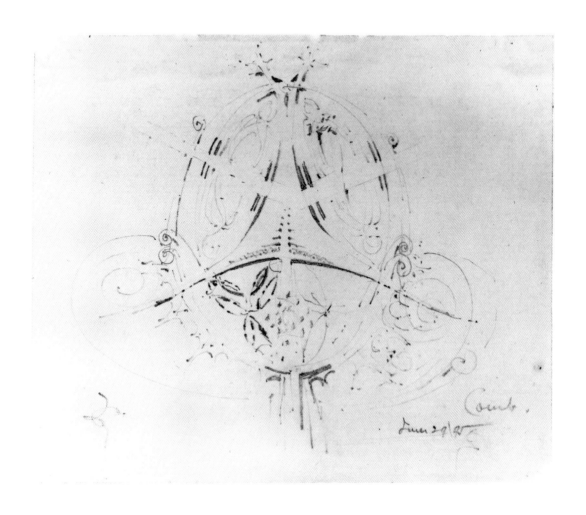

178. Design for comb (29 June 1895). Inscribed *Comb/June 29\95.*

Pencil on paper (10.8 x 13 cm.). Avery Library, Columbia University, FLLW/LHS 44;
purchased from Frank Lloyd Wright Foundation, 1965. W., S. 89.

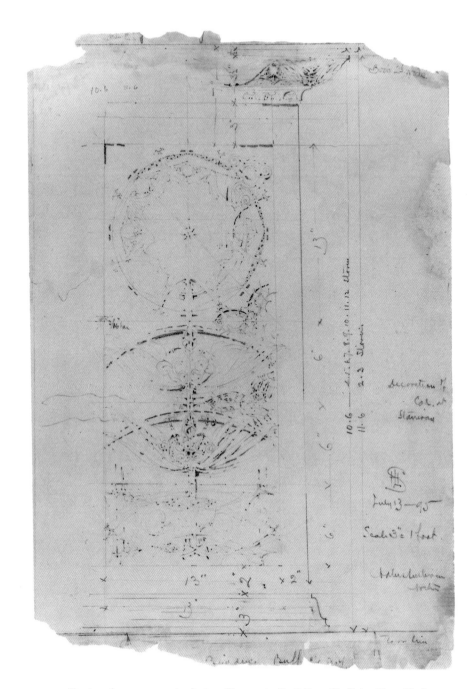

179. Design for ornament of pier, Guaranty Building, Buffalo, New York
(13 July 1895). Inscribed with dimensions; vertically: *10['].6["]4.5.6.7.8.9.10.11.12*
stories/11['].6["] 2.3 stories; on left-hand side of sheet: *Decoration of/Col.*
at/Stairway/LHS [monogram]/*July 13–95/Scale 3" = 1 foot/Adler & Sullivan/Archts;*
below design: [*Guaranty*] *Building Buffalo NY;* cropping marks in pencil by
Frank Lloyd Wright, for publication in *Genius and the Mobocracy* (1949).

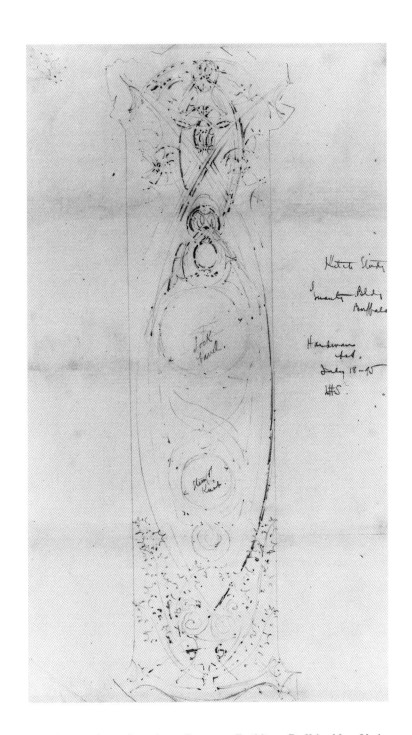

180. Design for a doorplate, Guaranty Building, Buffalo, New York
(18 July 1895). Inscribed on right-hand side of sheet:
Sketch Study/Guaranty Bldg/Buffalo/Hardware/A&S/July 18–95/LHS;
on drawing, above: *Lock/barrel*; on drawing, below: *Diam[eter] of/Knob*.
Pencil on paper (32.9 x 20.1 cm.). Avery Library, Columbia University, FLLW/LHS 124;
purchased from Frank Lloyd Wright Foundation, 1965. S. 97.

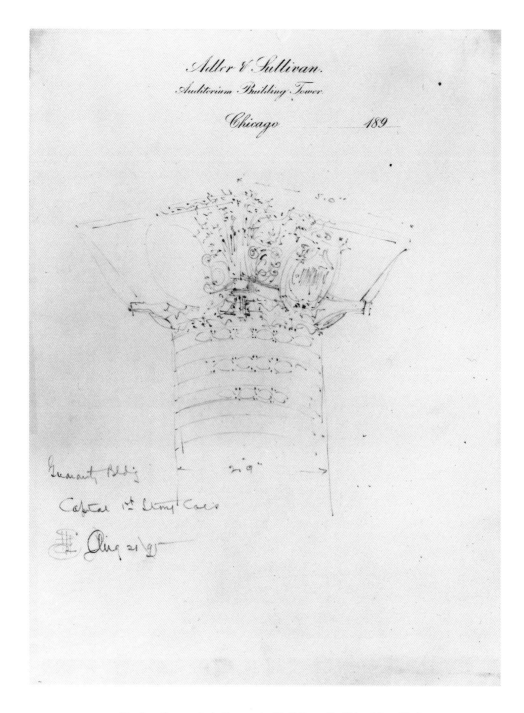

181. Design for capital, Guaranty Building, Buffalo, New York
(21 August 1895). Inscribed with dimensions on shaft; on lower left-hand
corner: *Guaranty Bldg/Capital 1st Story Cols/LHS* [monogram] *August. 21\95.*

Pencil on Adler & Sullivan imprinted stationery (27.5 x 20 cm.).
Avery Library, Columbia University, FLLW/LHS 75;
purchased from Frank Lloyd Wright Foundation, 1965. S. 98.

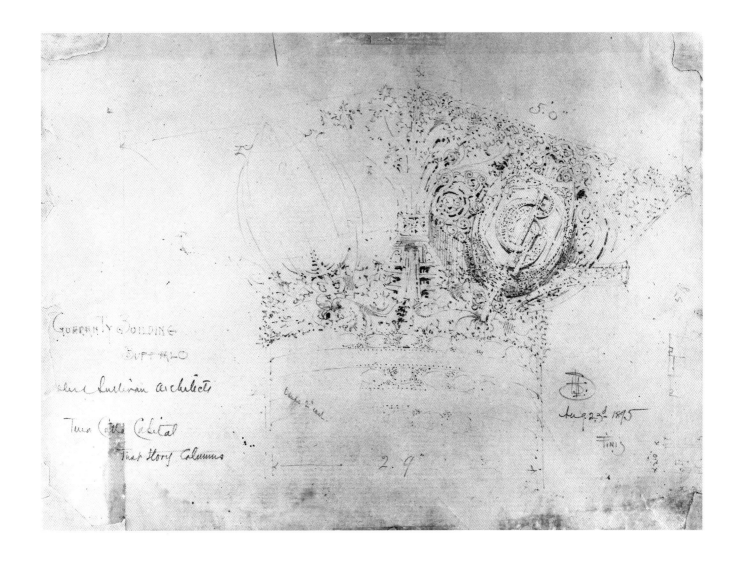

182. Design for capital, Guaranty Building Buffalo, New York (23 August
1895). Inscribed with dimensions on design; on left-hand side of sheet:
*Guaranty Building/Buffalo/Adler & Sullivan Architects/Terra Cotta Capital/
First Story Columns;* on right-hand side of sheet:
LHS [monogram]/*Aug. 23rd 1895/Finis.*

Pencil on paper (21.3 x 29.2 cm.). Avery Library, Columbia University, FLLW/LHS 76;
purchased from Frank Lloyd Wright Foundation, 1965. S. 99.

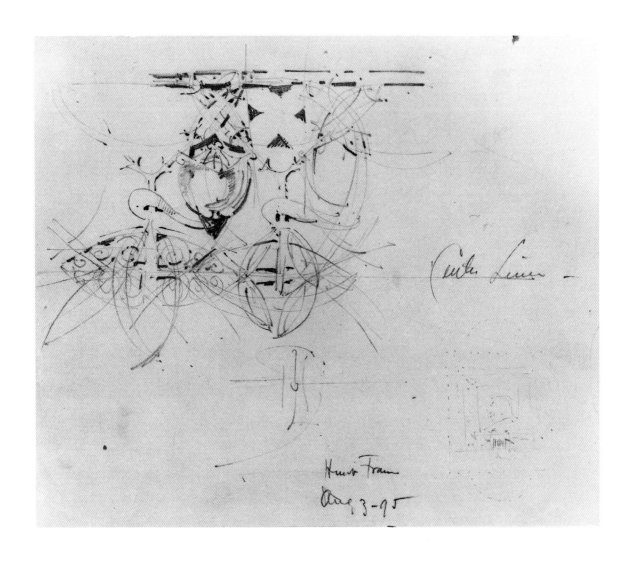

183. Study of ornamental frame for Richard Morris Hunt memorial
portrait for *Inland Architect* (7 August 1895). Inscribed
Center Line/Hunt Frame/Aug 3–95.

Pencil on paper (17 x 20.3 cm.). Avery Library, Columbia University, FLLW/LHS 123;
purchased from Frank Lloyd Wright Foundation, 1965. S 100.

184. Memorial portrait of Richard Morris Hunt with decorative
border by Sullivan for reproduction in *Inland Architect* (7 August 1895).

Photograph with mat with decorative border (21.6 x 20.3 cm.).
Art Institute of Chicago; gift of Richard Nickel, c. 1957; gift of Edgar Kaufmann jr.
to Richard Nickel on behalf of Frank Lloyd Wright, 1956. M. 272 (noted).

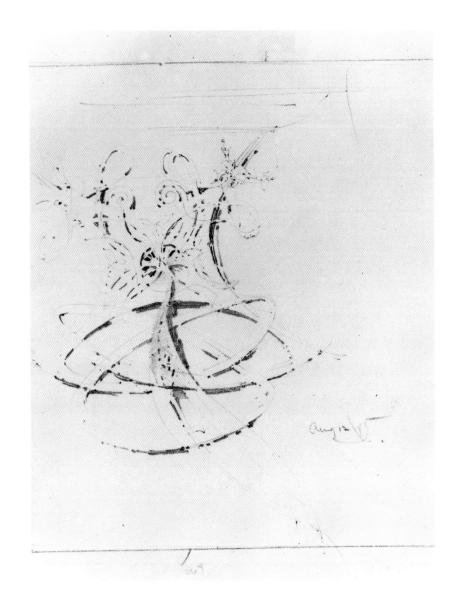

185. Design for ornament (12 August 1895). Dated.
Cropping marks in pencil by Frank Lloyd Wright, for publication in
Genius and the Mobocracy (1949).

Pencil on paper (17.4 x 13.9 cm.). Avery Library, Columbia University, FLLW/LHS 10;
purchased from Frank Lloyd Wright Foundation, 1965. W., S. 101.

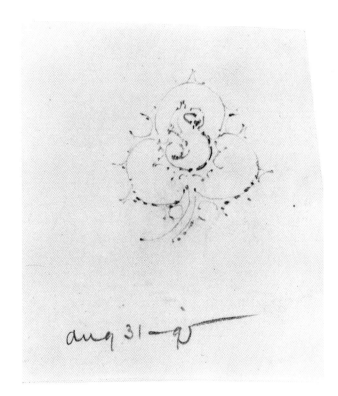

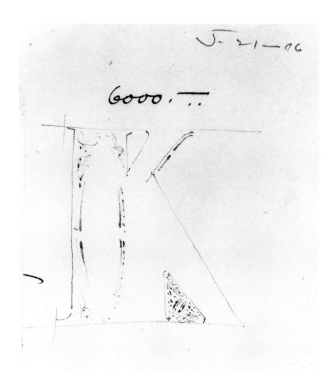

186. Design for ornamental letter S (31 August 1895). Dated.

Pencil on paper (6.8 x 6.5 cm.).
Avery Library, Columbia University, FLLW/LHS 103;
purchased from Frank Lloyd Wright Foundation, 1965. S. 102.

187. Design for ornamental letter K (21 May 1896).
Dated. Inscribed in ink: 6000.

Pencil on paper (7.7 x 7.1 cm.).
Avery Library, Columbia University, FLLW/LHS 105;
purchased from Frank Lloyd Wright Foundation, 1965. S. 103.

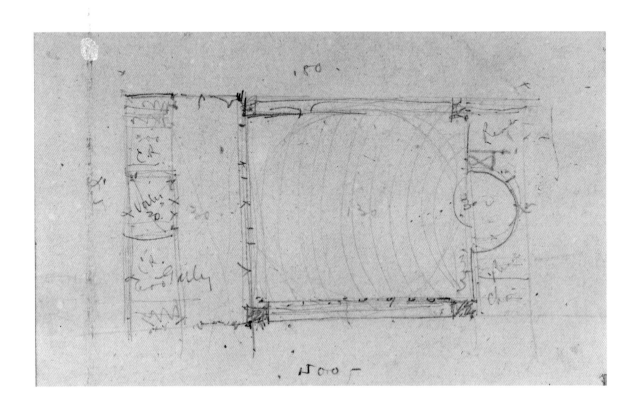

188. Sketch of plan, possibly for the First Church of Christ Scientist competition, Chicago, Illinois [1895]. Inscribed, left and right of apse: *reader*[,] *reader*[, and] *choir*; at right of entry: *gallery*; at entry: *vesti*[*bu*]*l*[*e*]; at left of entry: *C. R.* [coat room]; dimensions *85* [*feet x*] *180* [*feet*]; dimensions along center: *20*[,] *30*[, and] *130* [*feet*]; *1500* on bottom probably refers to seating capacity.

Pencil on buff card (7.6 x 12.7 cm.). Collection Tim Samuelson, Chicago; gift of Edgar Kaufmann jr. to Richard Nickel on behalf of Frank Lloyd Wright, 1956; gift of Richard Nickel to Tim Samuelson, 1971.

189. Sketch of elevation, possibly for the First Church of
Christ Scientist competition, Chicago, Illinois [1895].

Pencil on buff card (7.6 x 12.7 cm.). Collection Tim Samuelson, Chicago; gift of
Edgar Kaufmann jr. to Richard Nickel on behalf of Frank Lloyd Wright, 1956;
gift of Richard Nickel to Tim Samuelson, 1971.

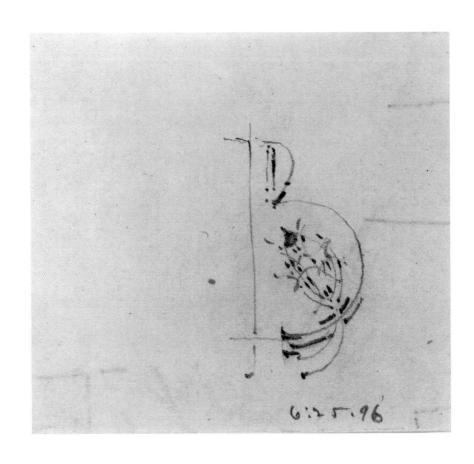

190. Design for ornamental letter B (25 June 1896). Dated.

Pencil on paper (5.7 x 7.6 cm.). Avery Library, Columbia University, FLLW/LHS 104;
purchased from Frank Lloyd Wright Foundation, 1965. S. 104.

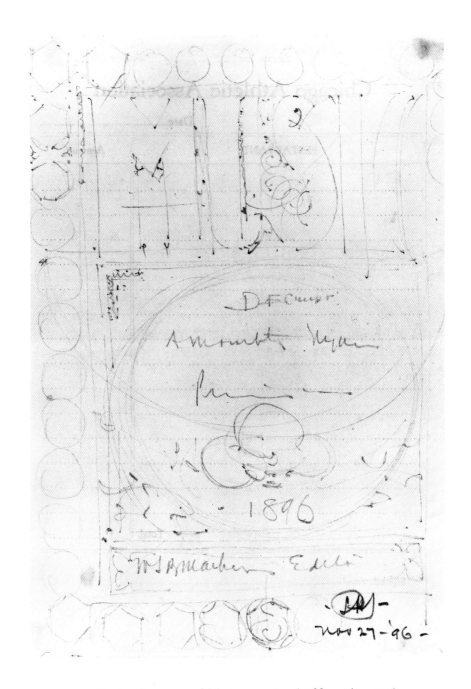

191. Design for cover of *Music* magazine (27 November 1896).
Inscribed on design: *MUSIC/D F C[. . .]/A Monthly Magazine/
P[. . .]/1896/W. S. B. Matthews Editor*; initialed *LHS* and dated on
lower right-hand side corner with softer pencil.

Pencil on back of a Chicago Athletic Association restaurant check (15.7 x 11.2 cm.).
Avery Library, Columbia University, FLLW/LHS 84;
purchased from Frank Lloyd Wright Foundation, 1965. S. 105.
(See No. 290 for illustration of printed cover.)

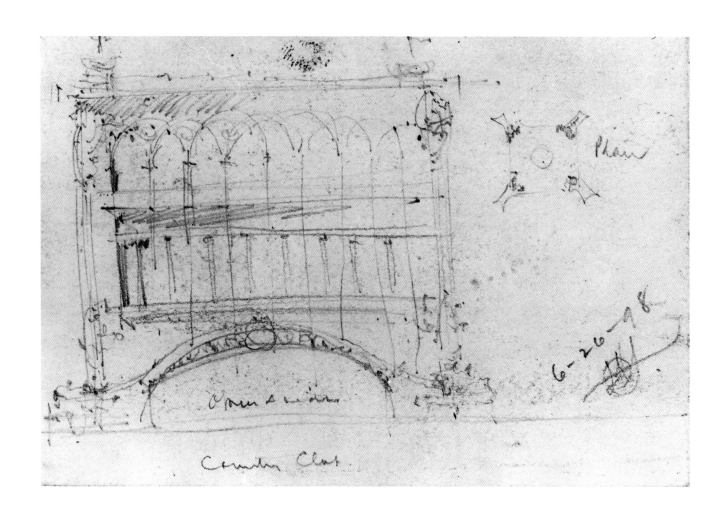

192. Elevation and plan of a country club (26 June 1898).
Dated and initialed with *LHS* monogram; inscribed on the elevation:
Open 4 sides; below the elevation: *Country Club*; next to the plan: *Plan*.

Pencil on back of a Louis H. Sullivan business card (5.7 x 8.7 cm.). Avery Library, Columbia
University, FLLW/LHS 116; purchased from Frank Lloyd Wright Foundation, 1965. S. 106.

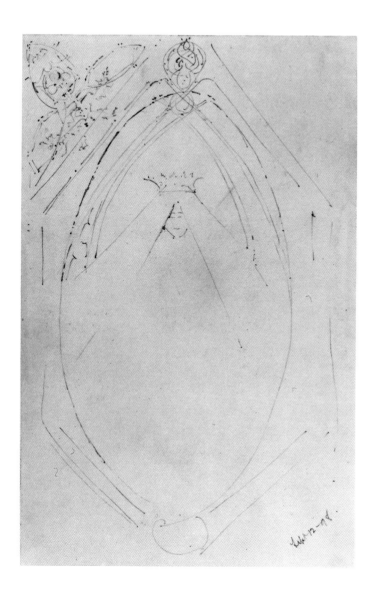

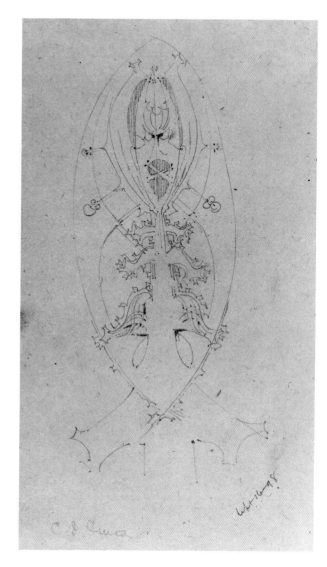

193. Design for ornament (12 September 1898). Dated.

Pencil on paper (21.2 x 13.8 cm.).
Avery Library, Columbia University, FLLW/LHS 120;
purchased from Frank Lloyd Wright Foundation, 1965. S. 107.

194. Design for a cast-iron fence (16 September 1898).
Dated. Inscribed *C. I. Fence*.

Pencil on paper (21.6 x 12.5 cm.).
Avery Library, Columbia University, FLLW/LHS 95;
purchased from Frank Lloyd Wright Foundation, 1965. S. 108.

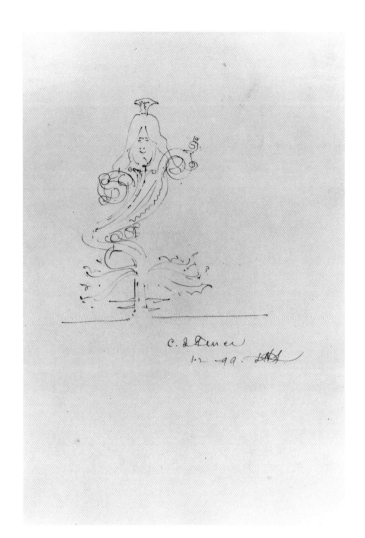

195. Design for a cast-iron fence (2 January 1899).
Inscribed *C. I. Fence/1.2–99 LHS*.

Ink on paper (21.2 x 13.7 cm.).
Avery Library, Columbia University, FLLW/LHS 86;
purchased from Frank Lloyd Wright Foundation, 1965. S. 109.

196. Design for an iron fence (2 January 1899). Inscribed
Iron Fence/Jan 2 99/ initialed with *LHS* monogram.

Ink on paper (21.2 x 13.7 cm.).
Avery Library, Columbia University, FLLW/LHS 87;
purchased from Frank Lloyd Wright Foundation, 1965. S. 110.

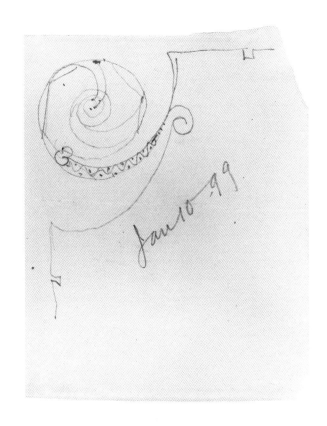

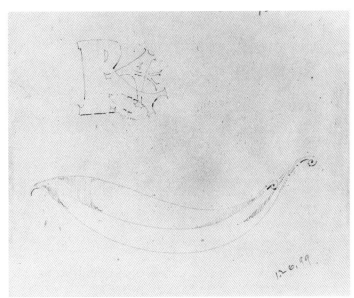

197. Design for ornament (10 January 1899). Dated.

Pencil on back of accounting paper (9.2 x 7.7 cm.).
Avery Library, Columbia University, FLLW/LHS 106;
purchased from Frank Lloyd Wright Foundation, 1965. S. 111.

198. Two designs for ornaments (26 January 1899). Dated.

Pencil on paper (12.4 x 15.3 cm.).
Avery Library, Columbia University, FLLW/LHS 115;
purchased from Frank Lloyd Wright Foundation, 1965. S.112.

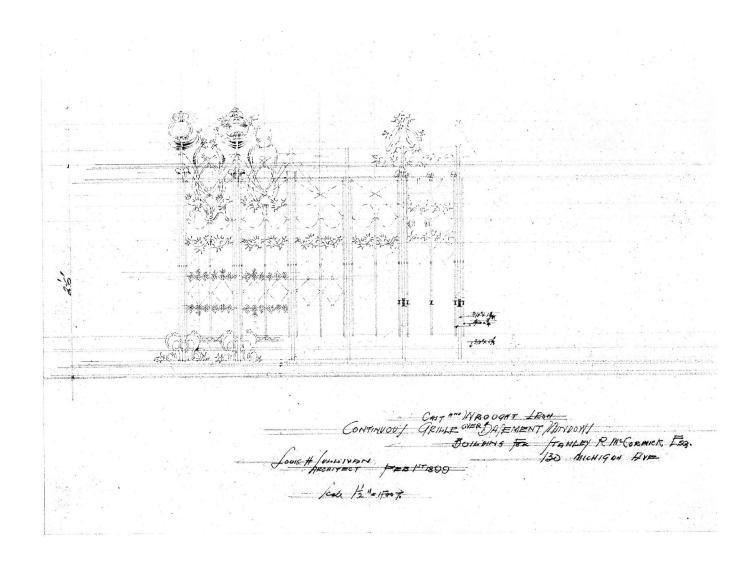

199. Design for continuous iron grille over basement windows, Gage Building,
Chicago (1 February 1899). Dimensions next to design; inscribed *CAST AND
WROUGHT IRON/CONTINUOUS GRILLE OVER BASEMENT WINDOWS/
Building for Stanley R. McCormick Esq./130 Michigan Ave/
Louis H. Sullivan, Architect Feb. 1st 1899/Scale 1 1/2" = 1 Foot.*

Pencil on paper (25.4 x 30.4 cm.). Collection of J. B. Muns and Jan Novie, Berkeley, California;
purchased from "the wife of a man whose nephew worked for Louis Sullivan at the turn of the century."

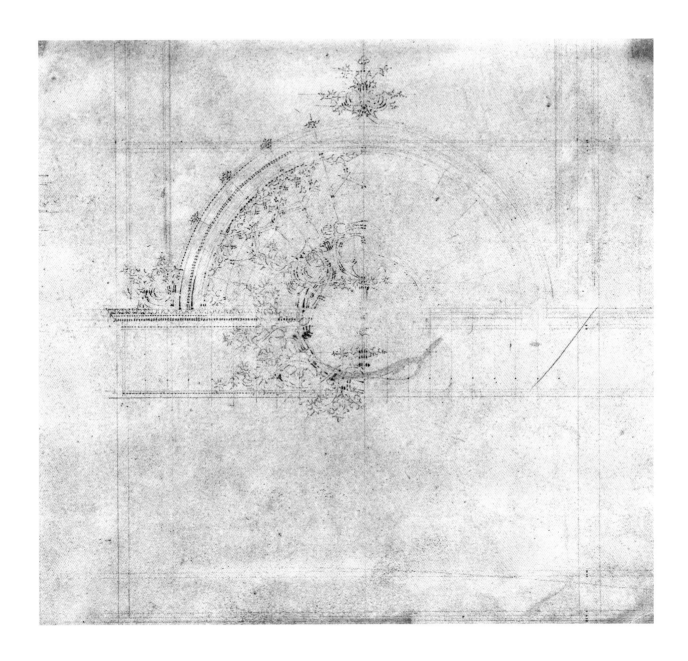

200. Design for a lunette, possibly for Gage Building, Chicago, Illinois [c. 1899].
Pencil on paper (16.8 x 18.2 cm.).
Avery Library, Columbia University, FLLW/LHS 97;
purchased from Frank Lloyd Wright Foundation, 1965. S. 113.

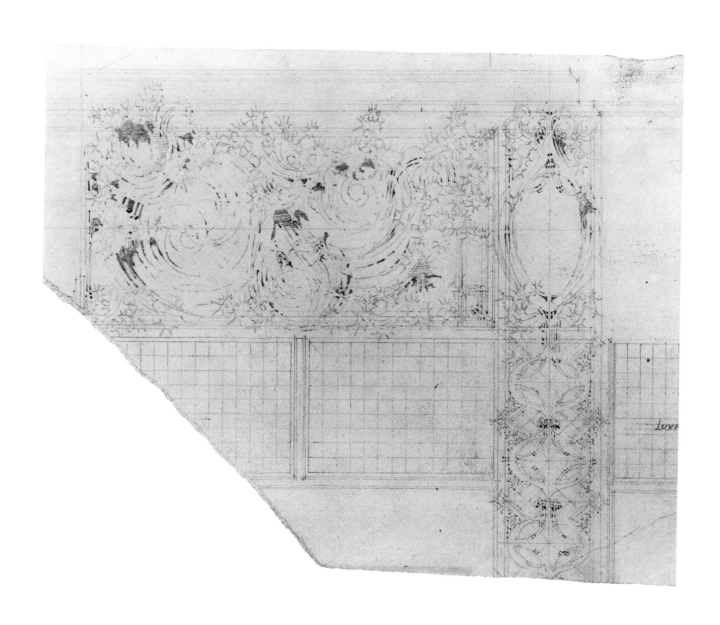

201. Design for iron spandrel, Schlesinger & Mayer Store,
Chicago, Illinois [n.d.]. Inscribed *LUXFE[R]*.

Pencil on paper (15.4 x 19.7 cm.). Avery Library, Columbia University, FLLW/LHS 100;
purchased from Frank Lloyd Wright Foundation, 1965. S. 114.

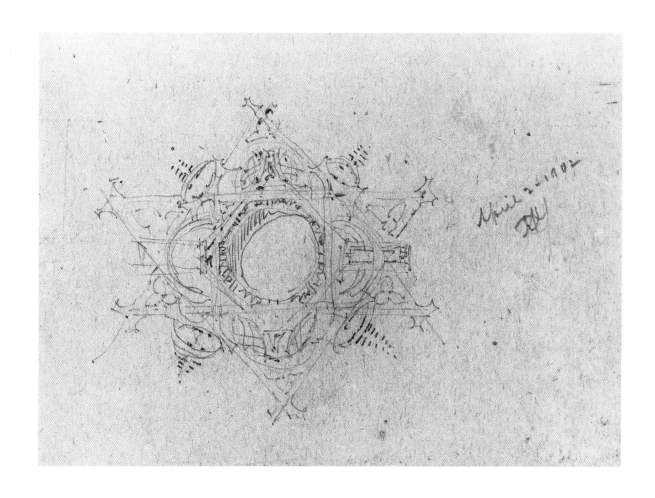

202. Design for ornament (2 April 1902).
Initialed with *LHS* monogram and dated.

Pencil on paper (9.7 x 13.5 cm.). Avery Library, Columbia University, FLLW/LHS 102;
purchased from Frank Lloyd Wright Foundation, 1965. S. 115.

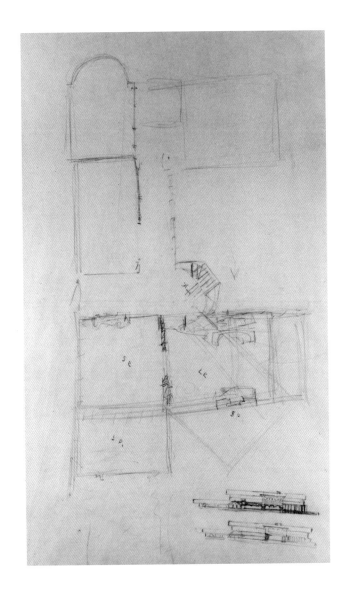

203. Plan and two sketches of elevation, Henry Babson House, Riverside, Illinois [1907].
Inscriptions on plan indicate location of stairs and room designations.

Pencil on paper (89 x 55 cm.). Collection Barbara G. Pine, New York.
Purchased by Ms. Pine from Leslie Hindman Galleries, Chicago, 1989 (on consignment by Scott Elliott of
Kelmscott Gallery, Chicago); purchased c. 1982 by Mr. Elliott from Robert L. Jacobson,
successor to the Niedecken–Walbridge Company, Milwaukee, Wisconsin; acquired by Mr. Jacobson in 1945 as
part of the holding of the Niedecken-Walbridge Company; acquired from Sullivan by
George Mann Niedecken probably at the time he worked on the interior decoration of the house.

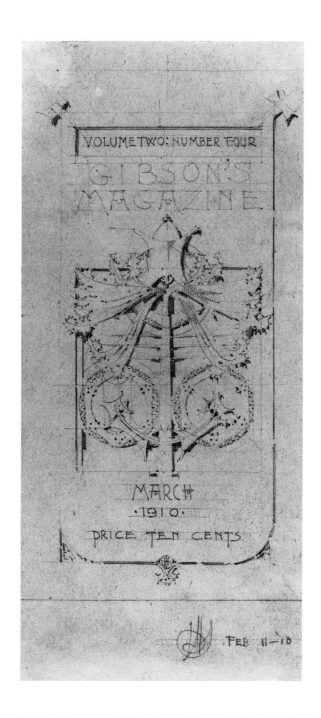

204. Design for cover of March 1910 issue of *Gibson's Magazine*
(11 February 1910). Inscribed on design: *VOLUME TWO: NUMBER
FOUR/GIBSON'S/MAGAZINE/MARCH/1910/PRICE TEN CENTS*;
initialed with *LHS* monogram and dated.

Pencil on paper (21.6 x 10.3 cm.). Avery Library, Columbia University, FLLW/LHS 82;
purchased from Frank Lloyd Wright Foundation, 1965. S. 122.

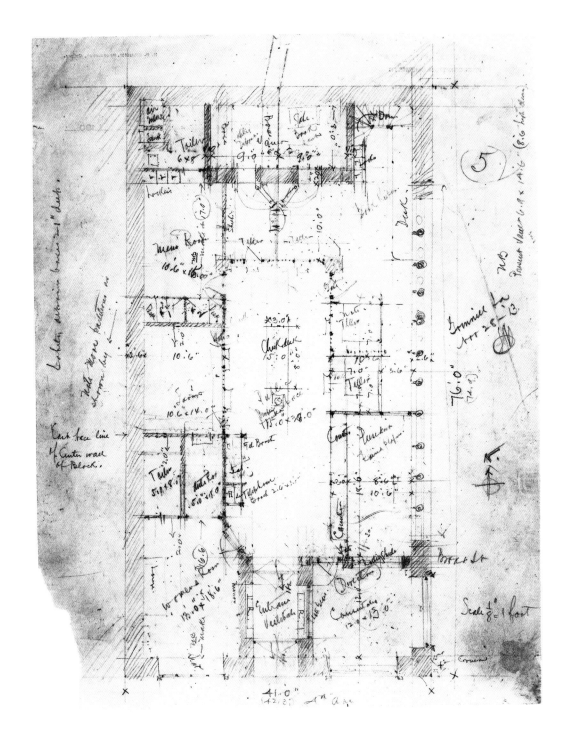

205. Merchants National Bank, Grinnell, Iowa, plan (28 November 1913).
Dated. Inscribed with numerous dimensions, labels, and notes.

Pencil on paper (28 x 21.4 cm.). Bentley Historical Library, University of Michigan; gift of
George Grant Elmslie, c. 1936, to Emil Lorch, for College of Architecture and Design,
University of Michigan; transferred to Bentley Historical Library, 1972.

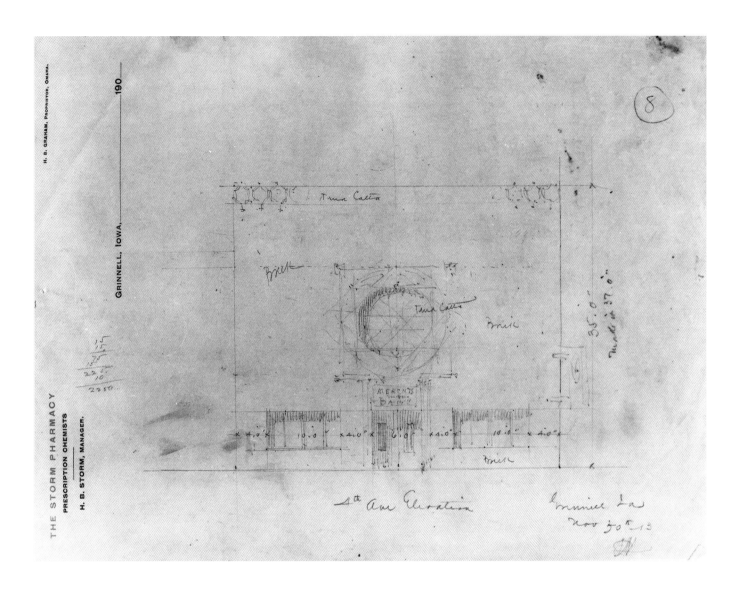

206. Merchants National Bank, Grinnell, Iowa, front (Fourth Avenue)
elevation (30 November 1913). Dated and initialed with *LHS* monogram.
Inscribed with dimensions, indications of materials, and title:
4th Ave. Elevation–Grinnell, Ia.

Pencil on imprinted Storm Pharmacy stationery (21.4 x 28 cm.). Bentley Historical Library,
University of Michigan; gift of George Grant Elmslie, c. 1936, to Emil Lorch, for College of
Architecture and Design, University of Michigan; transferred to Bentley Historical Library, 1972.

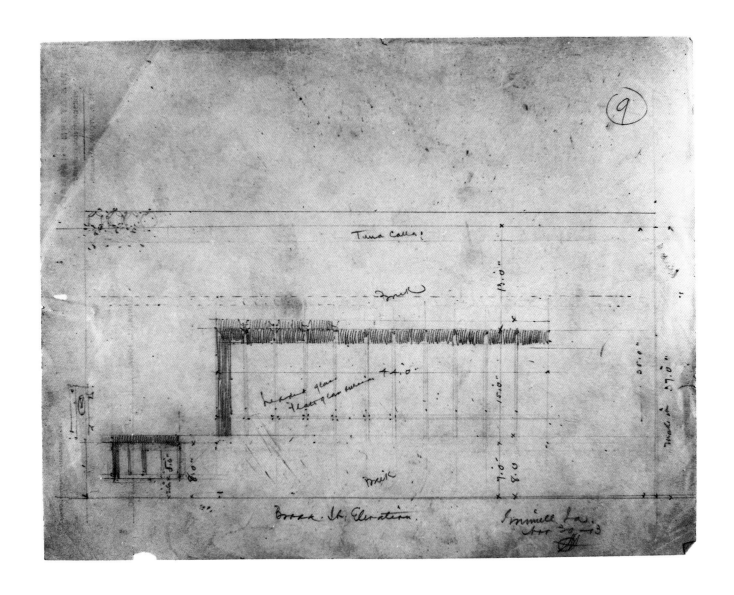

207. Merchants National Bank, Grinnell, Iowa, side (Broad Street) elevation
(30 November 1913). Dated and initialed with *LHS* monogram. Inscribed with
dimensions, indications of materials, and title: *Broad St. Elevation–Grinnell, Ia.*

Pencil on the back of imprinted Storm Pharmacy stationery (21.4 x 28 cm.). Bentley Historical
Library, University of Michigan; gift of George Grant Elmslie, c. 1936, to Emil Lorch, for College of
Architecture and Design, University of Michigan; transferred to Bentley Historical Library, 1972.

208. Design for plaster band in wood frieze, Peoples' Savings and Loan
Association, Sidney, Ohio (3 October 1917). Inscribed with dimensions;
on the lower right-hand side of sheet: *For Sidney* [in rectangular cartouche]
10\3\17/LHS [monogram]/*Plaster Band in Wood Frieze/Band Building*
for The Peoples Savings & Loan Assn.

Pencil on paper (20.4 x 30.4 cm.). Collection Wilbert and Marilyn Hasbrouck, Chicago;
gift of Louis Sullivan to William C. Presto; purchased from Sylvia (Mrs. William) Presto, c. 1971.

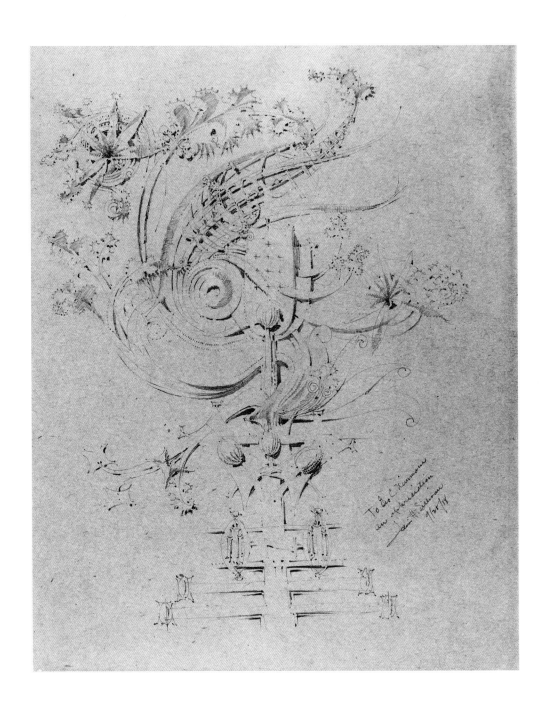

209. Study for ornament (25 September 1918). Inscribed
To Geo[.] C. Nimmons/an appreciation/Louis H. Sullivan/9\25\18.

Pencil on paper (28 x 22 cm.). Chicago Architecture Foundation;
gift of Rea Esgar, 1967; early provenance unknown.

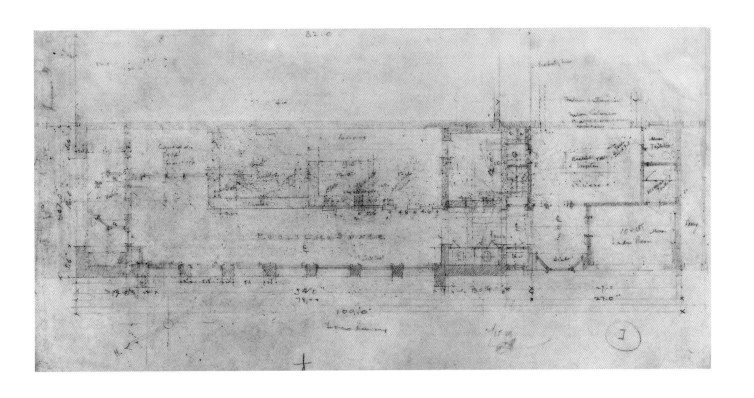

210. Farmers' & Merchants' Union Bank, Columbus, Wisconsin,
plan (15 February 1919). Inscribed with dimensions and room
labels; initialed with *LHS* monogram and dated.

Pencil on paper (20 x 41). Avery Library, Columbia University, 1936.001.00009;
gift of George Grant Elmslie, 1936.

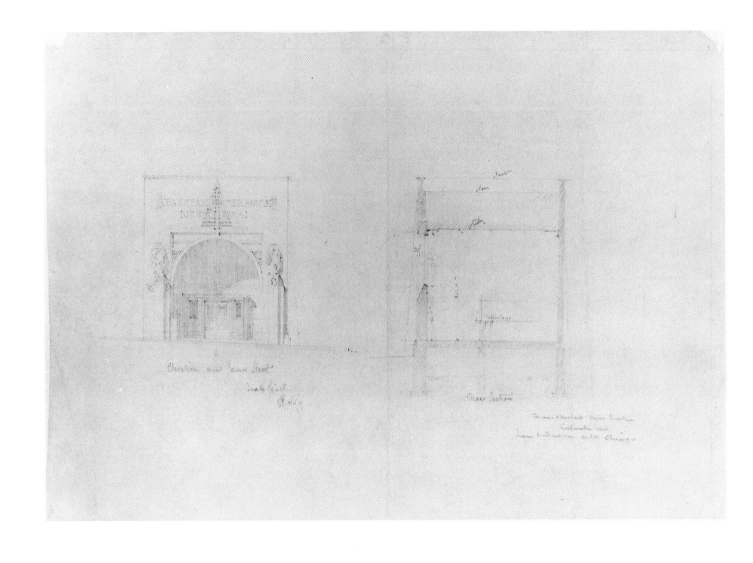

211. Farmers' & Merchants' Union Bank, Columbus, Wisconsin, elevation
and cross section (15 February 1919). Inscribed under elevation:
Elevation on James Street/Scale 1/8" = 1 F/LHS [monogram] *2\15\19;*
under cross section: *Cross Section/Farmers and Merchants Union Bank/
Columbus Wis/Louis H. Sullivan Archt Chicago.*

Pencil on paper (38 x 51 cm.). Art Institute of Chicago; gift of J. Russell Wheeler
(president of the Farmers' & Merchants' Union Bank), 1957. M. 100 (noted).

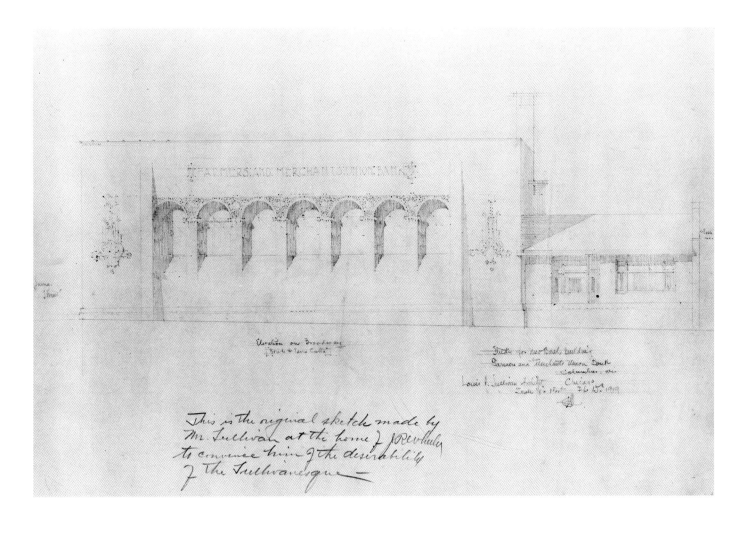

212. Farmers' & Merchants' Union Bank, Columbus, Wisconsin, side (Broadway)
elevation (15 February 1919). Inscribed on left-hand side of design: *James/Street*;
on right-hand side of design: *Gable/end*; across elevation:
FARMERS:AND:MERCHANTS:UNION:BANK; under elevation (left-hand side):
Elevation on Broadway/[Brick + Terra Cotta]; under elevation (right-hand side):
*Study for New Bank Building/Farmers and Merchants Union Bank/Columbus, Wis/
Louis H. Sullivan Architect Chicago/Scale 1/8" = 1 Foot Feb. 15th 1919/LHS* [monogram]; above
lower border of sheet, not in Sullivan's hand: *This is the original sketch made by/Mr. Sullivan
at the home of J. R. Wheeler/to convince him of the desirability/of the Sullivanesque.*

Pencil on paper (38 x 51 cm.). Art Institute of Chicago; gift of J. Russell Wheeler
(president of the Farmers' & Merchants' Union Bank), 1957. M. 100.

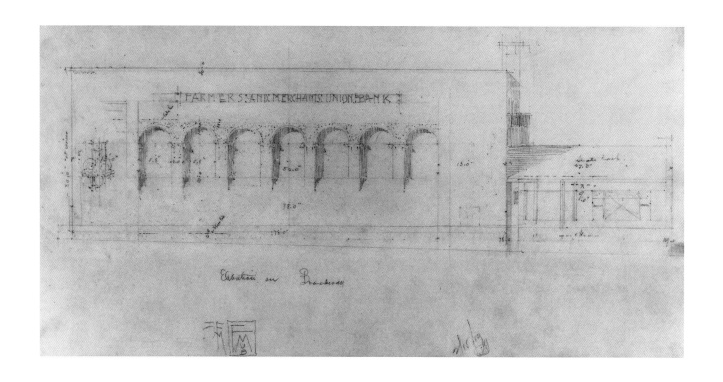

213. Farmers' & Merchants' Union Bank, Columbus Wisconsin, side
(Broadway) elevation (15 February 1919).
Inscribed with dimensions and indications of materials; across elevation:
FARMERS:AND:MERCHANTS:UNION:BANK; below drawing:
Elevation on Broadway; at bottom of sheet: studies for bank monogram;
dated and initialed with *LHS* monogram.

Pencil on paper (18.7 x 38.4 cm.). Avery Library, Columbia University, 1936.001.00002;
gift of George Grant Elmslie, 1936.

214. Farmers' and Merchants' Union Bank, Columbus, Wisconsin,
front (James Street) elevation (20 February 1919).
Inscribed *James Street Front/2\20\19/LHS* [monogram].

Pencil on paper (38 x 51 cm.). Art Institute of Chicago; gift of J. Russell Wheeler
(president of the Farmers' & Merchants' Union Bank), 1957 M. 100.

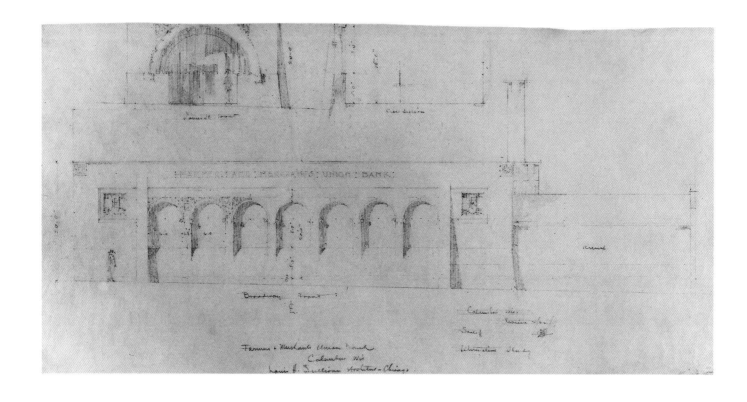

215. Farmers' and Merchants' Union Bank, Columbus, Wisconsin, front (James
Street) elevation, cross section, and side (Broadway) elevation (22 February 1919).
Inscribed with dimensions; under front elevation: *James St. Front*;
under cross section: *Cross Section*; under side elevation: *Broadway Front*;
on side elevation (right-hand side): *Annex*; under side elevation (center):
Farmers + Merchants Union Bank/Columbus Wis/Louis H. Sullivan Architect − Chicago;
under side elevation (right-hand side): *Columbus Wis/Revisions 2\22\19/
Scale 1/8 LHS/Alternative Study.*

Pencil on paper (19.4 x 40 cm.). Avery Library, Columbia University, 1936.001.00003;
gift of George Grant Elmslie, 1936. H.

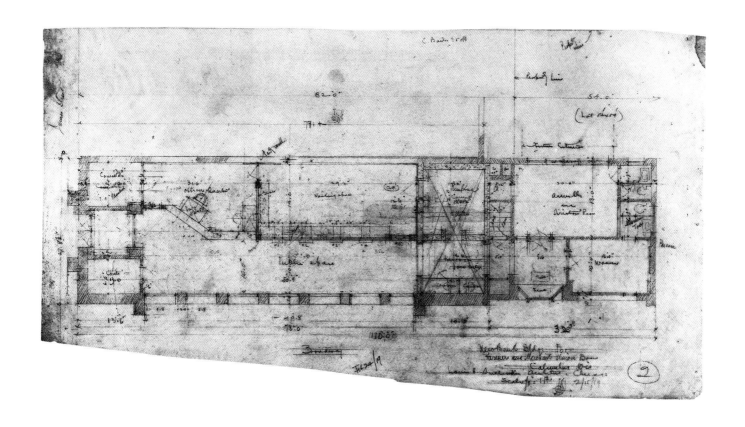

216. Farmers' & Merchants' Union bank, Columbus, Wisconsin, plan
(15 February 1919; revised, 24 February 1919). Inscribed with dimensions and
labels; on lower right-hand corner: *New Bank Building for/Farmers and
Merchants Union Bank/Columbus Wis/Louis H. Sullivan Architect − Chicago/Scale
1/8" = 1 Ft 2/15/19;* initialed with *LHS* monogram; on bottom center: *Feb 24/19.*

Pencil on paper (20.6 x 40 cm.). Avery Library, Columbia University, 1936.001.00010;
gift of George Grant Elmslie, 1936.

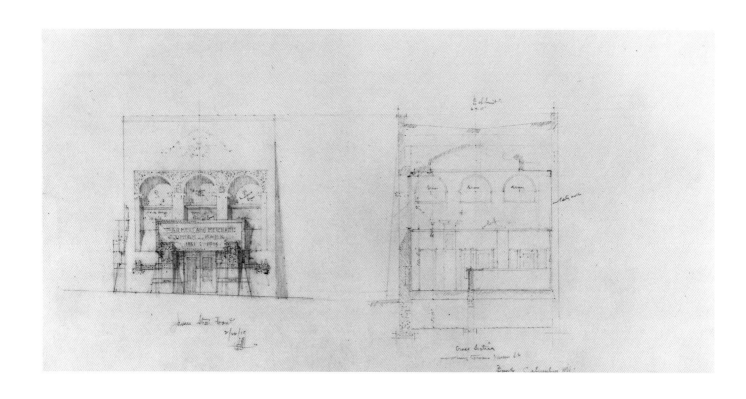

217. Farmers' and Merchants' Union Bank, Columbus, Wisconsin,
front (James Street) elevation and cross section (26 February 1919).
Inscribed with dimensions and labels on section; under elevation:
James Street Front/2\26\19\LHS; under section:
Cross Section/looking toward James Street/Bank Columbus Wis.

Pencil on paper (19.5 x 40 cm.). Avery Library, Columbia University, 1936.001.00004;
gift of George Grant Elmslie, 1936.

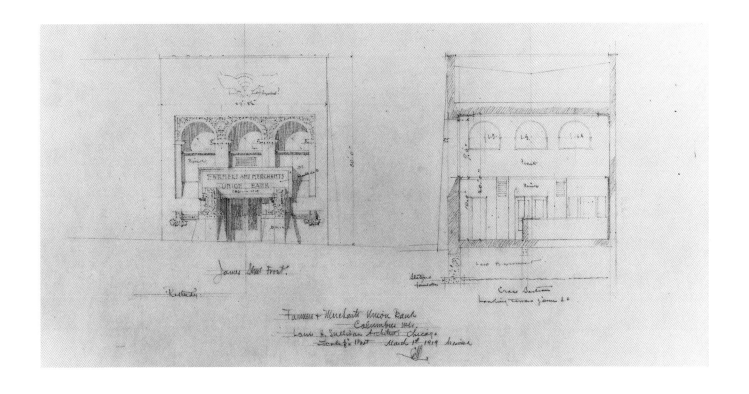

218. Farmers' & Merchants' Union Bank, Columbus, Wisconsin, front
(James Street) elevation and cross section (1 March 1919). Inscribed with
dimensions; under elevation: *James Street Front/Restudy*; under cross section:
Cross Section/Looking towards James St; on lower center of sheet:
*Farmers + Merchants Union Bank/Columbus Wis/Louis H. Sullivan Architect:
Chicago/Scale 1/8" = 1 Foot March 1st 1919 As revised/LHS.*

Pencil on paper (19.5 x 40 cm.). Avery Library, Columbia University, 1936.001.00005;
gift of George Grant Elmslie, 1936. H.

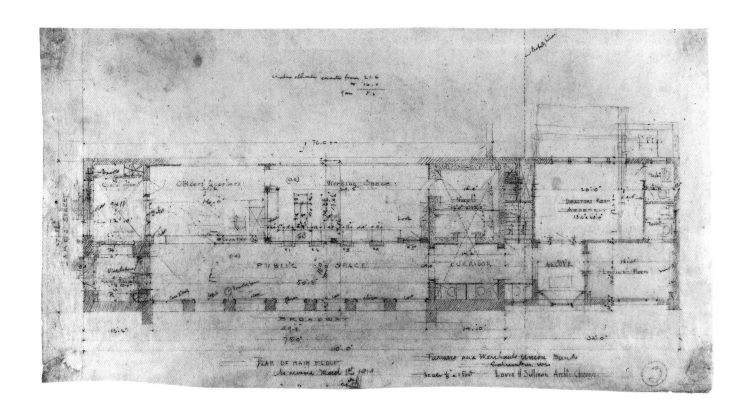

219. Farmers' & Merchants' Union Bank, Columbus, Wisconsin,
plan (revised 1 March 1919; revised 21 March 1919).
Inscribed with dimensions and labels; on lower right-hand corner:
*Farmers and Merchants Union Bank/Columbus Wis/Scale: 1/8" = 1 Foot −
Louis H. Sullivan Archt:Chicago*; on center bottom: *PLAN OF MAIN
FLOOR/As revised March 1st 1919/ " " " 21st.*

Pencil on paper (20.6 x 39.4 cm.). Avery Library, Columbia University, 1936.001.00011;
gift of George Grant Elmslie, 1936.

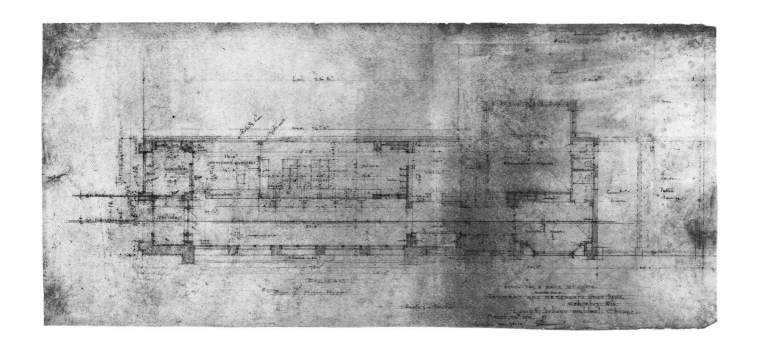

220. Farmers' & Merchants' Union Bank, Columbus, Wisconsin, plan
(24 March 1919; corrected 31 March 1919). Inscribed with dimensions and
labels; on lower right-hand corner: *STUDY FOR A BANK BUILDING/
COLUMBUS, WIS/Louis H. Sullivan Architect. Chicago/March 24th 1919/
Corrected March 31–'19*; initialed with *LHS* monogram.

Pencil on paper (22.7 x 51.8 cm.). Avery Library, Columbia University, 1936.001.00012;
gift of George Grant Elmslie, 1936. H.

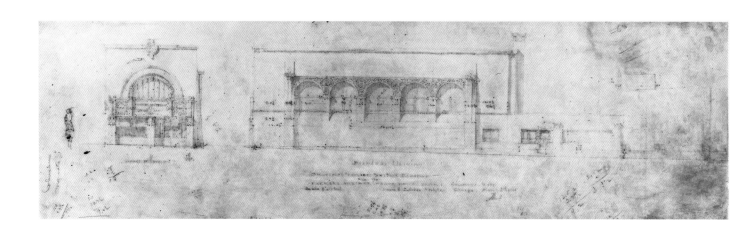

221. Farmers' & Merchants' Union Bank, Columbus, Wisconsin, front
(James Street) and side (Broadway) elevations (31 March 1919).
Inscribed with dimensions; under front elevations: *James St. Elevation*;
under side elevation: *Broadway Elevation*; at lower center of sheet:
*Study : For : Proposed : New : Bank : Building/For The/Farmers
Merchants Union Bank : Columbus Wis:/Scale 1/8" = 1 Foot
Louis H. Sullivan Architect Chicago. March 31st 1919/LHS*;
immediately above lower edge of sheet: *FINAL*.

Pencil on paper (20.2 x 64.7 cm.). Avery Library, Columbia University, 1936.001.00006;
gift of George Grant Elmslie, 1936. H.

222. Farmers' & Merchants' Union Bank, Columbus, Wisconsin,
front (James Street) elevation [n. d.].

Pencil on paper (17.6 x 39 cm.). Avery Library, Columbia University, 1936.001.00007;
gift of George Grant Elmslie, 1936. H.

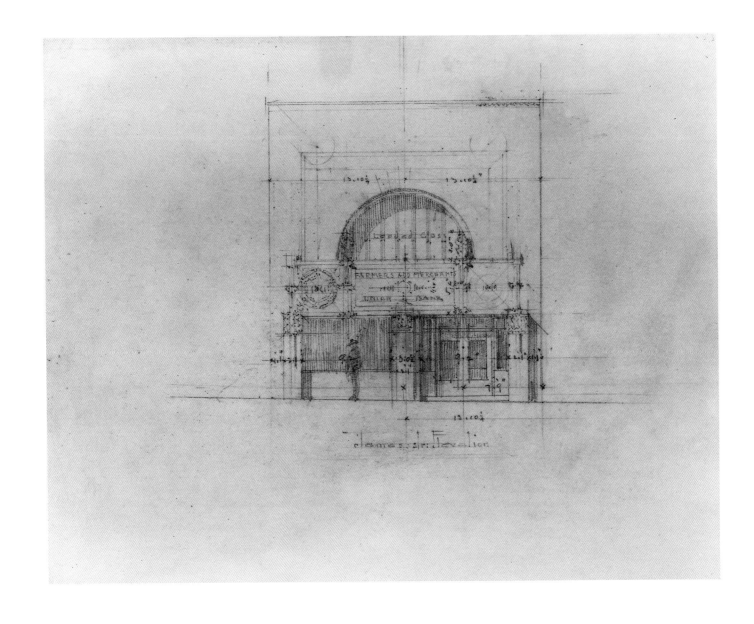

223. Farmers' & Merchants' Union Bank, Columbus, Wisconsin,
front (James Street) elevation [n. d.]. Inscribed with dimensions;
under design: *James : str : Elevation*.

Pencil on paper (20 x 41 cm.). Avery Library, Columbia University, 1936.001.00008;
gift of George Grant Elmslie, 1936. H.

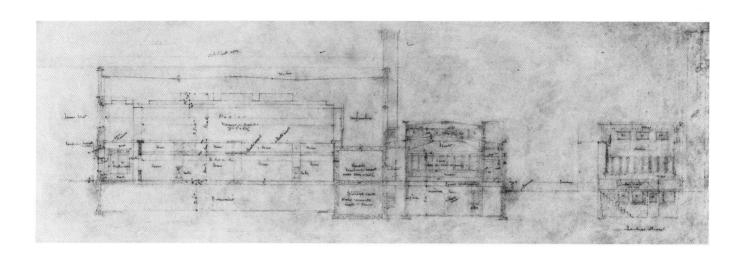

224. Farmers' & Merchants' Union Bank, Columbus, Wisconsin,
sections [n. d.]. Inscribed with dimensions and labels.

Pencil on paper (20 x 61 cm.). Avery Library, Columbia University, 1936.001.00015;
gift of George Grant Elmslie, 1936.

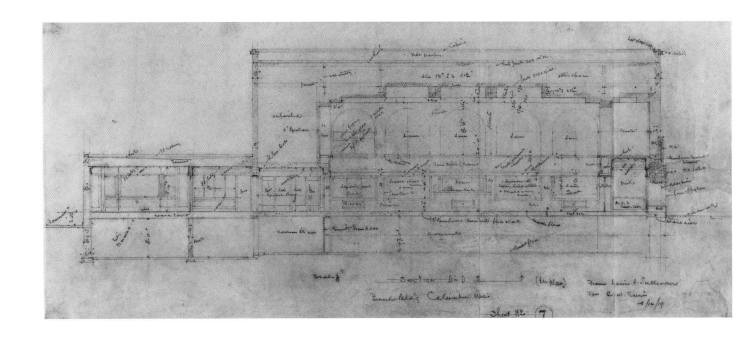

225. Farmers' & Merchants' Union Bank, Columbus, Wisconsin,
longitudinal section D-D, SHEET NO. 7 (14 April 1919). Dated.
Inscriptions on design concerning dimensions, materials, and methods of
construction; on lower center sheet: *Section D-D (In plan)/Bank Bldg
Columbus Wis/Sheet No. 7*; on right-hand corner of sheet:
From Louis H. Sullivan/For C. W. Ennis.

Pencil on paper (18.7 x 41.6 cm.). Avery Library, Columbia University, 1936.001.00014;
gift of George Grant Elmslie, 1936. H.

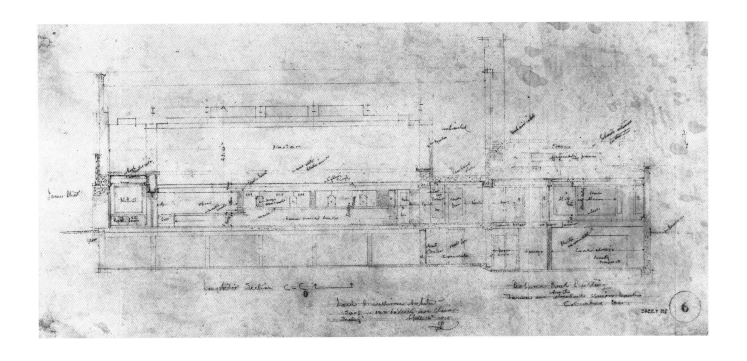

226. Farmers' & Merchants' Union Bank, Columbus, Wisconsin,
longitudinal section C-C, SHEET NO. 6 (16 April 1919). Inscriptions on design
concerning dimensions, materials, and methods of construction;
on lower center of sheet: *Longitudinal Section C-C/Louis H. Sullivan
Architect/2005-122 60 Mich Ave Chicago/Scale 1/8" April 16th 1919/ LHS*
[monogram]; on lower right-hand corner of sheet: *Proposed Bank Building/
for the/Farmers and Merchants Union Bank/Columbus Wis/SHEET NO. 6.*

Pencil on paper (20 x 42.2 cm.). Avery Library, Columbia University, 1936.001.00013;
gift of George Grant Elmslie, 1936. H.

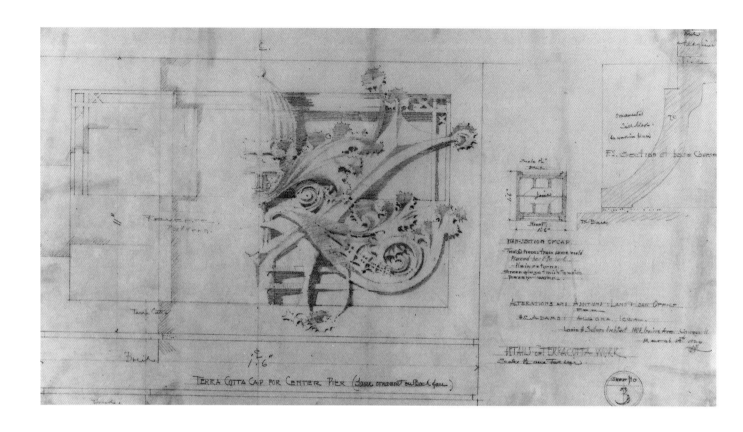

227. Alternations and additions to H. C. Adams & Co. Land and Loan Offices, Algona, Iowa, design for capital of pier, SHEET NO. 3 (14 March 1920). Inscriptions concerning materials and methods of construction; on lower center of sheet: *TERRA COTTA CAP FOR CENTER PIER (Same ornament on Back face)*; on lower right-hand corner of sheet: *ALTERATIONS AND ADDITIONS : LAND + LOAN OFFICE/FOR/H. C . ADAMS : ALGONA IOWA/Louis H. Sullivan Architect 1808 Prairie Ave. Chicago Il/March 14th 1920/LHS [monogram]/DETAILS OF TERRACOTTA WORK/Scale 1 1/2" and Full size/Sheet No/3.*

Pencil on paper (39.5 x 72.3 cm.). Avery Library, Columbia University, 1000.002.00001; gift of Richard Nickel, c. 1957; gift of Edgar Kaufmann jr. to Richard Nickel on behalf of Frank Lloyd Wright, 1956.

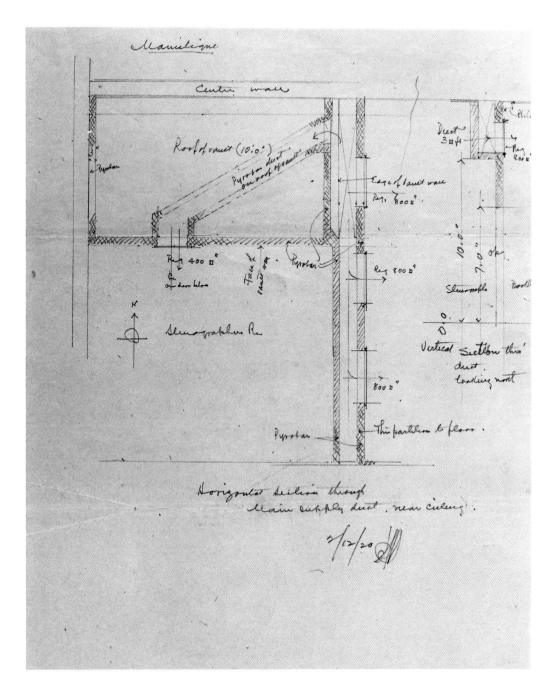

228. Remodeling of First National Bank, Manistique, Michigan, horizontal
section (12 February 1920). Inscriptions concerning materials and methods of
construction; near upper edge of sheet: *Manistique*; under design: *Horizontal
section through/main supply duct near ceiling/2\12\20/LHS* [monogram].

Pencil on paper (28 x 21.4 cm.). Art Institute of Chicago;
gift of Wilbert and Marilyn Hasbrouck, 1993; purchased from Sylvia (Mrs. William C.) Presto,
c. 1971; gift of Louis Sullivan to William C. Presto.

229. Remodeling of First National Bank, Manistique, Michigan,
plan of detail of exhaust from insurance room through roof
(12 February 1920). Inscriptions concerning room labels and construction
instructions; under design: *Route of Exhaust from Ins Rm thro' Roof/Scale 1/4"
2\12\20 LHS*; below: *Memo* (with technical information).

Pencil on paper (28 x 21.4 cm.). Art Institute of Chicago;
gift of Wilbert and Marilyn Hasbrouck, 1993; purchased from Sylvia (Mrs. William C.) Presto,
c. 1971; gift of Louis Sullivan to William C. Presto.

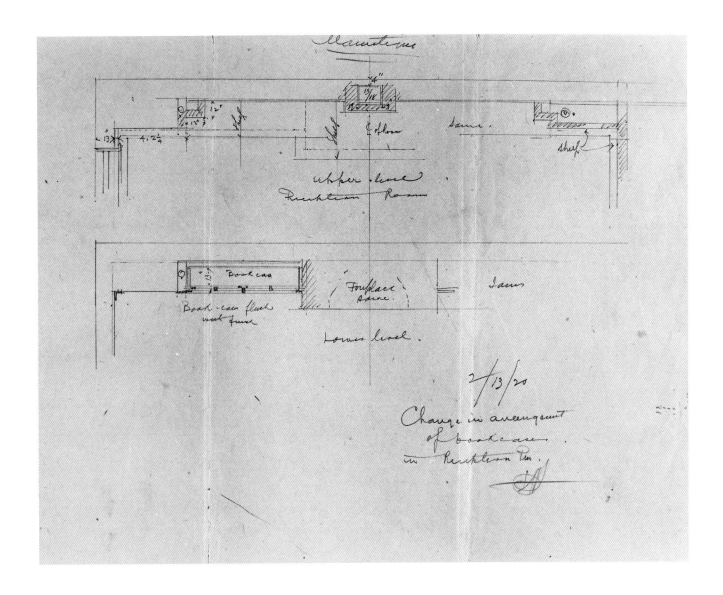

230. Remodeling of First National Bank, Manistique, Michigan, plans for
change in arrangement of bookcase in reception room (13 February 1920).
Inscribed: on top: *Manistique*; labels on drawings, principally:
Upper level/Reception Room and *Lower level*; at bottom: *2\13\20/*
Change in arrangement/of bookcase/in Reception Room/LHS.
Pencil on paper (21.4 x 28 cm.). Art Institute of Chicago;
gift of Wilbert and Marilyn Hasbrouck, 1993; purchased from Sylvia (Mrs. William C.) Presto,
c. 1971; gift of Louis Sullivan to William C. Presto.

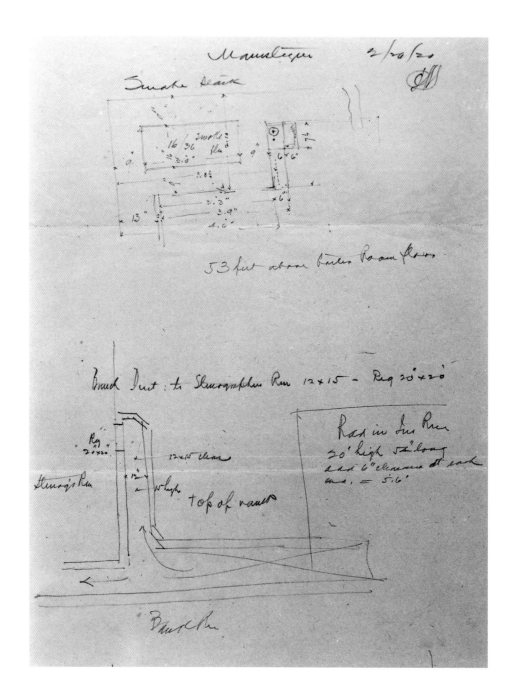

231. Remodeling of First National Bank, Manistique, Michigan, section through
smoke stack and plan of duct to stenographers' room (26 February 1920). Inscribed:
on top: *Manistique 2\26\20/LHS* [monogram]/*Smoke Stack*; dimensions and technical
labels on drawing; on upper part of drawing below: *Branch Duct: to Stenographers Rm
12 x 15 – Reg 20" x 20"*; dimensions and technical labels on drawing.

Pencil on paper (28 x 21.4 cm.). Art Institute of Chicago; gift of Wilbert and Marilyn Hasbrouck, 1993;
purchased from Sylvia (Mrs. William C.) Presto, c. 1971; gift of Louis Sullivan to William C. Presto.

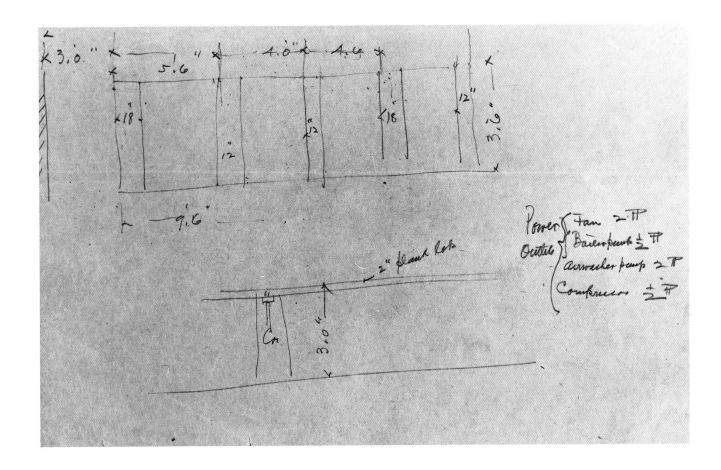

232. Remodeling of First National Bank, Manistique, Michigan, sketch
of location of power outlets on a wall [February 1920]. Inscribed with
dimensions on drawing; on right side: *purpose of outlets*.

Pencil on paper (21.4 x 28 cm.). Art Institute of Chicago;
gift of Wilbert and Marilyn Hasbrouck, 1993; purchased from Sylvia (Mrs. William C.)
Presto, c. 1971; gift of Louis Sullivan to William C. Presto.

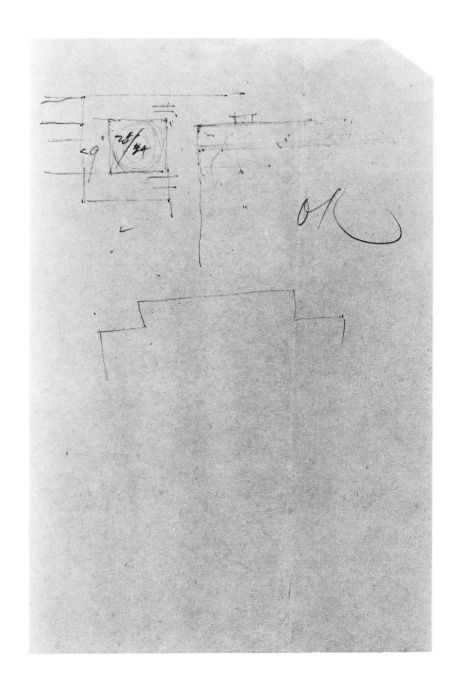

233. Remodeling of First National Bank, Manistique, Michigan, sketch
for unidentified purpose [February 1920].
Inscribed with dimensions on drawing; on the right-hand side: *OK*.

Pencil on paper (28 x 21.4 cm.). Art Institute of Chicago; gift of Wilbert and Marilyn
Hasbrouck, 1993; purchased from Sylvia (Mrs. William C.) Presto, c. 1971;
gift of Louis Sullivan to William C. Presto.

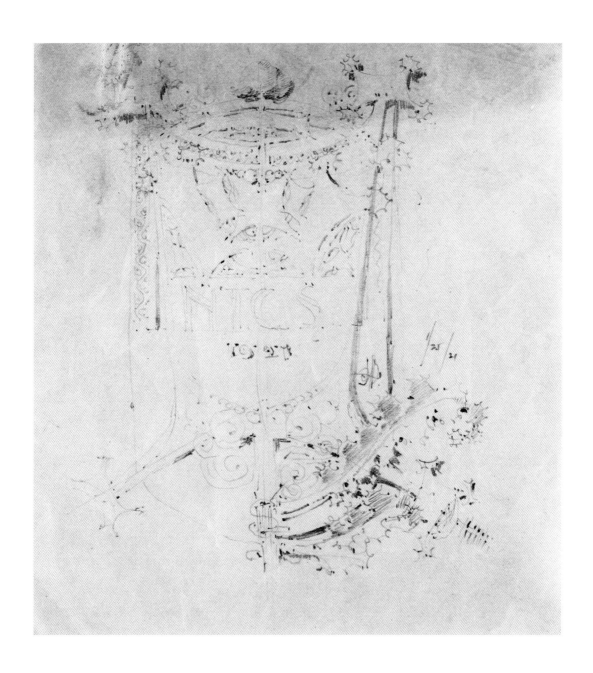

234. National Terra Cotta Society Monument, detail of preliminary design (25 January 1921). Dated and initialed with *LHS*
monogram on right-hand side of design. Inscribed: *NTCS/1921.*

Pencil on blue paper (15.2 x 14 cm.). Art Institute of Chicago;
gift of Robert Kueny and the University of Wisconsin–Parkside, 1992;
early provenance unknown. M. 183 (noted).

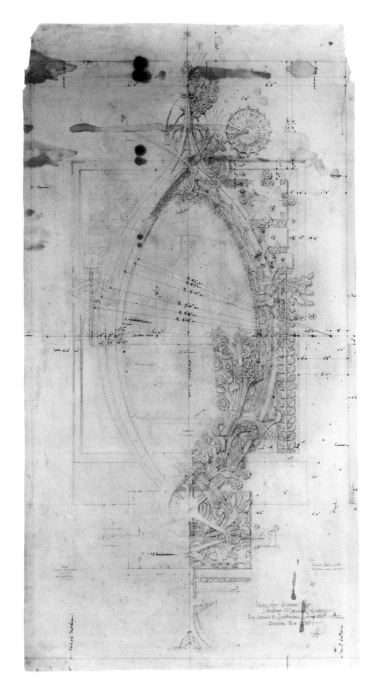

235. Design for screen for Andrew O'Connor, sculptor (1922).
Inscribed with dimensions; on lower right-hand corner of sheet:
Design for Screen for/Andrew O'Connor Sculptor/By Louis H. Sullivan Architect
1922/Scale 1 1/2" = 1 Foot/LHS [monogram].

Pencil and ink on paper (97.2 x 52.1 cm.). University of Michigan Museum of Art, Ann Arbor;
early provenance unknown; possibly a gift from the estate of Emil Lorch to College of Architecture
and Design, University of Michigan; transferred from College of Architecture and Design, 1972.

The Germ the Seat of Power.

A SYSTEM OF ARCHITECTURAL ORNAMENT

According with a philosophy of mans powers.

By Louis H Sullivan, Architect

THE GERM.

+ Cotyledon
Germ

Above is drawn a diagram of a typical seed
with two cotyledons. The cotyledons are specialized
rudimentary leaves: containing a supply of nourishment
sufficient for the initial stage of the development
of the germ.

The Germ is the real thing: the seat of identity. Within
its delicate mechanism lies the will to power; the
function which is to seek and eventually to find
its full expression in form.

The seat of power and the will to live constitute
the simple working idea upon which all that
follows is based - as to efflorescence

236. "A System of Architectural Ornament According
With a Philosophy of Man's Powers" (manuscript),
leaf 1 of 36 [January 1922]. Undated.

Pencil on paper (28 x 21.5 cm.). Art Institute of Chicago;
gift of George Grant Elmslie, 1932. Z. 47.

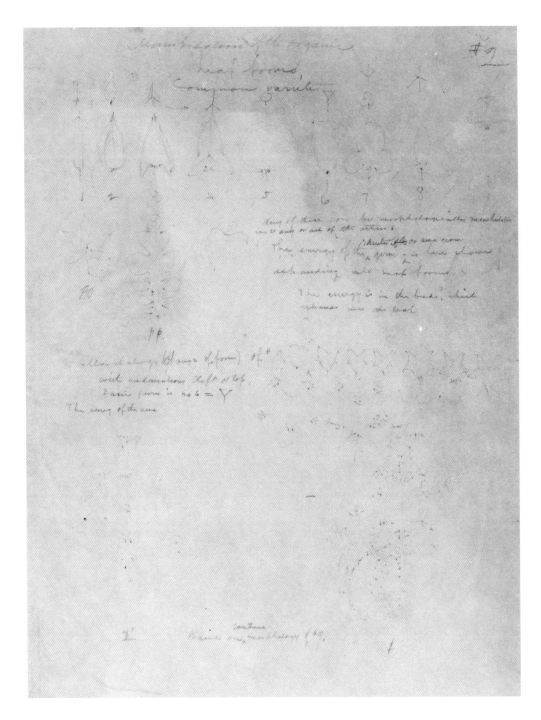

237. "A System of Architectural Ornament According
With a Philosophy of Man's Powers" (manuscript),
leaf 12 of 36 [late January–early February 1922]. Undated.

Pencil on paper (28 x 21.5 cm.). Art Institute of Chicago;
gift of George Grant Elmslie, 1932. Z. 69.

238. "A System of Architectural Ornament According
With a Philosophy of Man's Powers" (manuscript),
leaf 15 of 36 [late January–early February 1922]. Undated.

Pencil on paper (28 x 21.5 cm.). Art Institute of Chicago;
gift of George Grant Elmslie, 1932. Z. 75.

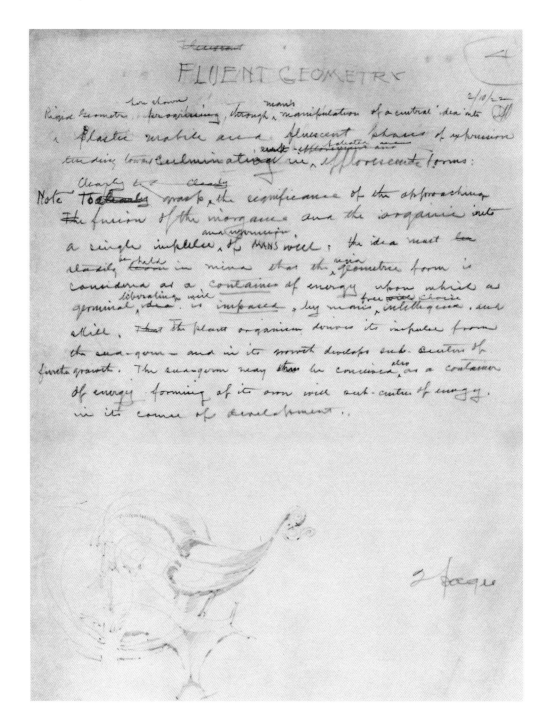

239. "A System of Architectural Ornament According
With a Philosophy of Man's Powers" (manuscript),
leaf 17 of 36 (10 February 1922). Dated.

Pencil on paper (28 x 21.5 cm.). Art Institute of Chicago;
gift of George Grant Elmslie, 1932. Z. 79.

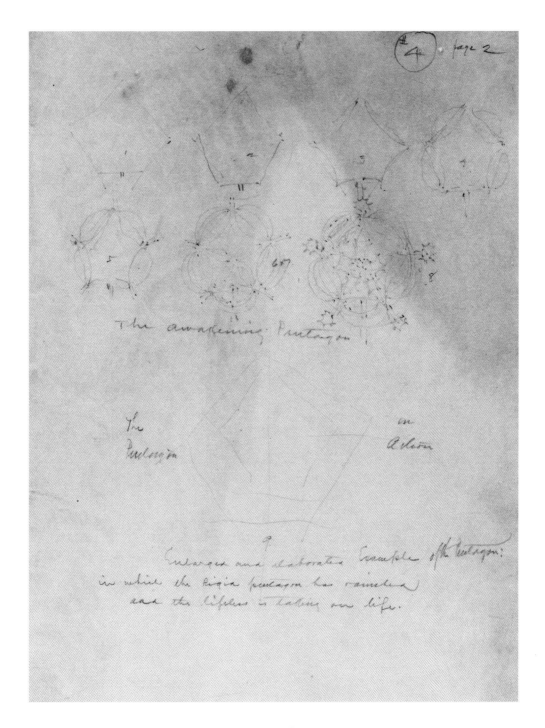

240. "A System of Architectural Ornament According With
a Philosophy of Man's Powers" (manuscript),
leaf 18 of 36 [mid–February 1922]. Undated.

Pencil on paper (28 x 21.5 cm.). Art Institute of Chicago;
gift of George Grant Elmslie, 1932. Z. 81.

241. "A System of Architectural Ornament According
With a Philosophy of Man's Powers" (manuscript),
leaf 19 of 36 (24 February 1922). Dated.

Pencil on paper (28 x 21.5 cm.). Art Institute of Chicago;
gift of George Grant Elmslie, 1932. Z. 83.

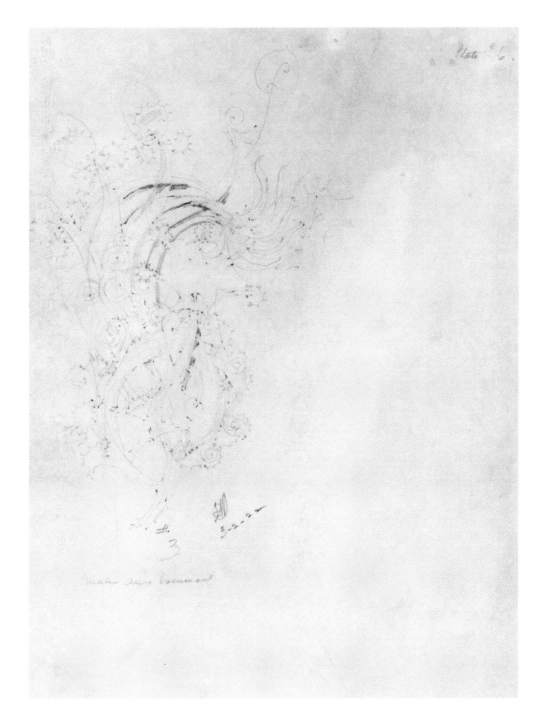

242. "A System of Architectural Ornament According With
a Philosophy of Man's Powers" (manuscript),
leaf 21 of 36 (2 March 1922). Dated.

Pencil on paper (28 x 21.5 cm.). Art Institute of Chicago;
gift of George Grant Elmslie, 1932. Z. 87.

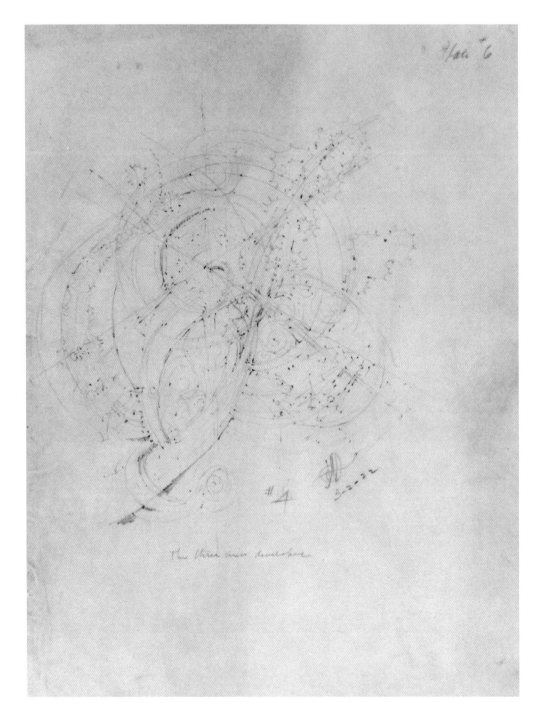

243. "A System of Architectural Ornament According
With a Philosophy of Man's Powers" (manuscript),
leaf 22 of 36 (2 March 1922). Dated.

Pencil on paper (28 x 21.5 cm.). Art Institute of Chicago;
gift of George Grant Elmslie, 1932. Z. 89.

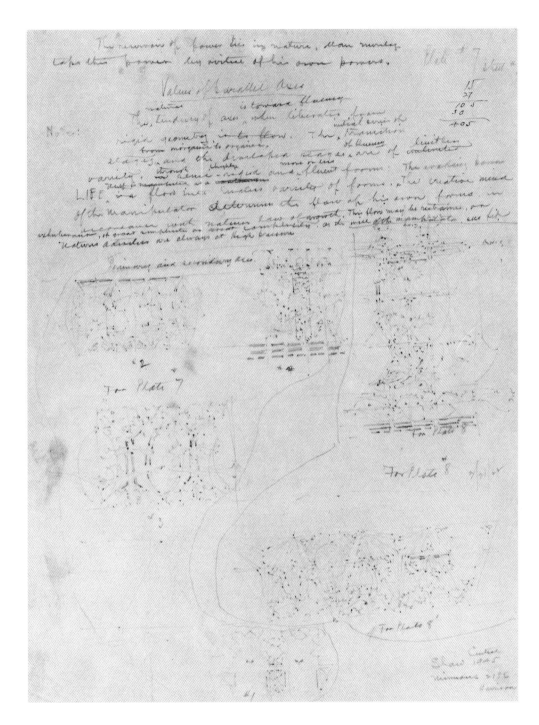

244. "A System of Architectural Ornament According
With a Philosophy of Man's Powers" (manuscript),
leaf 23 of 36 (21 March 1922). Dated.

Pencil on paper (28 x 21.5 cm.). Art Institute of Chicago;
gift of George Grant Elmslie, 1932. Z. 91.

245. "A System of Architectural Ornament According
With a Philosophy of Man's Powers" (manuscript),
leaf 25 of 36 (22 March 1922). Dated.

Pencil on paper (28 x 21.5 cm.). Art Institute of Chicago;
gift of George Grant Elmslie, 1932. Z. 95.

246. "A System of Architectural Ornament According
With a Philosophy of Man's Powers" (manuscript),
leaf 26 of 36 [late March 1922]. Undated.

Pencil on paper (28 x 21.5 cm.). Art Institute of Chicago;
gift of George Grant Elmslie, 1932. Z. 97.

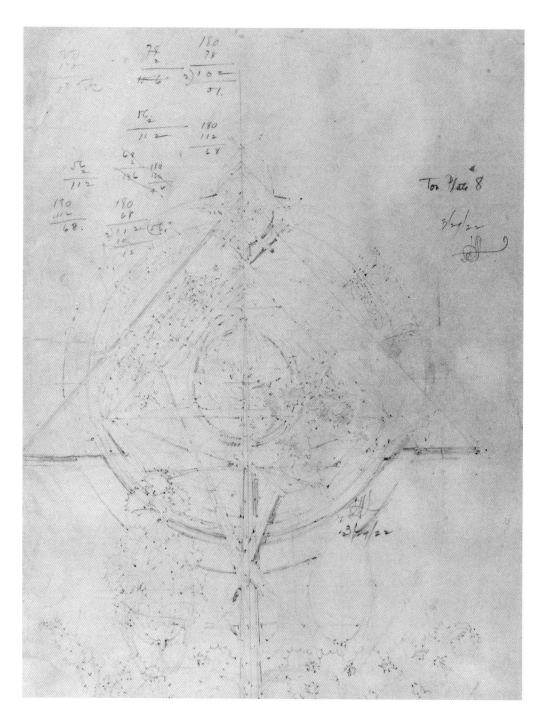

247. "A System of Architectural Ornament According
With a Philosophy of Man's Powers" (manuscript),
leaf 27 of 36 (29 March 1922). Dated.

Pencil on paper (28 x 21.5 cm.). Art Institute of Chicago;
gift of George Grant Elmslie, 1932. Z. 99.

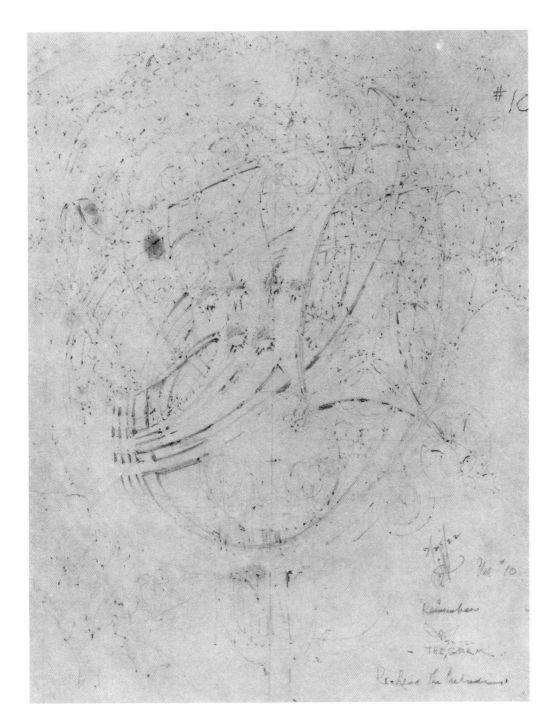

248. "A System of Architectural Ornament According
With a Philosophy of Man's Powers" (manuscript),
leaf 33 of 36 (28 March 1922). Dated.

Pencil on paper (28 x 21.5 cm.). Art Institute of Chicago;
gift of George Grant Elmslie, 1932. Z. 111.

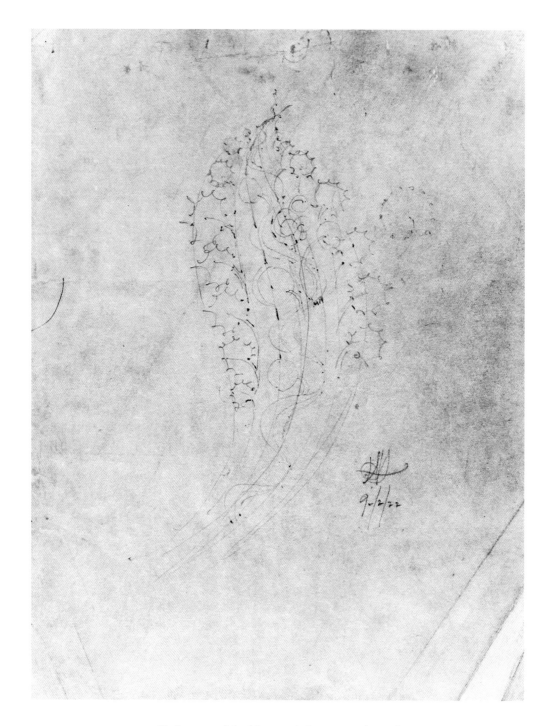

249. "A System of Architectural Ornament According
With a Philosophy of Man's Powers" (manuscript),
leaf 34 of 36 (2 September 1922). Dated.

Pencil on paper (28 x 21.5 cm.). Art Institute of Chicago;
gift of George Grant Elmslie, 1932. Z. 113.

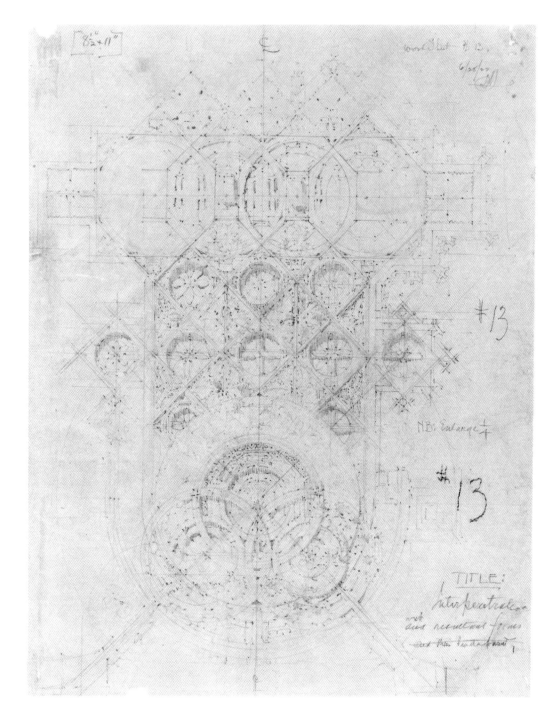

250. "A System of Architectural Ornament According
With a Philosophy of Man's Powers" (manuscript),
leaf 35 of 36 (28 June 1922). Dated.

Pencil on paper (28 x 21.5 cm.). Art Institute of Chicago;
gift of George Grant Elmslie, 1932. Z. 115.

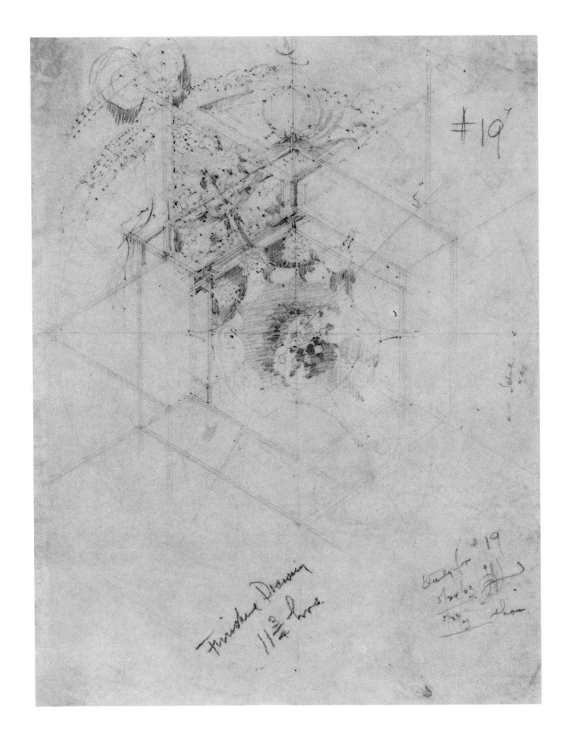

251. "A System of Architectural Ornament According
With a Philosophy of Man's Powers" (manuscript),
leaf 36 of 36 (24, 28 May 1923). Dated.

Pencil on paper (28 x 21.5 cm.). Art Institute of Chicago;
gift of George Grant Elmslie, 1932. Z. 117.

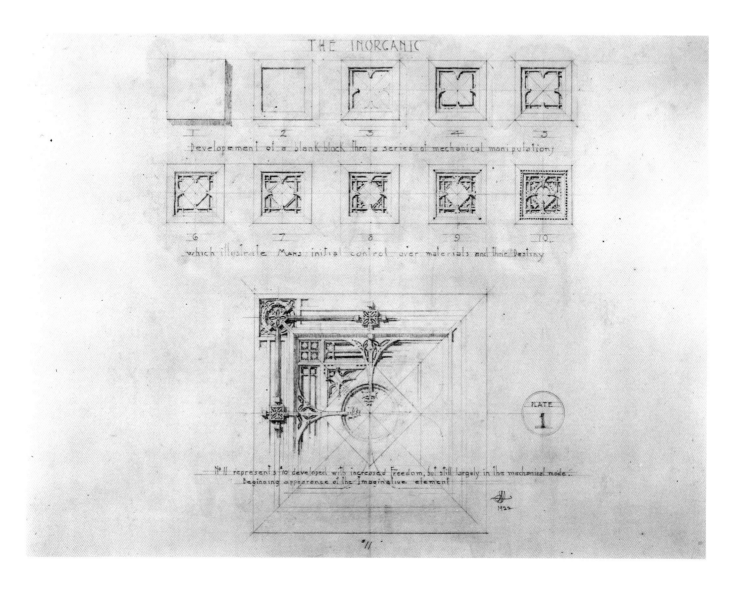

252. *A System of Architectural Ornament According With a Philosophy of Man's Powers,*
Plate 1. The Inorganic: Development of a Blank Block Through a Series of Mechanical Manipulations (1922). Dated and initialed with *LHS* monogram.

Pencil on paper (57.5 x 73.5 cm.). Art Institute of Chicago;
commissioned by Art Institute of Chicago. H, M. 186, Su, Z. 121.

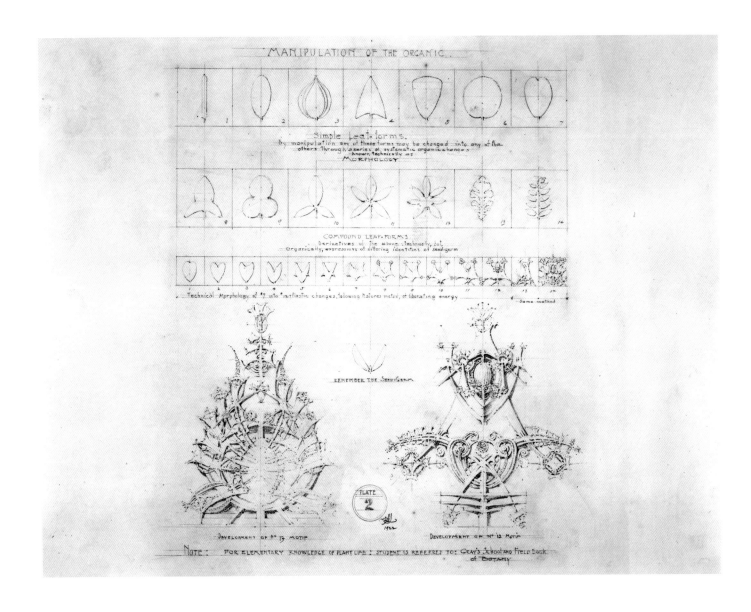

253. *A System of Architectural Ornament According With a Philosophy of Man's Powers*,
Plate 2. Manipulation of the Organic (1922). Dated and initialed with *LHS* monogram.

Pencil on paper (57.5 x 73.5 cm.). Art Institute of Chicago;
commissioned by Art Institute of Chicago. H, M. 187, Su, Z. 123.

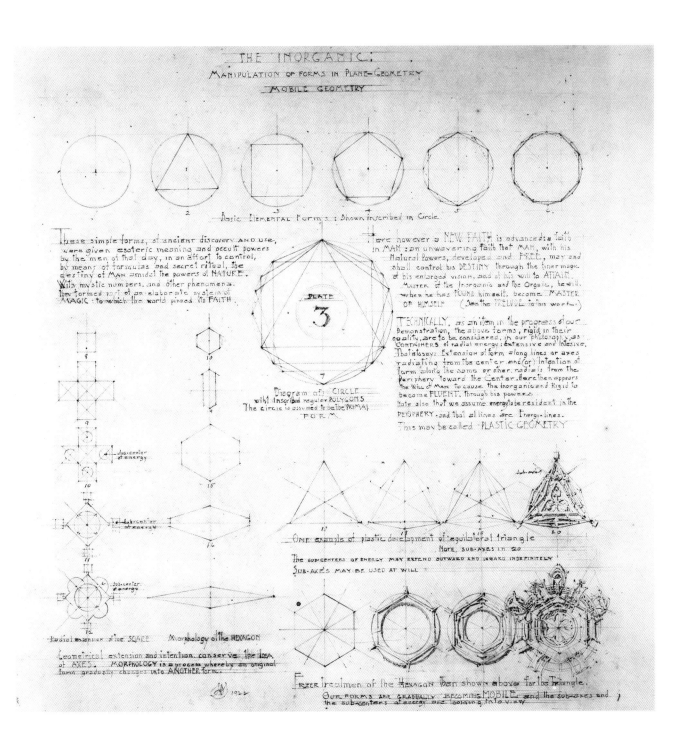

254. *A System of Architectural Ornament According With a Philosophy of Man's Powers,*
Plate 3. The Inorganic: Manipulation of Forms in Plane Geometry (1922).
Dated and initialed with *LHS* monogram.

Pencil on paper (57.5 x 73.5 cm.). Art Institute of Chicago;
commissioned by Art Institute of Chicago. H, M. 188, Su, Z. 125.

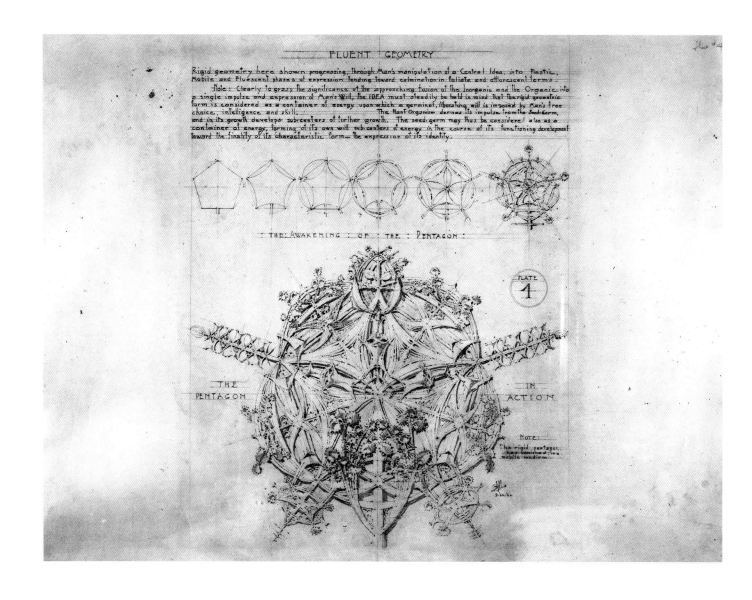

255. *A System of Architectural Ornament According With a Philosophy of Man's Powers*,
Plate 4. Fluent Geometry: The Awakening of the Pentagon (22 February 1922).
Dated and initialed with *LHS* monogram.

Pencil on paper (57.5 x 73.5 cm.). Art Institute of Chicago; commissioned by Art Institute of Chicago
H, M. 189, Su, Z. 127.

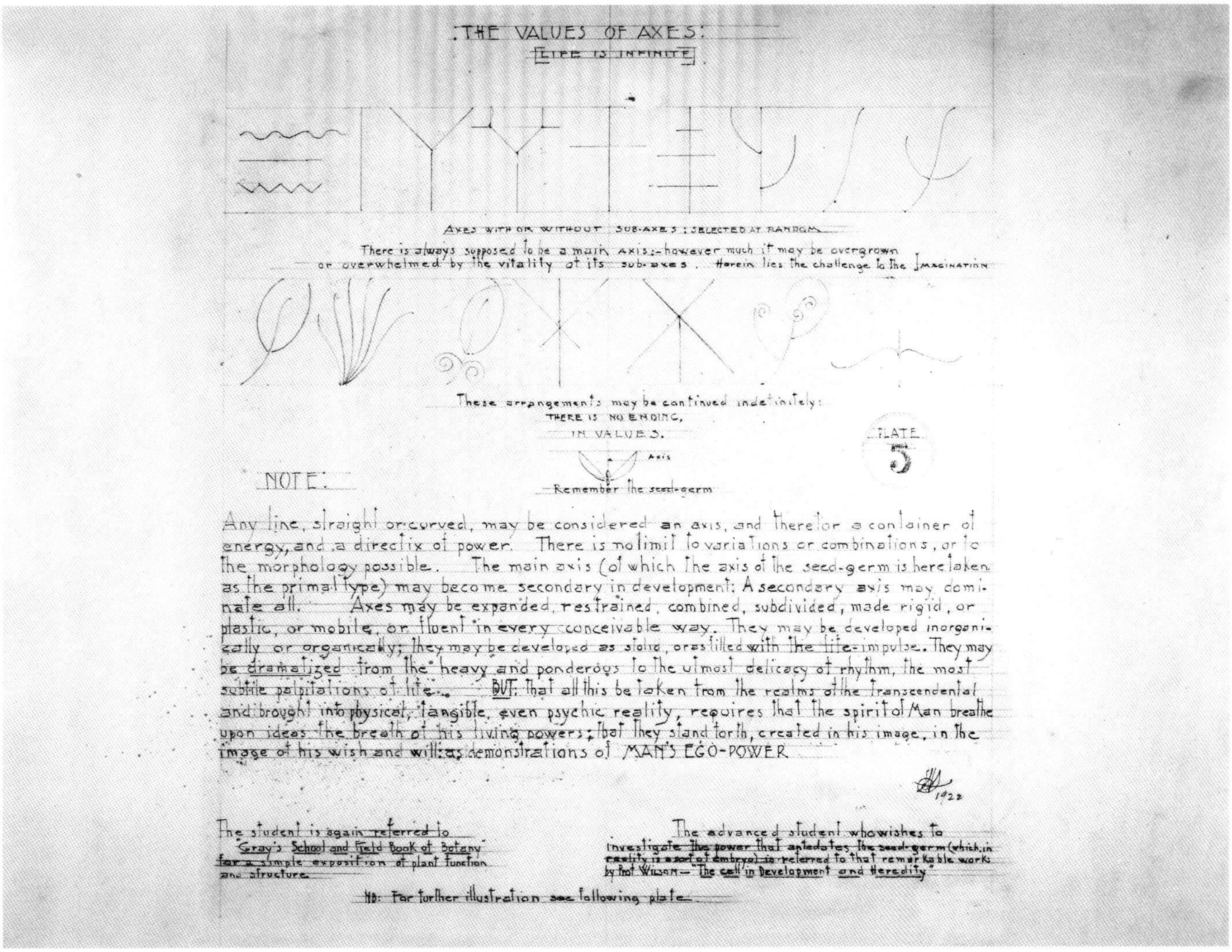

THE VALUES OF AXES:
LIFE IS INFINITE.

AXES WITH OR WITHOUT SUB-AXES ; SELECTED AT RANDOM.

There is always supposed to be a main axis;—however much it may be overgrown
or overwhelmed by the vitality of its sub-axes. Herein lies the challenge to the Imagination.

These arrangements may be continued indefinitely:
THERE IS NO ENDING,
IN VALUES.

PLATE
5

Axis

Remember the seed-germ

NOTE:

Any line, straight or curved, may be considered an axis, and therefor a container of
energy, and a directrix of power. There is no limit to variations or combinations, or to
the morphology possible. The main axis (of which the axis of the seed-germ is here taken
as the primal type) may become secondary in development: A secondary axis may dominate all. Axes may be expanded, restrained, combined, subdivided, made rigid, or
plastic, or mobile, or fluent in every conceivable way. They may be developed inorgani-
cally or organically; they may be developed as static, or as filled with the life-impulse. They may
be dramatized from the heavy and ponderous to the utmost delicacy of rhythm, the most
subtile palpitations of life. BUT; that all this be taken from the realms of the transcendental
and brought into physical, tangible, even psychic reality, requires that the spirit of Man breathe
upon ideas the breath of his living powers; that they stand forth, created in his image, in the
image of his wish and will; demonstrations of MAN'S EGO-POWER.

1922

The student is again referred to
"Gray's School and Field Book of Botany"
for a simple exposition of plant function
and structure.

The advanced student who wishes to
investigate the power that antedates the seed-germ (which in
reality is a sort of embryo) is referred to that remarkable work
by Prof Wilson— The cell in Development and Heredity.

N.B: For further illustration see following plate.

256. *A System of Architectural Ornament According With a Philosophy of Man's Powers*,
Plate 5. The Value of Axes (1922). Dated and initialed with *LHS* monogram.

Pencil on paper (57.5 x 73.5 cm.). Art Institute of Chicago;
commissioned by Art Institute of Chicago. H, M. 190, Su, Z. 129.

· 383 ·

257. *A System of Architectural Ornament According With a Philosophy of Man's Powers,*
Plate 6. Manipulation of Variants on a Given Axial Theme (1922).
Dated and initialed with *LHS* monogram.

Pencil on paper (57.5 x 73.5 cm.). Art Institute of Chicago;
commissioned by Art Institute of Chicago. H, M. 191, Su, Z. 131.

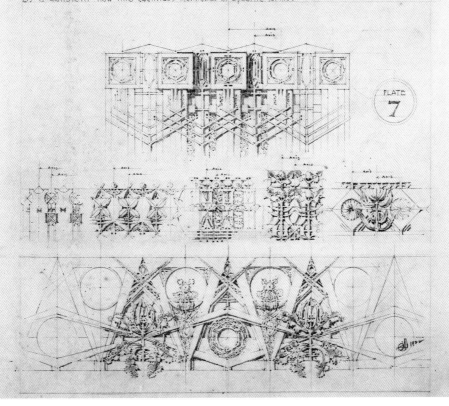

THE : VALUES
of
PARALLEL AXES

NOTE: The natural tendency of axes is toward fluency when once they are liberated from rigid geometry. The initial resultant-series of transition-stages from inorganic toward organic, and the developed stages of fluency, are, both, of limitless variety and scope, and there ceases to be visible a distinct line of demarcation between them. Thus we come upon the truth that the creative reality of form lies within a continuous series emanating from a single primal life-impulse seeking and finding manifold expression in form. LIFE, itself, is thus manifested as a constant flow into countless multitudes of specific forms.

PLATE

7

258. *A System of Architectural Ornament According With a Philosophy of Man's Powers,*
Plate 7. The Value of Parallel Axes (1922). Dated and initialed with *LHS* monogram.

Pencil on paper (57.5 x 73.5 cm.). Art Institute of Chicago;
commissioned by Art Institute of Chicago. H, M. 192, Su, Z. 133.

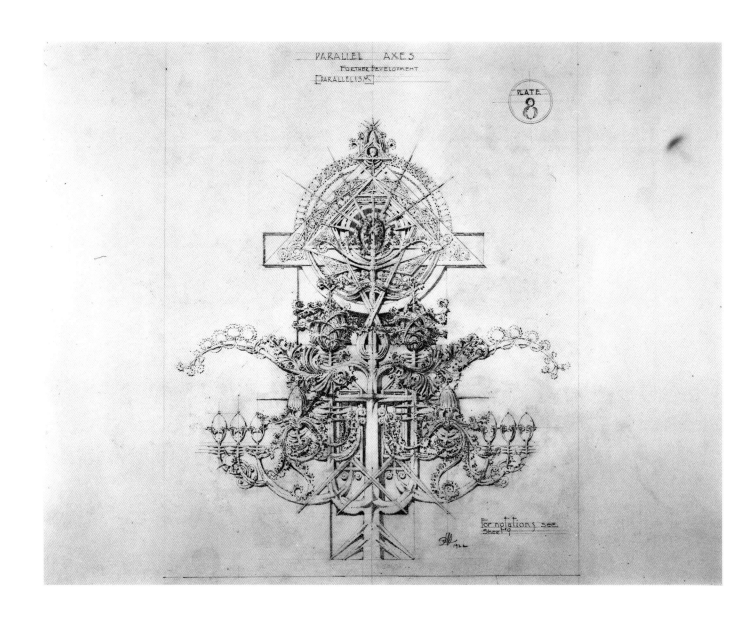

259. *A System of Architectural Ornament According With a Philosophy of Man's Powers,*
Plate 8. Parallel Axes: Further Development (1922).
Dated and initialed with *LHS* monogram.

Pencil on paper (57.5 x 73.5 cm.). Art Institute of Chicago;
commissioned by Art Institute of Chicago. H, M. 193, Su, Z. 135.

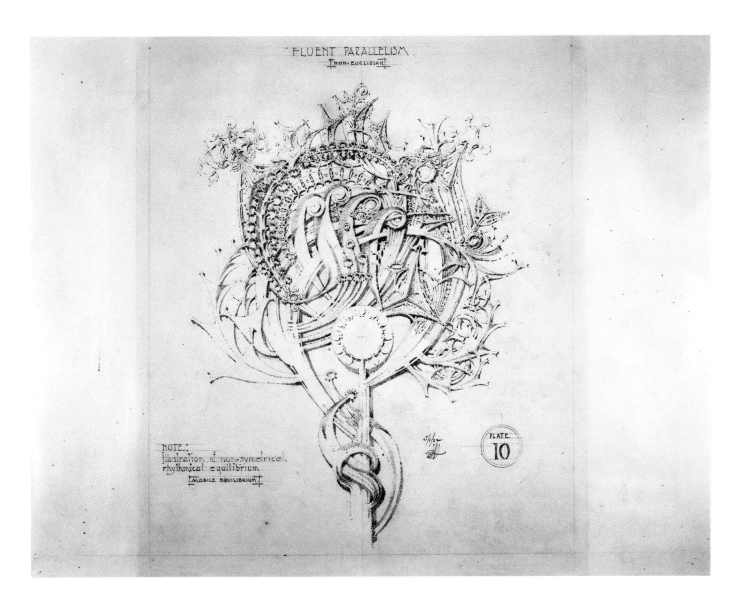

260. *A System of Architectural Ornament According With a Philosophy of Man's Powers,*
Plate 10. Fluent Parallelism (1922).
Dated and initialed with *LHS* monogram.

Pencil on paper (57.5 x 73.5 cm.). Art Institute of Chicago;
commissioned by Art Institute of Chicago. H, M. 195, Su, Z. 139.

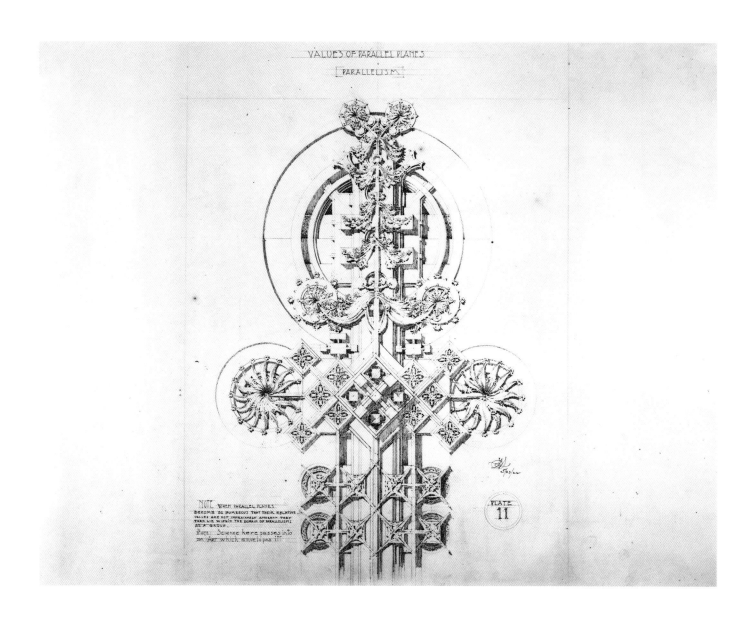

261. *A System of Architectural Ornament According With a Philosophy of Man's Powers*,
Plate 11. Values of Parallel Planes (1922).
Dated and initialed with *LHS* monogram.

Pencil on paper (57.5 x 73.5 cm.). Art Institute of Chicago;
commissioned by Art Institute of Chicago. H, M. 196, Su, Z. 141.

262. *A System of Architectural Ornament According With a Philosophy of Man's Powers,*
Plate 12. Values of Overlap and Overlay: A Study in Virtuosity (7 June 1922).
Dated and signed *Louis H. Sullivan Architect/Chicago Illinois.*

Pencil on paper (57.5 x 73.5 cm.). Art Institute of Chicago;
commissioned by Art Institute of Chicago. H, M. 197, Su, Z. 143.

263. *A System of Architectural Ornament According With a Philosophy of Man's Powers*,
Plate 13. Interpenetration: With Resultant Forms and Development (6 July 1922).
Dated and signed *Louis H. Sullivan fecit*.

Pencil on paper (57.5 x 73.5 cm.). Art Institute of Chicago;
commissioned by Art Institute of Chicago. H, M. 198, Su, Z. 145.

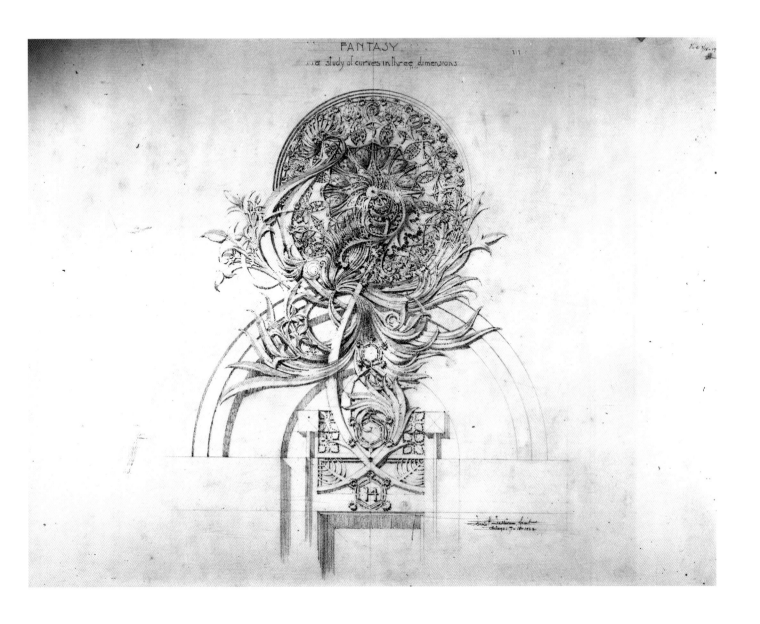

264. *A System of Architectural Ornament According With a Philosophy of Man's Powers,*
Plate 14. Fantasy: A Study of Curves in Three Dimensions (18 July 1922).
Dated and signed *Louis H. Sullivan fecit;*
inscribed on upper right-hand corner *7/11 to 7/18 − 1922/LHS* [monogram].

Pencil on paper (57.5 x 73.5 cm.). Art Institute of Chicago;
commissioned by Art Institute of Chicago. H, M. 199, Su, Z. 147.

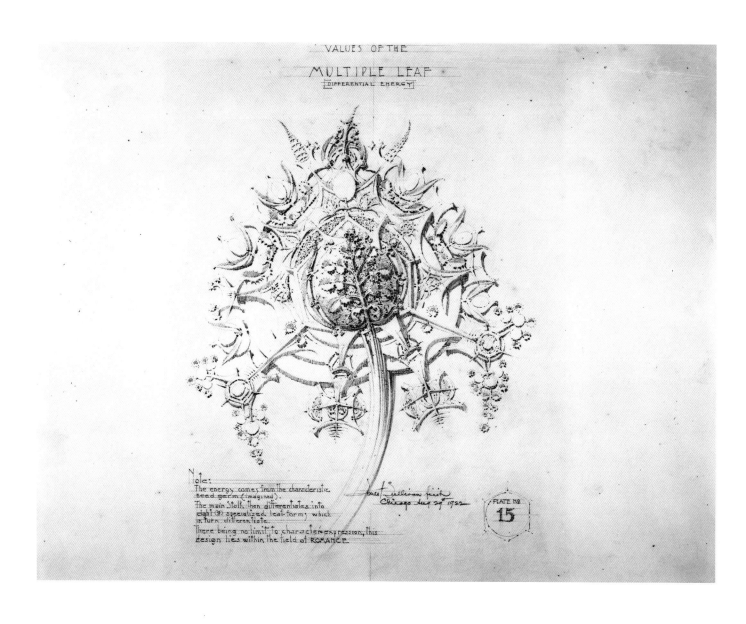

265. *A System of Architectural Ornament According With a Philosophy of Man's Powers,*
Plate 15. Values of the Multiple Leaf (29 August 1922).
Dated and signed *Louis H. Sullivan fecit.*

Pencil on paper (57.5 x 73.5 cm.). Art Institute of Chicago;
commissioned by Art Institute of Chicago. H, M. 200, Su, Z. 149.

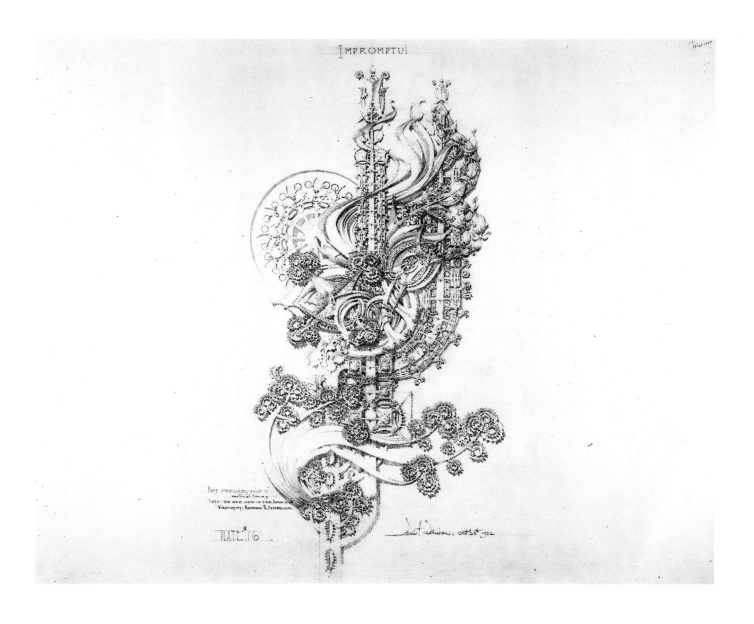

266. *A System of Architectural Ornament According With a Philosophy of Man's Powers*,
Plate 16. Impromptu! (28 October 1922).
Dated and signed *Louis H. Sullivan*.

Pencil on paper (57.5 x 73.5 cm.). Art Institute of Chicago;
commissioned by Art Institute of Chicago. H, M. 201, Su, Z. 151.

267. *A System of Architectural Ornament According With a Philosophy of Man's Powers,*
Plate 17. A Geometrical Playground (15 December 1922).
Dated and signed *Louis H. Sullivan del*[ineator].

Pencil on paper (57.5 x 73.5 cm.). Art Institute of Chicago;
commissioned by Art Institute of Chicago. H, M. 202, Su, Z. 153.

· 394 ·

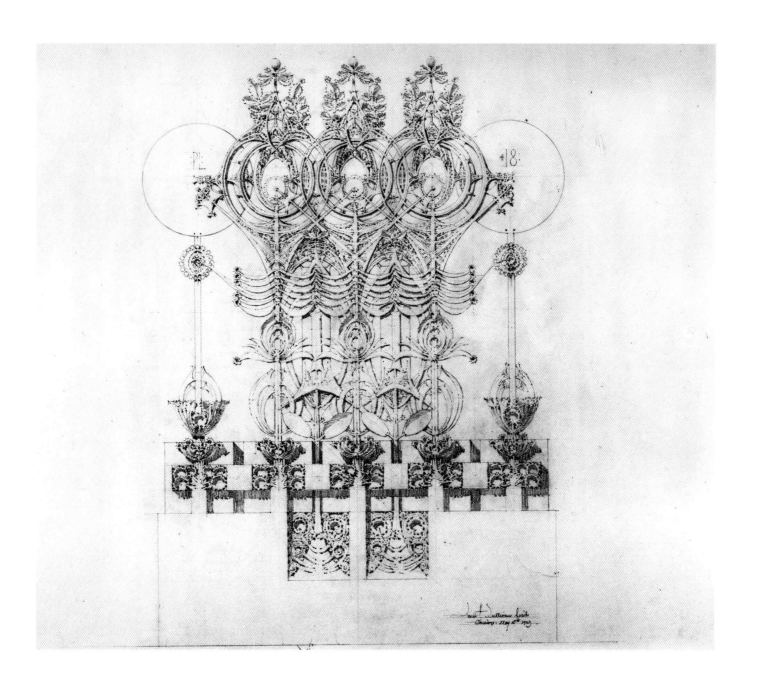

268. *A System of Architectural Ornament According With a Philosophy of Man's Powers,*
Plate 18. [Untitled] (15 May 1923).
Dated and signed *Louis H. Sullivan fecit.*

Pencil on paper (57.5 x 73.5 cm.). Art Institute of Chicago;
commissioned by Art Institute of Chicago. H, M. 203, Su, Z. 155.

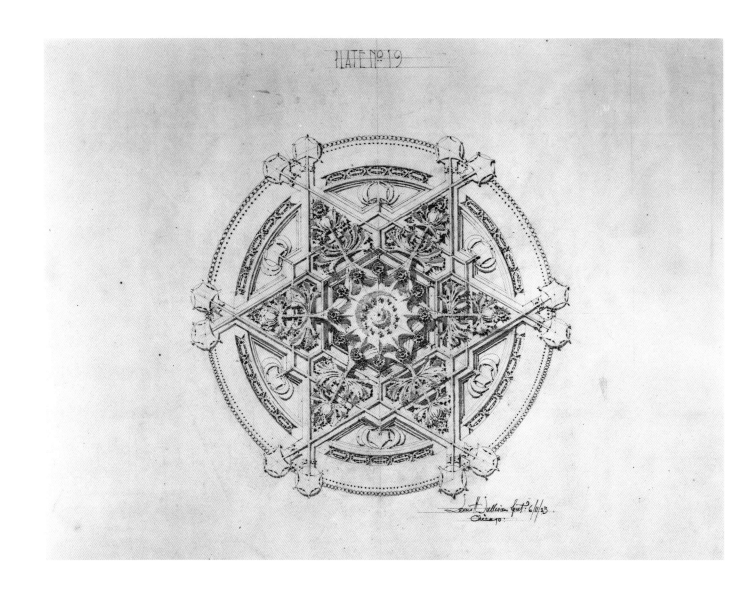

269. *A System of Architectural Ornament According With a Philosophy of Man's Powers,*
Plate 19. [Untitled] (11 June 1923).
Dated and signed *Louis H. Sullivan fecit.*

Pencil on paper (57.5 x 73.5 cm.). Art Institute of Chicago;
commissioned by Art Institute of Chicago. H, M. 204, Su, Z. 157.

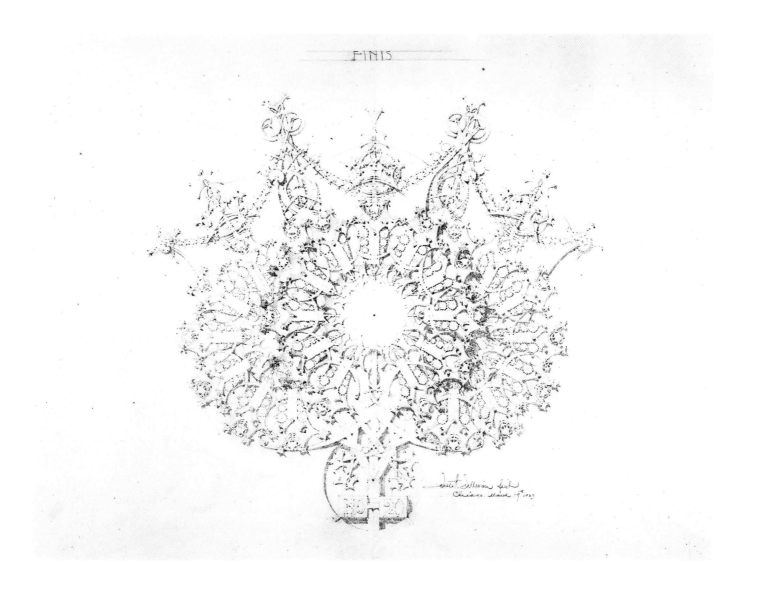

270. *A System of Architectural Ornament According With a Philosophy of Man's Powers,*
Plate 20. Finis (19 March 1923).
Dated and signed *Louis H. Sullivan fecit.*

Pencil on paper (57.5 x 73.5 cm.). Art Institute of Chicago;
commission by Art Institute of Chicago. H, M. 205, Su, Z. 159.

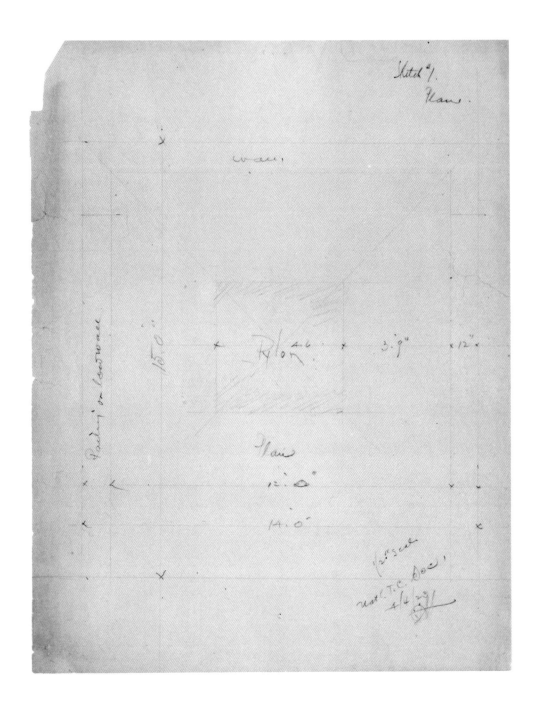

271. National Terra Cotta Society Monument, plan (4 April 1923).
Inscribed on upper right-hand corner: *Sketch #1/Plan*; dimensions and labels on design;
on lower right-hand corner: *1/2" Scale/Natl. T.C. Soc./4/4/23*; *LHS* monogram.

Pencil on paper (27.8 x 21.7 cm.). Art Institute of Chicago; gift of George Grant Elmslie to William Martin,
c. 1932–33; gift of William Martin to Robert Keuny, c. early 1960s; gift of Robert Keuny to University Archives
of the University of Wisconsin–Parkside, late 1960s; gift of Robert Kueny and the University Archives of the
University of Wisconsin–Parkside to Art Institute of Chicago, 1980. M. 183 (noted).

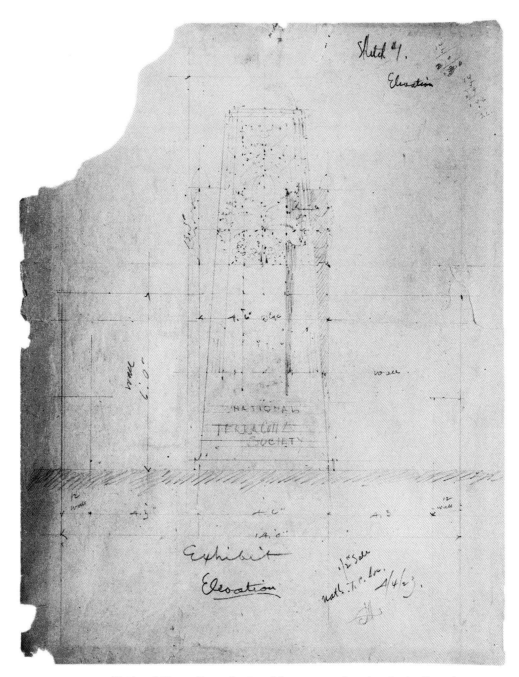

272. National Terra Cotta Society Monument, elevation (4 April 1923).
Inscribed with dimensions around design; on upper right-hand corner of sheet:
Sketch #1/Elevation; on lower center of sheet: *Exhibit/Elevation*; on lower right-hand
corner of sheet: *1/2" Scale/Natl. T. C. Ass.4/4/23/LHS* [monogram].

Pencil on paper (28 x 21.5 cm.). Art Institute of Chicago; gift of George Grant Elmslie to William Martin,
c. 1932–33; gift of William Martin to Robert Keuny, c. early 1960s; gift of Robert Keuny to University
Archives of the University of Wisconsin–Parkside, late 1960s; gift of Robert Kueny and the University
Archives of the University of Wisconsin–Parkside to Art Institute of Chicago, 1980. M. 183.

273. Horse. Undated.

Pencil on paper (31.7 x 19 cm.). Bentley Historical Library, University of Michigan;
gift of George Grant Elmslie, c. 1936, to Emil Lorch, for College of Architecture and
Design, University of Michigan; transferred to Bentley Historical Library, 1972.

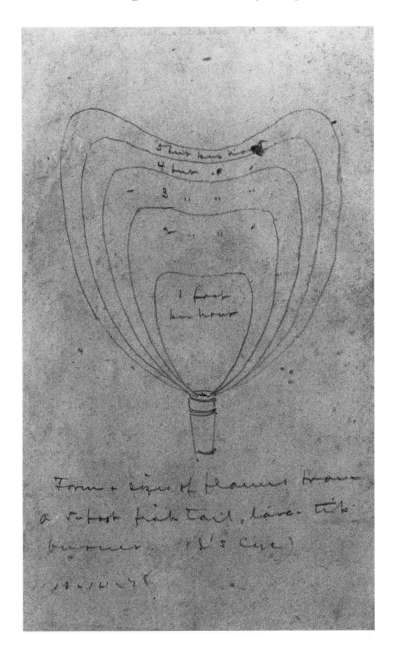

274. Study of a Flame (14 October 1878).
Inscribed on design: *5 feet per hour/4 feet " "/3 " " "/2 " " "/1 foot/per hour*, under
design: *Form + sizes of flames from/a 5-foot fish tail, bare tip/burner (F's Circ.)/10-14-78*.
Pencil on paper (18.2 x 10.2 cm.).
Last known to have been in Avery Library, Columbia University, FLLW/LHS 114;
purchased from Frank Lloyd Wright Foundation, 1965. S. 1. Courtesy of Paul E. Sprague.

275. *Detail.* (Design for frieze of the Wainwright Tomb, 1892.)
Published in *Catalogue, Seventh Annual Exhibition, Chicago Architectural Club.*
Art Institute, Chicago, May MCCCXCIV
(Chicago: Architectural Club, 1894) [page: 22 x 17.2 cm.; image: 9 x 11.4 cm.].
Courtesy of Art Institute of Chicago.

276. *Spring Song–A Decoration* (nude female figure emerging
from botanical motifs) [c. 1893]. Published in *The Chicago
Architectural Annual Published by the Chicago Architectural Club*
(Chicago: Architectural Club, 1902) [9.5 x 6.4 cm]. M. 272 (noted).

Courtesy of Art Institute of Chicago.

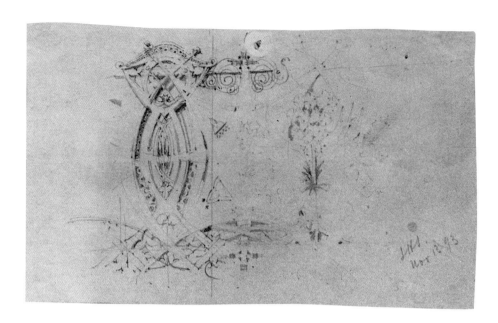

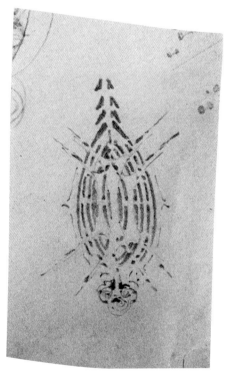

277. Design for ornament (13 November 1893).
Dated and initialed *LHS*.

Pencil on paper (8.3 x 14 cm.). Last known to have been in Avery
Library, Columbia University, FLLW/LHS 112; purchased from Frank
Lloyd Wright Foundation, 1965. S. 58. Courtesy of Paul E. Sprague.

278. Design for ornament [c. 1894].

Pencil on paper (7.9 x 5 cm.). Last known to have been in Avery
Library, Columbia University, FLLW/LHS 108; purchased from Frank
Lloyd Wright Foundation, 1965. S. 82. Courtesy of Paul E. Sprague.

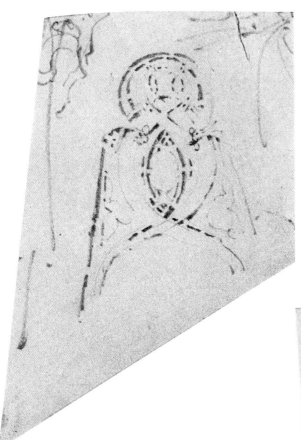

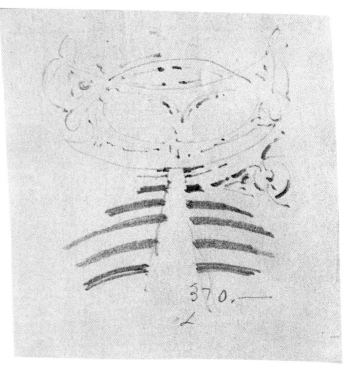

279. Design for ornament [c. 1894].

Pencil on paper (8.5 x 5.6 cm.). Last known to have been in Avery Library, Columbia University, FLLW/LHS 109; purchased from Frank Lloyd Wright Foundation, 1965. S. 83. Courtesy of Paul E. Sprague.

280. Design for ornament [c. 1894]. Inscribed: 370.

Pencil on paper (7.9 x 8.4 cm.). Last known to have been in Avery Library, Columbia University, FLLW/LHS 107; purchased from Frank Lloyd Wright Foundation, 1965. S. 84. Courtesy of Paul E. Sprague.

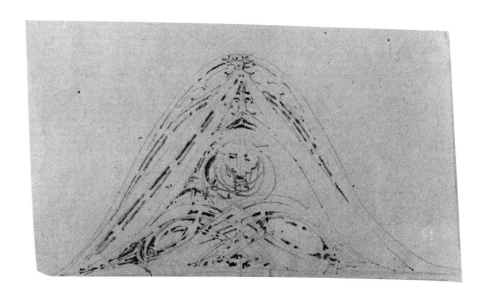

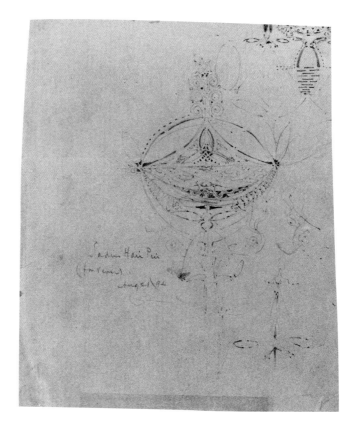

281. Design for ornament [c. 1894].

Pencil on paper (6 x 11.1 cm.). Last known to have been in Avery Library, Columbia University, FLLW/LHS 113; purchased from Frank Lloyd Wright Foundation, 1965. S. 85. Courtesy of Paul E. Sprague.

282. Design for a lady's hair pin (21 August 1894).
Inscribed: *Ladies Hair Pin/(for* [illegible]*)/Aug 21 94.*

Pencil on paper (15.7 x 13.3 cm.). Last known to have been in Avery Library, Columbia University, FLLW/LHS 110; purchased from Frank Lloyd Wright Foundation, 1965. S. 86. Courtesy Paul E. Sprague.

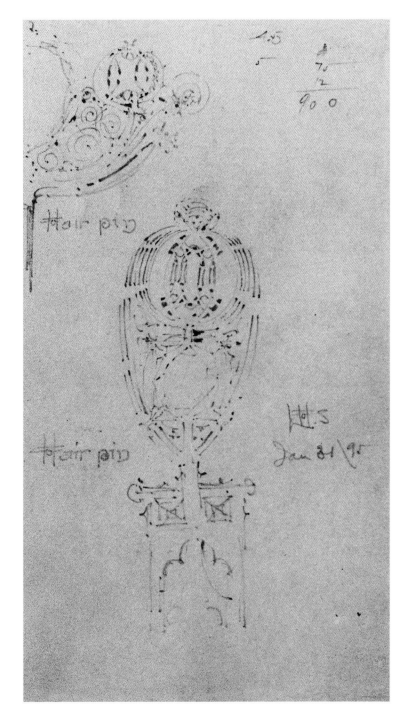

283. Two designs for hair pins (31 January 1895).
Initialed *LHS* [monogram] and dated; inscribed twice: *Hair pin*.

Pencil on paper (13.8 x 7.7 cm.). Last known to have been in Avery Library, Columbia
University, FLLW/LHS 111; purchased from Frank Lloyd Wright Foundation, 1965, S. 88.
Courtesy of Paul E. Sprague.

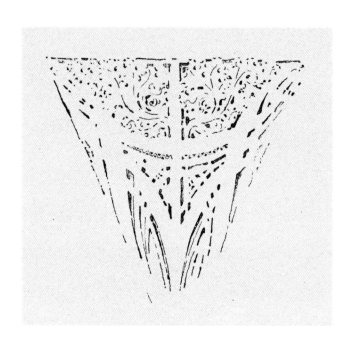

284. Printer's device after ornament of Guaranty Building, Buffalo (c. 1895).

Published in Louis H. Gibson, *Beautiful Houses* (New York and Boston: Thomas Y. Crowell, 1895), p. 89 [page: 22.6 x 16.3 cm.; image: 5.9 x 6.2 cm.]. Courtesy of Tim Samuelson.

285. Printer's device after ornament of Guaranty Building, Buffalo (c. 1895).

Published in Louis H. Gibson, *Beautiful Houses* (New York and Boston: Thomas Y. Crowell, 1895), p. 107 [page: 22. 6 x 16.3 cm.; image: 5.9 x 6.2 cm.]. Courtesy of Tim Samuelson.

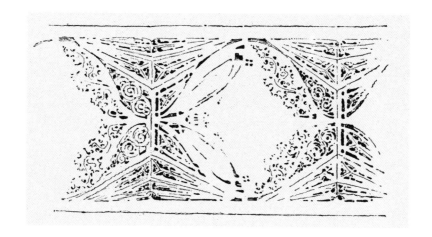

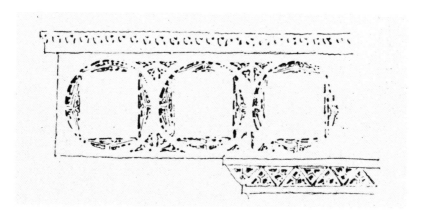

286. Printer's device after ornament of
Guaranty Building, Buffalo (c. 1895).

Published in Louis H. Gibson, *Beautiful Houses*
(New York and Boston: Thomas Y. Crowell, 1895),
p. 210 [page: 22.6 x 16.3 cm.; image: 3.9 x 7.1 cm.].
Courtesy of Tim Samuelson.

287. Printer's device after ornament of
Guaranty Building, Buffalo (c. 1895).

Published in Louis H. Gibson, *Beautiful Houses*
(New York and Boston: Thomas Y. Crowell, 1895),
p. 230 [page: 22.6 x 16.3 cm.; image: 2 x 7.8 cm.].
Courtesy of Tim Samuelson.

288. Printer's device after ornament of
Guaranty Building, Buffalo (c. 1895).

Published in Louis H. Gibson, *Beautiful Houses*
(New York and Boston: Thomas Y. Crowell, 1895),
p. 317 [page: 22.6 x 16.3 cm.; image: 2.4 x 4.9 cm.].
Courtesy of Tim Samuelson.

289. Design for a border inscribed *SWIMMING* [c. 1897].

Published: framing a photograph of Louis Sullivan on the cover of *Cherry Circle* 3 (1 April 1897);
in *Forms & Fantasies* (Chicago) 1 (June 1898); and as the frame of a Certificate of Merit of the First
Class for Swimming, Chicago Athletic Association, in *Interstate Architect and Builder* (Cleveland) 2
(8 December 1900), 8. Dimensions of original unknown.
Courtesy of Art Institute of Chicago.

290. Cover for *Music: A Monthly Magazine* (September 1898).

Blue ink on green paper [24.1 x 16.5 cm.].
All lettering as well as ornamentation within rectangle containing title possibly by others.
Courtesy of Art Institute of Chicago. M. 272 (noted).
(See No. 191 for preliminary sketch of cover.)

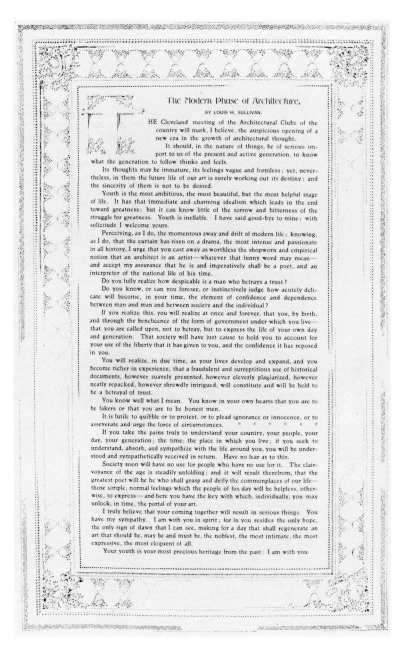

The Modern Phase of Architecture.

BY LOUIS H. SULLIVAN.

HE Cleveland meeting of the Architectural Clubs of the country will mark, I believe, the auspicious opening of a new era in the growth of architectural thought.

It should, in the nature of things, be of serious import to us of the present and active generation, to know what the generation to follow thinks and feels.

Its thoughts may be immature, its feelings vague and formless; yet, nevertheless, in them the future life of our art is surely working out its destiny; and the sincerity of them is not to be denied.

Youth is the most ambitious, the most beautiful, but the most helpful stage of life. It has that immediate and charming idealism which leads in the end toward greatness; but it can know little of the sorrow and bitterness of the struggle for greatness. Youth is ineffable. I have said good-bye to mine; with solicitude I welcome yours.

Perceiving, as I do, the momentous sway and drift of modern life; knowing, as I do, that the curtain has risen on a drama, the most intense and passionate in all history, I urge that you cast away as worthless the shopworn and empirical notion that an architect is an artist—whatever that funny word may mean—and accept my assurance that he is and imperatively shall be a poet, and an interpreter of the national life of his time.

Do you fully realize how despicable is a man who betrays a trust?

Do you know, or can you foresee, or instinctively judge how acutely delicate will become, in your time, the element of confidence and dependence between man and man and between society and the individual?

If you realize this, you will realize at once and forever, that you, by birth, and through the beneficence of the form of government under which you live—that you are called upon, not to betray, but to express the life of your own day and generation. That society will have just cause to hold you to account for your use of the liberty that it has given to you, and the confidence it has reposed in you.

You will realize, in due time, as your lives develop and expand, and you become richer in experience, that a fraudulent and surreptitious use of historical documents, however suavely presented, however cleverly plagiarized, however neatly repacked, however shrewdly intrigued, will constitute and will be held to be a betrayal of trust.

You know well what I mean. You know in your own hearts that you are to be fakers or that you are to be honest men.

It is futile to quibble or to protest, or to plead ignorance or innocence, or to asseverate and urge the force of circumstances. * * * * * *

If you take the pains truly to understand your country, your people, your day, your generation; the time; the place in which you live; if you seek to understand, absorb, and sympathize with the life around you, you will be understood and sympathetically received in return. Have no fear as to this.

Society soon will have no use for people who have no use for it. The clairvoyance of the age is steadily unfolding; and it will result therefrom, that the greatest poet will be he who shall grasp and deify the commonplaces of our life—those simple, normal feelings which the people of his day will be helpless, otherwise, to express—and here you have the key with which, individually, you may unlock, in time, the portal of your art.

I truly believe that your coming together will result in serious things. You have my sympathy. I am with you in spirit; for in you resides the only hope, the only sign of dawn that I can see, making for a day that shall regenerate an art that should be, may be and must be, the noblest, the most intimate, the most expressive, the most eloquent of all.

Your youth is your most precious heritage from the past: I am with you.

291. Border design.

Published in Louis Sullivan, "The Modern Phase of Architecture,"
Inland Architect 33 (June 1899), 40 [32.3 x 22.8 cm.].
Courtesy of Art Institute of Chicago.

292. Border design for Dankmar Adler's memorial portrait.
Published in *Inland Architect* 35 (May 1900), 33 [32.3 x 22.8 cm.].
Courtesy of Art Institute of Chicago.

293. Frontispiece of *The Chicago Architectural Annual Published by the Chicago Architectural Club* (Chicago: Architectural Club, 1902) [18.4 x 17.1 cm.].

Courtesy of Avery Library, Columbia University.

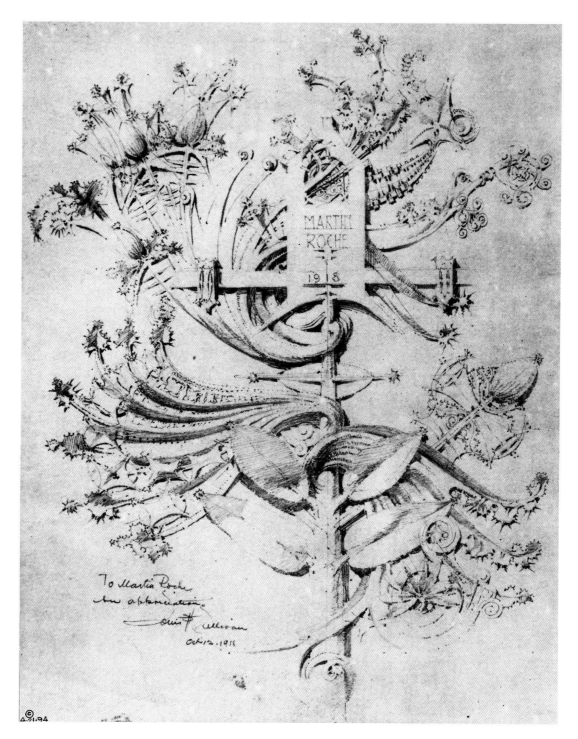

294. Ornamental design (12 October 1918).

Photograph [26 x 19.5 cm.] of a lost drawing.
Inscribed: *To Martin Roche/An Appreciation/Louis H. Sullivan/Oct. 12. 1918.*
Courtesy of William and Karen Schuster, Cedar Rapids, Iowa.

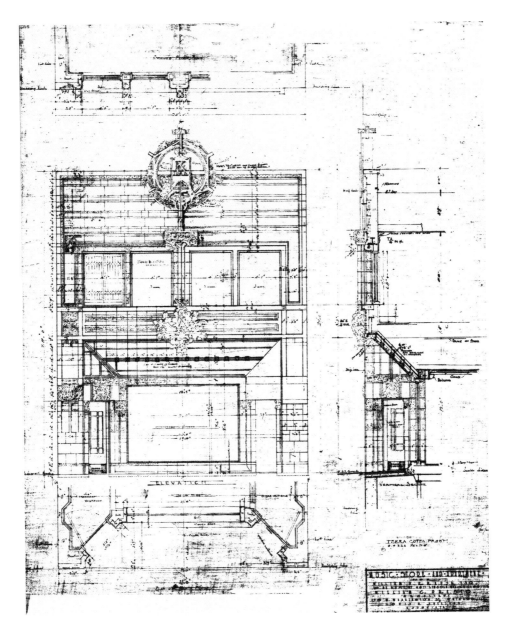

295. Plan, elevation, and section of terra-cotta front, Krause Music Store facade, Chicago, Illinois (25 January 1922). Inscriptions on design concerning dimensions, identification of features of design, and other information relevant to construction; initialed with *LHS* monogram and dated 1/25/22 on lower right-hand edge of sheet; on lower right-hand corner of sheet: *MUSIC STORE AND APARTMENT/FOR/WILLIAM P. KRAUSE, ESQ./TO BE BUILT AT 4611 LINCOLN ST. CHICAGO, ILL./WILLIAM C. PRESTO/ARCHITECT/175 W. WASHINGTON ST. CHICAGO, ILL./ LOUIS H. SULLIVAN/ASSOCATE/SCALE: 1/4" = 1'-0" DATE: FEBRUARY 27, 1922.*

Print of lost original [89 x 62 cm.]. Art Institute of Chicago, gift of Bernard C. Greengard, 1963; early provenance unknown. Courtesy of Art Institute of Chicago. M. 101.

296. The Christmas Spirit of Joy [1923].
Christmas card. Limited edition of 500.
Red proof of cover [14.3 x 10.1 cm., area of image].
Published as insert in *Common Clay*, Chicago,
American Terra-Cotta and Ceramic Company (December 1923). M. 272 (noted).
Courtesy of Art Institute of Chicago.

297. Design of cover for *International: An Illustrated Monthly Magazine*. Undated.

Printed in green and blue ink [26 x 18.4 cm]. M. 272 (noted). Courtesy of Art Institute of Chicago.
(It has not been possible to establish the date of this cover. There are collections of the magazine at the
Harold Washington Library, the Newberry Library, and the Chicago Historical Society Library;
all three removed the covers of the magazines prior to binding them into volumes.)

A Poet's Garden: Louis Sullivan's Vision for America

Portions of "A Poet's Garden" were originally published in different form in "Beyond Chicago: Louis Sullivan and the American West," *Pacific Historical Review* 54 (November 1985), and in "The Piazza in the Garden: Louis Sullivan's Attempt to Decolonize the West," in Rob Kroes, ed., *The American West as Seen by Europeans and Americans,* European Contributions to American Studies 16 (Amsterdam: Free University Press, 1989), or were presented in different form as the following papers:

"The Metaphysics of Louis Sullivan's Ornament," Chicago Historical Society, April 1986; "Tragic Facades: Five Dimensions of Louis Sullivan's Skyscrapers," Sorbonne, Paris, February 1988; "Louis Sullivan: The Vision of His Life," the Scholar's Convocation Address for "Louis Sullivan & the Architecture of Democracy: A Symposium," Grinnell University, Grinnell, Iowa, April 1989; "Louis Sullivan and the Poetry of Cultural Reform," Thomas Hoyne Buell Center for the Study of American Architectural History, Columbia University (New York), November 1989; and "Louis Sullivan's Concept of Democracy," Buell Center, Columbia University, November 1996.

1. Chicago Architect Jack Hartray, quoted in Cheryl Kent, "Minnesota Winners, Architects and Otherwise," *Inland Architect* 32 (January/February 1988): 31.

2. Louis H. Sullivan, "A Letter" (1901), Chat 25 in *Kindergarten Chats and Other Writings,* ed. Isabella Athey (New York: Wittenborn, 1947), 87; Sullivan, "What Is Architecture?" *Craftsman* 10 (May, June, July 1906), reprinted in Robert Twombly, ed., *Louis Sullivan: The Public Papers* (Chicago: University of Chicago Press, 1988), 191–92. Since all Sullivan speeches and essays cited in this text are reproduced in *Public Papers,* in these notes I refer readers to that volume by the initials *PP.*

3. Sullivan's words in section 1 of this essay are from "Natural Thinking, A Study in Democracy" (1904–8), later published as *Democracy, A Man-Search* (Detroit: Wayne State University Press, 1961), Group II, Chapter 2, "The Hermit"; Group II, Chapter 5, "Dance of Death"; and Group III, Chapter 3, "Democracy."

4. For biographical information consult Robert Twombly, *Louis Sullivan: His Life and Work* (New York: Elizabeth Sifton Books/Viking, 1986).

5. Sullivan to Monroe, April 10, 1905, Harriet Monroe Collection, University of Chicago Library.

6. Louis H. Sullivan, *The Autobiography of an Idea* (New York: Press of the American Institute of Architects, 1924), 197.

7. Dankmar Adler, "Autobiography of Dankmar Adler" (c. 1894–95), typescript in the Newberry Library, Chicago.

8. Sullivan's words in the remainder of this section are from *Kindergarten Chats,* 28, 76–78, 109–12. The Chats were published

in *The Interstate Architect and Builder* (Cleveland) in 1901 and 1902. Sullivan revised them in 1918 but they were not published in book form until 1934—Claude Bragdon, ed. (Lawrence, Kan.: Fraternity Press)—and then not definitively until by Isabella Athey (see note 2 above).

9. Ebenezer Howard, *To-morrow: A Peaceful Path to Real Reform* (1898), republished as *Garden Cities of To-morrow,* ed. F. J. Osborn (Cambridge, Mass.: MIT Press, 1965), 48.

10. "What Is Architecture?" (1906), *PP,* 191–92; *Democracy,* 379–80.

11. "Emotional Architecture as Compared with Intellectual: A Study in Subjective and Objective," *Inland Architect and News Record* 24 (November 1894), *PP,* 91.

12. "An Unaffected School of Modern Architecture: Will it Come?" *Artist* 24 (January 1899), and "The Modern Phase of Architecture," *Inland Architect* 33 (June 1899), *PP,* 122, 124–25; also see *Kindergarten Chats,* 87.

13. "Characteristics and Tendencies of American Architecture," *Inland Architect* 6 (November 1885), *PP,* 7.

14. "Emotional Architecture" (1894), *PP,* 92.

15. Unless otherwise noted, quotations in this section are from "May Not Architecture Again Become a Living Art?" (c. 1897), first published in *PP,* 113–18.

16. "Essay on Inspiration," *Inland Architect* 8 (December 1886), *PP,* 23–24.

17. *Real Estate and Building Journal* (Chicago), 31 (January 19, 1887): 35.

18. "What Is the Just Subordination, in Architectural Design, of Detail to Mass?" *Inland Architect* 9 (April 1887), *PP,* 30.

19. Ibid.

20. See O'Gorman, *H. H. Richardson: Architectural Forms for an American Society* (Chicago: University of Chicago Press, 1987), *passim.*

21. Lauro Martines, *Power and Imagination: City-States in Renaissance Italy* (New York: Viking Penguin, 1979), 356–58, 379–82. Also see Richard A. Goldthwaite, *The Building of Renaissance Florence: An Economic and Social History* (Baltimore: Johns Hopkins University Press, 1980), Chapters 1–2 and Conclusion.

22. Jeanne Chase, "Several Remarks on Design's Place in Society," unpublished version of a paper delivered to the Philadelphia College of Art, May 1974, later published in *Metropolis* (Paris).

23. Sullivan to Monroe, April 1905, Harriet Monroe Collection, University of Chicago Library.

24. "Education," *Inland Architect* 39 (June 1902), *PP,* 156.

25. Unless otherwise noted, Sullivan's words in this section are

from "The Tall Office Building Artistically Considered," *Lippincott's Magazine* 57 (March 1896), *PP*, 103–13.

26. "Characteristics and Tendencies" (1885), *PP*, 2–8.

27. *Democracy*, 151.

28. For a different treatment and numerous illustrations of Sullivan's skyscrapers see William Jordy, "The Tall Buildings," in Wim de Wit, ed., *Louis Sullivan: The Function of Ornament* (New York: W. W. Norton, 1986), 65–157.

29. The "false pier," a term that may or may not have been coined by Philip Johnson in "Is Sullivan the Father of Functionalism?" *Art News* 55 (December 1956), was employed by the architect at his Wainwright and Guaranty buildings, at the Burnet House Hotel remodeling, and at one of the Trust and Savings projects. Sullivan used them for visual effect and not as some sort of deception, as Johnson implied, writing during his "modernist" phase.

30. Sigfried Giedion, *Space, Time and Architecture* (1941; Cambridge, Mass.: Harvard Unviersity Press, 1970), 390 (quote), 392.

31. Jordy, "Tall Buildings," 137.

32. Sullivan's words in this section are from "The High Building Question," *The Graphic* 5 (December 19, 1891), *PP*, 76–79.

33. The sketch was not in Sullivan's or in any other professional renderer's hand. Probably drawn for *The Graphic* by an in-house or other commercial engraver, it must nevertheless have satisfied Sullivan, who was always meticulous in publishing matters.

34. "Architecture in Chicago: Adler & Sullivan," *Architectural Record*, special series, 4 (December 1895): 3–48. The Auditorium Building (and other pre-1896 structures mentioned in this essay) was, of course, designed with Dankmar Adler (1844–1900), for whom Sullivan worked part-time, full-time, and as a junior partner before becoming a principal in the reorganized firm of Adler & Sullivan on May 1, 1883. Although each architect had his own areas of responsibility—Adler dealt with clients and most technical matters while Sullivan took charge of facade and decorative design—the partnership was a true collaboration. With few exceptions—Sullivan's 1891 Transportation Building for the 1893 Chicago World's Fair being the most notable—the two developed programs and their components jointly, and neither proceeded in his own realm without closely consulting the other. In the Auditorium Theater, for example, Sullivan's ornamentation was partly determined by Adler's lighting, ventilation, and acoustical requirements, while Adler, in turn, had his own thoughts about the facade composition. Nevertheless, since exteriors were ultimately Sullivan's responsibility, I contend that the "democratic" imagery of their 1883 to 1895 partnership was entirely his. In omitting reference to Adler in this connection, I hope not to do him injustice.

35. "Natural Thinking" (1908), published as *Democracy* (1961), 377.

36. Sullivan's essay is "Lighting the People's Savings Bank,

Cedar Rapids, Iowa: An Example of American Twentieth Century Ideas of Architecture and Illumination," *Illuminating Engineer* 6 (February 1912), *PP*, 205–8.

37. Hofstadter's analysis appears in "Beard and the Constitution," *American Quarterly* 2 (Fall 1950): 195–213; *The Age of Reform: From Bryan to FDR* (New York: Alfred A. Knopf, 1961), especially p. 200; and *The Progressive Historians: Turner, Beard, Parrington* (New York: Alfred A. Knopf, 1968), especially p. 184.

38. "The Image of Progressive Banking" in de Wit, ed., *Function of Ornament*, 159–97.

39. Sullivan's words in this section are from the foreword to *Suggestions in Artistic Brick* (St. Louis: Hydraulic-Press Brick Co., c. 1910), *PP*, 200–205.

40. Quoted in Linda Mason Hunter, "A Lesson in Democracy," *Inland Architect* 35 (September/October 1991): 24. The most comprehensive account of the banks is Lauren Weingarden, *Louis H. Sullivan: The Banks* (Cambridge, Mass.: MIT Press, 1987).

41. Sullivan's words in this and the following paragraphs are from "Ornament in Architecture," *Engineering Magazine* 3 (August 1892), *PP*, 79–85.

42. Narciso Menocal, *Architecture as Nature: The Transcendentalist Idea of Louis Sullivan* (Madison: University of Wisconsin Press, 1981), especially section 2.

43. Twombly, *Louis Sullivan*, 103–5.

44. Menocal, *Architecture as Nature*, 106–11. On the Goodrich, McCormick, and Bennett projects, I am indebted to Menocal's analyses.

45. Quoted in Robert A. Warn, "Louis H. Sullivan: '. . . an air of finality,'" *Prairie School Review* 10 (Fourth Quarter 1973): 9.

46. Larry Millett, *The Curve of the Arch: The Story of Louis Sullivan's Owatonna Bank* (St. Paul: Minnesota Historical Society Press, 1985), 9, 11.

47. Quoted in ibid., 110.

48. Quoted in Warn, "Louis H. Sullivan," 10.

49. Menocal, *Architecture as Nature*, 126.

50. Warn, "Louis H. Sullivan," 8; quoting Fitch, 9.

51. Ibid., 11; H. Allen Brooks, *The Prairie School: Frank Lloyd Wright and His Midwest Contemporaries* (Toronto: University of Toronto Press, 1972), 228; Millett, *Curve of the Arch*, 108.

52. Quoted in Warn, "Louis H. Sullivan," 10.

53. Quoted in Menocal, *Architecture as Nature*, 120.

54. Published in "On Scholarship" (Kindergarten Chat 40), *Interstate Architect and Builder* (1901), repr. Athey, ed., *Kindergarten Chats*, 130, 248. Here Sullivan replied to Robert S. Peabody, the AIA president, who in his address had attacked Sullivan for his remarks about architectural educators published in the *Chicago Tribune* and then as "Reality in the Architectural Art" in *Interstate Architect and Builder* 2 (August 11, 1900), *PP*, 144–49.

55. These projects were described in the *Chicago Tribune* (February 14, 1908) p. 1; and *Real Estate and Building Journal* (Chicago), 42 (February 15, 1908): 11 and 43 (March 6, 1909): 7. Visual depictions apparently no longer exist.

56. Between 1896 and 1902, Sullivan produced at least seven schemes for the expanding Schlesinger & Mayer Store, of which two, from 1898 and 1902, constitute his portion of the present Carson Pirie Scott Store. For an excellent analysis see Joseph Siry, *Carson Pirie Scott: Louis Sullivan and the Chicago Department Store* (Chicago: University of Chicago Press, 1988). Sullivan's accounts—in part attempts to demonstrate his technical expertise in order to generate new commissions—are "Sub-structure at the New Schlesinger & Mayer Store Building, Chicago," *Engineering Record* 47 (February 21, 1903), *PP*, 158–67, and "Basements and Sub-basements," *Economist* (Chicago), 31 (February 20, 1904), *PP*, 167–69.

57. Christopher Lasch, *The New Radicalism in America, 1889–1963: The Intellectual as a Social Type* (New York: Alfred A. Knopf, 1965), xiv–xv.

The Iconography of Architecture: Sullivan's View

Introduction

1. Xavier Zubiri, *Naturaleza, historia, Dios* (Madrid: Editora Nacional, 1944), 492–93, 507.

2. Plato, *Epinomis* 975.b-c, in *The Collected Dialogues of Plato, Including the Letters*, ed. Edith Hamilton and Huntington Cairns, Bollingen Series LXXI (New York: Pantheon, 1961), 1518–19.

3. Ralph Waldo Emerson, "Thoughts on Art" (January 1841), in *The Works of Ralph Waldo Emerson*, 4 vols. (New York: Tudor, n.d.), 4:56–71; quotation, 64.

4. George Grant Elmslie (1871–1952), born in a farm near Huntley, Scotland, was Sullivan's assistant for many years. He arrived in Chicago with his family in 1884, at age thirteen. Four years later, in 1888, he entered the office of J. Lyman Silsbee, where he met Frank Lloyd Wright, and a year later went on to Adler & Sullivan, becoming chief draftsman in 1893 and then staying on with Louis Sullivan until 1909. Becoming Sullivan's "right hand," Elmslie was responsible for ornamental designs for major Sullivan buildings as well as for the design of the Henry Babson house in Riverside, Illinois (1907), and the Harold and Josephine Crane Bradley house in Madison, Wisconsin (1909). After leaving Sullivan, he joined into a partnership with William Gray Purcell and George Feick Jr. in Minneapolis. The 1909 firm of Purcell, Feick & Elmslie became Purcell & Elmslie in 1913 and dissolved in 1922. Purcell and Elmslie were responsible for important Prairie School public buildings and residences. See, by David Gebhard, "William Gray Purcell and George Grant Elmslie and the Early Progressive Movement from 1900 to 1920" (Ph.D. diss., University of Minnesota, 1957); *Purcell and Elmslie: Architects* (Minneapolis, Minn.: Walker Art Center, 1953; *A Guide to the Existing Buildings of Purcell and Elmslie* (Roswell, N.M.: Roswell Museum and Art Center, 1960); "Louis Sullivan and George Grant Elmslie," *Journal of the Society of Architectural Historians* 19 (1960): 62–68; *The Work of Elmslie and Purcell, Architects* (Park Forest, Ill.: Prairie School Press, 1965); "Purcell and Elmslie, Architects," *Prairie School Review* 2 (First Quarter 1965): 5–15; and "A Guide to the Architecture of Purcell and Elmslie," *ibid.*, 16–24. See also H. Allen Brooks, *The Prairie School: Frank Lloyd Wright and His Midwestern Contemporaries* (Toronto: University of Toronto Press, 1972).

1: Normative Years: 1872–80

1. For French romantic rationalism, see, by Neil Levine, "Architectural Reasoning in the Age of Positivism: The Néo-Grec Idea of Henri Labrouste's Bibliothèque Sainte-Geneviève" (Ph.D. diss., Yale University, 1975); "The Romantic Idea of Architectural Legibility: Henri Labrouste and the Neo-Grec," in Arthur Drexler, ed., *The Architecture of the Ecole des Beaux-Arts* (New York: Museum of Modern Art, 1977); and "The Competition for the Grand Prix in 1824," in Robin Middleton (ed.), *The Beaux-Arts and Nineteenth Century French Architecture* (Cambridge, Mass.: MIT Press, 1982). By David Van Zanten, see "Architectural Composition at the Ecole des Beaux-Arts from Percier to Charles Garnier," in Drexler; "Félix Duban and the Buildings of the Ecole des Beaux-Arts," *Journal of the Society of Architectural Historians* 37 (October 1978): 161–74; and *Designing Paris: The Architecture of Duban, Labrouste, Duc, and Vaudoyer* (Cambridge, Mass.: MIT Press, 1987). There are other essays relevant to the question in Drexler and Middleton. Another useful work is Donald Drew Egbert, *The Beaux-Arts Tradition in France*, ed. David Van Zanten (Princeton, N.J.: Princeton University Press, 1980). For Sullivan and French romantic rationalism, see Van Zanten, "Sullivan to 1890," in Wim de Wit, ed., *Louis Sullivan: The Function of Ornament* (New York: W. W. Norton, 1986), 13–55.

2. John Ruskin, "The Lamp of Obedience" VII, *The Seven Lamps of Architecture*, 2nd ed. (London: Smith, Elder, and Co., 1855), 192. In "The Lamp of Power" I (p. 57), Ruskin makes a distinction between the beautiful and the sublime in architecture: "In thus reverting to the memories of those works of architecture by which we have been most pleasurably impressed, it will generally happen that they fall into two broad classes: the one characterized by an exceeding preciousness and delicacy, to which we recur with a sense of affectionate admiration; and the other by a severe, and, in many cases mysterious, majesty, which we remember with an undiminished awe, like that felt at the presence and operation of some great Spiritual Power." All four styles Ruskin recommended so that they would progressively lead architects into an English style fell within the category of the beautiful, as he described it.

3. Robert Twombly, *Louis Sullivan: His Life and Work* (New York: Elizabeth Sifton Books/Viking, 1986), 26–27.

4. For the school of architecture at MIT, see Caroline Shillaber, *Massachusetts Institute of Technology, School of Architecture and Planning, 1861–1961: A Hundred Year Chronicle* (Cambridge, Mass.: MIT Press, 1963).

5. William R. Ware, *Modern Perspective: A Treatise Upon the Principles and Practice of Plane and Cylindrical Perspective* (Boston: J. R. Osgood, 1883); Ware, *Shades and Shadows, with Applications to Architectural Details, and Exercises in Drawing Them with the Brush or Pen*, 2 vols. (Scranton: International Textbook Company, 1912–13); and Ware, *The American Vignola*, 2 vols. (Boston: American Architect and Building News Company, 1902–6).

6. Shillaber, *Massachusetts Institute of Technology*, 12–15.

7. Louis Sullivan, *The Autobiography of an Idea* (New York: Press of the American Institute of Architects, 1924), 185.

8. Ibid., 188.

9. Ibid., 187.

10. Ibid., 188.

11. Ibid. For some of Sullivan's school drawings of the orders see the Catalogue of the Drawings, pls. 3–6.

12. Sullivan, *Autobiography*, 188.

13. Ruskin, "The Lamp of Power" I–VI, *Seven Lamps of Architecture*, 61–69.

14. Henry-Russell Hitchcock, "Foreign Influences in American Painting and Architecture," in John K. Howat, ed., *The Shaping of Art and Architecture in Nineteenth-Century America* (New York: Metropolitan Museum of Art, 1972), 59.

15. Sullivan, *Autobiography*, 189.

16. Ibid., 189–90.

17. Twombly, *Louis Sullivan*, 39.

18. For the Moore house, see George E. Thomas et al., eds., *Frank Furness: The Complete Works* (New York: Princeton Architectural Press, 1991), 169.

19. Sullivan, *Autobiography*, 193. For Notman, see Constance M. Greiff, *John Notman, Architect: 1810–1865* (Philadelphia: The Athenaeum of Philadelphia, 1979). There is no monograph on George Watson Hewitt (1841–1916); entry in Henry F. Withey and Elsie Rathburn Withey, *Biographical Dictionary of American Architects (Deceased)* (Los Angeles: Hennessey & Ingalls, 1970), 282.

20. For Furness's body of work in 1873, see Thomas et al., eds., *Frank Furness*, 160–80.

21. Sullivan, *Autobiography*, 193.

22. For information on the Union Banking Company Building, see Thomas et al., eds., *Frank Furness*, 176.

23. Sullivan, *Autobiography*, 197.

24. Ibid., 202.

25. However, on the issue of aesthetic economy one must remember that to cut down cost the design was reduced from eight floors to four and a mansard roof was deleted.

26. Theodore Turak, *William Le Baron Jenney: A Pioneer of Modern Architecture* (Ann Arbor, Mich.: UMI Research Press, 1986), 169.

27. Sullivan, *Autobiography of an Idea*, 202. There is no monograph on Adolph Cudell (1850–1910). He was born in Aachen, was educated in Germany, and settled in Chicago as a young man. He is best known for his residential work, among which were the Louvre-inspired mansion of Cyrus McCormick on Rush Street (1877) and later, when he was associated with the Hungarian Arthur Hercz, the very grand German rococo Francis Dewes residence on Wrightwood Avenue (1896). Richard E. Schmidt, Hugh Garden's partner, served an apprenticeship under Cudell. For Cudell, see Withey, *Biographical Dictionary*, 152; John Drury, *Old Chicago Houses* (Chicago: University of Chicago Press, 1941), 97–101, 340–43; and John Zukowsky, ed., *Chicago Architecture, 1872–1922: Birth of a Metropolis* (Munich: Prestel-Verlag, in association with the Art Institute of Chicago, 1987), 98, 100, 437.

28. Turak, *William Le Baron Jenney*, 169.

29. This point is made in ibid., 166.

30. Ibid., 134.

31. Sullivan, *Autobiography of an Idea*, 203.

32. Sigfried Giedion, *Space, Time and Architecture: The Growth of a New Tradition* (1941; Cambridge, Mass.: Harvard University Press, 1967), 370–72; Carl W. Condit, *The Chicago School of Architecture: A History of Commercial and Public Buildings in the Chicago Area, 1875-1925* (Chicago: University of Chicago Press, 1964), 79–94. Condit's book is a revised and enlarged version of his earlier *The Rise of the Skyscraper* (Chicago: University of Chicago Press, 1952).

33. As an example, see Giedion, *Space, Time, and Architecture*, 371.

34. Sullivan, *Autobiography of an Idea*, 203–4.

35. Twombly, *Louis Sullivan*, 55.

36. Richard Chafee, "The Teaching of Architecture at the Ecole des Beaux-Arts," in Arthur Drexler, ed., *The Architecture of the Ecole des Beaux-Arts* (New York: Museum of Modern Art, 1977), 82.

37. Van Zanten, "Sullivan to 1890," 26.

38. At age twenty-five, in 1854, Joseph-Auguste-Emile Vaudremer (1829–1914) won a Grand Prix at the Ecole des Beaux-Arts with the design of a tomb based on Hadrian's Mausoleum, a building that was the subject for his fourth-year *envoi* from the French Academy in Rome, an assigned archaeological study. After working under Victor Baltard and Félix Duban, the architect of the Ecole des Beaux-Arts buildings and one of the principal practitioners of romantic rationalism, Vaudremer was appointed city architect in the thirteenth and fourteenth arrondissements in Paris. Principally an architect of churches (Saint-Pierre de Montrouge and Notre-Dame d'Auteuil) and *lycées* (high schools), Vaudremer delighted in making manifest, volumetrically, the different parts of a building, following a hierarchy of functions; and in expressing the supportive character of walls, which he would render as large planes and volumes of masonry with as little ornamentation as possible. In his obituary of Vaudremer, Loys Brachet wrote:

"In his architecture Vaudremer has a certain sincerity, often to the point of ingenuousness, a loyalty to his point of view which has the coldness of a demonstrated theorem, or of a constructive syllogism where the premises and the conclusions are absolutely clear. But in this architecture is apparent a forceful truth of expression as between the exterior and the interior of his buildings, between the plan and its elevations, which is insisted upon minutely and rigorously, without motives introduced for effect only." In his summary paragraph, Brachet also wrote that Vaudremer's work "breathes a deep breath of truth, of moral and material honesty." For Vaudremer, see Jacques Hermant, "Emile Vaudremer," *L'Architecture* 27 (1914), 65–68; Louis Hautecoeur, *Histoire de l'architecture classique en France*, vol. 7 (Paris: Picard, 1957), 360–71; and Barry Bergdol, "Emil Vaudremer," in Adolf K. Placzek, ed., *Macmillan Encyclopedia of Architects* (New York: Free Press, 1982), 4:301. For Loy Brachet's obituary of Vaudremer, see *Journal of the American Institute of Architects* 3 (July 1915): 294–98. This is part of a group of three obituaries appearing under the title "Emile Vaudremer," 293–99.

39. Louis Sullivan to Albert Sullivan, 7 December 1874, quoted in Willard Connely, *Louis Sullivan: The Shaping of American Architecture* (New York: Horizon Press, 1960), 61–63; this quotation, 62.

40. Louis Sullivan to Albert Sullivan, 7 December 1874.

41. Sullivan, *Autobiography*, 238. The announcement of the competition for the Church of the Sacré-Coeur was published while Sullivan was in Paris. See *Revue générale d'architecture et des travaux publiques* 31 (1874): 47.

42. Sullivan, *Autobiography*, 239.

43. For Ernest-Georges Coquard (1831–1903), see Louis Hautecoeur, *Histoire de l'architecture classique en France*, vol. 7, *La fin de l'architecture classique, 1848–1900* (Paris: Editions A. et J. Picard et Cie., 1957), 424. For Coquard's work as architect of the Ecole des Beaux-Arts, see C. Marmoz, "The Building of the École des Beaux-Arts," in Robin Middleton, ed., *The Beaux-Arts and Nineteenth-Century French Architecture* (Cambridge, Mass.: MIT Press, 1982), 134.

44. A chronology of events of that year in Paris is as follows. 11 July 1874: Sullivan sails from New York aboard the SS *Britannic*; passage takes ten days. Arrives in Liverpool, where he stays for one or two days. Spends two weeks in London. Arrives in Paris in mid-August not knowing the nature of the entrance exams at the Ecole, finds a room in the attic of 17 rue Racine at the corner of rue Monsieur-le-Prince, near the Boulevard Saint-Michel; on advice of the American Legation, engages Monsieur Clopet as instructor of mathematics; also engages in succession three instructors of French "to acquire the language of the man on the street." On 11 September, Emile Vaudremer (Eugène Letang's *patron* and consequently the architect whose atelier former MIT students favored) sponsors Sullivan's application to the Ecole. 24 September: Passes the entrance examinations. 22 October: Formally admitted at the Ecole; enrolls in Vaudremer's atelier, where there were three other Americans. 29 November: Date of first

design of fresco for Edelmann. 7 December: Date of a pen-and-ink sketch of a landscape and of faces of popular types. That same day: Letter to his brother, Albert, saying that he is working on a design project due on 28 December. 18 January 1875: Possible date for his finishing reading vol. 1 of Taine's *Philosophie de l'art* (another possible date is in August–September 1874, "during his preparatory work"). Mid-January to mid-March: Possible period for travels. Visit to Italy prompted by his reading of Taine (three days in Rome and six weeks in Florence), followed by trip to the Riviera and Nice. Mid-March: Back in Paris. 29 March: Date of eight pen-and-ink drawings of brothel scenes, a cocotte and a painter, and models. 1 April: Date of second design of fresco for Edelmann. Early May: Leaves Paris. 24 May 1875: Arrives in New York. This chronology has been culled from Sullivan, *Autobiography*, 213–40; Twombly, *Louis Sullivan*, 55–76; Van Zanten, "Sullivan to 1890," 13–55; Connely, *Louis Sullivan*, 54–68; Paul Sprague, *The Drawings of Louis Henry Sullivan* (Princeton, N.J.: Princeton University Press, 1979), 23–24; and Sarah C. Mollman, ed., *Louis Sullivan in the Art Institute of Chicago: The Illustrated Catalogue of Collections* (New York: Garland, 1989), 229–32.

45. Some religious buildings were designed and constructed, such as Moody's Tabernacle and the Sinai Synagogue by Johnston and Edelmann, as well as Patrick Keely's Holy Name Cathedral (1874–75); St. James's Church (1875–80); and St. Stanislaus Kostka's Church (1877–81). Also during this period Willcox and Miller built the Olivet Baptist Church (1875–76). See George A. Lane, *Chicago Churches and Synagogues* (Chicago: Loyola University Press, 1981), 36–43.

46. For information on the frescoes, see Twombly, *Louis Sullivan*, 87–92. Sullivan began developing ideas for the frescoes in Paris (Catalogue, pls. 9, 11–13, 27) and continued working on them after he arrived in the United States (pl. 39). In January 1876 he was working on the fresco of the Sinai Synagogue (pls. 40–42). The pen-and-ink drawing of May 1876 may also be for the synagogue (pl. 43).

47. Sullivan, *Autobiography*, 246–49. For the Eads Bridge, see Carl W. Condit, *American Building Art: The Nineteenth Century* (New York: Oxford University Press, 1960), 185–90. For the bridge at Dixville, see ibid., 155–56.

48. Twombly, *Louis Sullivan*, 92, 94–96.

49. This was not true; Edelmann was still in Cleveland at that time. See Donald D. Egbert and Paul E. Sprague, "In Search of John Edelmann," *Journal of the American Institute of Architects* 45 (February 1966): 37.

50. Sullivan, *Autobiography*, 255–57. In fact, Sullivan places the partnership of Johnston and Edelmann at this time rather than in 1874–76. He also misnamed Johnston, calling him "Johnson." Ibid., 255.

51. Twombly, *Louis Sullivan*, 92. William L. Strippelman (1843–1912) was born in Germany and studied at the University of Marburg. He came to the United States at age nineteen, arriving in Nashville, Tennessee, shortly before the Civil War. After the war, Strippelman worked in New Orleans first and then in Galveston, Texas. He arrived in Chicago in 1868 and

stayed there the rest of his life, designing mostly stores and industrial buildings. Strippelman does not appear in any of the standard histories of Chicago architecture. For a note on his life see Withey, *Biographical Dictionary,* 580.

2: A Search for an Architecture: 1880–93

1. For Adler's role as designer of buildings in the firm, see my dissertation, "Louis Sullivan: His Theory, Mature Development, and Theme" (Urbana: University of Illinois, 1974), 51–60.

2. Hugh Morrison, *Louis Sullivan: Prophet of Modern Architecture* (New York: W. W. Norton, 1935), 295.

3. Mardges Bacon, *Ernest Flagg: Beaux-Arts Architect and Urban Reformer* (New York: Architectural History Foundation, 1986), 175–83.

4. Hans Frei, *Louis Henry Sullivan* (Zürich: Artemis Verlags-AG, 1992), 29.

5. See Margot Gayle and Edmund V. Gillon Jr., *Cast-Iron Architecture in New York* (New York: Dover, 1974), 86–87, 140–41.

6. *Revue générale de l'architecture et des travaux publics* 16 (1858), cols. 46, 73–78, 115–26; pls. 15–20. The house was commissioned in June 1856 (col. 76); the facade carried the date of 1857, in Roman numerals, on the pediment (pl. 16). For information on the history of the rue Malesherbes, where the house stands, see Jacques Hillairet, *Dictionnaire historique des rues de Paris,* 2 vols. (Paris: Editions de Minuit, 1963), 2:93. Antoine-Anatole Jal was born in Paris on 20 September 1823, entered the Ecole des Beaux-Arts on 27 November 1846 as a student of Vaudoyer's, presented a *Projet d'une maison de commissaire de police, pour chacun des quartiers de la ville de Paris* at the Salon of 1850, and died at the age of forty-two in May 1866. For Jal, see Emile Bellier de la Chavignerie, *Dictionnaire générale des artistes de l'école française,* 2 vols. (Paris: Librairie Renouard, 1882), 1:818, and Louis Hautecoeur, *Histoire de l'architecture classique en France,* vol. 7, *La fin de l'architecture classique, 1848–1900* (Paris: Editions A. et J. Picard et Cie., 1957), 387; for Jollivet, see mainly Ulrich Thieme and Felix Becker, eds., *Allgemeines Lexikon der Bildenden Künstler* (Leipzig: Verlag von E. a. Seemann, 1926), 19:104–5, and David Van Zanten, "Jacques Ignace Hittorf," in Adolf Placzek, ed., *Macmillan Encyclopedia of Architects* (New York: Free Press, 1982), 2:393. I am grateful to Christopher Henige for photographing the house. For Baudelaire's review of *Le Massacre des Innocents,* a painting by Jollivet, see Charles Baudelaire, *Salon de 1845,* in Charles Baudelaire, *Oeuvres complètes,* texte établi et annoté par Y.-G. Le Dantec (Paris: Bibliothèque de la Pléiade, 1961), 835.

7. Hautecoeur, *Histoire de l'architecture 7:* 388.

8. Item 189 in *Auction Catalogue of the Household Effects, Library, Oriental Rugs, Paintings, Etc. of Louis H. Sullivan, Nov. 29 1909* (Chicago: Williams, Barker & Severn Company, 1909), Burnham Library, Art Institute of Chicago.

9. Egbert and Sprague, "In Search of John Edelmann," 41.

10. His system of construction presented extraordinary features. See Morrison, *Louis Sullivan,* 89–99.

11. Egbert and Sprague, "In Search of John Edelmann," 39.

12. See William H. Jordy, *American Buildings and Their Architects,* vol. 3, *Progressive and Academic Ideals at the Turn of the Twentieth Century* (Garden City, N.Y.: Doubleday, 1972), 110–11 and fig. 50.

13. Sullivan, "Characteristics and Tendencies of American Architecture" (1885), in Sullivan, *Kindergarten Chats and Other Writings,* ed. Isabella Athey (New York: Wittenborn, 1947), 179, 178.

14. Sullivan to Claude Bragdon, 8 November 1903, in Claude Bragdon, "Letters from Louis Sullivan," *Architecture* 64 (July 1931), 9; Wright, *Genius and the Mobocracy* (1949; New York: Horizon, 1971), 75; Elmslie to William Gray Purcell, undated draft of a letter marked "Revision No. 1," Northwest Architectural Archives, University of Minnesota.

15. Among other buildings, one thinks of Biagio Rossetti's Palazzo dei Diamanti, Giuliano da Sangallo's Palazzo Strozzi, Raphael's Villa Madama, Peruzzi's Villa Farnesina, Giulio Romano's Palazzo del Tè, and Sansovino's Library of St. Mark's and Palazzo Corner della Cà Grande.

16. Vitruvius, Bk. III, ch. 3.

17. Montgomery Schuyler, "Architecture in Chicago: Adler & Sullivan," in Montgomery Schuyler, *American Architecture and Other Writings,* ed. William H. Jordy and Ralph Coe, 2 vols. (Cambridge, Mass.: Belknap Press/Harvard University Press, 1961), 2:390.

18. Eugène Viollet-le-Duc, *Discourses on Architecture,* trans. Benjamin Bucknall, 2 vols. (Boston: Ticknor, n.d.), 2:128.

19. This paragraph contains a revised version of an argument I presented in my *Architecture as Nature: The Transcendentalist Idea of Louis Sullivan* (Madison: University of Wisconsin Press, 1981), 46–50.

20. Montgomery Schuyler, "Architecture in Chicago: Adler & Sullivan," in Montgomery Schuyler, *American Architecture,* 2:390; Barr Ferree, "The High Building and Its Art," *Scribner's Magazine* 15 (March 1894): 297–318, and "The Modern Office Building," *Inland Architect* 27 (February 1896): 4–5, (April 1896): 23–25, (May 1896): 34–35, and (June 1896): 45–47.

21. Louis Sullivan, *The Autobiography of an Idea,* (New York: Press of the American Institute of Architects, 1924), 298.

22. Claude Bragdon, "Louis H. Sullivan," *Journal of the American Institute of Architects* 12 (May 1924): 241; Robert Craik McLean, "Louis Henry Sullivan: An Appreciation," *Western Architect* 23 (May 1924): 53–55; Frank Lloyd Wright, "Louis Sullivan: Beloved Master," ibid. (June 1924): 63–66; Irving K. Pond, "Louis Sullivan's *The Autobiography of an Idea:* A Review and an Estimate," ibid., 67–69; Wallace Rice, "Louis Sullivan as Author," ibid., 70–71; and Fiske Kimball, "Louis Sullivan: An Old Master," *Architectural Record* 57 (April 1925): 289–304.

23. W. A. Starrett, *Skyscrapers and the Men Who Build Them* (New York: Charles Scribner's Sons, 1928); and Francisco Mujica, *History of the Skyscraper* (1929; New York: DaCapo Press, 1977).

24. Erich Mendelsohn, *Amerika: Bilderbuch eines Architekten* (Berlin: R. Mosse, 1928), 178: "In vielem noch abhängig von der Ueberlieferung, aber doch schon ein ehrlicher Versuch, den neuen Bedingungen auch in der Form gerecht zu werden." While on first inspection there would seem to be no possible relationship between the Neue Sachlichkeit and Mendelsohn's opinion on Sullivan's architecture, an indirect connection might be established. The Neue Sachlichkeit, as a mid-1920s pictorial movement, insisted on "objectivity" partly as a reaction against Expressionism. It also influenced photographers, making them more conscious of their subject as an object instead of as a metaphorical entity standing for something else. This is the kind of photography that Mendelsohn took for his *Amerika: Bilderbuch eines Architekten*. While there is no study as yet on the relationship of the Neue Sachlichkeit and architecture, it might be argued that the insistence on "objectivity" was a factor in the new views on functionalism that appeared in the late 1920s and then colored the architecture of the 1930s. For the Neue Sachlichkeit, see Hans-Jurgen Buderer, *Neue Sachlichkeit, Bilder auf der Suche nach der Wirlichkeit: Figurative Malerei der Zwanziger Jahre* (Munich: Prestel, 1994); Wolf-Dieter Dube, *The Expressionists,* trans. Mary Whittall (London: Thames & Hudson, 1972); Jost Hermand, "Unity within Diversity? The History of the Concept 'Neue Sachlichkeit,'" in Keith Bullivant, ed., *Culture and Society in the Weimar Republic* (Manchester, Britain: Manchester University Press, 1977), 166–82; Helmut Lethen, *Neue Sachlichkeit: 1924–1932* (Stuttgart: Metzler, 1975); Orrel P. Reed, Jr., *German Expressionist Art* (Los Angeles: University of California/Frederick S. Wight Art Gallery, 1977); and Peter Vergo, *Twentieth-Century German Painting* (New York: Rizzoli, 1992). For the relationship of the Neue Sachlichkeit and photography, see Sergiusz Michalski, *Neue Sachlichkeit: Malerei, Graphik, und Photographie in Deutschland, 1919–1923* (Cologne: B. Taschen, 1992).

25. Frank Lloyd Wright, *An Autobiography* (New York: Longmans, Green, 1932), 267.

26. Morrison, *Louis Sullivan,* 154.

27. Sullivan, "The Tall Office Building Artistically Considered," *Kindergarten Chats,* 202–13.

28. Ibid., 208.

29. Ibid., 203.

30. Morrison, *Louis Sullivan,* 147.

31. Irving K. Pond, "Louis Sullivan's 'The Autobiography of an Idea': A Review and an Estimate," *Western Architect* 33 (June 1924): 67–69.

32. Ibid., 69.

33. Schuyler, "Architecture in Chicago," 2:390.

34. Robert Twombly, *Louis Sullivan: His Life and Work* (New York: Elizabeth Sifton Books/Viking, 1986), 284–85.

35. Sullivan to Claude Bragdon, 8 November 1903, in Bragdon, "Letters from Louis Sullivan," *Architecture* 64 (July 1931): 9.

36. Paul Goldberger, *The Skyscraper* (New York: Knopf, 1982), 18.

37. William C. Maclintock, J. P. Ellacott, and Norman Totten, "Fraternity Temple: An Announcement to the Independent Order of Odd Fellows of Chicago and the State of Illinois" (September 1891), a brochure partially reproduced in *Industrial Chicago,* 2 vols. (Chicago: Goodspeed Publishing Company, 1891), 2:593–95, and "Plans for the Odd Fellows Temple," *Chicago Tribune,* 6 September 1891, p. 29, quoted in Twombly, *Louis Sullivan,* 302.

38. Morrison, *Louis Sullivan,* 303.

39. Twombly, *Louis Sullivan,* 315.

3: Genesis of an Iconography

1. For the story of the publishing of *The Autobiography of an Idea,* see George E. Pettengill, "The Biography of a Book: Correspondence Between Sullivan and *The Journal,*" *AIA Journal* 63 (June 1975), 42–45.

2. Sherman Paul, *Louis Sullivan: An Architect in American Thought* (Englewood Cliffs, N.J.: Prentice-Hall, 1962), 132.

3. Charles Whitaker to Louis Sullivan, 26 September 1923, Burnham Library, Chicago.

4. In *Architecture as Nature* I proposed an influence of Viollet-le-Duc's *Histoire d'un dessinateur* in the "Kindergarten Chats" (Narciso G. Menocal, *Architecture as Nature: The Transcendentalist Idea of Louis Sullivan* [Madison: University of Wisconsin Press, 1981], 89–92). It is possible that such an influence extended into the *Autobiography.*

5. Louis Sullivan, *The Autobiography of an Idea* (New York: Press of the American Institute of Architects, 1924), 14, 36.

6. Ibid., 36.

7. Ibid., 92–93.

8. Ibid., 11.

9. Ibid., 68.

10. Ibid., 27.

11. Ibid., 28.

12. Ibid., 171.

13. Ibid., 19–20.

14. Ibid., 176.

15. Ibid., 208–9.

16. Ibid., 183.

17. Ibid., 179–80.

18. Ibid., 11–12.

19. Ibid., 60.

20. Ibid., 42.

21. Ibid.

22. Ibid., 164–65.

23. Ibid., 168.

24. Ibid., 166.

25. For William Henry Furness, see Charles Gordon Ames, "William Henry Furness," *Harvard Graduate's Magazine* 4 (June 1896): 545–50; "Obituary Notice of the Rev. Dr. William Henry Furness," *Proceedings of the American Philosophical Society, Memorial Volume I* 1 (1900): 9–17; Edward Everett Hale, "Reminiscences of the Unitarian Pulpit, III: William Henry Furness," *Christian Register* 78 (2 March 1899): 230–43; Perry Miller, ed., *The Transcendentalists: An Anthology* (Cambridge, Mass.: Harvard University Press, 1950), 124–29; Elizabeth M. Geffen, *Philadelphia Unitarianism, 1796–1861* (Philadelphia: University of Pennsylvania Press, 1961); and Mark B. Orlowski, "Frank Furness: Architecture and the Heroic Ideal" (Ph.D. diss. University of Michigan, 1986), 10–44. William Henry Furness's address to the American Institute of Architects, 9 November 1870, is in Don Gifford, ed., *The Literature of Architecture: The Evolution of Architectural Theory and Practice in Nineteenth-Century America* (New York: Dutton, 1966), 390–404; a comment on it is in George E. Thomas et al., *Frank Furness: The Complete Works* (New York: Princeton Architectural Press, 1991), 33–35.

26. For Clopet, see David Van Zanten, "Sullivan to 1890," in Wim de Wit, ed., *Louis Sullivan: The Function of Ornament* (New York: W. W. Norton, 1986), 58, note 37.

27. Sullivan, *Autobiography*, 221 (emphasis in the original).

28. Ibid., 179.

29. Ibid., 272.

30. Ibid., 23.

31. Ibid., 247.

32. Ibid., 248.

33. Ibid., 79.

34. Ibid., 85.

35. Ibid., 86–87.

36. For Edelmann, see Donald D. Egbert and Paul E. Sprague, "In Search of John Edelmann," *Journal of the American Institute of Architects* 45 (February 1966): 35–41; and Willard Connely, *Louis Sullivan as He Lived: The Shaping of American Architecture* (New York: Horizon, 1960), chaps. 5–6. According to Egbert and Sprague, John Edelmann was born in Cleveland, Ohio, in 1852. He was in Chicago by 1872, a draftsman at Burling, Adler & Company. A year later he was the foreman in William LeBaron Jenney's office and met Sullivan there. In 1874–75 he established a partnership with Joseph S. Johnston (also formerly of Jenney's office). Johnston & Edelmann designed Moody's Tabernacle (interior decoration by Sullivan) and some other eight unbuilt projects. Edelmann became a member of the Lotos Club at this time. A decline in the partnership business and his father's final illness caused him to move to Cleveland in 1876, where he worked as a draftsman. Shortly after, because of bad health (epilepsy), he moved either to Iowa or Wisconsin to breed horses. In the years 1877–79 he developed his ideas on radical socialism. He was back in Chicago early in 1880 and became foreman at Dankmar Adler & Company. He returned to Cleveland in 1881 and there joined the firm of Coburn & Barnum, as foreman and supervisor of construction. Moving again to Chicago in 1883, he would stay there until 1886, working in Beman's office and also at Adler & Sullivan. His enthusiasm for radical causes increased during this time, and in 1886 he moved to New York to take part in Henry George's unsuccessful campaign for mayor of New York. He was unsuccessful at establishing an independent practice in New York and worked as a draftsman. About 1890 he married Rachell Krimont, also a radical and supporter of Henry George. They joined the Socialist Labor Party and had two children. In the years 1891–93 Edelmann was employed by Alfred Zucker, a New York architect, and in April 1892 he published his article "Pessimism of Modern Architecture" (in *The Engineering Magazine*), arguing that Richardson and Sullivan were the only good architects in the United States. In 1892, along with some friends, Edelmann was expelled from the Socialist Labor Party because of his anarchist views and founded the Socialist League, patterned after that founded by Karl Marx's daughter in London. He then began to contribute to *Solidarity*, an anarchist paper that soon folded. In 1894 he built a house for his family in Arlington (now a part of Kearny, New Jersey). From September 1896 to the end of 1897 he worked at the firm of McKim, Mead & White. When Prince Peter Koprotkin was in New York to deliver two lectures, in 1897, he stayed at Edelmann's house and handed him the lecture fees to revive *Solidarity*. In the years 1898–1900 Edelmann once more attempted to establish an independent practice in New York, was not successful (possibly because of his ill health), and worked at times as superintendent of construction for other architects. He died suddenly, of a heart attack, on 12 July 1900. Shortly after, his wife moved to England with the two children to live with a well-to-do brother.

37. Robert Twombly, *Louis Sullivan: His Life and Work* (New York: Elizabeth Sifton Books/Viking, 1986), 78–83.

38. Frank Lloyd Wright, *Genius and the Mobocracy* (1949; New York: Horizon, 1971), 70.

39. Sullivan, *Autobiography*, 206.

40. Ibid.

41. J. H. Fichte, *Johann Gottlieb Fichte's Sämmtliche Herausgegeben J. H. Fichte*, 8 vols. (Berlin: Veit und Comp., 1845–46), 5:182ff., 210ff. Friedrich Schiller, *Werke*, 6 vols. (Zurich: Stauffacher, 1967), 1:195–207 ("Die Künstler"), 341ff. ("Über die Ästhetische Erziehung des Menschen"), 433ff. ("Über das Patetische").

42. Jean-Jacques Rousseau, *Emile, Or the Treatise on Education*, trans. W. H. Payne (New York: Appleton, 1908), 1–5; and Friedrich Froebel, *The Education of Man*, trans. W. N. Hailmann (New York: Appleton, 1887), 5–7.

43. For Sullivan's consideration of Edelmann as the author of the theory, see Sullivan, *Autobiography*, 207.

44. For Sullivan's and Edelmann's drawings, see "Lotos Club Notebook," Avery Library, leaves 94, 97, and 217; for Eakins, see

Gordon Hendricks, *The Photography of Thomas Eakins* (New York: Grossman, 1972).

45. Sullivan, *Autobiography*, 211.

46. Ibid., 234–35.

47. Ibid., 248.

48. Ibid., 207, 220–21, 232–40, 248–50.

49. Ibid., 248.

50. Ibid., 207.

51. Ibid., 248–49.

52. Ibid., 253.

53. Ibid., 259.

54. For the full text of the letter, see Paul, *Louis Sullivan,* 1–3.

55. *Inland Architect* 14 (October 1889), 38–39.

56. Sullivan, "Inspiration," in Menocal, *Architecture in Nature,* 165.

57. Ibid., 166.

58. Ibid., 166–67.

59. In this paragraph I discuss ideas I presented in *Architecture as Nature*, 10–11.

60. For the minutes of the meeting, see *Inland Architect* 9 (March 1887), 23–26; Sullivan's participation, 26.

61. *Inland Architect* 6 (November 1885): 58–59; reprinted in Sullivan, *Kindergarten Chats,* 177–81; this quotation, 177.

62. Hippolyte Taine, *Lectures on Art*, 3rd American ed., trans. John Durand (New York: Henry Holt, 1889), 162.

63. Sullivan, *Autobiography*, 167, 233; for a further discussion of Taine's influence on Sullivan, see Paul, 20, 41–42, 77.

64. Taine, *Lectures on Art,* 76.

65. Ibid., 87, 222–23. The idea loses in translation. The original text reads: "L'oeuvre d'art est determinée par un ensemble que c'est l'état général de l'esprit et de moeurs environnantes." 16th French ed. (Paris: Hachette, 1918), 1:49.

66. For these ideas of Ruskin, see "The Lamp of Sacrifice" I; "The Lamp of Beauty" II, XII, XV, *The Seven Lamps of Architecture*, 2nd ed. (London: Smith, Elder and Company, 1855), 7–8, 94–95, 106–7.

67. Ibid., "The Lamp of Sacrifice" I, 7–8.

68. Ibid., II–VI, 8–15.

69. Ibid., "The Lamp of Power" II, 64.

70. For Sullivan and Ruskin, see also Lauren Weingarden, "The Colors of Nature: Louis Sullivan's Architectural Polychromy and Nineteenth-Century Color Theory," *Winterthur Portfolio* 24 (Winter 1985): 243–60; and "Naturalized Nationalism: A Ruskinian Discourse on the Search for an American Style of Architecture," ibid. 24 (Spring 1989): 43–68.

71. Ruskin, "The Lamp of Beauty" III, 96 (emphasis in the original).

72. Ibid., XXXVI, 126–27.

73. Ibid., XXXV, 125.

74. Ibid., XXXVI, 126.

75. Ralph Waldo Emerson, *Complete Works* (Boston: Houghton Mifflin, 1903), I:214.

76. In the "The Lamp of Obedience" VII, 192, Ruskin argued that the four best styles of architecture were the Pisan Romanesque, the Early Gothic of the Western Italian Republics, Venetian Gothic "in its purest development," and English Earliest Decorated because these were the periods when architecture best imitated nature and consequently they furnished architects with the best lessons in how to design a building.

77. Sullivan, "Style," *Inland Architect* 11 (May 1888): 59–60.

78. Eugène Viollet-le-Duc, *Entretiens sur l'architecture*, (Paris: A Morel, 1863), I, 184.

79. In the *Entretiens*, I, 183, Viollet-le-Duc wrote: "Dans tout ce qu'elle produit, la nature a toujours du style, parce que, si variées que soient ses productions, celles-ci sont toujours soumises à des lois, à des principes invariables. Une feuille d'arbuste, une fleur, un insecte, ont du style, parce qu'ils croissent, se développent, se conservent par des lois essentiellement logiques. On ne peut rien enlever à une fleur, car dans son organisation chaque partie accuse une fonction en adoptant la forme qui convient à cette fonction." ("In all it creates, nature always has style because its productions, however varied they may be, are always subjected to laws, to invariable principles. A leaf from a bush, a flower, an insect have style because they grow, develop, and live thanks to laws that are essentially logical. One cannot take anything out from a flower because, as in any organized entity, each part of the whole expresses a function by adopting the form that is convenient to that function.")

80. In respect to the empiricism of Positivism, Renan had said: "La seule fonction de la science est de connaître la réalité, non de réaliser l'idéal. Comment, d'ailleurs, le pourrait-elle? La réalité est une, l'idéal est divers, il varie d'homme à homme." ("The only function of science is to know reality, not to realize the ideal. How, anyway, could it be otherwise? Reality is one, the ideal is manyfold, it varies from man to man.") Quoted in Jean Bourdeau, *Les maîtres de la pensée contemporaine* (Paris: Félix Alcan, 1907), 63. In general terms, the Positivist idea was based on a use of scientific methods for humanity to acquire knowledge up a pyramid of increasingly general and all-embracing empirical concepts. The final truth of the universe—from which everything derives—would be at the top. For Positivism, see Donald Geoffrey Charlton, *Positivist Thought in France During the Second Empire, 1852–1870* (Oxford: Clarendon Press, 1959); Walter Michael Simon, *European Positivism in the Nineteenth Century* (Ithaca, N.Y.: Cornell University Press, 1963); and Juliette Grange, *La philosophie d'Auguste Comte: science, politique, religion* (Paris: Presses Universitaires de France, 1996).

81. "Our teacher, my dear Sullivan, would roll his eyes wide if he could see you committing such heresies, such lies!"

82. Hermant had come to Chicago to supervise construction of the French Pavilion at the Columbian Exposition, which he had designed. Also, he wrote one of the most perceptive views on American architecture of the period. See Jacques Hermant, "L'Art à l'exposition de Chicago," *Gazette des beaux-arts* (troisième période), 10 (September 1893): 237–53; (November 1893): 416–25, (December 1893): 441–61; and 11 (February 1894): 149–69. Quotation on Sullivan, 246–47.

83. "neither in the composition of the whole nor in those smallest details of the building to be constructed." Viollet-le-Duc, *Entretiens,* I, 485.

84. For Viollet-le-Duc's conception of *l'architecte savant* and *l'architecte dessinateur,* see ibid., I, 477–78; II, 55, 74–75, 112.

85. Ruskin, "The Lamp of Truth" VI, 32. Viollet-le-Duc, I, 18.

86. For Eidlitz, see mainly Biruta Erdmann, "Leopold Eidlitz's Architectural Theories and American Transcendentalism" (Ph.D. diss., University of Wisconsin–Madison, 1977). H. Allen Brooks, "Leopold Eidlitz (1823–1908)" (M.A. thesis, Yale University, 1955) is also useful. For Eidlitz's architecture, see Montgomery Schuyler, "A Great American Architect: Leopold Eidlitz," *Architectural Record* 24 (September 1908): 164–79, (October 1908): 277–92, and (November 1908): 365–78. For Eidlitz's involvement in the design of the Albany Capitol, see H.-R. Hitchcock, *The Architecture of H. H. Richardson and His Times,* rev. ed. (Cambridge, Mass.: MIT Press, 1961), 161–71. I discussed Eidlitz in *Architecture as Nature,* 64-66.

87. In 1843, the year Eidlitz arrived in America, Horatio Greenough expanded some of Emerson's ideas in "American Architecture," *United States Magazine and Democratic Review* 13 (August 1843): 206–10; reedited in Gifford, ed., *Literature of Architecture,* 141–51. By Greenough, see also his *Form and Function: Remarks on Art, Design and Architecture,* ed. Harold A. Small (Berkeley: University of California Press, 1966). For the correspondence between Greenough and Emerson, see Nathalia Wright, "Ralph Waldo Emerson and Horatio Greenough," *Harvard Library Bulletin* 12 (1958): 91–116. Greenough was also a friend of the Reverend William Henry Furness.

88. John Root, whose opinions Sullivan held in high regard, considered that of all definitions of art, Eidlitz's was "the most nearly true." See John Wellborn Root, "Broad Art Criticism," *Inland Architect* 11 (February 1888): 2–6.

89. Leopold Eidlitz, *The Nature and Function of Art, More Especially of Architecture* (New York: Armstrong & Son, 1881), 57.

90. Ibid., 72, 196.

91. Sullivan, *Kindergarten Chats and Other Writings,* ed. Isabel Athey (New York: Wittenborn, 1947), 46.

92. Eidlitz, *Nature and Function of Art,* 222–23.

93. Ibid., 223, 92. Since those ideas find a basis in German transcendentalism, Hegel and Schopenhauer provide a good starting point for discussing the origins of Eidlitz's thought. In spite of their differences in other matters, both Hegel and Schopenhauer endorsed a typical early-nineteenth-century neoclassicist attitude toward architecture, considering that its main function was to express gravity through the post-and-lintel system. Such opinions were soon outmoded. By mid-century, romantic ideas of associationism and the belief that a building should reflect the function it served modified earlier, stricter views. A second generation of transcendentalists, whom Eidlitz seems to have followed, argued in favor of the accidental and the typical. In that respect, a consideration of Friedrich Vischer's philosophical work would clarify Edlitz's views. Vischer (1807–87), in his youth a follower of Hegel, established in his *Aesthetik oder Wissenschaft des Schönen* (1846–54) one of the clearest enunciations of the architectural theory resulting from a conflation of romanticism and transcendentalism. Vischer understood that such a mixture led to incongruity. Functional and essential realities were to produce individual solutions proper to each design, but at the same time architecture was to express universal objectivity. To solve that dilemma, Vischer brought into use a self-contradicting term, *subjective idealism.* With it he denoted a simultaneous portrayal of the typical and the universal in a synthesis Hegel would have probably disavowed. For Vischer, an evocation of tectonics in design was the means of joining together those mutually exclusive ideas. Protruding and receding volumes would indicate the relative importance of each part of a building while massive compositions standing for the universal idea of matter would arouse the idea of geomorphism. As Vischer explained it, architectural elements considered until then as inert came to have dynamic characteristics shared with the observer's life—vertical lines now "soared upwardly" and horizontal ones "broadened out." This notion of dynamic expression is at the core of his idea of *Einfühlung,* or empathy: an act of inner imitation, the lending of our humanity to forms without souls, the reading of ourselves into inorganic nature. Architecture, besides expressing the universal idea of matter as well as the individual characteristics of each building, became symbolic of the movements of man and, by extension, of man himself. In the opinion of the day, this identification was the highest degree of poetry that architecture could achieve. For Hegel, see his *Philosophy of Art,* 4 vols., trans. F. P. Osmaston (London: G. Bell & Sons, 1920), especially Part III. For Schopenhauer, see his *The World as Will and as Representation,* 2 vols., trans. C. F. J. Payne (New York: Dover, 1969), 1:214–18; 2:chap. 35. For Friedrich Vischer, see his *Aesthetik oder Wissenschaft des Schönen,* 3 parts in 4 vols. (Reutlingen and Leipzig: Carl Mäcken, 1846–51; Stuttgart: Carl Mäcken, 1852–54), especially the section devoted to architecture, "Die subjectiv-objectiv Wirklichkeit des Schönen," III, 173–338, and within that section, "Die untergeordnete Tektonik," III, 331–38. Vischer was responsible for systematizing ideas on empathic architecture. According to his theory, the principal aesthetic aim of architecture was to evoke shapes of inorganic nature and to idealize them by means of anthropomorphic association. This notion was at the base of his theory of *Einfühlung.* On this respect, see his *Vorträge,* published posthumously by his son (Stuttgart: J. B. Gotha, 1898), especially the section "Das Schöne und Kunst."

94. Eidlitz, *Nature and Function of Art,* 287.

95. Sullivan, *Kindergarten Chats*, 29–30.

96. Ibid., 49.

97. Sullivan, "Inspiration," in Menocal, *Architecture as Nature*, 166.

98. Sullivan, "What Is the Just Subordination, in Architectural Design, of Details to Mass?" *Kindergarten*, 184.

99. Sullivan, *Autobiography*, 42.

100. Donald Hoffmann, *The Architecture of John Wellborn Root* (Baltimore: Johns Hopkins University Press, 1973), 13.

101. Thomas S. Hines, *Burnham of Chicago: Architect and Planner* (New York: Oxford University Press, 1974), 3–5, 135, 326.

102. The Swedenborg Publishing Association, Philadelphia, distributed free of charge a twelve-volume *Swedenborg Library*, a compendium of Swedenborg's writings. There were also shorter anthologies, such as the one-volume *Compendium of the Writings of Emanuel Swedenborg* (New York: Lippincott, 1879). The New Jerusalem Tract Society, Manchester, England, translated and published Swedenborg's *Complete Works*. These were reedited in New York by the American Swedenborg Printing and Publishing Society beginning in 1850. There were, furthermore, such introductory surveys as T. Parsons, *Outlines of the Religion and Philosophy of Swedenborg* (Boston: Roberts Brothers, 1876), and W. White, *Life of Emanuel Swedenborg, Together with a Brief Synopsis of His Writings Both Philosophical and Theological* (Philadelphia: Lippincott, 1877). For twentieth-century works, see Martin Lamm, *Swedenborg: Eine Studie über seine Entwicklung zum Mystiker und Geisterseher*, trans. Ilse Meyer-Lüne (Leipzig: Verlag von Felix Meiner, 1922), still the standard monograph; Paul Valéry, "Svedenborg," in Paul Valéry, *Oeuvres*, ed. Jean Hytier, 2 vols. (Paris: Gallimard, 1957), 1:867–83 (preface to the French translation of Lamm's book); and Karl Jaspers, *Strindberg and Van Gogh: An Attempt at a Pathographic Analysis with Reference to Parallel Cases of Swedenborg and Hölderin*, trans. Oskar Grunow (Tucson: University of Arizona Press, 1977), 115–31.

103. See mainly, in this respect, Emanuel Swedenborg, *Angelic Wisdom: Concerning the Divine Love and the Divine Wisdom* (New York: American Swedenborg Printing and Publishing Society, 1875), pars. 1–60; and *Marriage and the Sexes in Both Worlds: From the Writings of Emanuel Swedenborg*, ed. B. F. Barrett, vol. 9 of the *Swedenborg Library* (Philadelphia: Claxton, 1881), 61–63. Other works in which Swedenborg expounded on his correspondences were *The Apocalypse Explained* (3 vols.); *The Heavenly Arcana* (2 vols.); *A Dictionary of Correspondences, Representatives and Significatives Derived from the World of the Lord*; *The Divine Attributes Including Also the Divine Trinity*; and *Heaven and Its Wonders and Hell: From Things Heard and Seen*, in which Swedenborg gives a firsthand account of his visits to Heaven and Hell.

104. Herbert Spencer, *First Principles of a New System of Philosophy*, 2nd ed. (New York: Appleton, 1872), chap. 24. Sullivan began reading Spencer while he was quite young; see Paul, *Louis Sullivan*, 18.

105. Sullivan, "Inspiration," in Menocal, *Architecture as Nature*, 166.

4: Birth of an Iconography: 1890–92

1. Frank Lloyd Wright, *Genius and the Mobocracy* (1949; New York: Horizon, 1971), 95.

2. Louis Sullivan, "Ornament in Architecture," *Kindergarten Chats and Other Writings*, ed. Isabella Athey (New York: Wittenborn, 1947), 187.

3. David Van Zanten, "Sullivan to 1890," in Wim de Wit, ed., *Louis Sullivan: The Function of Ornament* (New York: W. W. Norton, 1986), 19, 21.

4. Allison Owen, "Remembering Louis Sullivan," *Journal of the American Institute of Architects* 6 (August 1946): 90.

5. For the Dresden synagogue, see Carole Hersey Krinsky, *Synagogues of Europe: Architecture, History, Meaning* (Cambridge, Mass.: MIT Press, 1985), 276–79.

6. Lauren Weingarden, "Synagogue Architecture in Illinois," in Maurice Spertus Museum of Judaica, ed., *Faith and Form* (Chicago: Spertus College Press, 1976), 37–80.

7. As a type, the *qubba* is essentially an Islamic cubic one-room building or space surmounted by a dome. In the sense I use the term here it refers to a tomb, but a *qubba* may serve any function—bedroom, garden pavilion, tomb, hall of justice, and so on.

8. Van Zanten to Menocal, 25 June 1979.

9. Dimitri Tselos, "The Chicago Fair and the Myth of the 'Lost Cause,'" *Journal of the Society of Architectural Historians* 26 (December 1967): 264.

10. Inigo Jones expressed this rule admirably in 1615 when he wrote in his sketchbook: "In all designing of ornament one must first design the ground plan as it is for use, and then adorn and compose it with decorum according to its use. . . . For as outwardly every wise man carries himself gravely in public places, yet inwardly has imagination and fire which sometimes flies out to delight or amuse us, to move us to laughter, contemplation, or even horror; so in architecture the outward ornament is to be solid, proportionable according to rule, masculine, and unaffected." Quoted in Sacheverell Sitwell, *British Architects and Craftsmen: A Survey of Taste, Design and Style During Three Centuries, 1600 to 1830* (1945; London: Batsford, 1947), 35.

11. Pierre du Colombier, *Jean Goujon* (Paris: Éditions Albin Michel, 1949), 53–58.

12. "Colour Decoration at the Chicago Exhibition," *Builder* (London) 65 (19 August 1893): 152.

13. Avery Library, FLLW/LHS No. 28. Paul Sprague, *The Drawings of Louis Henry Sullivan* (Princeton, N.J.: Princeton University Press, 1979), no. 54.

14. Sprague, *Drawings*, 44.

15. For a list of Sullivan's nonbotanical or geometrical ornamental figures, see note 39 for section 7

5: Growth of an Iconography: The Skyscrapers of 1892–1903

1. Jacques Hermant, "L'Art à l'exposition de Chicago," *Gazette des beaux-arts* (troisième période), 10 (September 1893): 237–53; (November 1893): 416–25; (December 1893): 441–61; 11 (February 1894): 149–69. Vaudremer's motto in (September 1893), 246.

2. Louis Sullivan, "The Tall Office Building Artistically Considered," *Kindergarten Chats and Other Writings,* ed. Isabella Athey (New York: Wittenborn, 1949), 203.

3. Louis Sullivan, *Autobiography of an Idea* (New York: Press of the American Institute of Architects, 1924), 240.

4. As did other architects. Leroy Buffington's claim to the invention of the skyscraper comes to mind. See Muriel B. Branham, "How Buffington Staked His Claim," and Dimitri Tselos, "The Enigma of Buffington's Skyscraper," both in *Art Bulletin* 26 (March 1944): 13–24 and 3–12, respectively.

5. Sullivan, *Autobiography,* 313–14.

6. Sullivan, *Kindergarten Chats,* 99.

7. This is the building Jordy identified as "scheme 'B,' St. Louis, ca. 1892," but Twombly identified as the first design for the Trust and Savings Building. See William Jordy, "The Tall Buildings," in Wim de Wit, ed., *Louis Sullivan: The Function of Ornament* (New York: W. W. Norton, 1986), 117; and Robert Twombly, *Louis Sullivan: His Life and Work* (New York: Elizabeth Sifton Books/Viking, 1986), 310–13.

8. Designed in September 1894 and originally named the Taylor Building after Hascal L. Taylor (1830–94), who commissioned it as "the largest and best in the city," the building changed names before construction after Taylor died and the Guaranty Construction Company of Chicago (which was to construct the building for Taylor) bought the property and completed the project. Construction began in March 1895 and the building was ready for occupancy exactly one year later. In 1898 it changed names once more when the Prudential Insurance Company refinanced it. See Olaf W. Shelgren et al., *The Prudential Building* (Buffalo: Niagara Frontier Landmarks, 1977), n. p.

9. Philip Johnson, "Is Sullivan the Father of Functionalism?" *Art News* 55 (December 1956): 45–46, 56–57; this quotation, p. 57.

10. Paul E. Sprague, "The Architectural Ornament of Louis Sullivan and His Chief Draftsmen" (Ph.D. diss., Princeton University, 1969), 422.

11. Sullivan told his friend Claude Bragdon that the Bayard Building was his best skyscraper. Bragdon reported Sullivan's statement to Lewis Mumford, who published it in his *Roots of Contemporary Architecture,* 2nd ed. (1952; New York: Grove Press, 1959), 21.

12. Sullivan, *Autobiography,* 246.

13. The floor-to-ceiling heights of the floors of the Bayard Building are as follows: first floor, 15 feet; second floor, 13 feet; third floor, 12 feet; fourth and fifth floors, 11 feet each; sixth through eleventh floors, 10 feet each; twelfth floor, 9 feet 6 inches; thirteenth floor, 14 feet 6 inches. Sullivan, *The Bayard Building,* real estate brochure (New York: Rost Printing and Publishing Company, n.d.), n. p., Avery Library, New York.

14. Norval White and Elliot Willensky, *AIA Guide to New York City,* rev. ed. (New York: Macmillan, 1978), 94. That error has remained uncorrected in the latest (3rd) ed. (New York: Harcourt Brace Jovanovich, 1988), 151.

15. For the Salle de Sept Cheminées, see mainly Christiane Aulanier, *Histoire du palais et du musée du Louvre: Le pavillon du roi et les appartements de la reine* (Paris: Musées Nationaux, 1958), 96–104.

16. Catalogue of the Drawings, plate 192.

17. "Brick and Terra-Cotta Work in American and Foreign Cities, Manufacturers' Department and Miscellany," *Brickbuilder* 8 (December 1899): 253–54.

18. Hugh Morrison, *Louis Sullivan: Prophet of Modern Architecture* (New York: W. W. Norton, 1935), 195–96. For Luxfer Prisms, see Henry Crew and Olin H. Basquin, eds., *Pocket Handbook of Electro-Glazed Luxfer Prisms* (Chicago: Luxfer Prism Companies, 1898).

19. This interpretation was made earlier in Menocal, *Architecture as Nature: The Transcendentalist Idea of Louis Sullivan* (Madison: University of Wisconsin Press, 1981), 69.

20. R. D. Johnson, "The Gage Panels, from Contractor's Scrap to Museum Display," *Prairie School Review* 1 (Third Quarter 1964): 15–16.

21. The best work on this building is Joseph Siry, *Carson Pirie Scott: Louis Sullivan and the Chicago Department Store* (Chicago: University of Chicago Press, 1988). See also "Appendix B: A Chronology of the Construction of the Schlesinger and Mayer Building (Carson Pirie Scott)" in Menocal, *Architecture as Nature,* 168–78.

22. This interpretation was made in Menocal, *Architecture as Nature,* 69.

23. For the lingering of transcendentalism in Chicago after it had been discarded in the East, see Hugh D. Duncan, *Culture and Democracy* (Totowa, N.J.: Bedminster Press, 1965); and Helen L. Horowitz, *Culture and the City: Cultural Philanthropy in Chicago from the 1880s to 1917* (Lexington: University of Kentucky Press, 1976).

24. Sullivan, "What Is Architecture: A Study in the American People of Today," *Kindergarten Chats,* 227–41.

25. Ibid., 233.

26. Sullivan, "Is Our Art a Betrayal Rather Than an Expression of American Life?" *Craftsman* 15 (January 1909): 402–4.

27. Claude Bragdon, "Architecture in the United States—I," *Architectural Record* 25 (June 1909): 432.

6: Culmination of an Iconography: The Banks, 1906–24

This section appeared in different form in John S. Garner, ed., *The Midwest in American Architecture* (Urbana: University of Illinois Press, 1991), 99–134.

1. Wim de Wit, "The Image of Progressive Banking," in Wim de Wit, ed., *Louis Sullivan: The Function of Ornament* (New York: W. W. Norton, 1986), 159–97.

2. H. Allen Brooks, *The Prairie School* (Toronto: University of Toronto Press, 1972) , 135–38.

3. Larry Millet, *The Curve of the Arch: The Story of Louis Sullivan's Owatonna Bank* (St. Paul: Minnesota Historical Society Press, 1985), 54.

4. For the influence of Impressionist music and of Symbolist poetry in Sullivan's aesthetic thought of about 1906, see Narciso Menocal, *Architecture as Nature: The Transcendentalist Idea of Louis Sullivan* (Madison: University of Wisconsin Press, 1981), 128–29.

5. I refer to perhaps the three clearest examples of the progressivist tradition: Siegfried Giedion, *Space, Time and Architecture: The Growth of a New Tradition* (Cambridge, Mass.: Harvard University Press, 1941); Nikolaus Pevsner, *Pioneers of Modern Design: From William Morris to Walter Gropius* (New York: Museum of Modern Art, 1949); and Bruno Zevi, *Storia dell'architettura moderna.* (Turin: Einaudi, 1950).

6. Kenneth Frampton, Foreword to Lauren S. Weingarden, *Louis H. Sullivan: The Banks* (Cambridge, Mass.: MIT Press, 1987), viii.

7. John Szarkowski, *The Idea of Louis Sullivan* (Minneapolis: University of Minnesota Press, 1956).

8. Louis Sullivan, *Suggestions in Artistic Brick* (St. Louis: Hydraulic-Press Brick Company, 1910); reprinted in *Prairie School Review* 4 (Second Quarter 1967): 24–26, the edition I use.

9. Ibid., 24.

10. Ibid.

11. Frampton, Foreword, x, makes the same point. John Wellborn Root, a friend of Sullivan's, had translated Semper into English. *Inland Architect* 14 (December 1889): 76–78; 15 (February 1890): 5–6. See also Donald Hoffmann, *The Architecture of John Wellborn Root* (Baltimore: Johns Hopkins University Press, 1973), 91.

12. Sullivan, *Suggestions,* 24.

13. Ibid., 24–25.

14. Ibid., 24.

15. Viollet-le-Duc, *Discourses on Architecture*, trans. Henry Van Brunt (Boston: James R. Osgood, 1875), 179.

16. For Sullivan's problems with residential floor plans see Menocal, *Architecture as Nature,* 102–27.

17. De Wit, "Image of Progressive Banking," 173–77. For the types of plan, see Philip Sawyer, "The Planning of Bank Buildings," *Architectural Review* 12 (1905): 25–31. That article is followed by two others concerning banks: M. S. Kelley, "Modern Bank Furniture and Fittings" (pp. 32–34); and Frederick S. Holmes, "The Design and Construction of Modern Bank Vaults" (pp. 35–38). Then, pp. 39–108 consist entirely of photographs and drawings of recent bank buildings Sullivan may also have seen.

18. I have previously advanced the explanation of Sullivan's new aesthetic that follows. See Menocal, *Architecture as Nature,* 128–29. For an excellent study of the Owatonna bank, see Millet, *Curve of the Arch.*

19. For Hovey, and his influence on Frank Lloyd Wright, see Anthony Alofsin, "Taliesin: 'To Fashion Worlds in Little,'" in Narciso G. Menocal, ed., *Wright Studies, I* (Carbondale: Southern Illinois University Press, 1992), 44–65.

20. Carl K. Bennett to Louis Sullivan, quoted in Robert R. Warn, "Part II: Louis H. Sullivan, 'an air of finality,'" *Prairie School Review* 10 (Fourth Quarter, 1973): 6.

21. For a description of the Transportation Building, see "Colour Decoration at the Chicago Exhibition," *Builder* (London) 65 (26 August 1893): 151–52, my source for the quotation in this sentence.

22. Carl K. Bennett, "A Bank Built for Farmers: Louis Sullivan Designs a Building Which Marks a New Epoch in American Architecture," *Craftsman* 15 (November 1908): 184.

23. Paul Sprague, "The National Farmers' Bank, Owatonna, Minnesota," *Prairie School Review* 4 (Second Quarter 1967): 7–11. See also David Gebhard, "Louis Sullivan and George Grant Elmslie," *Journal of the Society of Architectural Historians* 19 (May 1960): 66.

24. Montgomery Schuyler, "The New National Park Bank," *Architectural Record* 17 (April 1905): 319–28.

25. Ibid., 328.

26. Some examples are his correlating his early ornamentation to the work of French and English ornamentalists; his applying the lesson of Richardsons's Marshall Field Wholesale Store to the Chicago Auditorium and to all his subsequent Richardsonian buildings; his deriving the general composition of two of his three tombs from the North African *al-qubba* type; his borrowing of Viollet-le-Duc's interior elevation of Notre-Dame and his adapting Duban and Coquart's courtyard of the Ecole des Beaux-Arts for the Transportation Building; his synthesizing the interior elevation of Notre-Dame and of the west wall of Reims into the facade of the Wainwright Building; his transforming Burnham's design of the Ashland Block into the Chicago Stock Exchange Building; his making the upper area of the bays of the Bayard Building facade dependent upon thirteenth-century English plate tracery; his designing the winged figures on the upper spandrels of that same building after those of Duban in the Salle des Sept Cheminées at the Louvre; and his basing the final design of the Schlesinger & Mayer Store on that of Paul Sedille's Au Printemps department store in Paris. For these compositional affiliations, see Menocal, *Architecture as Nature.*

27. Russell Sturgis, "Good Things in Modern Architecture," *Architectural Record* 8 (July–September 1898): 94–97 and 100–1. Sturgis offered the Law Library as an example of his statement "Things might be better if architects were allowed to build very plainly for awhile" (p. 93).

28. Louis Hautecoeur, *Histoire de l'architecture classique en France,* vol. 7, *La fin de l'architecture classique: 1848–1900* (Paris: Picard, 1957), 108–9, 346, 348, 378.

29. Sullivan had been in Paris during the academic year 1874–75; construction of the Law Library began in 1876.

30. Mardges Bacon, *Ernest Flagg: Beaux-Arts Architect and Urban Reformer* (Cambridge, Mass.: MIT Press, 1986), 172.

31. Ibid., 173.

32. Schuyler, "The People's Savings Bank of Cedar Rapids, Iowa," *Architectural Record* 31 (January 1912): 48.

33. Robert Twombly, *Louis Sullivan: His Life and Work* (New York: Elizabeth Sifton Books/Viking, 1986), 407.

34. Ibid.

35. Ibid., 408.

36. Ibid., 409.

37. Schuyler, "People's Savings Bank," 54.

38. Sullivan, *The Bayard Building,* real estate brochure (New York: Rost Printing and Publishing Company, n.d.), 7.

39. For Sullivan's belief that the subjective and the objective naturally transform themselves into one another, see Sullivan, *Kindergarten Chats and Other Writings,* ed. Isabella Athey (New York: Wittenborn, 1947), 99.

40. For the basic literature on the Bradley and Babson houses, see Menocal, *Architecture as Nature,* 216–17.

41. For the basic literature on these buildings, see ibid., 213, 217.

42. For the basic literature on the Algona Land and Loan Offices, see ibid., 213.

43. For the basic literature of the Krause Music Store, see ibid., 214.

7: Meanings of an Iconography

1. Frank Lloyd Wright, "Review of Hugh Morrison, *Louis Sullivan: Prophet of Modern Architecture,*" *Saturday Review of Literature* 13 (4 December 1935): 6.

2. Louis H. Sullivan, *Democracy: A Man-Search,* ed. Elaine Hedges (Detroit: Wayne State University Press, 1961), 379–80, emphasis in the original.

3. It is to be noted that *Democratic Vistas,* published in 1871, was "new" in the decade of Sullivan's most intense intellectual development.

4. Walt Whitman, *Democratic Vistas,* in *The Complete Writings of Walt Whitman,* 10 vols. (New York: Putnam's, 1902), 5:51.

5. Ibid., 5:139.

6. Ibid.

7. Ibid., 5:52–53.

8. Ibid.

9. The ms. remained unpublished until 1949, when the Free Public Library of Louisville, Kentucky, published a microcard edition supervised by Walter L. Creese and with an introduction by Hugh Morrison. It was subsequently published in book form, edited by Elaine Hedges, the text I use (see note 2 above). What follows is an adaptation of my argument about the book in my *Architecture as Nature: The Transcendentalist Thought of Louis Sullivan* (Madison: University of Wisconsin Press, 1981), 96–99.

10. Sullivan, *Democracy,* 141. See also pp. 39–40 for Sullivan's ideas on political revolution. Compare these passages with G. W. Friedrich Hegel, *Philosophy of History,* trans. J. Sibree (New York: Collier, 1902), 169–71.

11. Sullivan, *Democracy,* 59–60.

12. Ibid., 60.

13. Ibid., 97.

14. Ibid., 46.

15. Ibid., 143–44.

16. Ibid., 64.

17. Ibid., 151.

18. Ibid., 148–49, 223–24.

19. Ibid., 151.

20. Ibid., 385–86.

21. Water stains, which begin to appear on leaf 3 and increasingly become larger, finally make some words illegible from leaf 40 to the end. The manuscript, in the Sullivania collection of the Art Institute of Chicago, appears in print and translated into English for the first time in the present publication. The only other time it has been discussed is in Lauren S. Weingarden, "Louis H. Sullivan: Investigation of a Second French Connection," *Journal of the Society of Architectural Historians* 39 (December 1980): 297–303.

22. André Bouilhet, "L'Exposition de Chicago: Notes de voyage d'un orfèvre," *Revue des arts décoratifs* 14 (1893–94), 65–79.

23. Ibid., 68. My translation. "Une petite brochure . . . sorte de dithyrambe en l'honneur de son art, [ou] on retrouve l'exposé de ses idées sous une forme un peu nuageuse, mais à coup sûr très poétique."

24. Ibid. My translation. "M. Sullivan est un artiste, c'est un poète, c'est un rêveur doublé d'un homme pratique; il est très agréable de le suivre dans le développement de ses théories artistiques, et il met un tel feu à vous les exposer, qu'il vous entraîne avec lui et vous convainc."

25. Ibid, 69. My translation. "Si M. Sullivan est venu en France, s'il a étudié à notre École des Beaux-Arts, il est resté bien Américain, et son oeuvre n'a nullement l'air d'un concours de Prix de Rome."

26. Ibid., 72. My translation. "La décoration en est tout à fait originale et nouvelle pour nous. . . . M. Sullivan a tenu à donner à son ornementation un caractère personnel et n'empruntant rien aux styles connus."

27. Ibid., 79. My translation. "Ils pensent qu'à pays neuf il faut du nouveau, et ils ont créé ce style composite un peu barbare, un peu sauvage peut-être, que j'appellerais volontiers le style américain, et qui n'est ni de l'hindou, ni de l'arabe, ni du japonais, mais un peu de tout cela à la fois, renouvelé par une étude curieusement fouillée de la plante, rajeuni par une franche conception de la nature, qu'ils admirent."

28. Sullivan, "Etude sur l'inspiration," leaf 1: "C'est ici que l'art atteint son couronnement et le point culminant de son existence."

29. Ibid., leaves 2–3 (emphasis in the original): "En resumé, qu'il s'agisse de l'art créateur lui-même, ou qu'il s'agisse de la jouissance et de l'analyse des produits de cet art par le spectateur, — la base fondamentale est toujours la même: c'est la *spiritualisation du sentiment de la nature.*

30. Ibid., leaf 5: "L'art véritable est le produit de la fécondation de l'âme humaine par l'âme de la nature."

31. Ibid., leaf 7: "Il faut laisser disparaître cet art qui a fait son temps." Leaf 8: "Mais cette mort n'est que temporaire. Après un sonmeil plus ou moins prolongé, se lève une ère nouvelle." Leaf 9: "Chaque école d'art se met en harmonie avec l'époque qui la voit naître."

32. Ibid., leaf 10: "Il semble aujourd'hui que nous touchons au terme d'un long interrègne artistique et que nous allons assister à l'éclosion d'une jeune école."

33. Ibid., leaf 30: "Ainsi à tout jamais une grande âme s'engloutit sous les ténèbres profondes et jamais cette âme ne revivra."

34. Ibid., leaf 31: "Si la mort est inévitable, la résurrection est certaine."

35. Ibid., leaf 34: "Ainsi, dans la génération éclose, et croissant sous le même soleil, circule une même vie, l'âme de son époque; le souffle d'un commun génie mène tous ses membres à l'unique labeur, l'incarnation du rêve d'art qui les marquera de son sceau héraldique."

36. Ibid., leaf 13: "Seul, le coeur de l'homme . . . qui enfante les merveilles, fait la forêt puissante et merveilleuse."

37. Ibid., leaf 14. The title of the second subsection of "Proposition" is "Fécondité de l'âme de l'homme unie à l'âme de la nature."

38. My assessment of the development of Sullivan's ornamental design partly coincides with that of Paul Sprague, "The Architectural Ornament of Louis Sullivan and His Chief Draftsman" (Ph.D. diss., Princeton University, 1969), especially what he called "Sullivan's first ornamental period of 1873–1890" (pp. 168–79). Sprague also noted carefully the thematic variations of what he called the second period (1890–1918), "with graceful curvilinear plants and delicate geometrical abstractions" (p. 167); and the third period (1919–23), "best described as random, centrifugal, and contradictory" (p. 168). For his argument on these two periods, see pp. 179–87; see pp. 187–96 for his discussion of Sullivan's two-dimensional ornamentation.

39. A list of Sullivan ornamental figures that are not botanical or geometrical is as follows. Winged female figures: Transportation Building, Chicago (1892); unknown hotel project (1892–93); Trust and Savings Bank Building, St. Louis, first design (1892); Burnet House remodeling, Cincinnati (1894); Bayard Building, New York (1897–98); and Island City amusement park project, Philadelphia (1907). Nude male and female figures: Transportation Building, Chicago (c. 1891–92), fountains. Lion heads: Transportation Building, Chicago (1892), fountains; and Bayard Building, New York (1897–98), twelfth-floor spandrels. Lions rampant: Design for a capital of an ornamental gallery, 5 June 1892 (Catalogue, pl. 145). Lions *sejant érectes*: Union Trust Building, St. Louis (1892), winged; Peoples Savings Bank, Cedar Rapids, Iowa (1910–11) winged; Merchants National Bank, Grinnell, Iowa (1913–14) winged; Peoples' Savings and Loan Association, Sidney, Ohio (1916–18), winged; and Farmers' & Merchants' Union Bank, Columbus, Wisconsin (1919–20), wingless; wingless lions appear also in a preliminary design of 15 February, an undated facade c. March, and the final design of 31 March 1919 of the Columbus bank (pls. 211, 221–22). Eagles: Farmers' & Merchants' Union Bank, Columbus, Wisconsin (1919–20), preliminary designs of 20 February, 26 February, and 1 March 1919 have each a wing-spread eagle (pls. 214, 217, 218), and the design of 31 March 1919 carries an eagle with the wings tucked in (pl. 221). Angels: St. Paul's Methodist Episcopal Church, Cedar Rapids, Iowa (1910), first design.

40. The best edition is the latest: Sullivan, *Louis H. Sullivan: A System of Architectural Ornament*, ed. John Zukowsky and Susan Glover Godlewski, with an essay by Lauren S. Weingarden (New York: Rizzoli, 1990).

41. Ibid., 7.

42. Ibid., 124.

43. Ibid., 128.

44. Ibid., 133.

45. Ibid., 137.

46. Sullivan, "Ornament in Architecture," *Kindergarten Chats and Other Writings*, ed. Isabella Athey (New York: Wittenborn, 1947), 189.

47. George Hersey, *The Lost Meaning of Classical Architecture* (Cambridge, Mass.: MIT Press, 1988), 149.

48. Hyginus, *Hygini Fabulae*, ed. Bernhardus Bunte (Lipsiae: Sumptibus Librariae Dykianae, 1857), 170. Gaius Julius Hyginus (c. 64 B.C.–A.D. 17) was a Spanish freedman of Augustus and a friend of Ovid. One of the great scholars of his time, he was appointed by Augustus head of his newly founded library. Besides the *Fabulae* (a collection of myths), he wrote a treatise on astronomy and a commentary on Virgil. His authorship of these works is in question, however, and some ascribe them to other *grammatici* who also bore the name Hyginus.

49. See, by Mircea Eliade, *The Myth of the Eternal Return, or Cosmos and History* (Princeton, N.J.: Princeton University Press, 1954); *The Sacred and the Profane: The Nature of Religion* (New York: Harcourt, Brace & World, 1959); and *Myth and Reality* (New York: Harper & Row, 1963).

Introduction to Study on Inspiration

1. Lauren S. Weingarden, "Louis H. Sullivan: Investigation of a Second French Connection," *Journal of the Society of Architectural Historians* 39 (December 1980): 300 (f. 10).

2. Donald D. Egbert and Paul E. Sprague, "In Search of John Edelmann: Architect and Anarchist," *American Institute of Architects Journal* 45 (February 1966): 39.

3. Quoted in Weingarden, "Louis H. Sullivan," 300.

4. Ibid., 301 (f. 16), 303. For further discussion of Bouilhet and of Sullivan's "Etude," see Narciso Menocal's essay in this volume.

5. Weingarden, "Louis H. Sullivan," 301.

Catalogue of the Drawings

1. We have also chosen to exclude those drawings that Sullivan may have made in the "Lotos Club Notebook," Avery Library, Columbia University. It is impossible to tell which are by Sullivan and which by John Edelmann or others.

2. This information appeared on two pages from Sullivan's diary which George Grant Elmslie allowed Hugh Morrison to transcribe. Morrison gave Richard Nickel a thermofax copy of his transcription. In turn, Nickel allowed Tim Samuelson to make a photocopy of the thermofax. We are grateful to Mr. Samuelson for this information.

3. See mainly Sarah C. Mollman, ed., *Louis Sullivan in The Art Institute of Chicago: The Illustrated Catalogue of Collections* (New York: Garland, 1989), 15–67 for Adler and Sullivan and 68–101 for Louis Sullivan, Architect. This volume contains a substantial number of illustrations of the buildings as well as a large selection of the drawings.

4. Fourteen of these drawings are at the Avery Library and the fifteenth is at the Art Institute of Chicago. For the Avery drawings, see Paul E. Sprague, *The Drawings of Louis Henry Sullivan: A Catalogue of the Frank Lloyd Wright Collection of the Avery Architectural Library* (Princeton, N.J.: Princeton University Press, 1979), cat. nos. 116, 117, 118, 119, 120, and 121 for Elmslie, 56 and 61 for Wright, and 31, 47, 48, 50, 54, and 90 for others. For the Art Institute drawing, see Mollman, ed., *Louis Sullivan*, 15, where it is listed as "possibly in Sullivan's hand."

5. Mollman, ed., *Louis Sullivan*, 15.

6. Robert Twombly, *Louis Sullivan: His Life and Work* (New York: Elizabeth Sifton Books/Viking, 1986), 442.

7. The arithmetic gets complicated here. Wright received a total of 132 drawings: 117 by Sullivan and fifteen by draftsmen. Wright gave away eight by Sullivan (reducing the number from 117 to 109) and one by a draftsman (going from fifteen drawings to fourteen). Consequently, the Avery Library bought 123 drawings, 109 by Sullivan and fourteen by draftsmen.

8. In 1931: Nos. 1, 2, 31, 34-38, 43, 44, 46-49, 56, 57, 59-66, 68-73, 75, 78, 83-85, 91, 99-101, 103, 104, 106, and 107. In 1932: No. 80. In 1933: Nos. 3–6 and 14–25. At the date unknown: No. 58.

9. Nos. 271–72. In the early 1960s, Mr. Martin gave his two drawings to Robert Keuny, an architect in Kenosha, Wisconsin. Mr. Keuny, in turn, gave these, along with another Sullivan drawing he had acquired (No. 234), to the University of Wisconsin–Parkside, which, recognizing it had no facilities to store them properly, gave all three to the Art Institute with Mr. Keuny's consent.

10. Nos. 11–13, 26, 39–42, 45, 67, 86, 111, 142–44, 205–7, 235, and 273.

11. Nos. 210, 213, and 215–26.

12. Nos. 10, 32, 50–55, 74, 76, and 98.

13. Nos. 211, 212, and 214.

14. No. 82.

15. These seven drawings were purchased by Wilbert and Marilyn Hasbrouck of Chicago from Sylvia Presto. The Hasbroucks gave six to the Art Institute (Nos. 228–33) in 1993, retaining one in their collection (No. 208), and also donated a print of the plan, elevation, and section of the Krause Music Store to the Art Institute (No. 295).

16. Although *A System of Architectural Ornament* contains twenty plates, we are not including Plate 9 in this inventory since it consists entirely of text.

17. This figure of 109 drawings includes the 101 that are now in the Avery Library, the seven Wright gave to Richard Nickel, and the one he gave to Douglas Haskell. The total excludes the eight drawings stolen from the Avery, which we list in the second section of the catalogue, "Lost Drawings."

18. This drawing suggests that the houses in Ocean Springs were designed by Sullivan and not by Wright as has often been suggested, for instance in Bruce Brooks Pfeiffer and Yukio Futagawa, *Frank Lloyd Wright Monograph: 1887–1901* (Tokyo: A.D.A. Edita, 1986), 4.

19. Louis H. Sullivan, *The Autobiography of an Idea* (New York: Press of the American Institute of Architects, 1924), 236.

20. Sullivan to Claude Bragdon, 8 November 1903, in Bragdon, "Letters from Louis Sullivan," *Architecture* 64 (July 1931): 9.

21. *Saturday Review of Literature* 13 (4 December 1935): 6.

22. This edition of *A System of Architectural Ornament* is even better than Sullivan's original because of the quality of reproduction and because it publishes for the first time the thirty-six leaves of the first draft to complement the final twenty plates. Huxtable's edition of *A System* is listed here because in it she also published drawings of the Farmers' & Merchants' Union Bank, Columbus, Wisconsin, that George Grant Elmslie gave the Avery Library in 1936.

INDEX